Teen Titans
BEAST BOYS
& GIRLS

Dan DiDio VP-Executive Editor
Eddie Berganza Editor-original series
Maureen McTigue
Tom Palmer, Jr.
Associate Editors-original series
Robert Greenberger
Senior Editor-collected edition
Robbin Brosterman Senior Art Director
Paul Levitz President & Publisher
Georg Brewer VP-Design & Retail
Product Development
Richard Bruning
Senior VP-Creative Director
Patrick Caldon
Senior VP-Finance & Operations
Chris Caramalis VP-Finance
Terri Cunningham VP-Managing Editor
Stephanie Fierman
Senior VP-Sales & Marketing
Alison Gill VP-Manufacturing
Rich Johnson VP-Book Trade Sales
Hank Kanalz VP-General Manager,
WildStorm
Lillian Laserson Senior VP &
General Counsel

Paula Lowitt Senior VP-Business &
Legal Affairs
Jim Lee VP-Editorial Director-WildStorm
David McKillips
VP-Advertising & Custom Publishing
John Nee VP-Business Development
Gregory Noveck
Senior VP-Creative Affairs
Cheryl Rubin
Senior VP-Brand Management
Bob Wayne VP-Sales

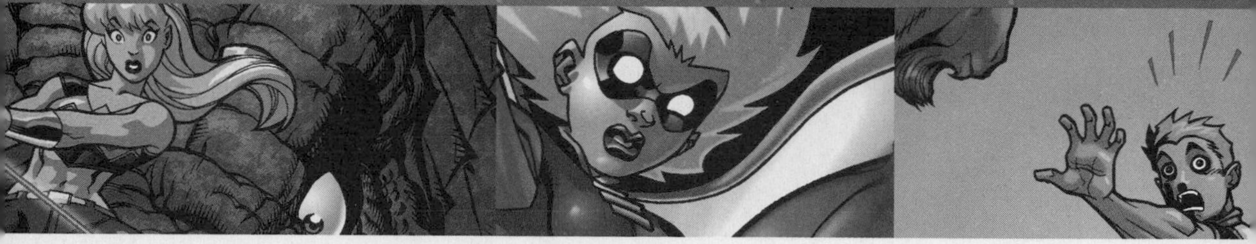

INTRODUCTION

BEAST BOY

He's always been a favorite character of mine. Changing into animals is cool, but it goes beyond the powers. We all can take life too seriously because, well, it can be serious. But despite the horrible luck Gar Logan has had, Beast Boy still wears a smile on his face. He's not just a human zoo delivering a joke a minute; he's there to remind the Titans to lighten up and roll with the punches. Without him, I don't think the Tower would be as much fun.

Today, thanks to Cartoon Network's Teen Titans, Beast Boy is more famous now than he's ever been. He's graduated to a class of DC heroes that is pretty exclusive – those my niece and nephew know and love.

Gar Logan was introduced in DOOM PATROL #99 back in 1965 as a mischievous green-skinned kid who broke into the team's headquarters. The Doom Patrol was made up of a family of freaks — every member had suffered a horrible accident that left them shunned by society and faced with a choice: live in seclusion or use their odd abilities to help a world they were no longer a part of.

So Beast Boy fit right in.

When he was a kid, his parents, Mark and Marie Logan, took Gar on a trek through Africa, where they were researching genetic coding. When Gar came down with a rare tropical disease (and I'd love to know where the name of this came from) called sakutia he became horribly sick. Apparently, only animals could survive sakutia. Working to save his son's life, Mark Logan created a machine that was intended to identify the missing link between man and animal. Although Gar was saved, he became a living missing link. Left with green skin and the ability to change into any animal imaginable, Gar became known as the Beast Boy.

And for a while life wasn't too good for young Gar. His parents were killed in an accident, he was adopted by a horrible legal guardian and forced to live a life of crime. It wasn't until he found the Doom Patrol that Gar got some semblance of a family life. As Beast Boy, Gar wore a purple mask to hide his green-skinned face to keep his identity secret. (I'm sure it made sense at the time.) During his tenure with

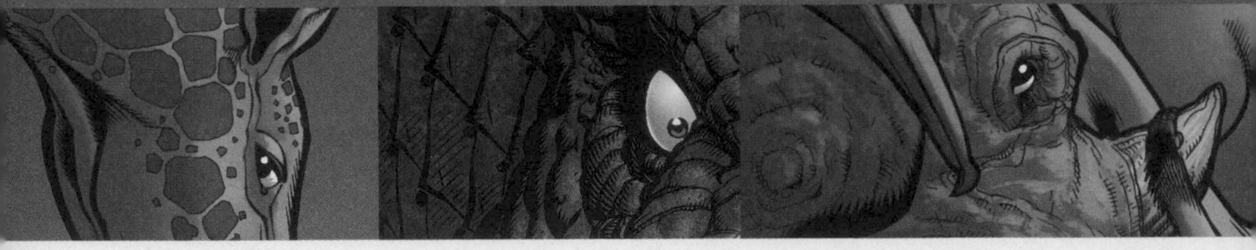

the misfit heroes, he even got a chance to meet the original Teen Titans in TEEN TITANS #6 in 1966.

But before Gar could even begin to feel at home with his new adoptive parents, the Doom Patrol sacrificed their lives to save a small town. Gar was once again left without a family, and he disappeared with the DOOM PATROL comic in 1968.

Eight years later, Gar got a new lease on life when the Titans took him in. This time, after a stint as a failed Hollywood child actor, Gar joined with a bunch of other Teen Titan wannabes calling themselves Titans West. After a few appearances in 1976, Beast Boy again vanished.

The biggest break this character got was when Marv Wolfman and George Pérez added him to their NEW TEEN TITANS lineup which debuted in DC COMICS PRESENTS #26 in 1980. Along with Cyborg, Starfire, and Raven, Beast Boy – now calling himself the Changeling – joined the cast of familiar characters like Robin and Wonder Girl. If anyone knows anything about comics, they know that the NEW TEEN TITANS was one of the biggest comics of the 1980s, rivaling the X-Men on many occasions. For years he was a mainstay in the NEW TEEN TITANS. He finally found his family.

Now let's leap ahead 19 years to 1999. I had just gotten into comics writing and STARS & S.T.R.I.P.E. was launching while I was starting to work on JSA with David Goyer. It was then that I spoke with Eddie Berganza about doing a BEAST BOY miniseries to spin out of the current TITANS book. At the same time, as this happens more often than you'd think, they'd also asked writer Ben Raab to pitch a BEAST BOY miniseries. A few weeks later Eddie gave me a call. He offered me the series, with one catch – I'd be co-writing with Ben Raab. You see our pitches, as strange as it seems, had a few things in common.

Well, actually a lot in common.

We both had Gar going back to L.A., looking for a new career in Hollywood, feeling like he was washed up. We both had a female super-hero supporting cast member. In Ben's case it was Aura, a short-lived character from SUPERBOY AND THE RAVERS. In mine, I chose former Titans West member Flamebird. Because of the Titans connection, we went with Flamebird. We both wanted to see her as a more capable hero, with motivations beyond that of wanting to be famous and be Nightwing's girlfriend. Flamebird actually got more of the spotlight as the series continued.

The problem was, Ben and I had never met. He lived in New York. I live in L.A. But we were willing to give co-writing coast-to-coast a try. And you know what? It worked out pretty well. Ben and I would talk on the phone for hours, plot out the issue and take turns breaking it down and dialoguing it. For someone I had never spoken to or known, I was shocked by how easy it went. Ben is very much Beast Boy in a lot of ways when it comes to humor.

Eddie had this artist he was working with on TITANS on occasion named Justiniano that he chose for the series. Today, I've had the pleasure of working with him on THE FLASH and he's now pencilling one of DC's bigger series of 2005 – DAY OF VENGEANCE.

With BEAST BOY, you'll get a glimpse of Gar Logan's adventures between his first run with the Titans and his current run with the TEEN TITANS, a time when he was doing his best to find a new family. But his real family will always be with the Titans.

Geoff Johns
February 1, 2005

BEAST BOY

Ben Raab Geoff Johns Writers

Justiniano Penciller & Original Covers

Chris Ivy Inker

Comicraft Letterer

Jason Wright Colorist

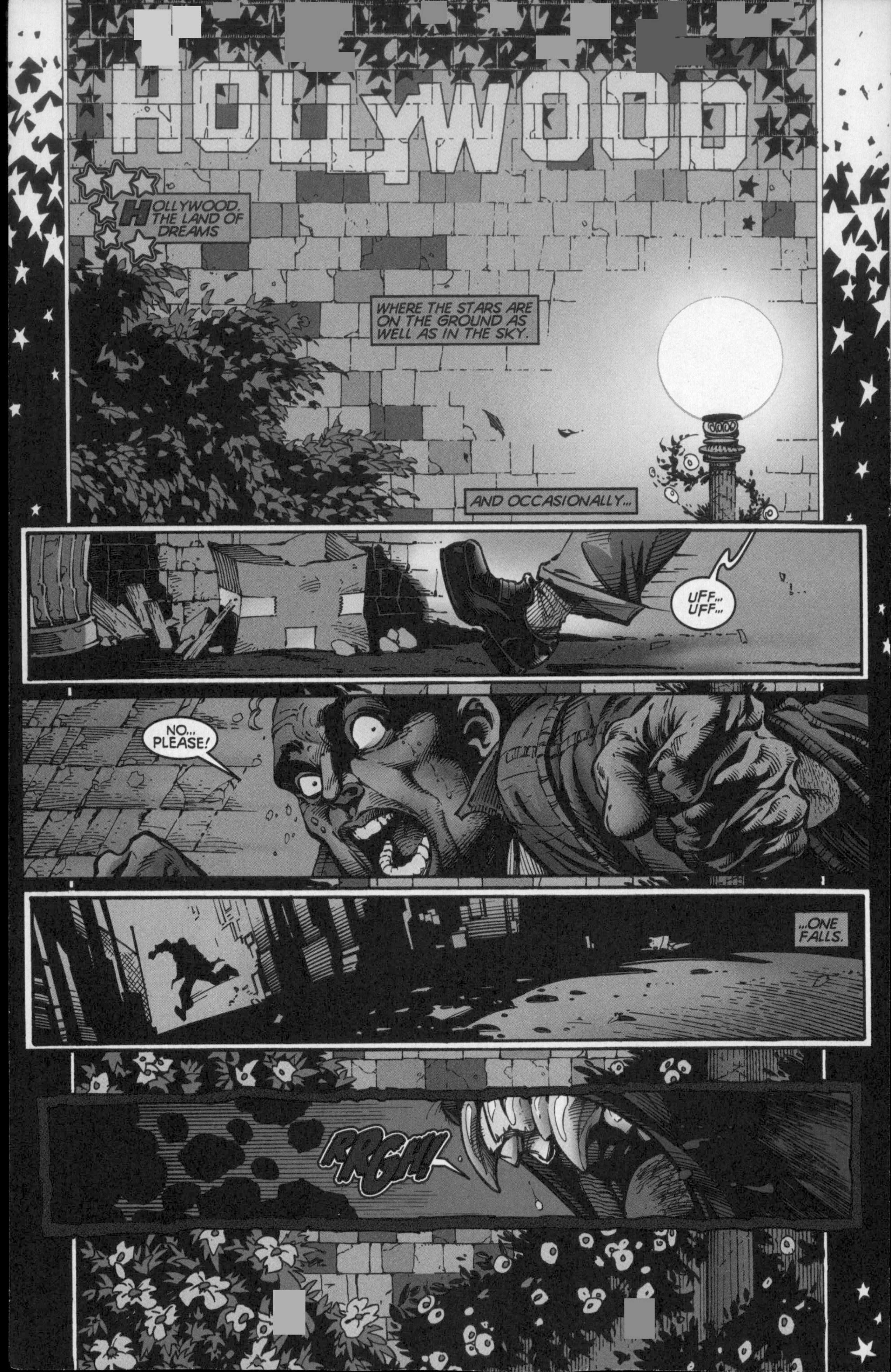
HOLLYWOOD
HOLLYWOOD. THE LAND OF DREAMS
WHERE THE STARS ARE ON THE GROUND AS WELL AS IN THE SKY.
AND OCCASIONALLY...
UFF... UFF...
NO... PLEASE!
...ONE FALLS.
RRGH!

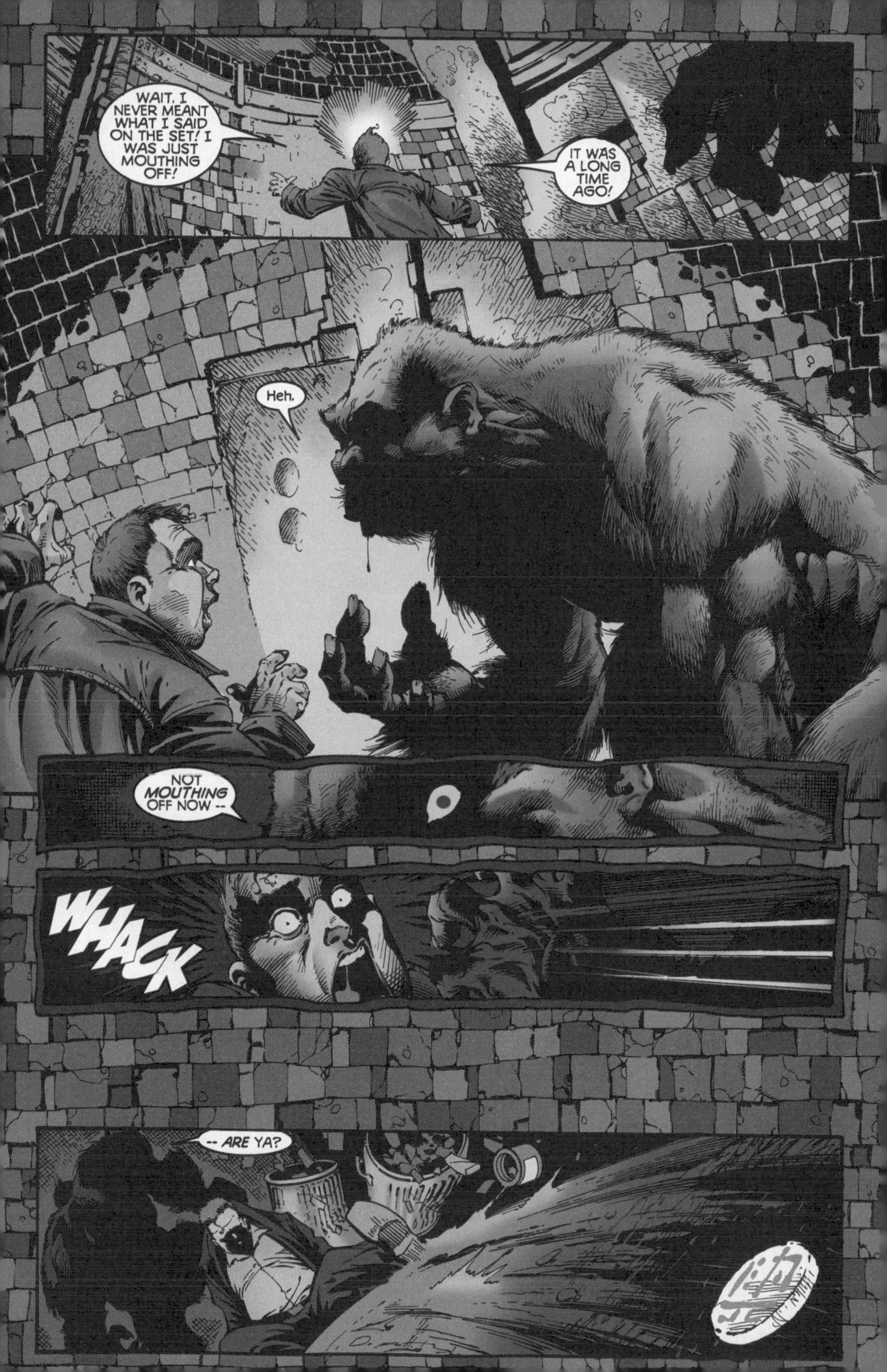
WAIT. I NEVER MEANT WHAT I SAID ON THE SET! I WAS JUST MOUTHING OFF!
IT WAS A LONG TIME AGO!
Heh.
NOT *MOUTHING* OFF NOW --
WHACK
-- *ARE YA?*

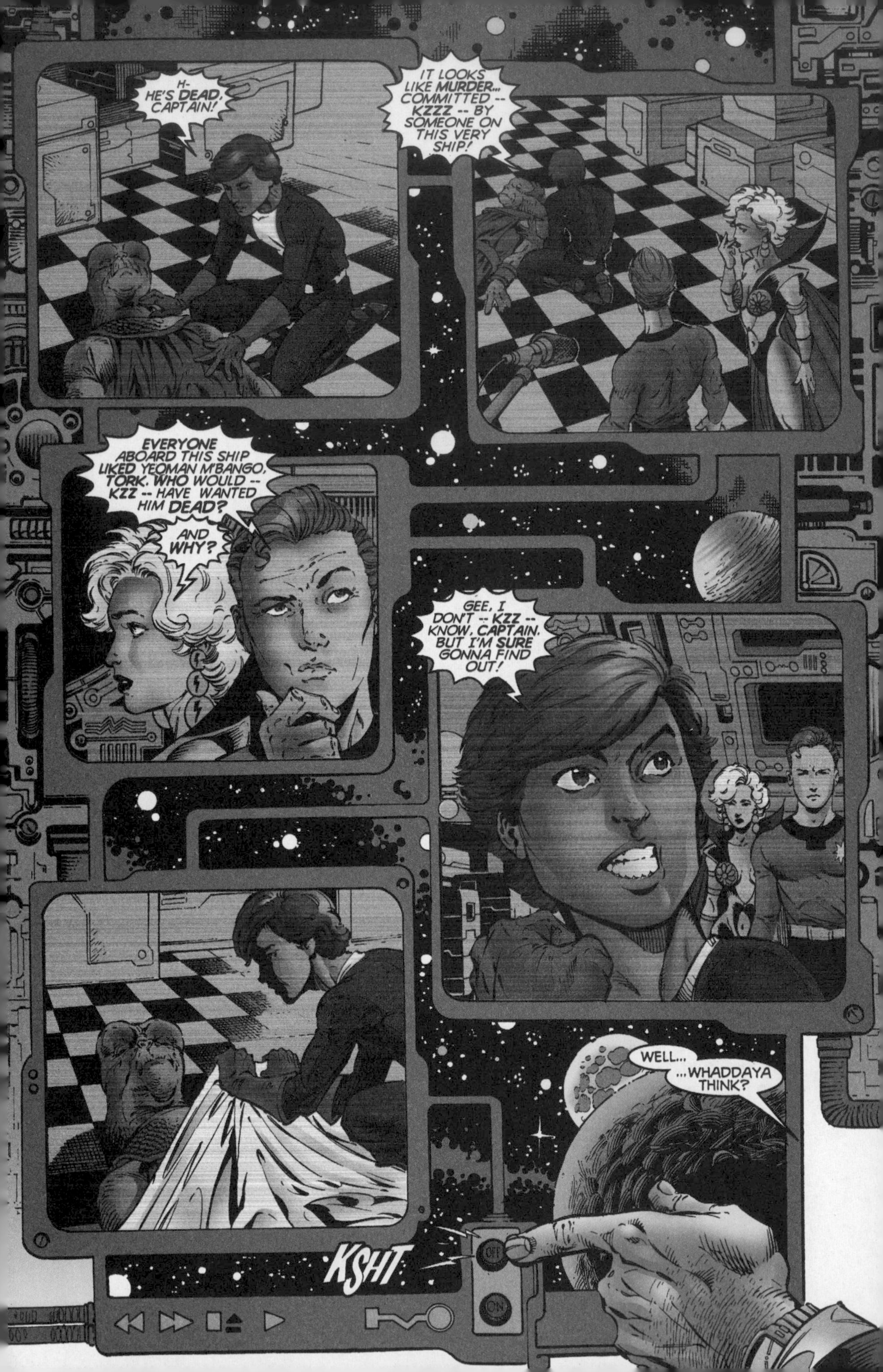
H- HE'S DEAD, CAPTAIN!
IT LOOKS LIKE MURDER... COMMITTED -- KZZZ -- BY SOMEONE ON THIS VERY SHIP!
EVERYONE ABOARD THIS SHIP LIKED YEOMAN M'BANGO, TORK. WHO WOULD -- KZZ -- HAVE WANTED HIM DEAD?
AND WHY?
GEE, I DON'T -- KZZ -- KNOW, CAPTAIN. BUT I'M SURE GONNA FIND OUT!
WELL...
...WHADDAYA THINK?
KSHT
OFF
ON

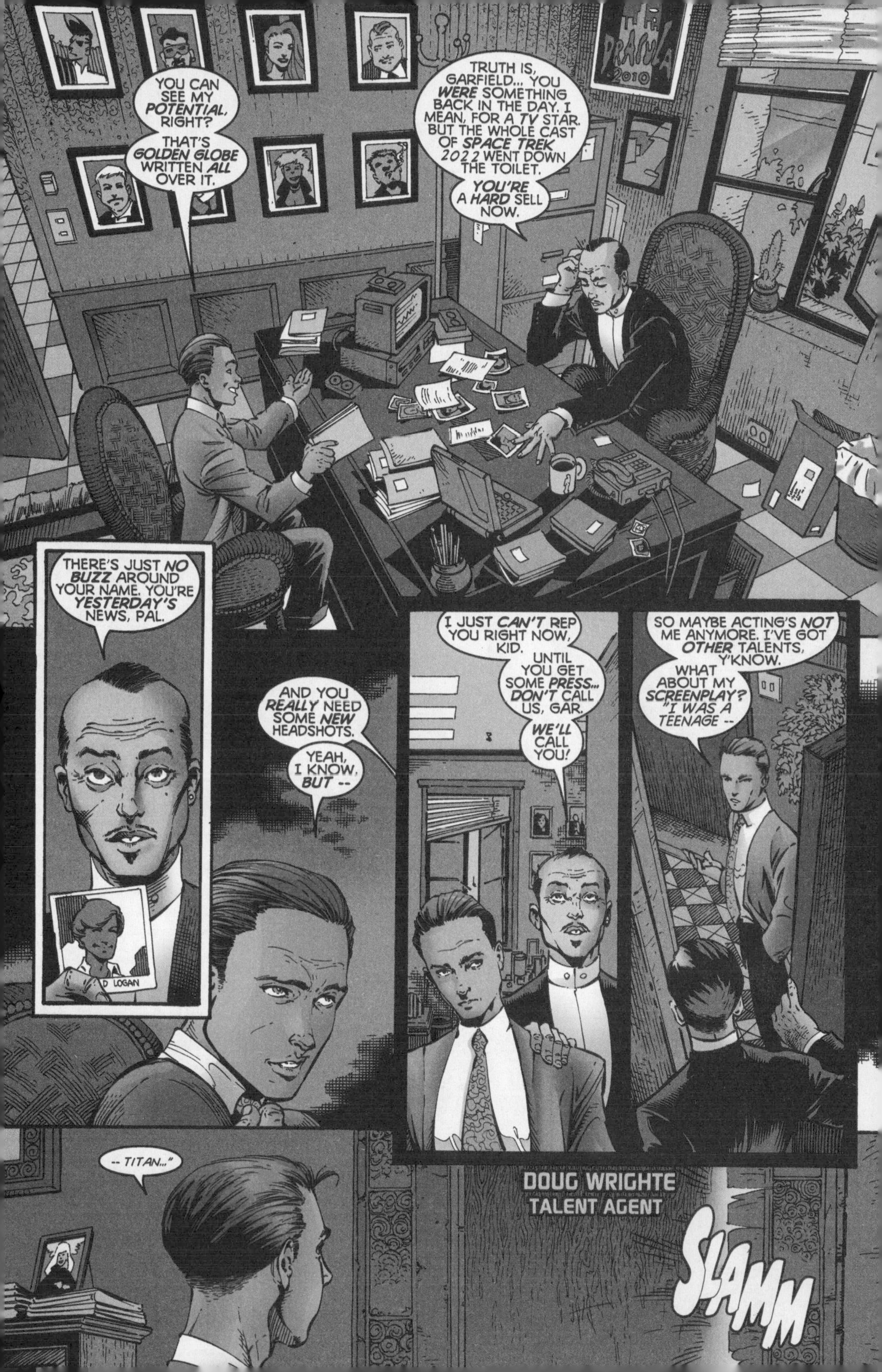
YOU CAN SEE MY POTENTIAL, RIGHT?
THAT'S GOLDEN GLOBE WRITTEN ALL OVER IT.
TRUTH IS, GARFIELD... YOU WERE SOMETHING BACK IN THE DAY. I MEAN, FOR A TV STAR. BUT THE WHOLE CAST OF SPACE TREK 2022 WENT DOWN THE TOILET.
YOU'RE A HARD SELL NOW.
DRACULA 2010
THERE'S JUST NO BUZZ AROUND YOUR NAME. YOU'RE YESTERDAY'S NEWS, PAL.
D LOGAN
AND YOU REALLY NEED SOME NEW HEADSHOTS.
YEAH, I KNOW, BUT --
I JUST CAN'T REP YOU RIGHT NOW, KID.
UNTIL YOU GET SOME PRESS... DON'T CALL US, GAR.
WE'LL CALL YOU!
SO MAYBE ACTING'S NOT ME ANYMORE. I'VE GOT OTHER TALENTS, Y'KNOW.
WHAT ABOUT MY SCREENPLAY? "I WAS A TEENAGE --
-- TITAN..."
DOUG WRIGHTE
TALENT AGENT
SLAMM

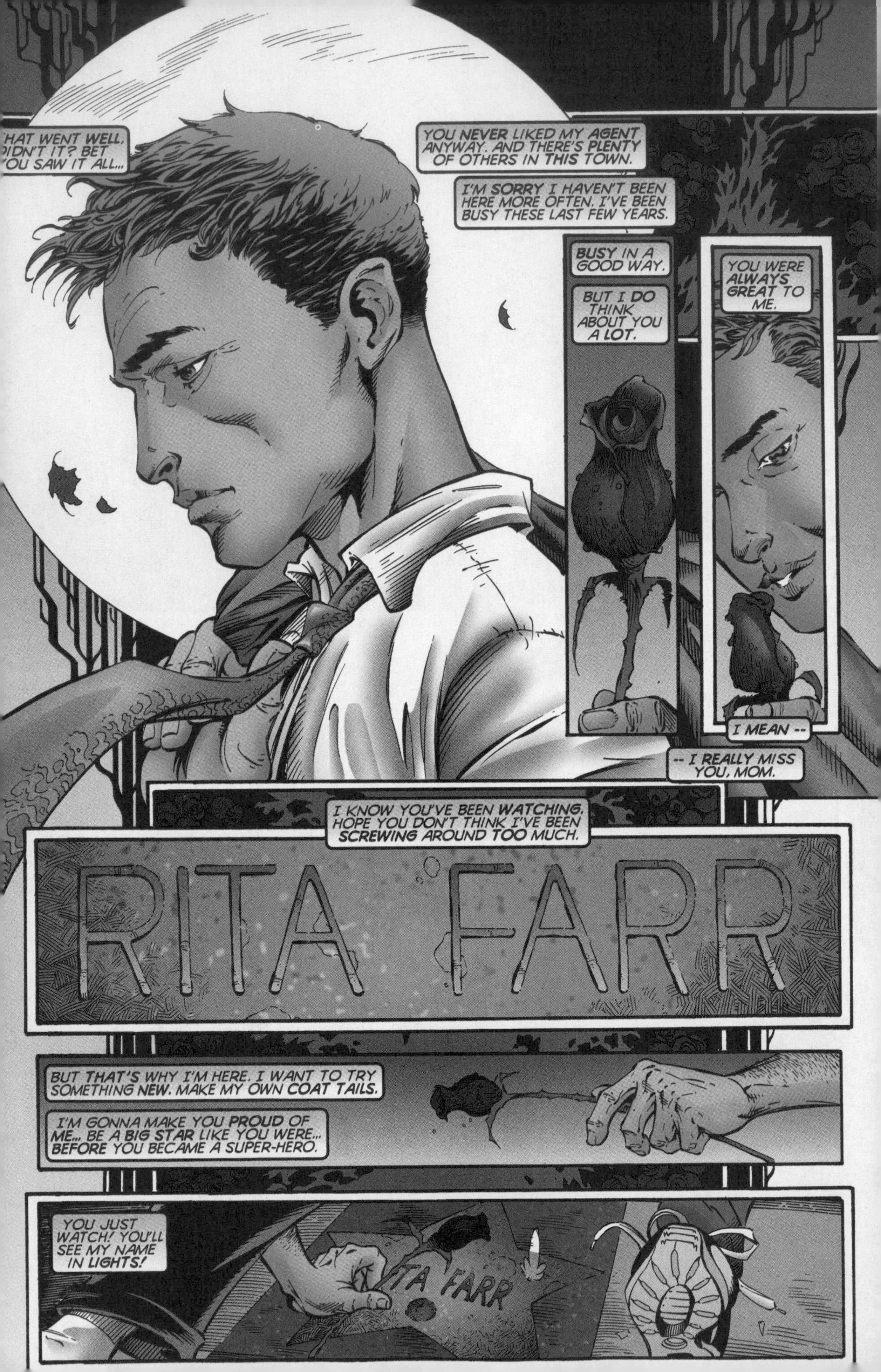

HAT WENT WELL, DIDN'T IT? BET YOU SAW IT ALL...
YOU NEVER LIKED MY AGENT ANYWAY. AND THERE'S PLENTY OF OTHERS IN THIS TOWN.
I'M SORRY I HAVEN'T BEEN HERE MORE OFTEN. I'VE BEEN BUSY THESE LAST FEW YEARS.
BUSY IN A GOOD WAY.
BUT I DO THINK ABOUT YOU A LOT.
YOU WERE ALWAYS GREAT TO ME.
I MEAN --
-- I REALLY MISS YOU, MOM.
I KNOW YOU'VE BEEN WATCHING. HOPE YOU DON'T THINK I'VE BEEN SCREWING AROUND TOO MUCH.
RITA FARR
BUT THAT'S WHY I'M HERE. I WANT TO TRY SOMETHING NEW. MAKE MY OWN COAT TAILS.
I'M GONNA MAKE YOU PROUD OF ME... BE A BIG STAR LIKE YOU WERE... BEFORE YOU BECAME A SUPER-HERO.
YOU JUST WATCH! YOU'LL SEE MY NAME IN LIGHTS!
TA FARR

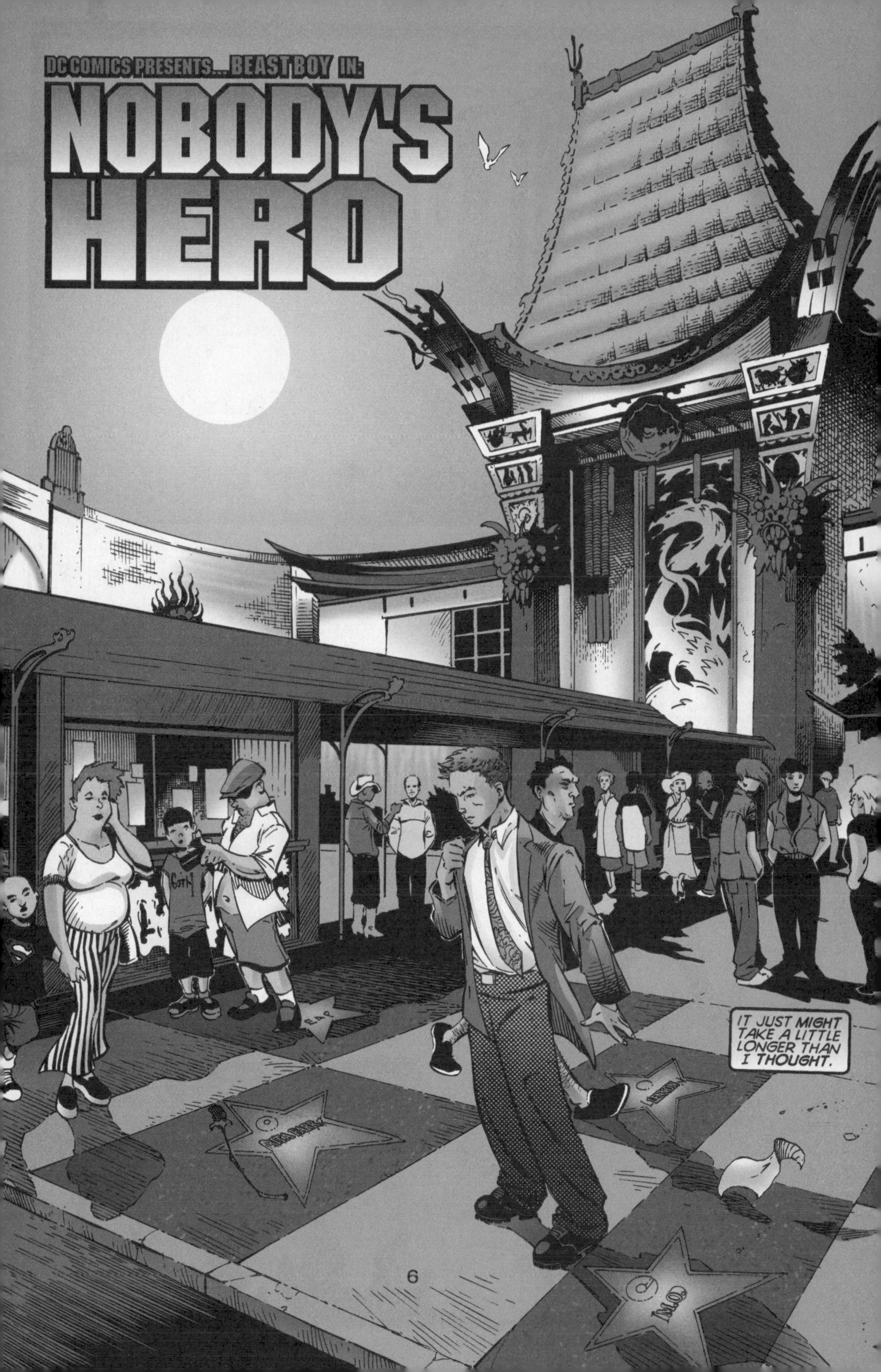

DC COMICS PRESENTS... BEAST BOY IN:
NOBODY'S HERO
IT JUST MIGHT TAKE A LITTLE LONGER THAN I THOUGHT.

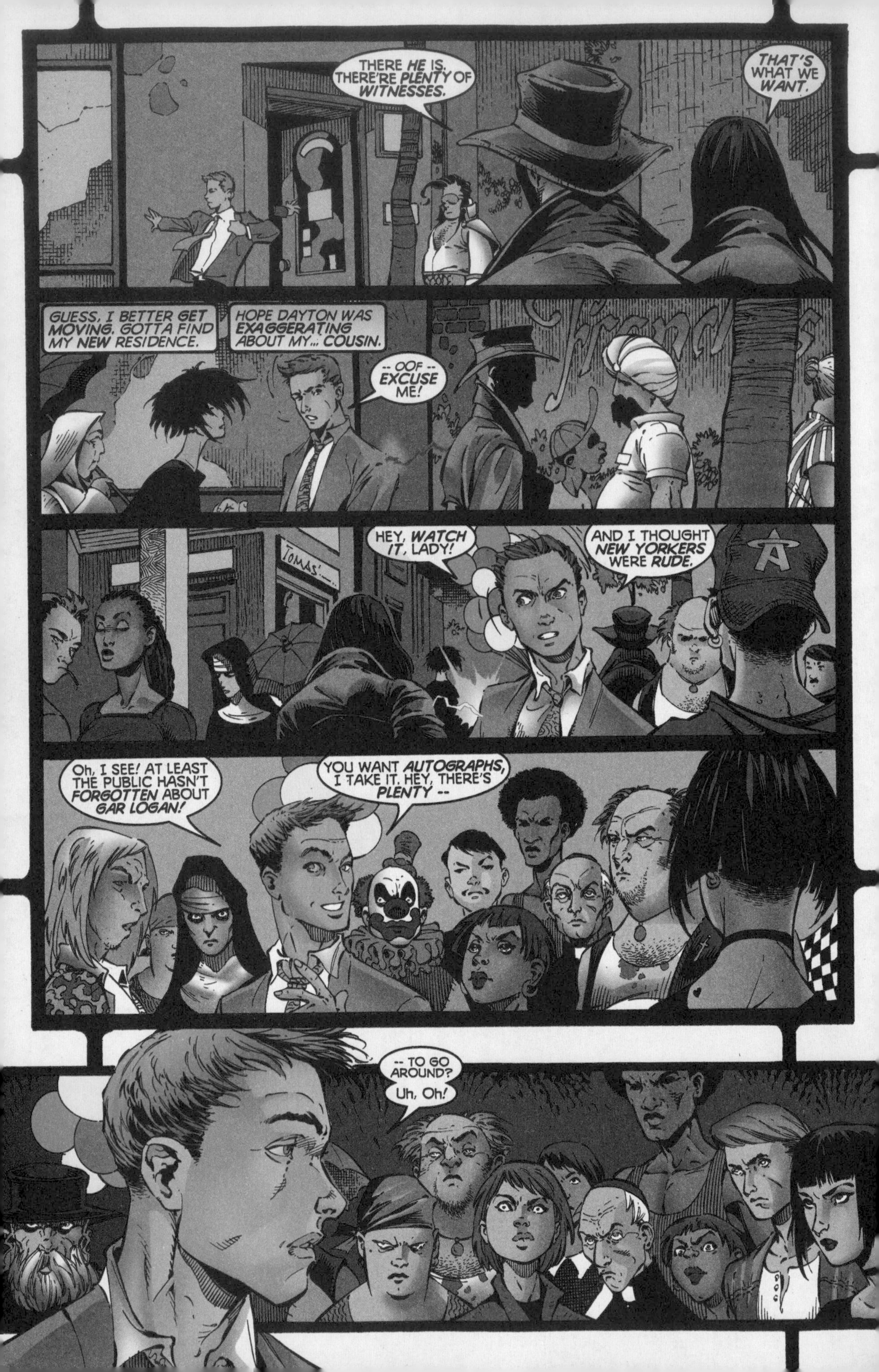
THERE HE IS. THERE'RE PLENTY OF WITNESSES.
THAT'S WHAT WE WANT.
GUESS, I BETTER GET MOVING. GOTTA FIND MY NEW RESIDENCE.
HOPE DAYTON WAS EXAGGERATING ABOUT MY... COUSIN.
-- OOF -- EXCUSE ME!
HEY, WATCH IT, LADY!
AND I THOUGHT NEW YORKERS WERE RUDE.
Oh, I SEE! AT LEAST THE PUBLIC HASN'T FORGOTTEN ABOUT GAR LOGAN!
YOU WANT AUTOGRAPHS, I TAKE IT. HEY, THERE'S PLENTY --
-- TO GO AROUND?
Uh, Oh!

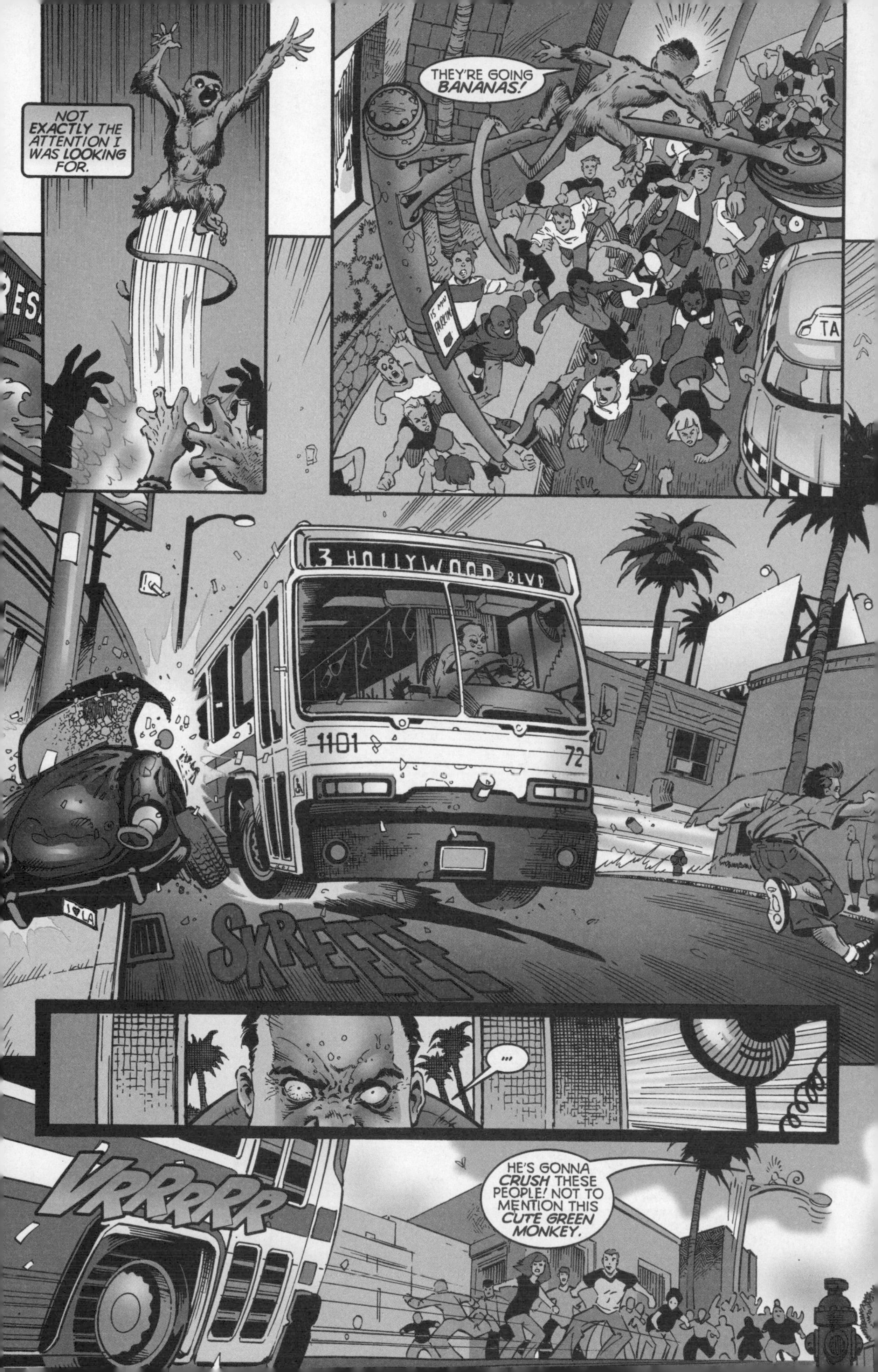
NOT EXACTLY THE ATTENTION I WAS LOOKING FOR.
THEY'RE GOING BANANAS!
3 HOLLYWOOD BLVD
1101
72
I ♥ LA
SKREEE
...
VRRRRR
HE'S GONNA CRUSH THESE PEOPLE! NOT TO MENTION THIS CUTE GREEN MONKEY.

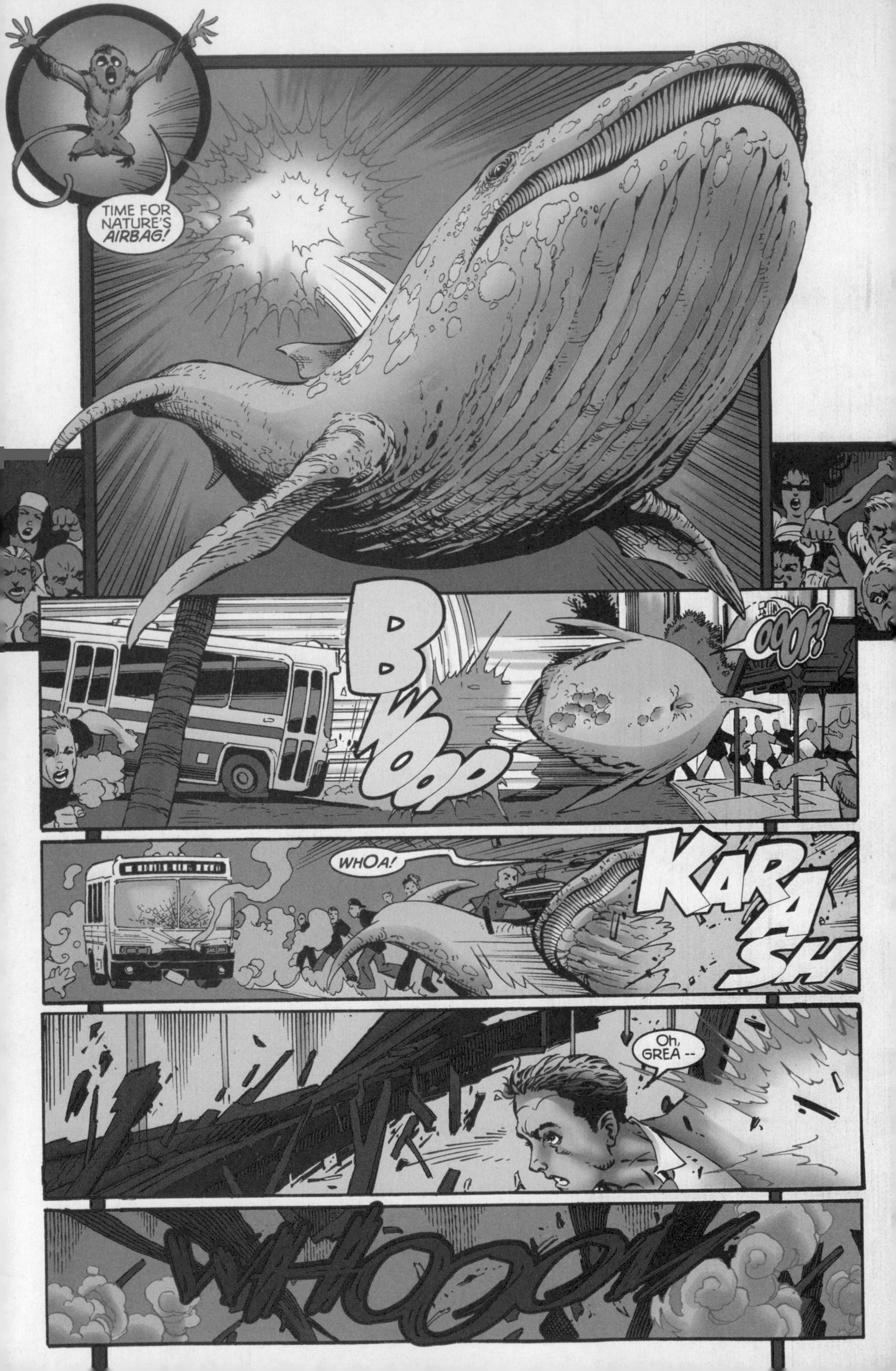
TIME FOR NATURE'S AIRBAG!
BWOOP
OOOF!
WHOA!
KARASH
Oh, GREA --
WHOOOOM

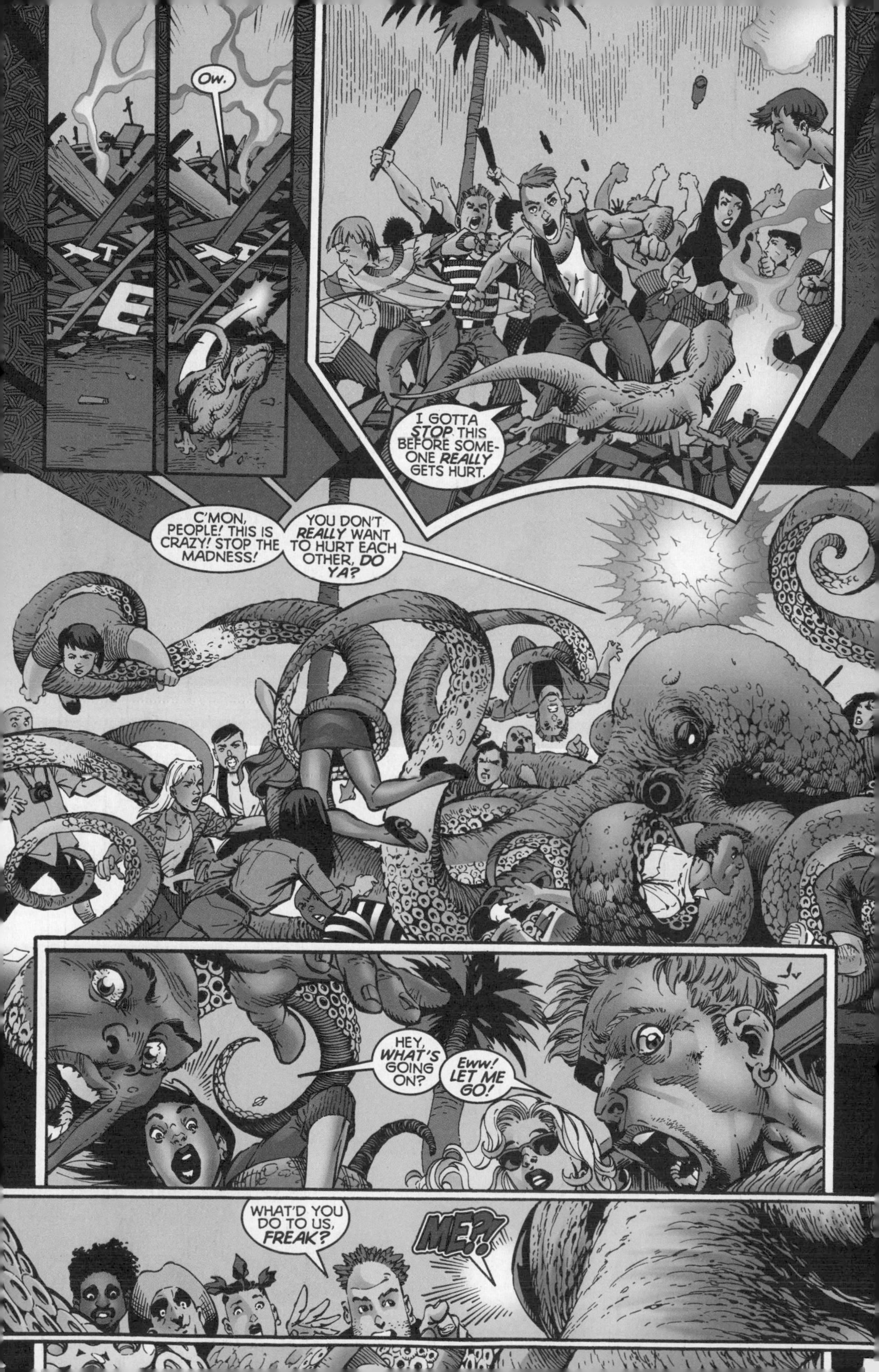
Ow.
I GOTTA STOP THIS BEFORE SOME-ONE REALLY GETS HURT.
C'MON, PEOPLE! THIS IS CRAZY! STOP THE MADNESS!
YOU DON'T REALLY WANT TO HURT EACH OTHER, DO YA?
HEY, WHAT'S GOING ON?
Eww! LET ME GO!
WHAT'D YOU DO TO US, FREAK?
ME?!

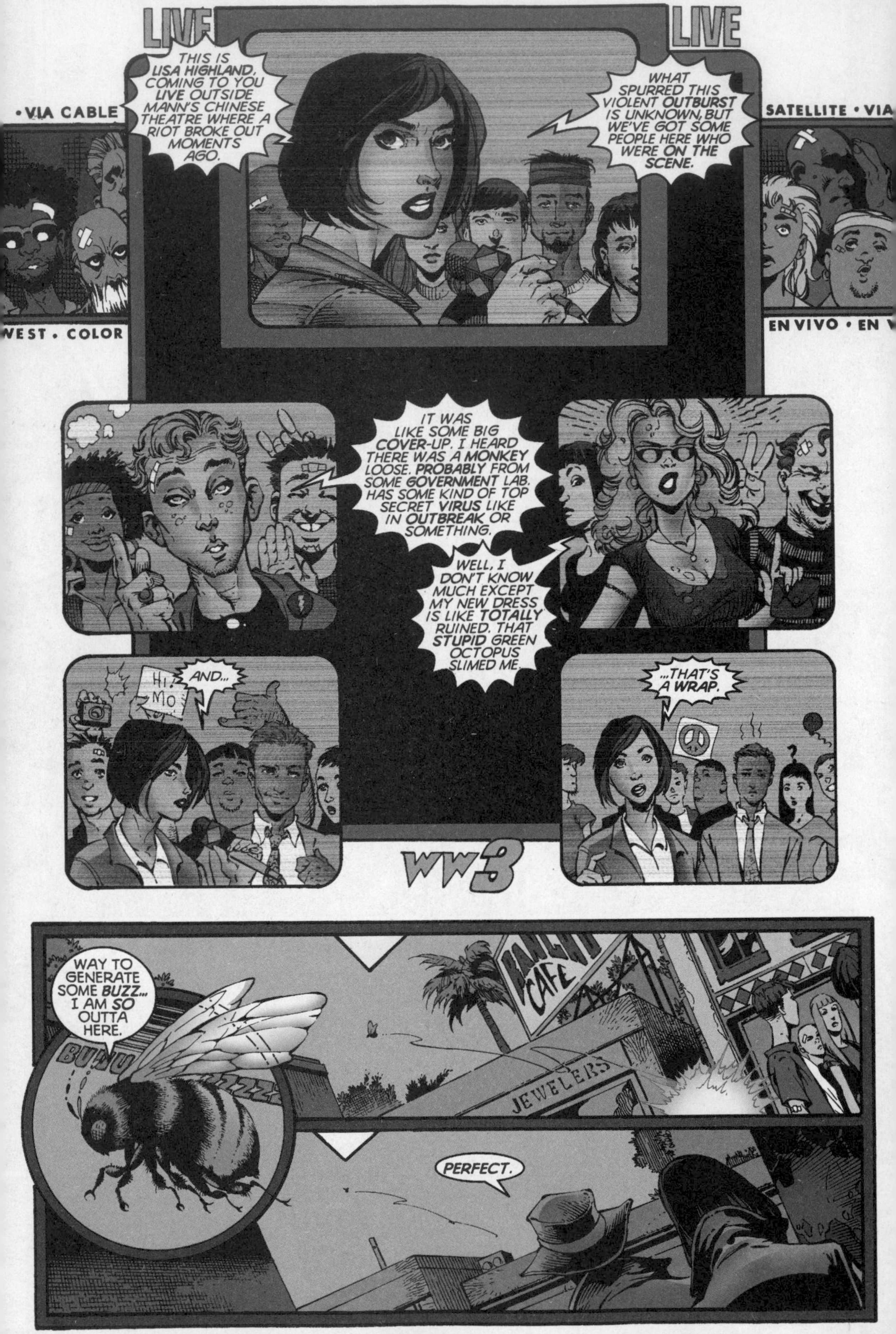

LIVE
LIVE
• VIA CABLE
SATELLITE • VIA
WEST • COLOR
EN VIVO • EN V
THIS IS USA HIGHLAND, COMING TO YOU LIVE OUTSIDE MANN'S CHINESE THEATRE WHERE A RIOT BROKE OUT MOMENTS AGO.
WHAT SPURRED THIS VIOLENT OUTBURST IS UNKNOWN, BUT WE'VE GOT SOME PEOPLE HERE WHO WERE ON THE SCENE.
IT WAS LIKE SOME BIG COVER-UP. I HEARD THERE WAS A MONKEY LOOSE. PROBABLY FROM SOME GOVERNMENT LAB. HAS SOME KIND OF TOP SECRET VIRUS LIKE IN OUTBREAK OR SOMETHING.
WELL, I DON'T KNOW MUCH EXCEPT MY NEW DRESS IS LIKE TOTALLY RUINED. THAT STUPID GREEN OCTOPUS SLIMED ME.
HI MO
AND...
...THAT'S A WRAP.
WW3
WAY TO GENERATE SOME BUZZ... I AM SO OUTTA HERE.
CAFE
JEWELERS
PERFECT.

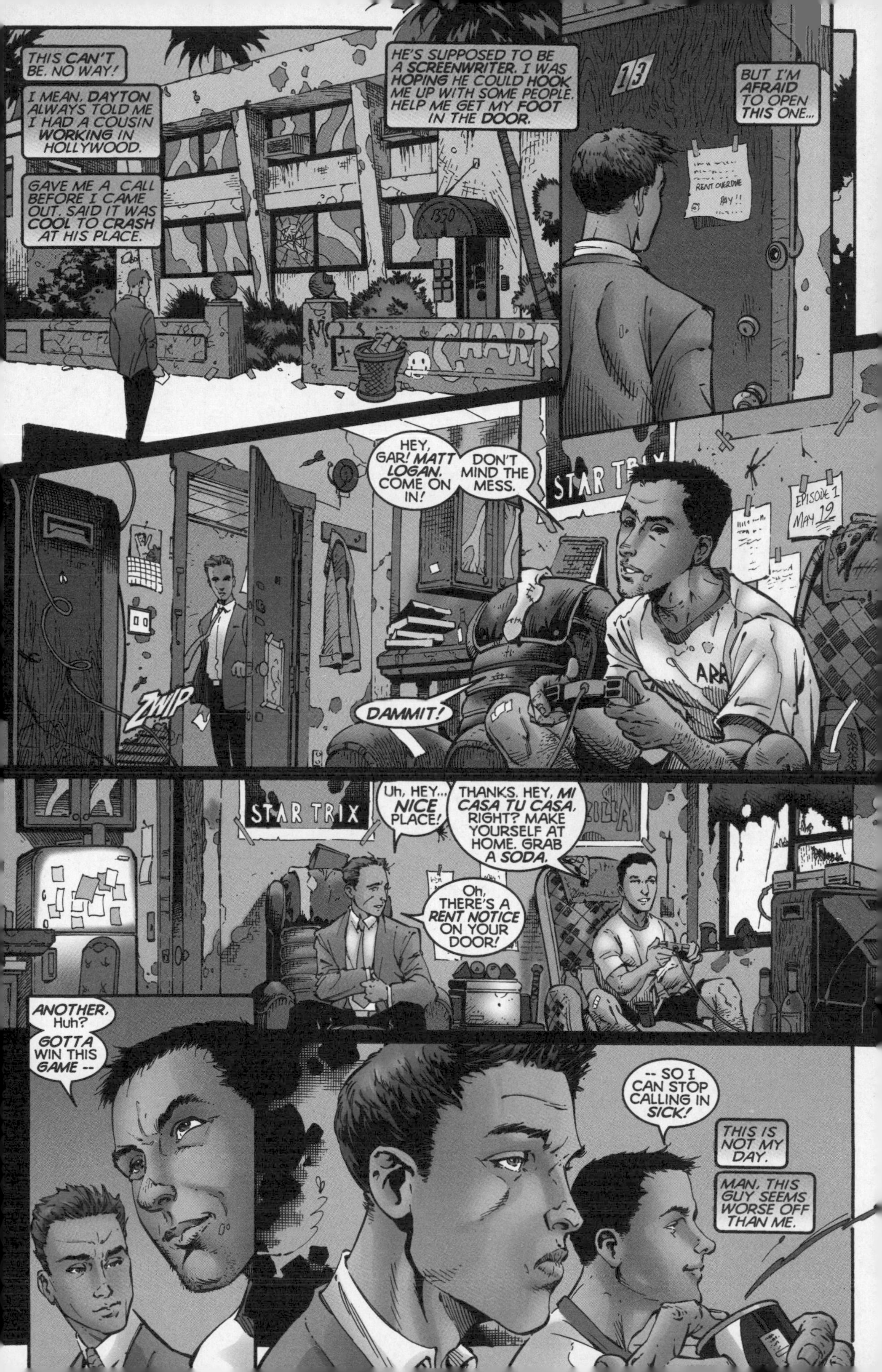

THIS CAN'T BE. NO WAY!
I MEAN, DAYTON ALWAYS TOLD ME I HAD A COUSIN WORKING IN HOLLYWOOD.
GAVE ME A CALL BEFORE I CAME OUT. SAID IT WAS COOL TO CRASH AT HIS PLACE.
HE'S SUPPOSED TO BE A SCREENWRITER. I WAS HOPING HE COULD HOOK ME UP WITH SOME PEOPLE. HELP ME GET MY FOOT IN THE DOOR.
13
BUT I'M AFRAID TO OPEN THIS ONE...
RENT OVERDUE PAY!!
HEY, GAR! MATT LOGAN. COME ON IN!
DON'T MIND THE MESS.
STAR TRIX
EPISODE 1 May 19
ZWIP
DAMMIT!
STAR TRIX
Uh, HEY... NICE PLACE!
THANKS. HEY, MI CASA TU CASA, RIGHT? MAKE YOURSELF AT HOME. GRAB A SODA.
Oh, THERE'S A RENT NOTICE ON YOUR DOOR!
ANOTHER, Huh? GOTTA WIN THIS GAME --
-- SO I CAN STOP CALLING IN SICK!
THIS IS NOT MY DAY.
MAN, THIS GUY SEEMS WORSE OFF THAN ME.

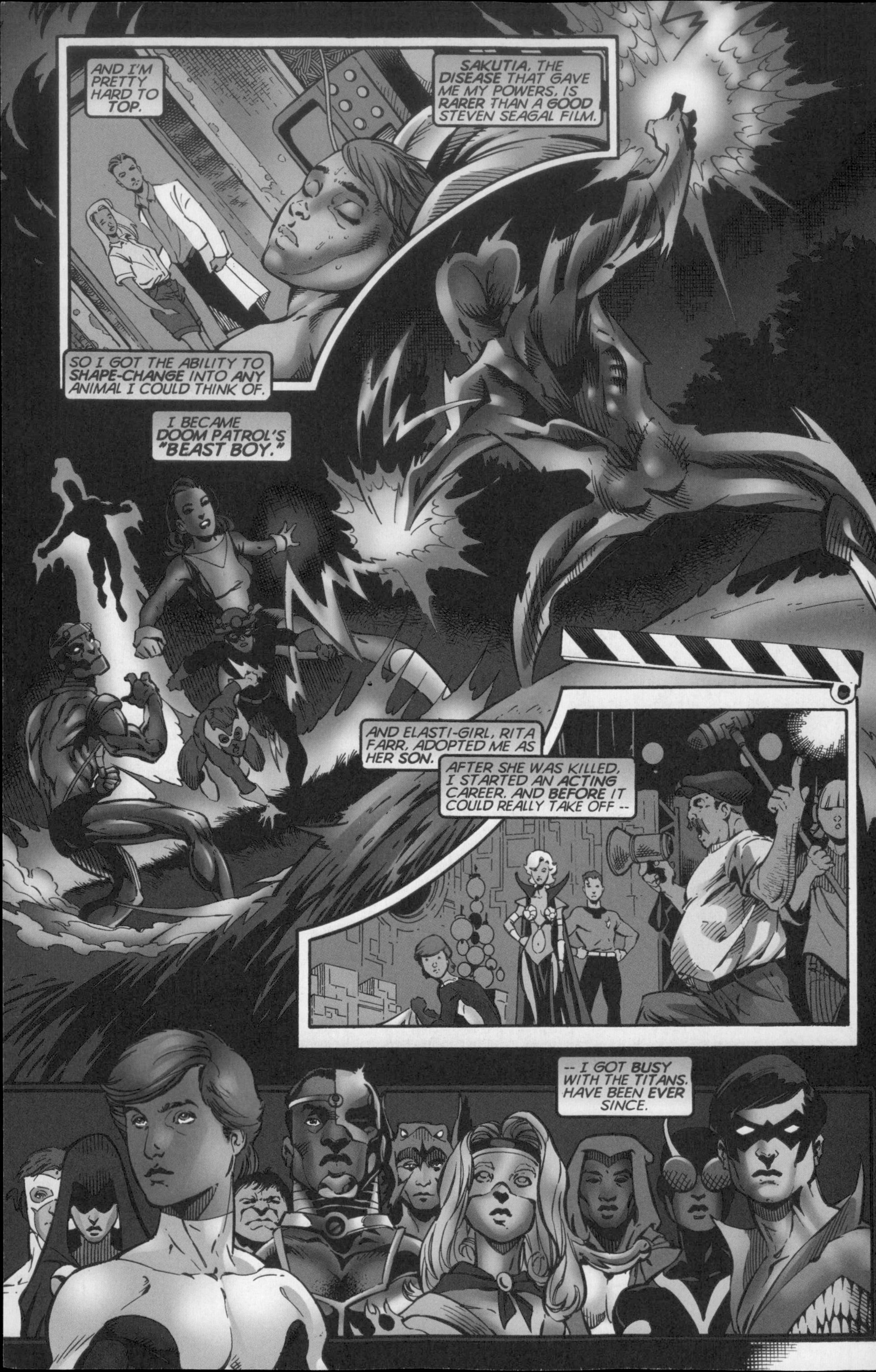
AND I'M PRETTY HARD TO TOP.
SAKUTIA, THE DISEASE THAT GAVE ME MY POWERS, IS RARER THAN A GOOD STEVEN SEAGAL FILM.
SO I GOT THE ABILITY TO SHAPE-CHANGE INTO ANY ANIMAL I COULD THINK OF.
I BECAME DOOM PATROL'S "BEAST BOY."
AND ELASTI-GIRL, RITA FARR, ADOPTED ME AS HER SON.
AFTER SHE WAS KILLED, I STARTED AN ACTING CAREER. AND BEFORE IT COULD REALLY TAKE OFF --
-- I GOT BUSY WITH THE TITANS. HAVE BEEN EVER SINCE.

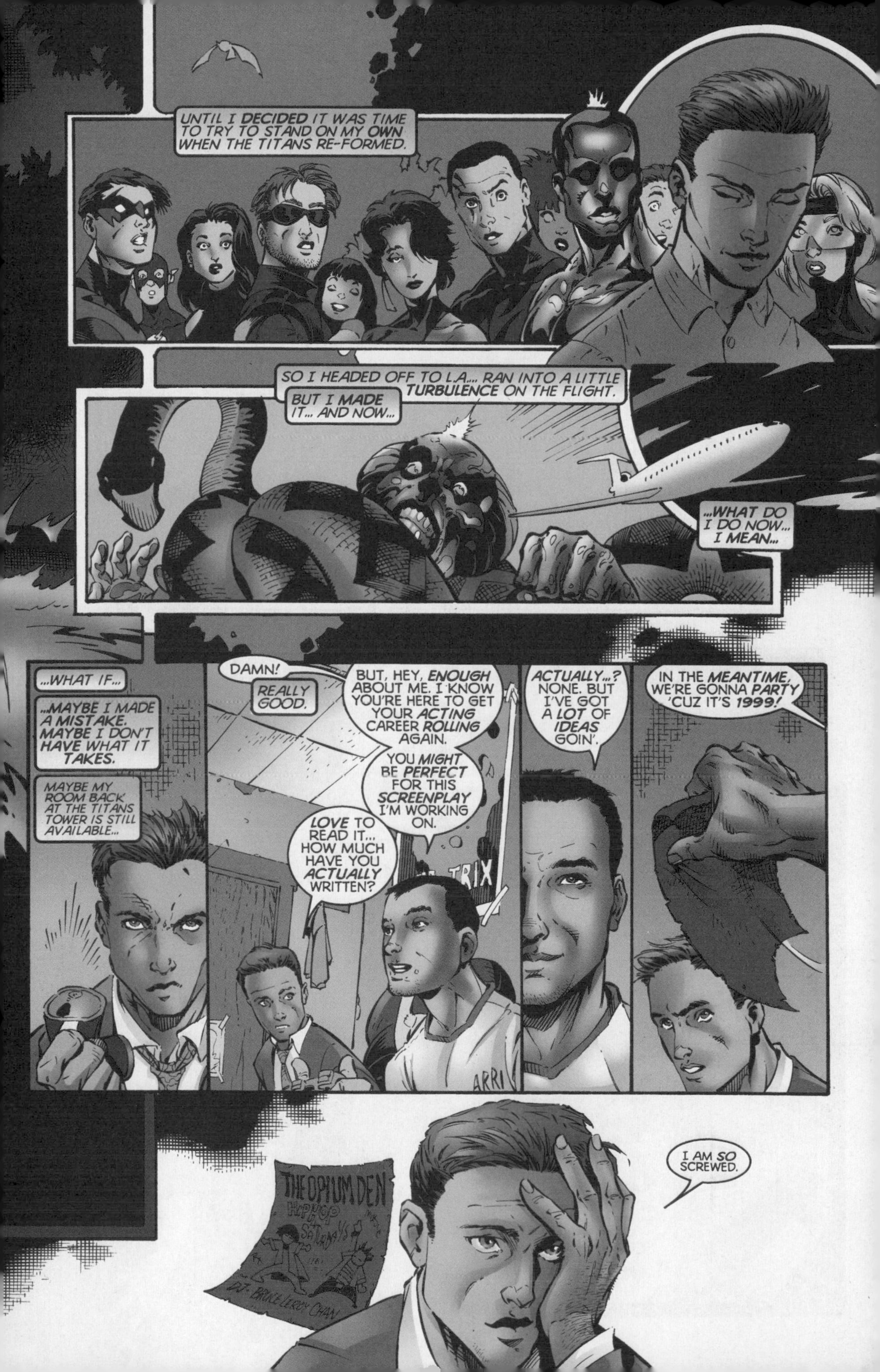
UNTIL I DECIDED IT WAS TIME TO TRY TO STAND ON MY OWN WHEN THE TITANS RE-FORMED.
SO I HEADED OFF TO L.A.... RAN INTO A LITTLE TURBULENCE ON THE FLIGHT.
BUT I MADE IT... AND NOW...
...WHAT DO I DO NOW... I MEAN...
...WHAT IF...
...MAYBE I MADE A MISTAKE. MAYBE I DON'T HAVE WHAT IT TAKES.
MAYBE MY ROOM BACK AT THE TITANS TOWER IS STILL AVAILABLE...
DAMN!
REALLY GOOD.
BUT, HEY, ENOUGH ABOUT ME. I KNOW YOU'RE HERE TO GET YOUR ACTING CAREER ROLLING AGAIN.
YOU MIGHT BE PERFECT FOR THIS SCREENPLAY I'M WORKING ON.
LOVE TO READ IT... HOW MUCH HAVE YOU ACTUALLY WRITTEN?
ACTUALLY...? NONE. BUT I'VE GOT A LOT OF IDEAS GOIN'.
IN THE MEANTIME, WE'RE GONNA PARTY 'CUZ IT'S 1999!
THE OPIUM DEN
HIP HOP SATURDAYS
DJ - BRUCE LEROY CHAN
I AM SO SCREWED.

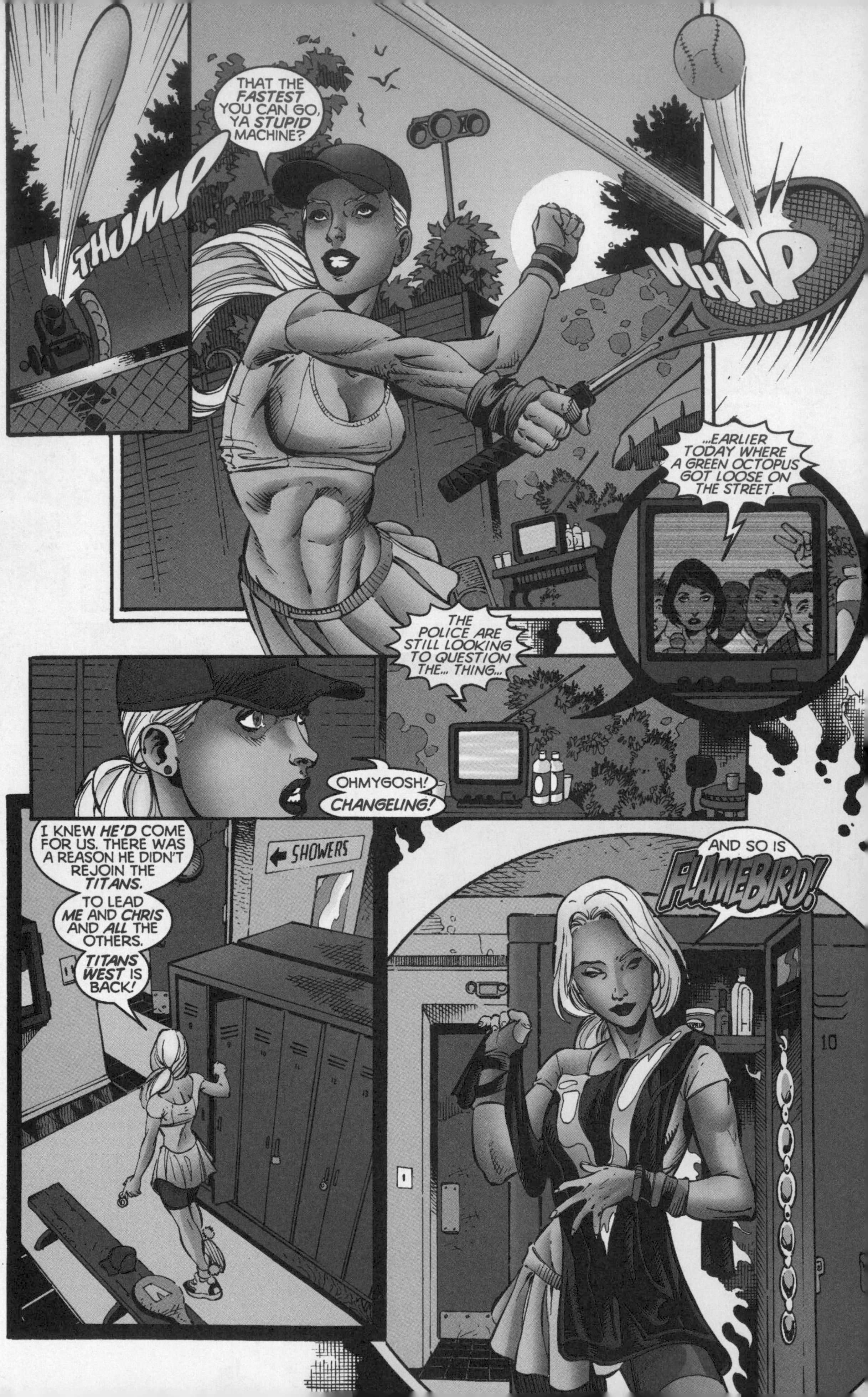
THUMP
THAT THE FASTEST YOU CAN GO, YA STUPID MACHINE?
WHAP
...EARLIER TODAY WHERE A GREEN OCTOPUS GOT LOOSE ON THE STREET.
THE POLICE ARE STILL LOOKING TO QUESTION THE... THING...
OHMYGOSH!
CHANGELING!
I KNEW HE'D COME FOR US. THERE WAS A REASON HE DIDN'T REJOIN THE TITANS.
TO LEAD ME AND CHRIS AND ALL THE OTHERS.
TITANS WEST IS BACK!
SHOWERS
AND SO IS FLAMEBIRD!

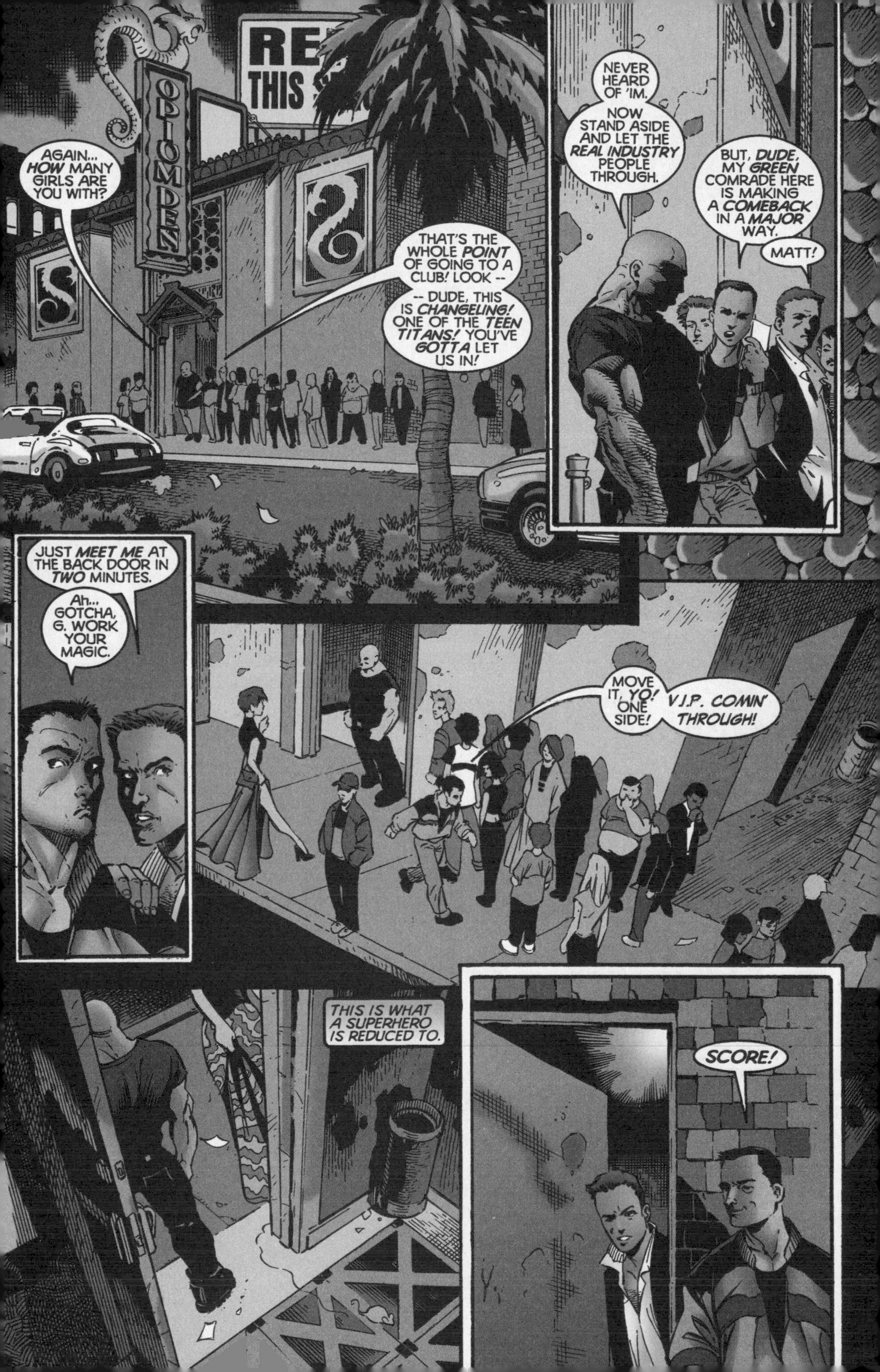

OPIUM DEN
RE
THIS
AGAIN... HOW MANY GIRLS ARE YOU WITH?
THAT'S THE WHOLE POINT OF GOING TO A CLUB! LOOK --
-- DUDE, THIS IS CHANGELING! ONE OF THE TEEN TITANS! YOU'VE GOTTA LET US IN!
NEVER HEARD OF 'IM.
NOW STAND ASIDE AND LET THE REAL INDUSTRY PEOPLE THROUGH.
BUT, DUDE, MY GREEN COMRADE HERE IS MAKING A COMEBACK IN A MAJOR WAY.
MATT!
JUST MEET ME AT THE BACK DOOR IN TWO MINUTES.
Ah... GOTCHA, G. WORK YOUR MAGIC.
MOVE IT, YO! ONE SIDE!
V.I.P. COMIN' THROUGH!
THIS IS WHAT A SUPERHERO IS REDUCED TO.
SCORE!

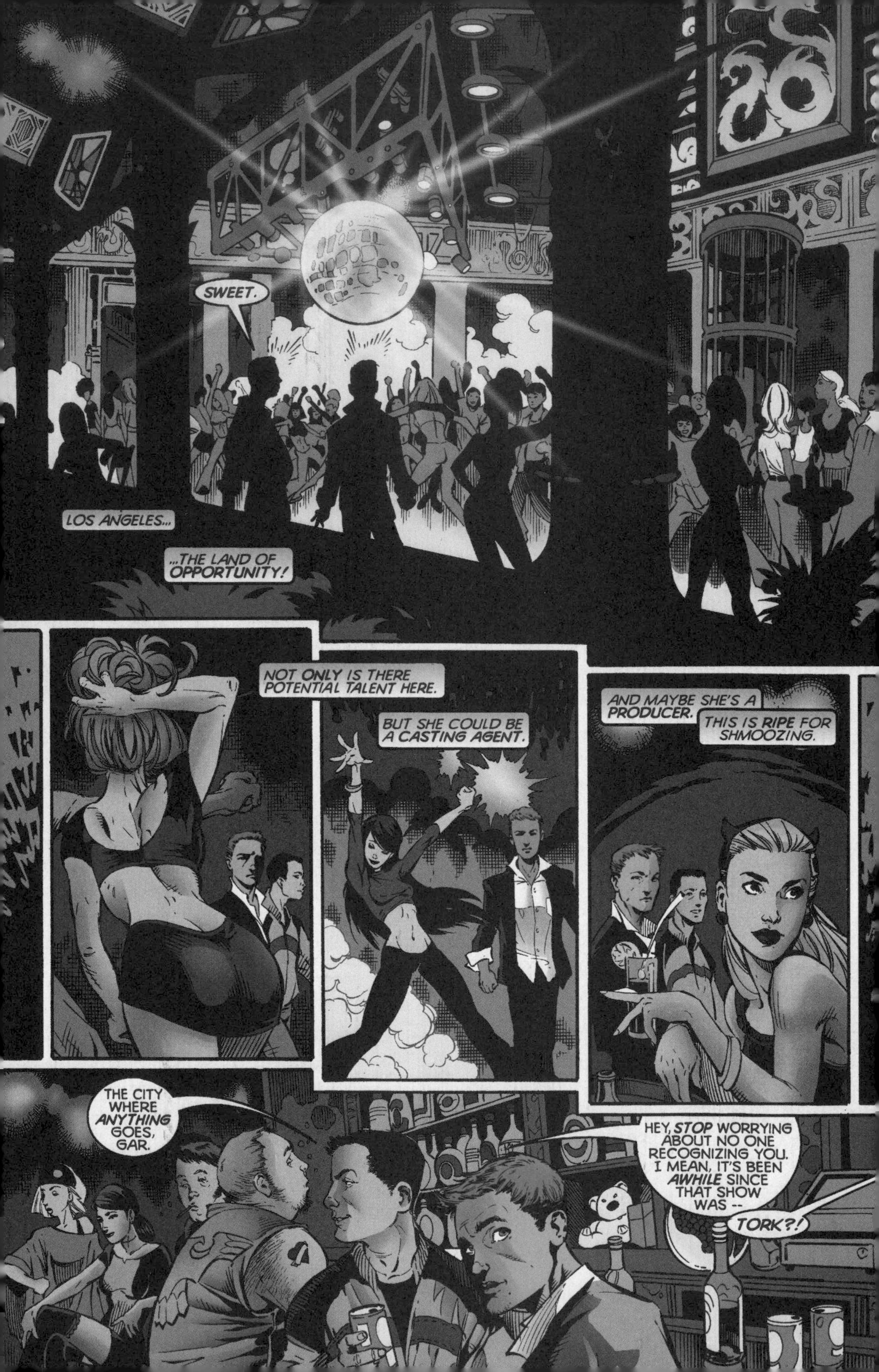

SWEET.
LOS ANGELES...
...THE LAND OF OPPORTUNITY!
NOT ONLY IS THERE POTENTIAL TALENT HERE.
BUT SHE COULD BE A CASTING AGENT.
AND MAYBE SHE'S A PRODUCER.
THIS IS RIPE FOR SHMOOZING.
THE CITY WHERE ANYTHING GOES, GAR.
HEY, STOP WORRYING ABOUT NO ONE RECOGNIZING YOU. I MEAN, IT'S BEEN AWHILE SINCE THAT SHOW WAS --
TORK?!

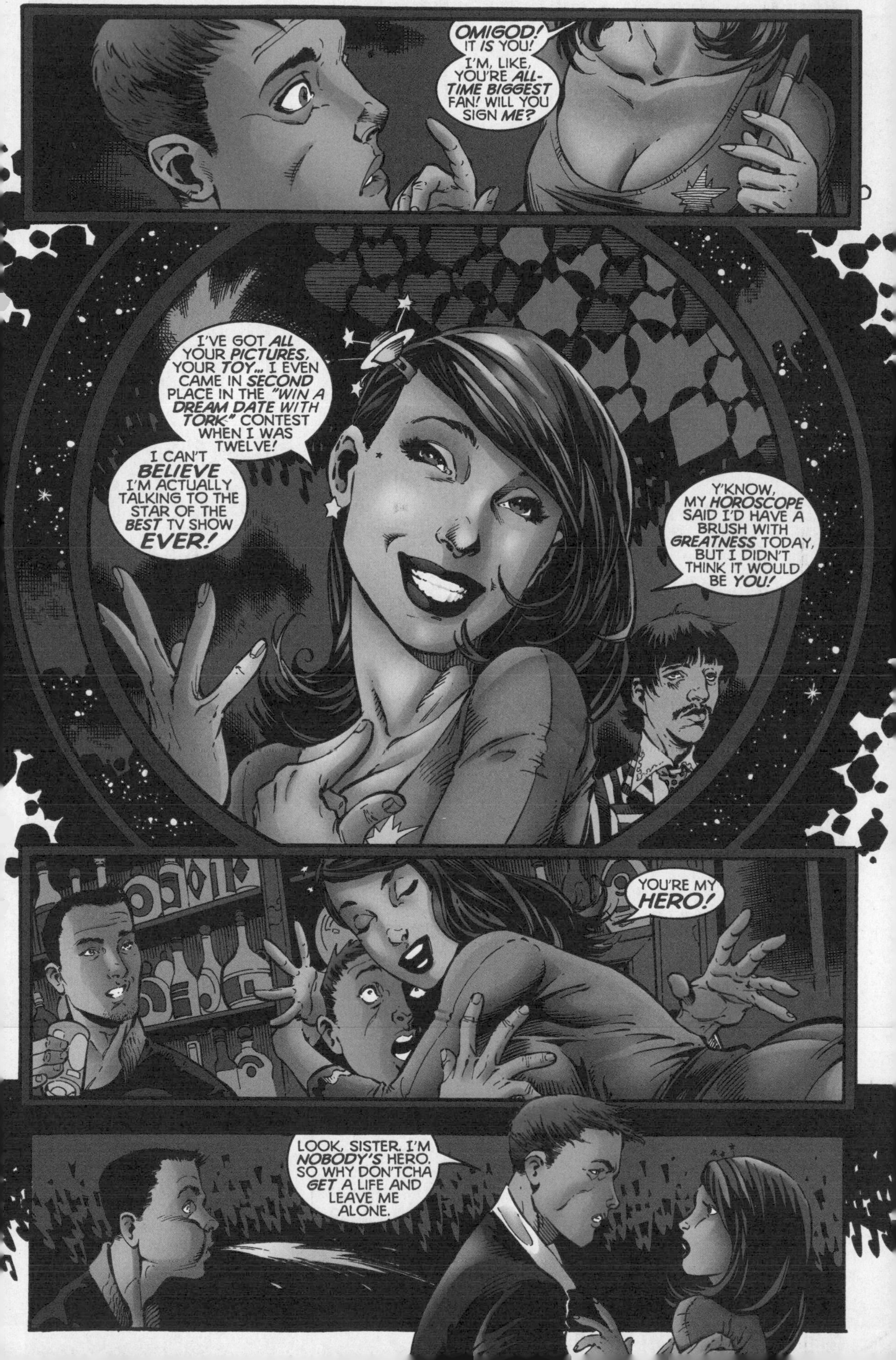
OMIGOD! IT IS YOU! I'M, LIKE, YOU'RE ALL-TIME BIGGEST FAN! WILL YOU SIGN ME?
I'VE GOT ALL YOUR PICTURES, YOUR TOY... I EVEN CAME IN SECOND PLACE IN THE "WIN A DREAM DATE WITH TORK" CONTEST WHEN I WAS TWELVE!
I CAN'T BELIEVE I'M ACTUALLY TALKING TO THE STAR OF THE BEST TV SHOW EVER!
Y'KNOW, MY HOROSCOPE SAID I'D HAVE A BRUSH WITH GREATNESS TODAY, BUT I DIDN'T THINK IT WOULD BE YOU!
YOU'RE MY HERO!
LOOK, SISTER. I'M NOBODY'S HERO. SO WHY DON'TCHA GET A LIFE AND LEAVE ME ALONE.

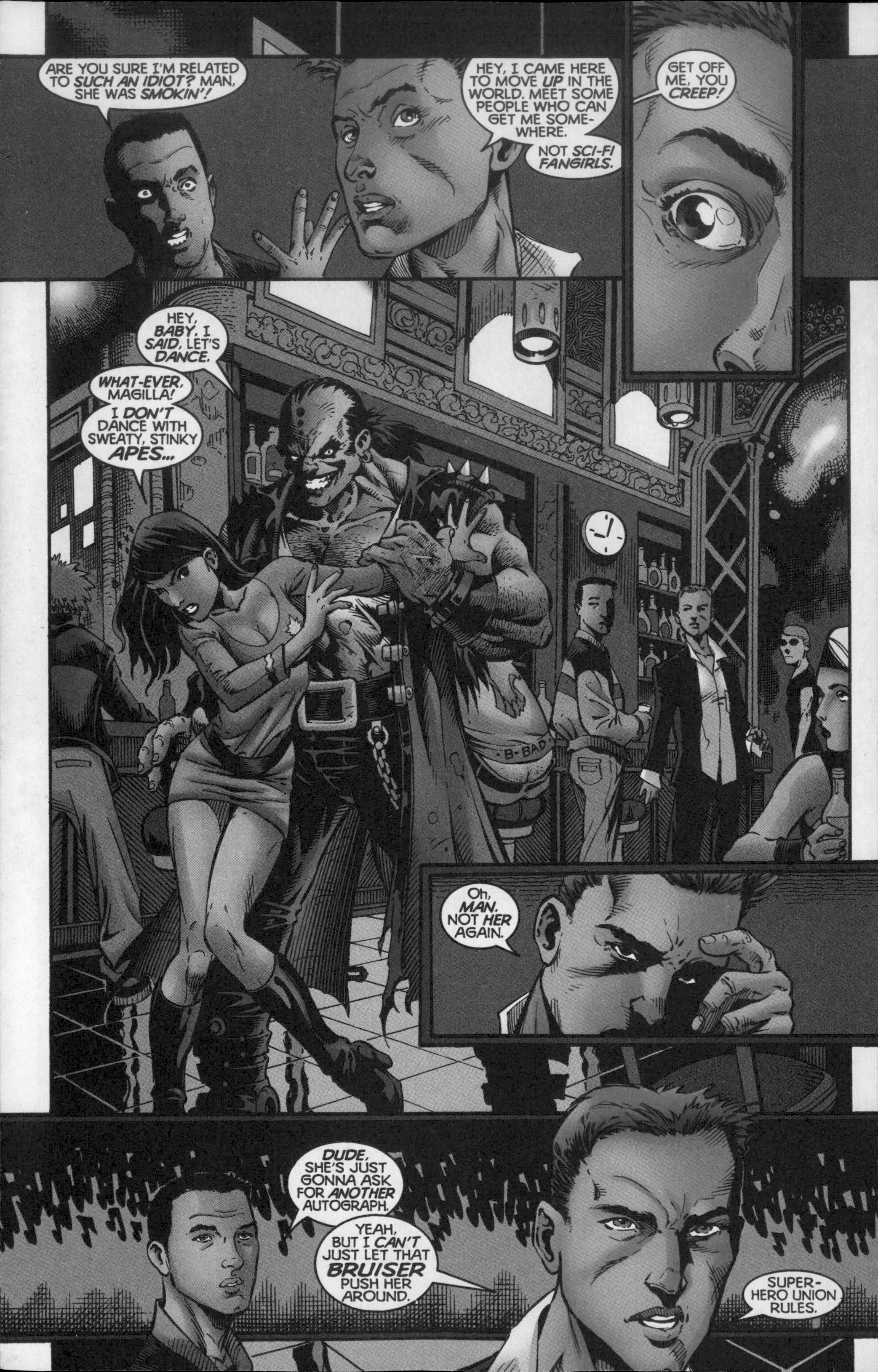
ARE YOU SURE I'M RELATED TO SUCH AN IDIOT? MAN, SHE WAS SMOKIN'!
HEY, I CAME HERE TO MOVE UP IN THE WORLD. MEET SOME PEOPLE WHO CAN GET ME SOME-WHERE.
NOT SCI-FI FANGIRLS.
GET OFF ME, YOU CREEP!
HEY, BABY. I SAID, LET'S DANCE.
WHAT-EVER, MAGILLA!
I DON'T DANCE WITH SWEATY, STINKY APES...
B-BAD
Oh, MAN. NOT HER AGAIN.
DUDE, SHE'S JUST GONNA ASK FOR ANOTHER AUTOGRAPH.
YEAH, BUT I CAN'T JUST LET THAT BRUISER PUSH HER AROUND.
SUPER-HERO UNION RULES.

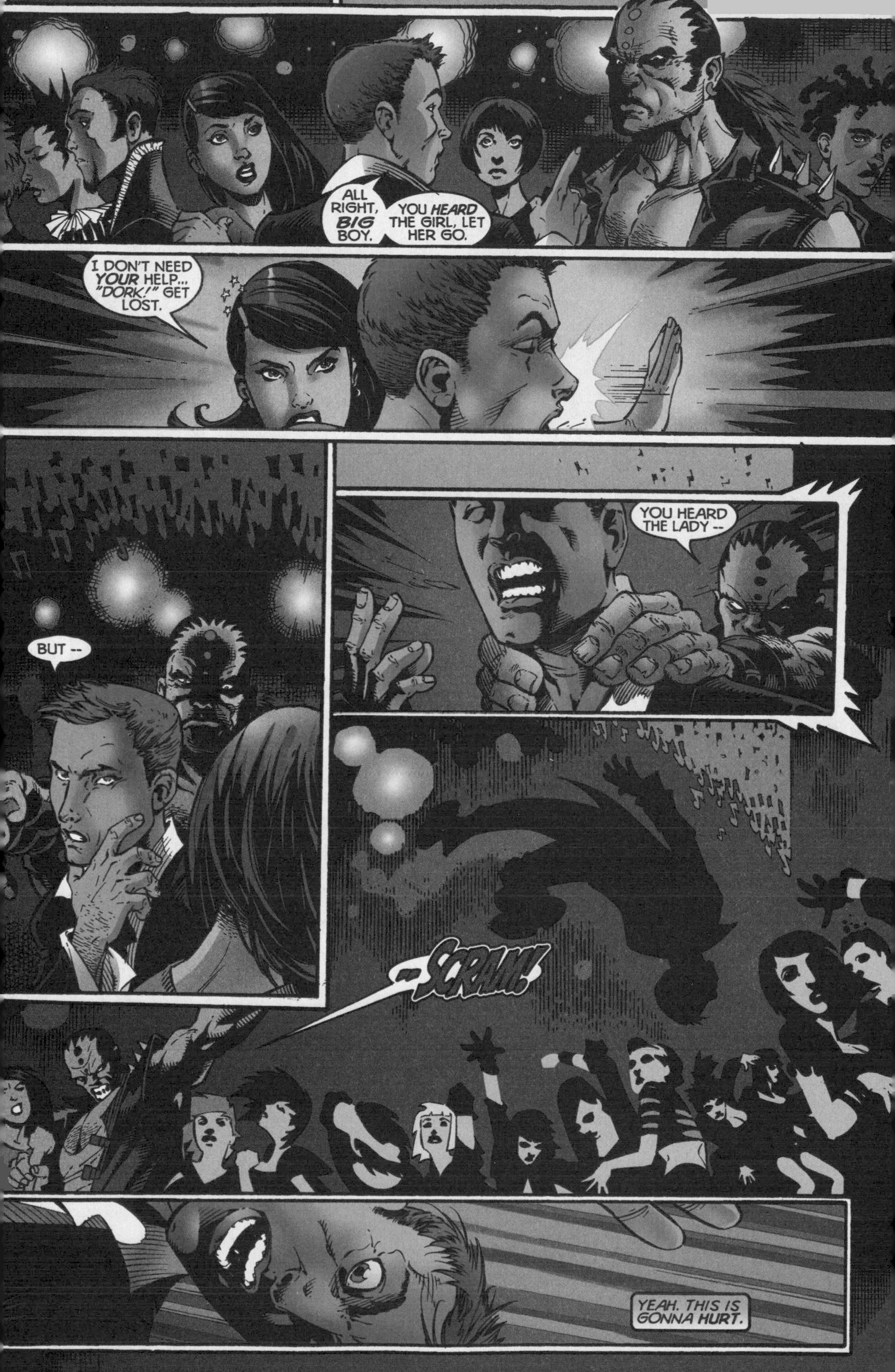

ALL RIGHT, BIG BOY.
YOU HEARD THE GIRL, LET HER GO.
I DON'T NEED YOUR HELP... "DORK!" GET LOST.
BUT --
YOU HEARD THE LADY --
-- SCRAM!
YEAH. THIS IS GONNA HURT.

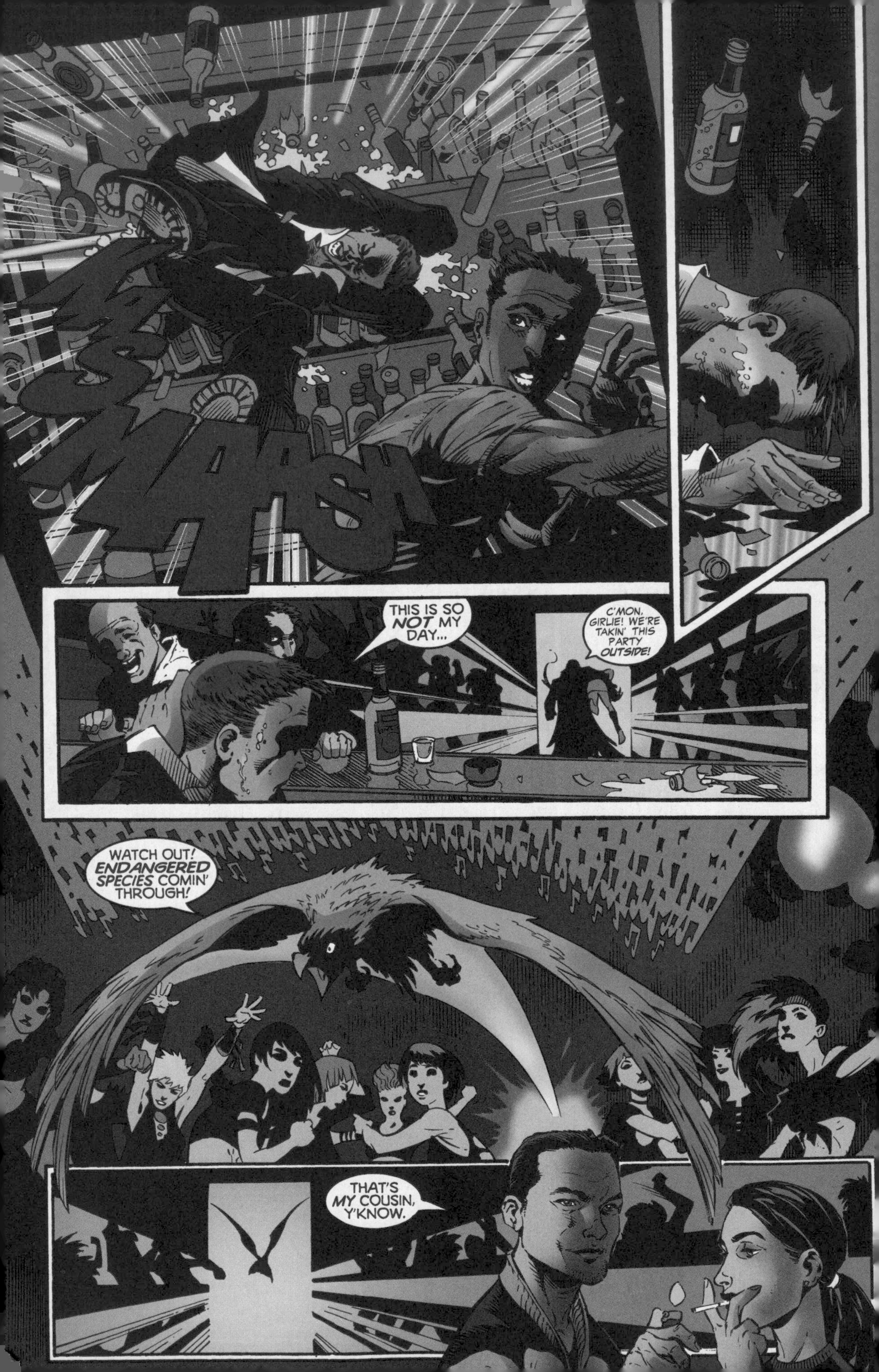
SMASH
THIS IS SO NOT MY DAY...
C'MON, GIRLIE! WE'RE TAKIN' THIS PARTY OUTSIDE!
WATCH OUT! ENDANGERED SPECIES COMIN' THROUGH!
THAT'S MY COUSIN, Y'KNOW.

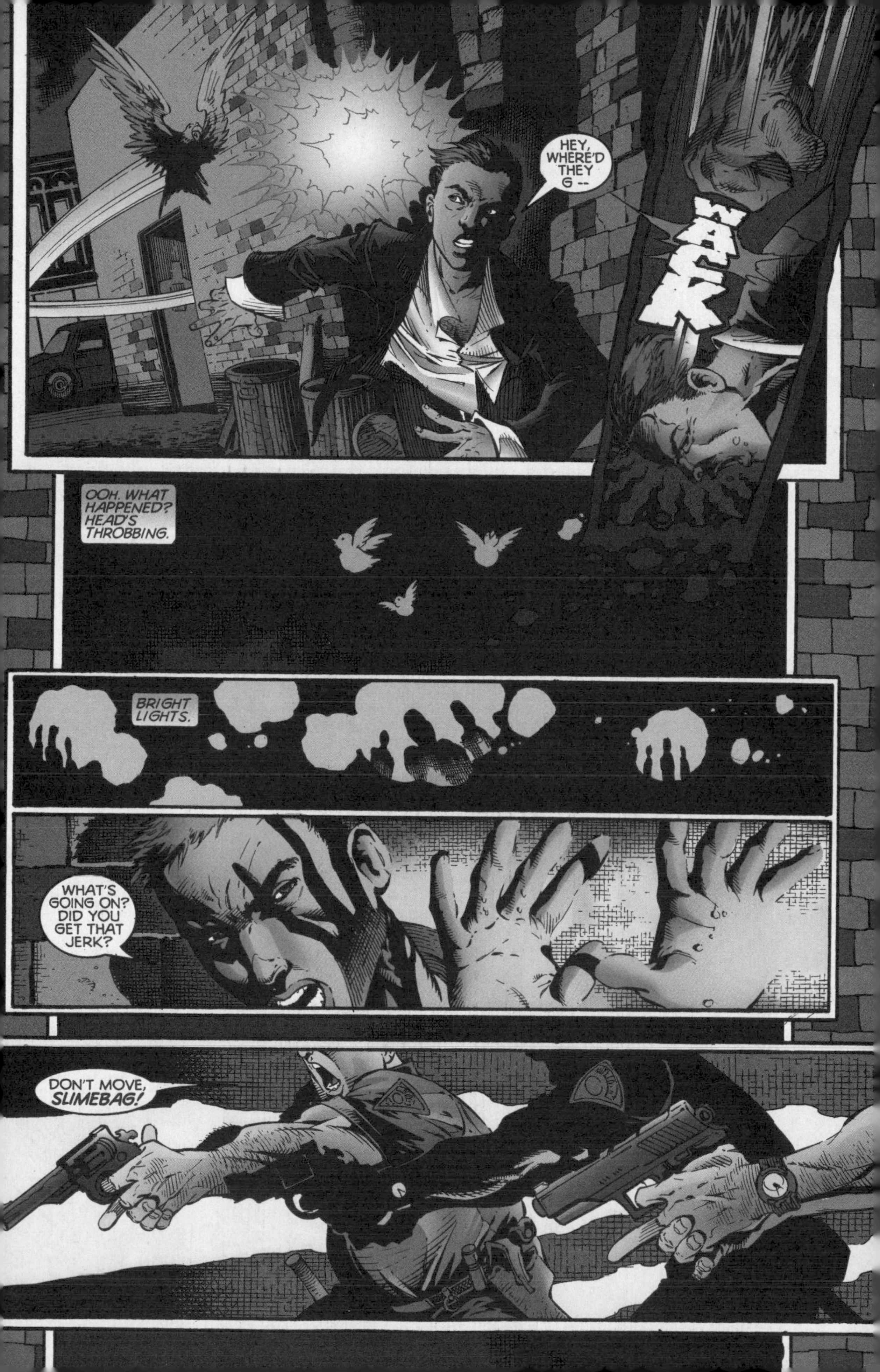

HEY, WHERE'D THEY G --
WACK
OOH. WHAT HAPPENED? HEAD'S THROBBING.
BRIGHT LIGHTS.
WHAT'S GOING ON? DID YOU GET THAT JERK?
DON'T MOVE, SLIMEBAG!

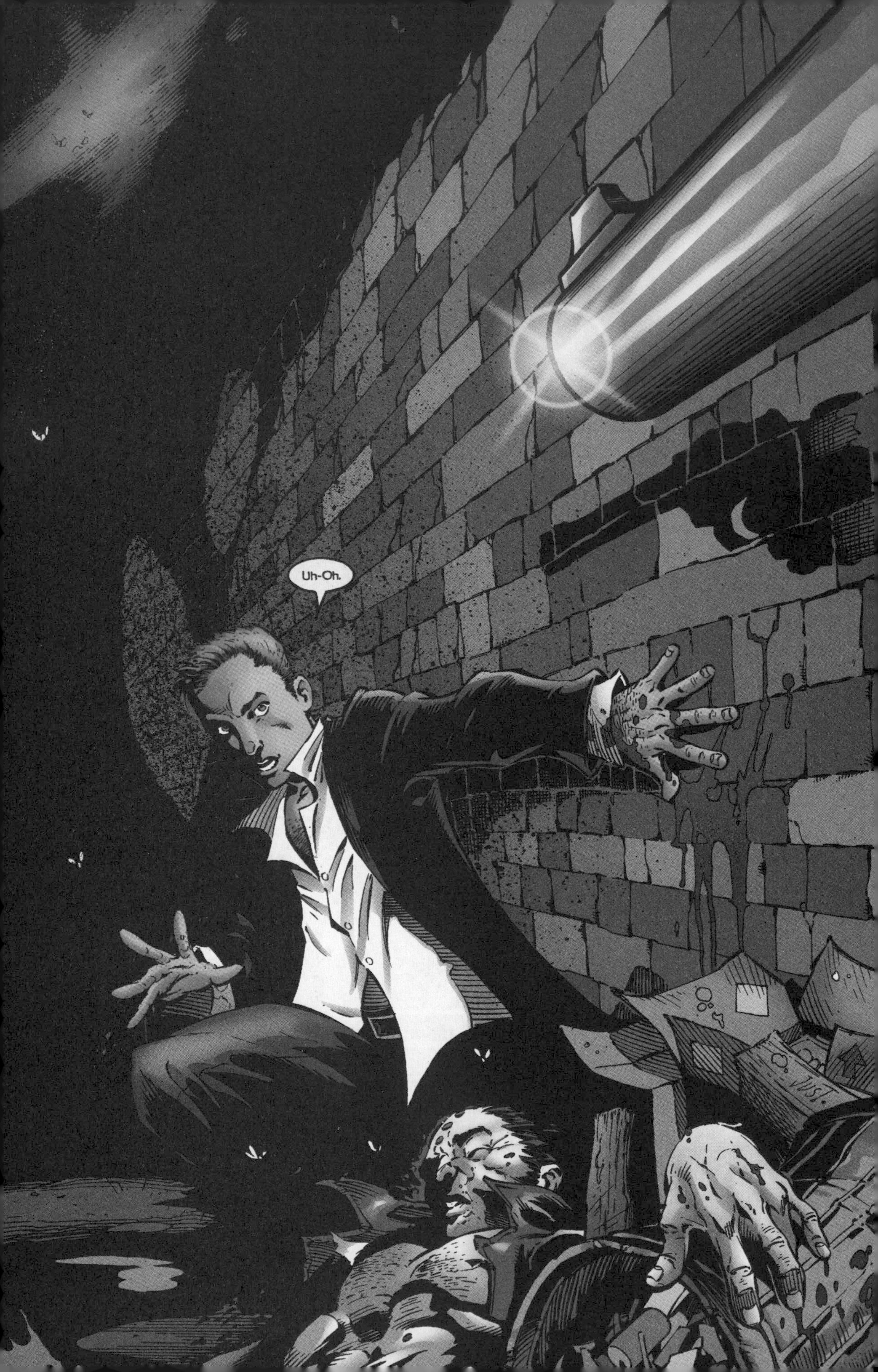
Uh-Oh.

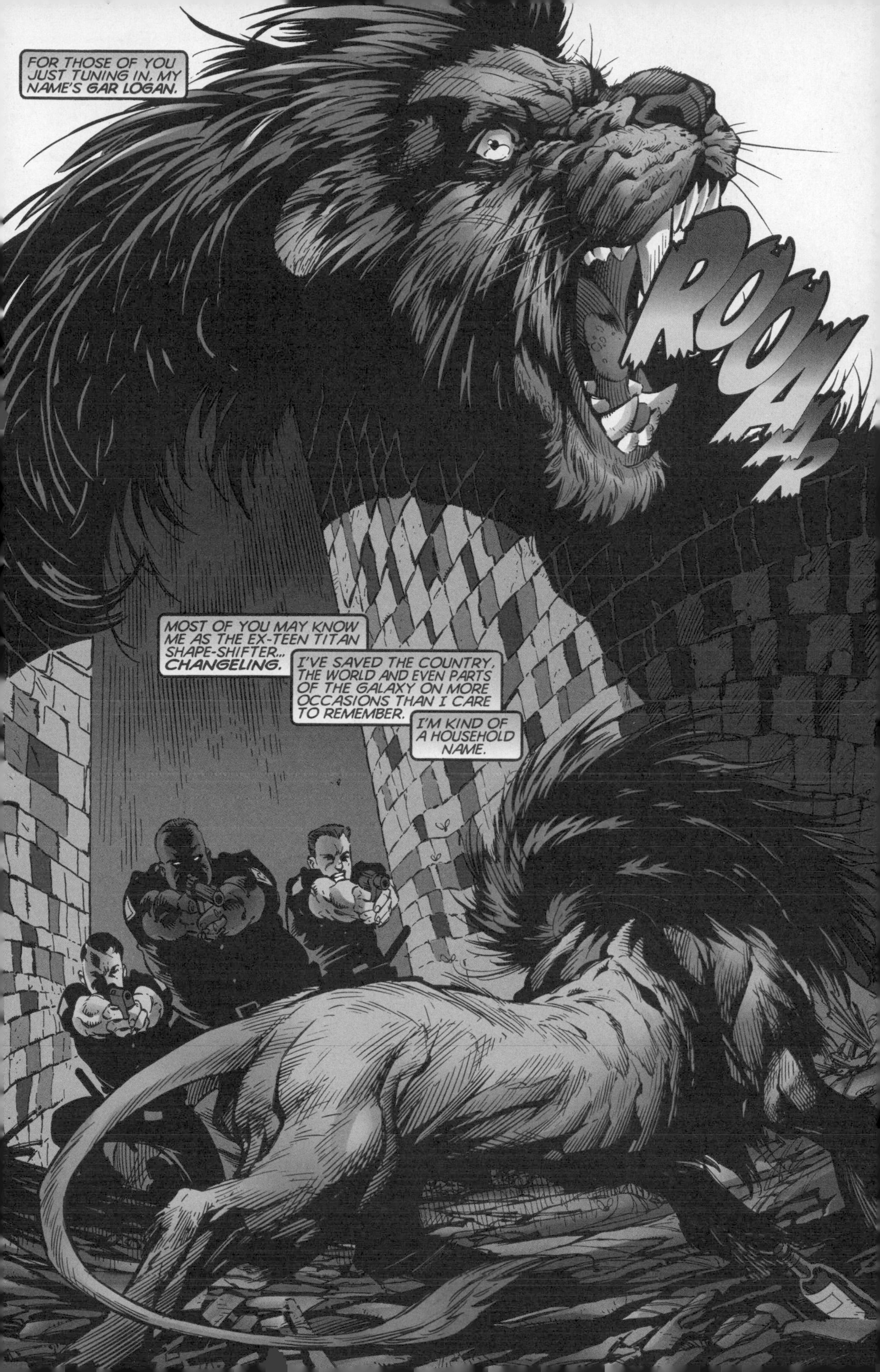
FOR THOSE OF YOU JUST TUNING IN, MY NAME'S GAR LOGAN.
ROOOAAR
MOST OF YOU MAY KNOW ME AS THE EX-TEEN TITAN SHAPE-SHIFTER... CHANGELING.
I'VE SAVED THE COUNTRY, THE WORLD AND EVEN PARTS OF THE GALAXY ON MORE OCCASIONS THAN I CARE TO REMEMBER.
I'M KIND OF A HOUSEHOLD NAME.

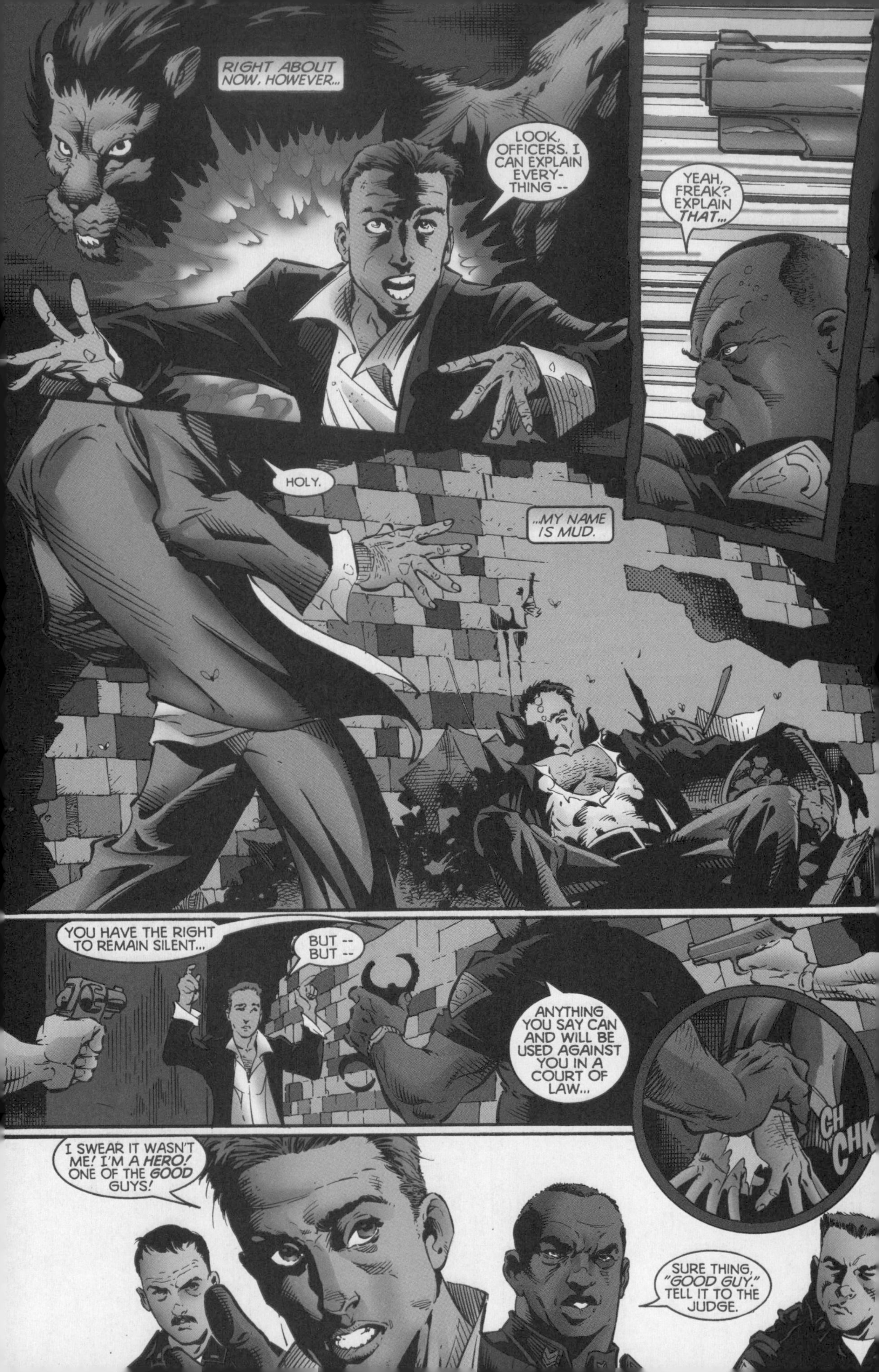
RIGHT ABOUT NOW, HOWEVER...
LOOK, OFFICERS. I CAN EXPLAIN EVERY-THING --
YEAH, FREAK? EXPLAIN THAT...
HOLY.
...MY NAME IS MUD.
YOU HAVE THE RIGHT TO REMAIN SILENT...
BUT -- BUT --
ANYTHING YOU SAY CAN AND WILL BE USED AGAINST YOU IN A COURT OF LAW...
CH CHK
I SWEAR IT WASN'T ME! I'M A HERO! ONE OF THE GOOD GUYS!
SURE THING, "GOOD GUY." TELL IT TO THE JUDGE.

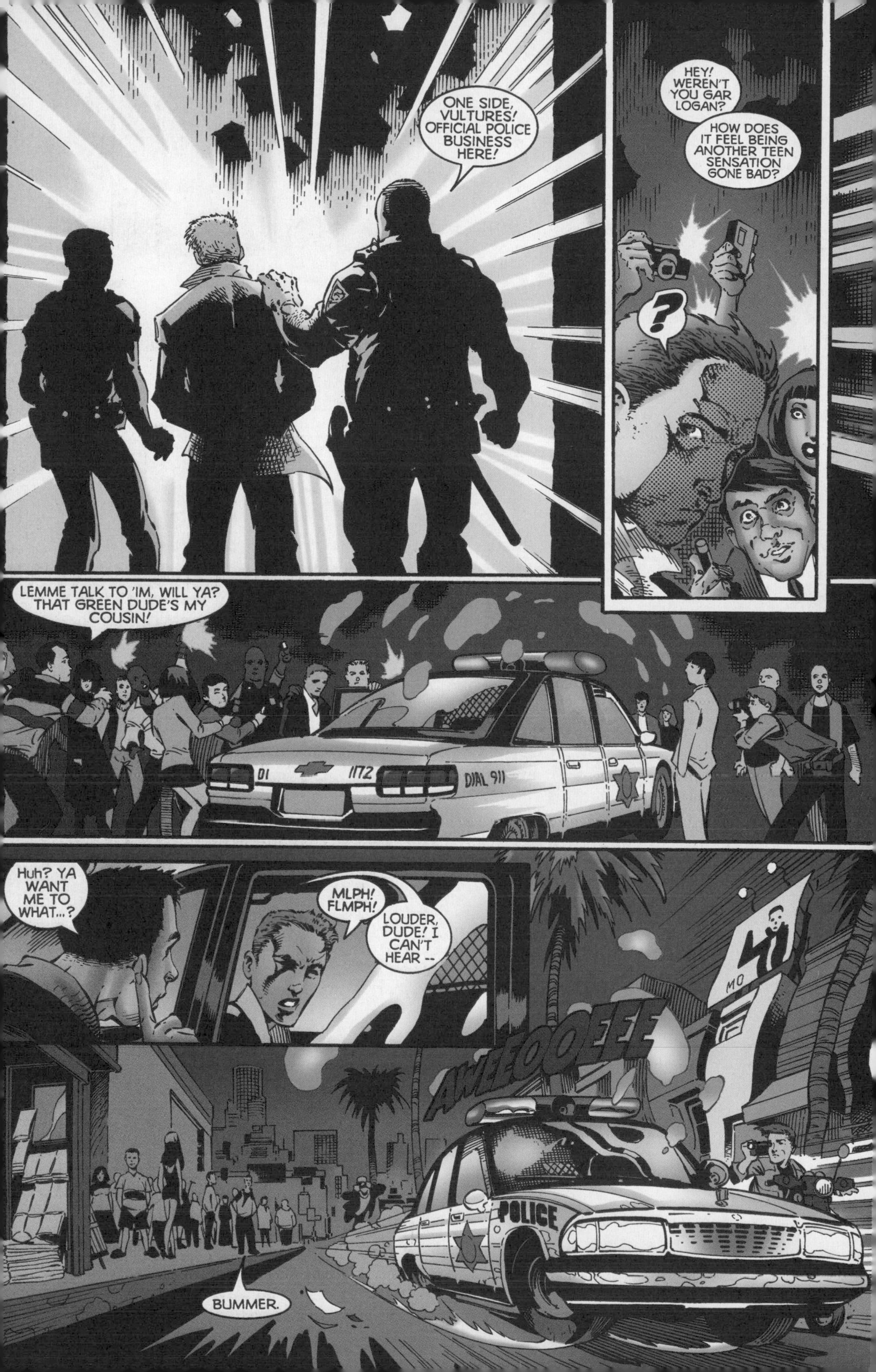
ONE SIDE, VULTURES! OFFICIAL POLICE BUSINESS HERE!
HEY! WEREN'T YOU GAR LOGAN?
HOW DOES IT FEEL BEING ANOTHER TEEN SENSATION GONE BAD?
?
LEMME TALK TO 'IM, WILL YA? THAT GREEN DUDE'S MY COUSIN!
01
1172
DIAL 911
Huh? YA WANT ME TO WHAT...?
MLPH! FLMPH!
LOUDER, DUDE! I CAN'T HEAR --
AWEEOOEEE
POLICE
BUMMER.

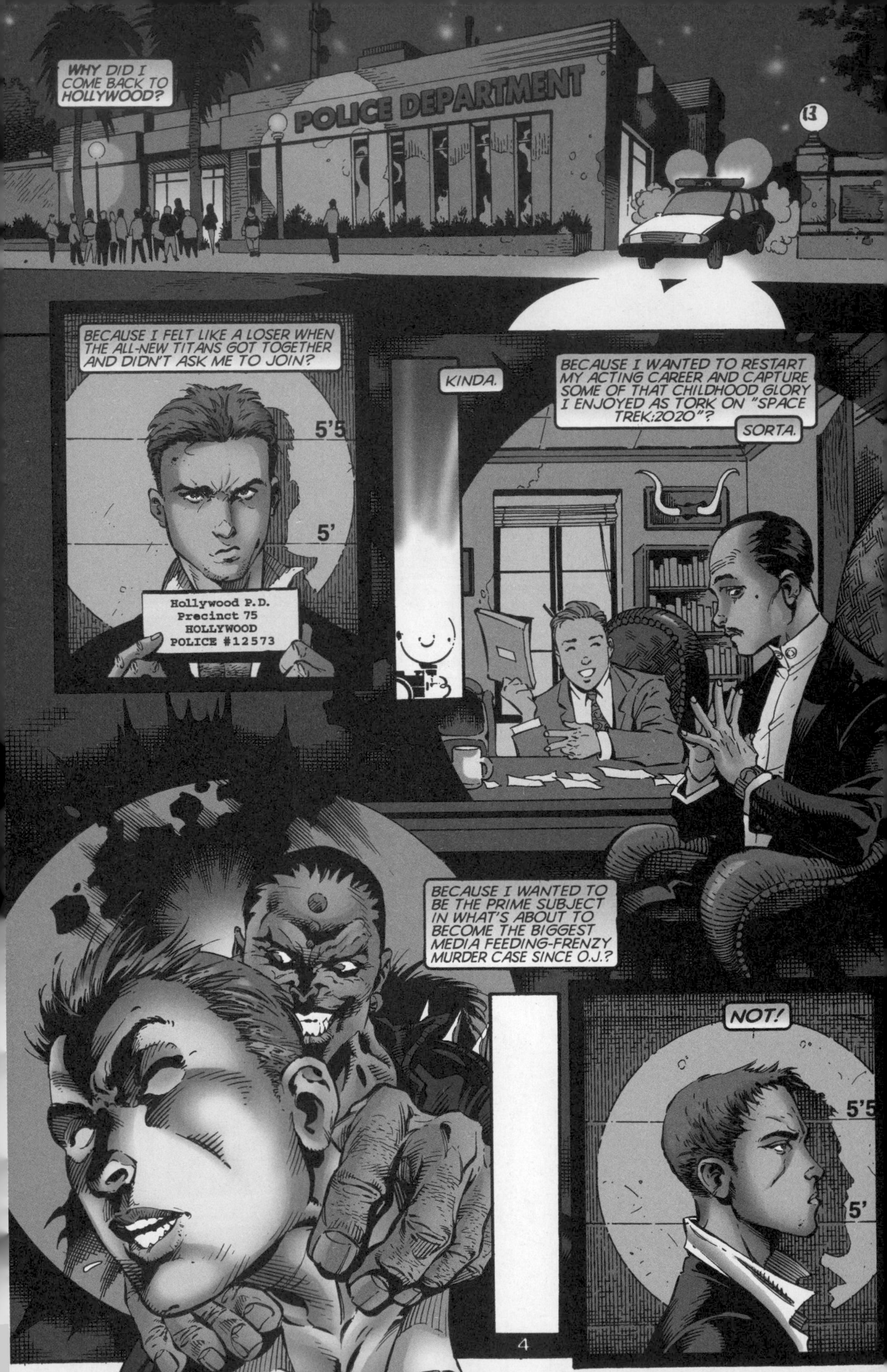
WHY DID I COME BACK TO HOLLYWOOD?
POLICE DEPARTMENT
BECAUSE I FELT LIKE A LOSER WHEN THE ALL-NEW TITANS GOT TOGETHER AND DIDN'T ASK ME TO JOIN?
KINDA.
5'5
5'
Hollywood P.D.
Precinct 75
HOLLYWOOD
POLICE #12573
BECAUSE I WANTED TO RESTART MY ACTING CAREER AND CAPTURE SOME OF THAT CHILDHOOD GLORY I ENJOYED AS TORK ON "SPACE TREK:2020"?
SORTA.
BECAUSE I WANTED TO BE THE PRIME SUBJECT IN WHAT'S ABOUT TO BECOME THE BIGGEST MEDIA FEEDING-FRENZY MURDER CASE SINCE O.J.?
NOT!
5'5
5'

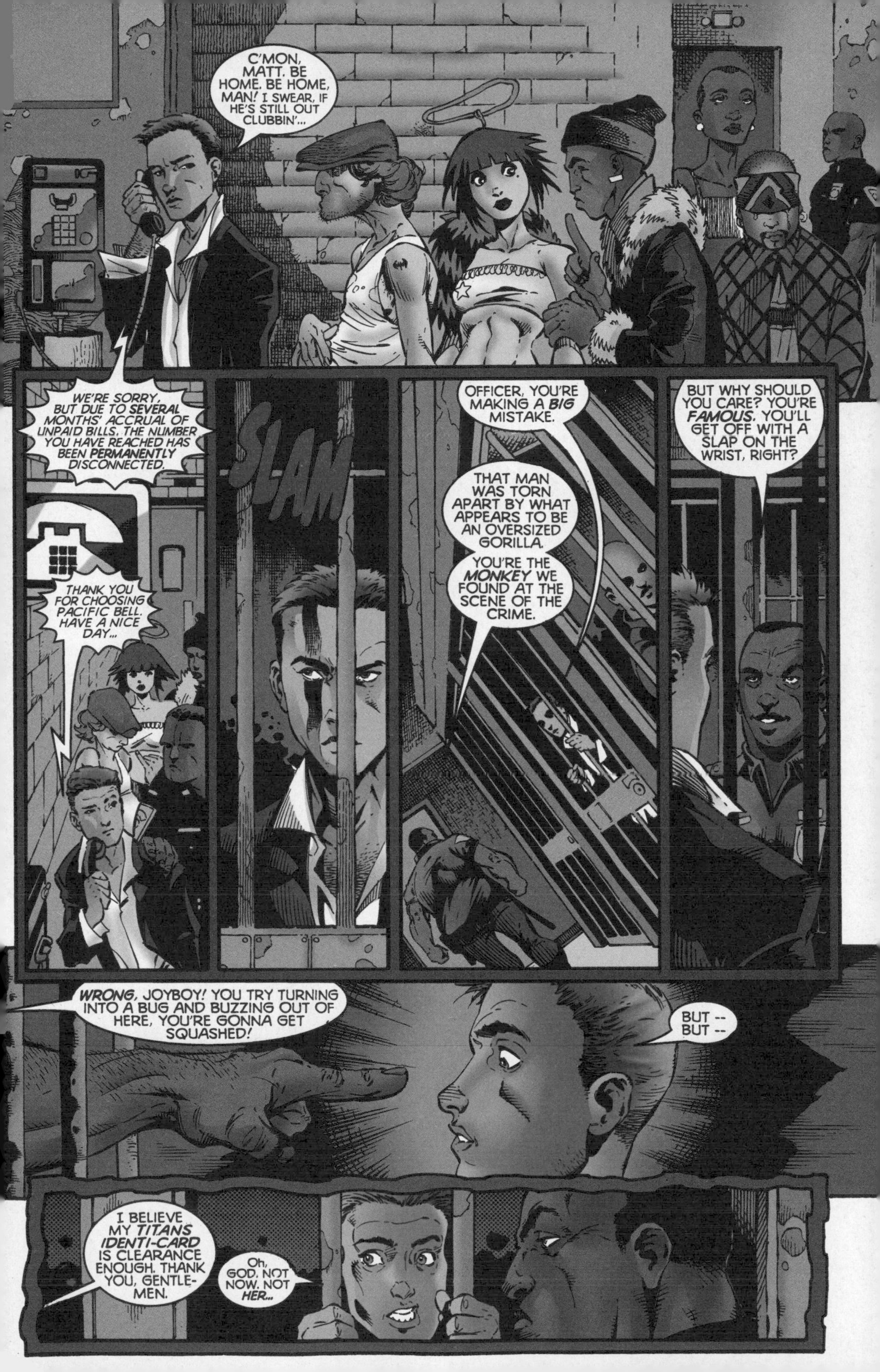
C'MON, MATT. BE HOME. BE HOME, MAN! I SWEAR, IF HE'S STILL OUT CLUBBIN'...
WE'RE SORRY, BUT DUE TO SEVERAL MONTHS' ACCRUAL OF UNPAID BILLS, THE NUMBER YOU HAVE REACHED HAS BEEN PERMANENTLY DISCONNECTED.
THANK YOU FOR CHOOSING PACIFIC BELL. HAVE A NICE DAY...
SLAM
OFFICER, YOU'RE MAKING A BIG MISTAKE.
THAT MAN WAS TORN APART BY WHAT APPEARS TO BE AN OVERSIZED GORILLA.
YOU'RE THE MONKEY WE FOUND AT THE SCENE OF THE CRIME.
BUT WHY SHOULD YOU CARE? YOU'RE FAMOUS. YOU'LL GET OFF WITH A SLAP ON THE WRIST, RIGHT?
WRONG, JOYBOY! YOU TRY TURNING INTO A BUG AND BUZZING OUT OF HERE, YOU'RE GONNA GET SQUASHED!
BUT -- BUT --
I BELIEVE MY TITANS IDENTI-CARD IS CLEARANCE ENOUGH. THANK YOU, GENTLE-MEN.
Oh, GOD. NOT NOW. NOT HER...

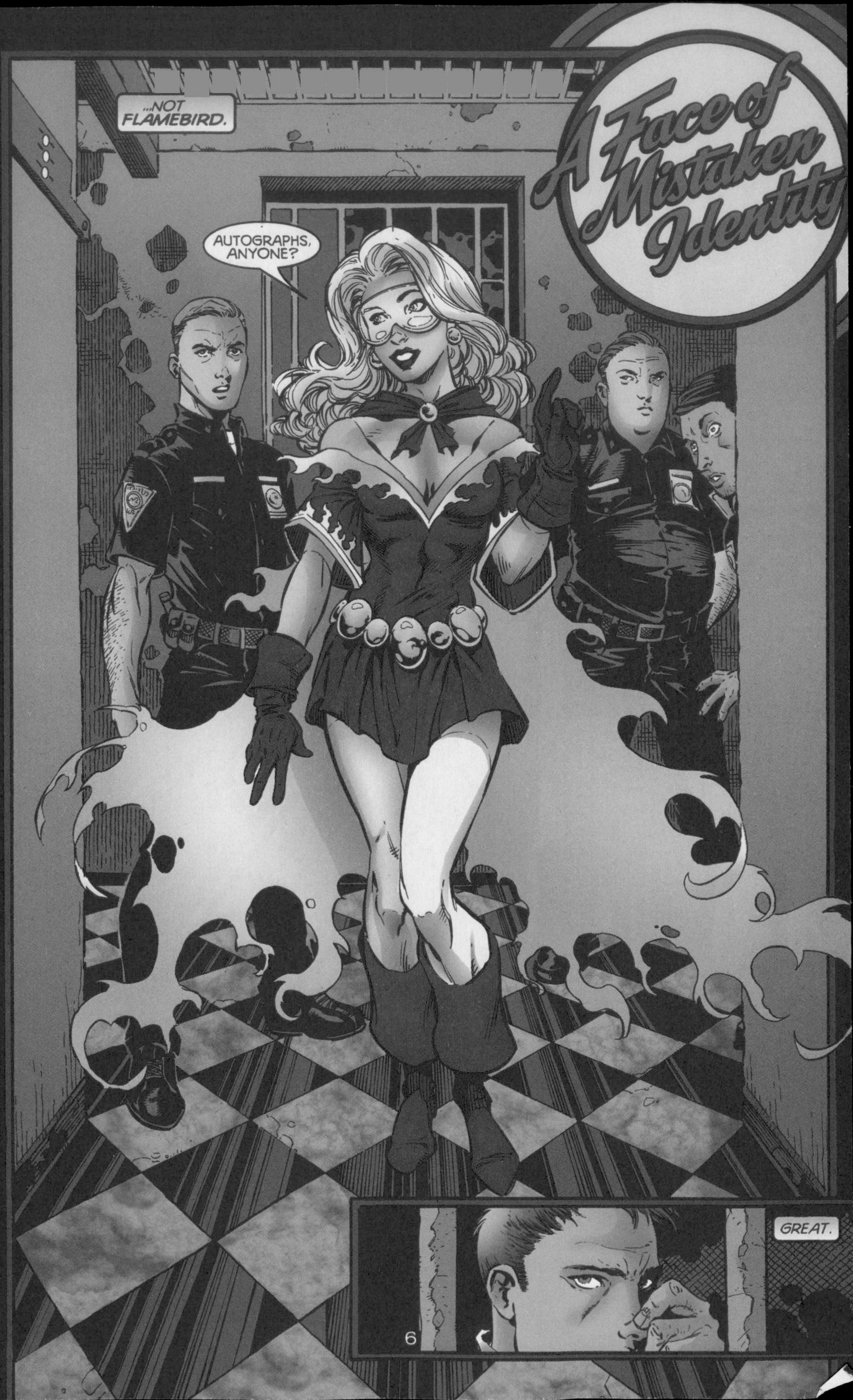
...NOT FLAMEBIRD.
A Face of Mistaken Identity
AUTOGRAPHS, ANYONE?
GREAT.

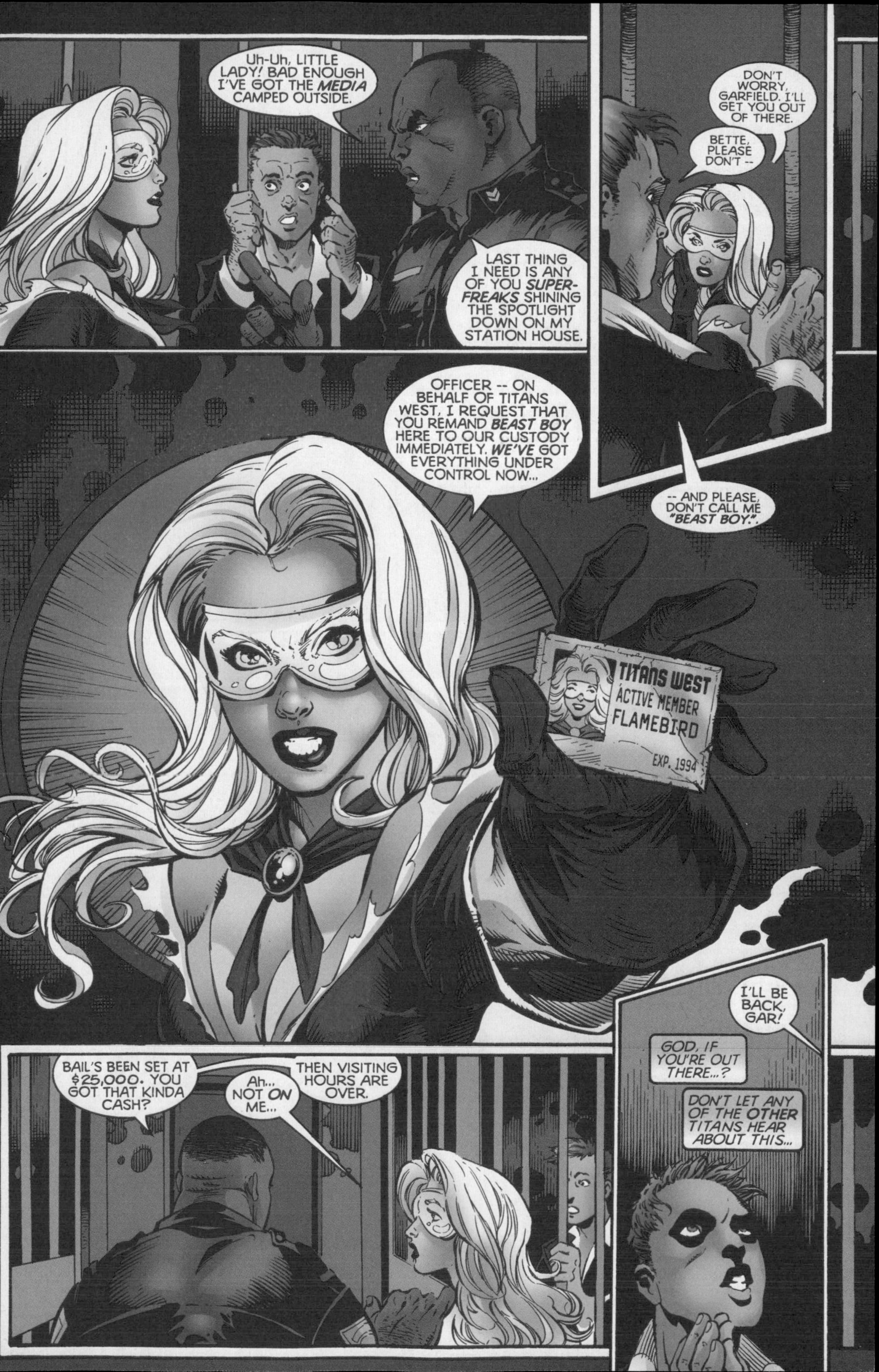

Uh-Uh, LITTLE LADY! BAD ENOUGH I'VE GOT THE MEDIA CAMPED OUTSIDE.
LAST THING I NEED IS ANY OF YOU SUPER-FREAKS SHINING THE SPOTLIGHT DOWN ON MY STATION HOUSE.
DON'T WORRY, GARFIELD. I'LL GET YOU OUT OF THERE.
BETTE, PLEASE DON'T --
OFFICER -- ON BEHALF OF TITANS WEST, I REQUEST THAT YOU REMAND BEAST BOY HERE TO OUR CUSTODY IMMEDIATELY. WE'VE GOT EVERYTHING UNDER CONTROL NOW...
-- AND PLEASE, DON'T CALL ME "BEAST BOY."
TITANS WEST
ACTIVE MEMBER
FLAMEBIRD
EXP. 1994
BAIL'S BEEN SET AT $25,000. YOU GOT THAT KINDA CASH?
Ah... NOT ON ME...
THEN VISITING HOURS ARE OVER.
I'LL BE BACK, GAR!
GOD, IF YOU'RE OUT THERE...?
DON'T LET ANY OF THE OTHER TITANS HEAR ABOUT THIS...

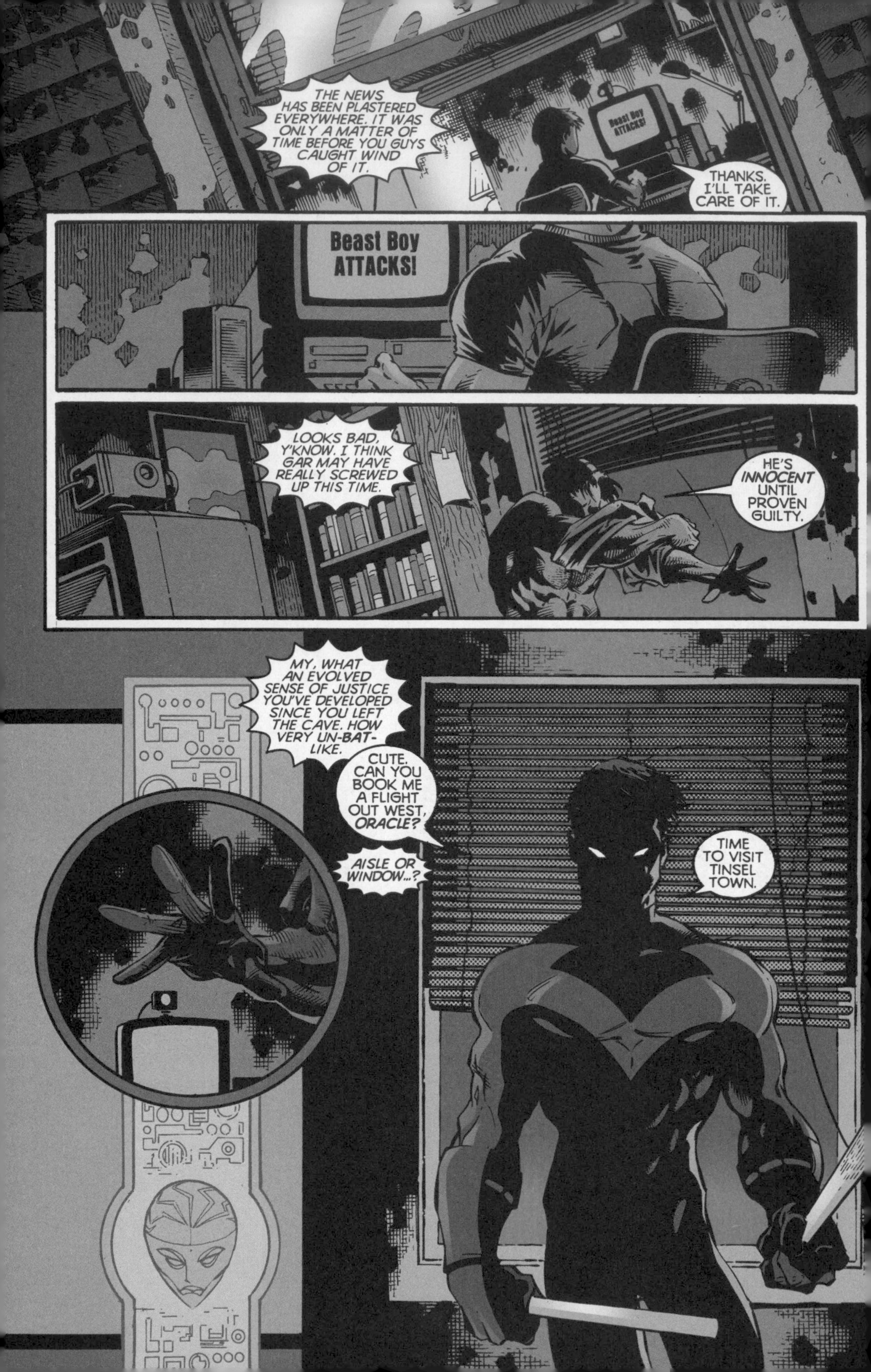
THE NEWS HAS BEEN PLASTERED EVERYWHERE. IT WAS ONLY A MATTER OF TIME BEFORE YOU GUYS CAUGHT WIND OF IT.
Beast Boy ATTACKS!
THANKS. I'LL TAKE CARE OF IT.
Beast Boy ATTACKS!
LOOKS BAD, Y'KNOW. I THINK GAR MAY HAVE REALLY SCREWED UP THIS TIME.
HE'S INNOCENT UNTIL PROVEN GUILTY.
MY, WHAT AN EVOLVED SENSE OF JUSTICE YOU'VE DEVELOPED SINCE YOU LEFT THE CAVE. HOW VERY UN-BAT-LIKE.
CUTE. CAN YOU BOOK ME A FLIGHT OUT WEST, ORACLE?
AISLE OR WINDOW...?
TIME TO VISIT TINSEL TOWN.

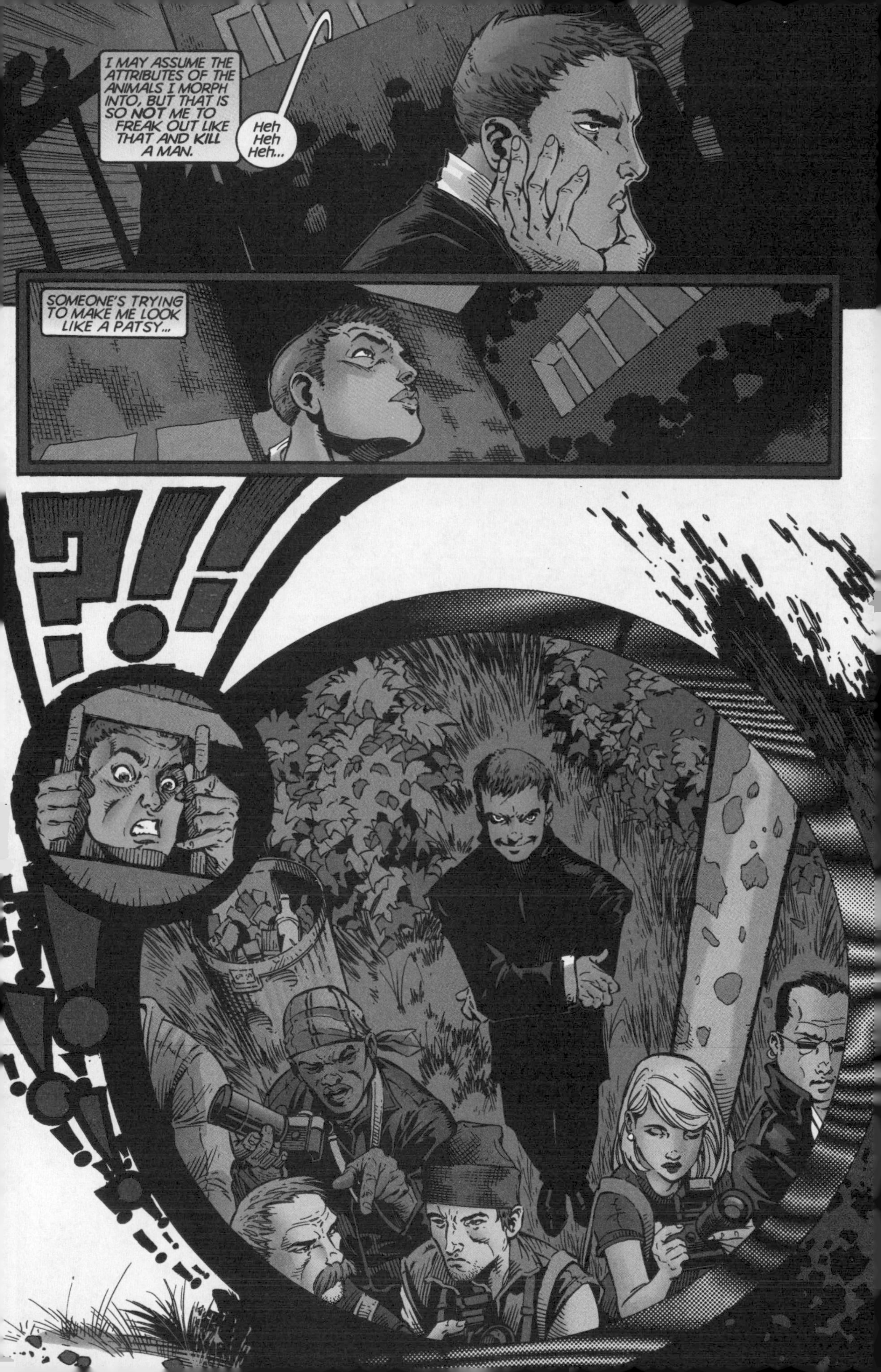
I MAY ASSUME THE ATTRIBUTES OF THE ANIMALS I MORPH INTO, BUT THAT IS SO NOT ME TO FREAK OUT LIKE THAT AND KILL A MAN.
Heh Heh Heh...
SOMEONE'S TRYING TO MAKE ME LOOK LIKE A PATSY...
?!!
!

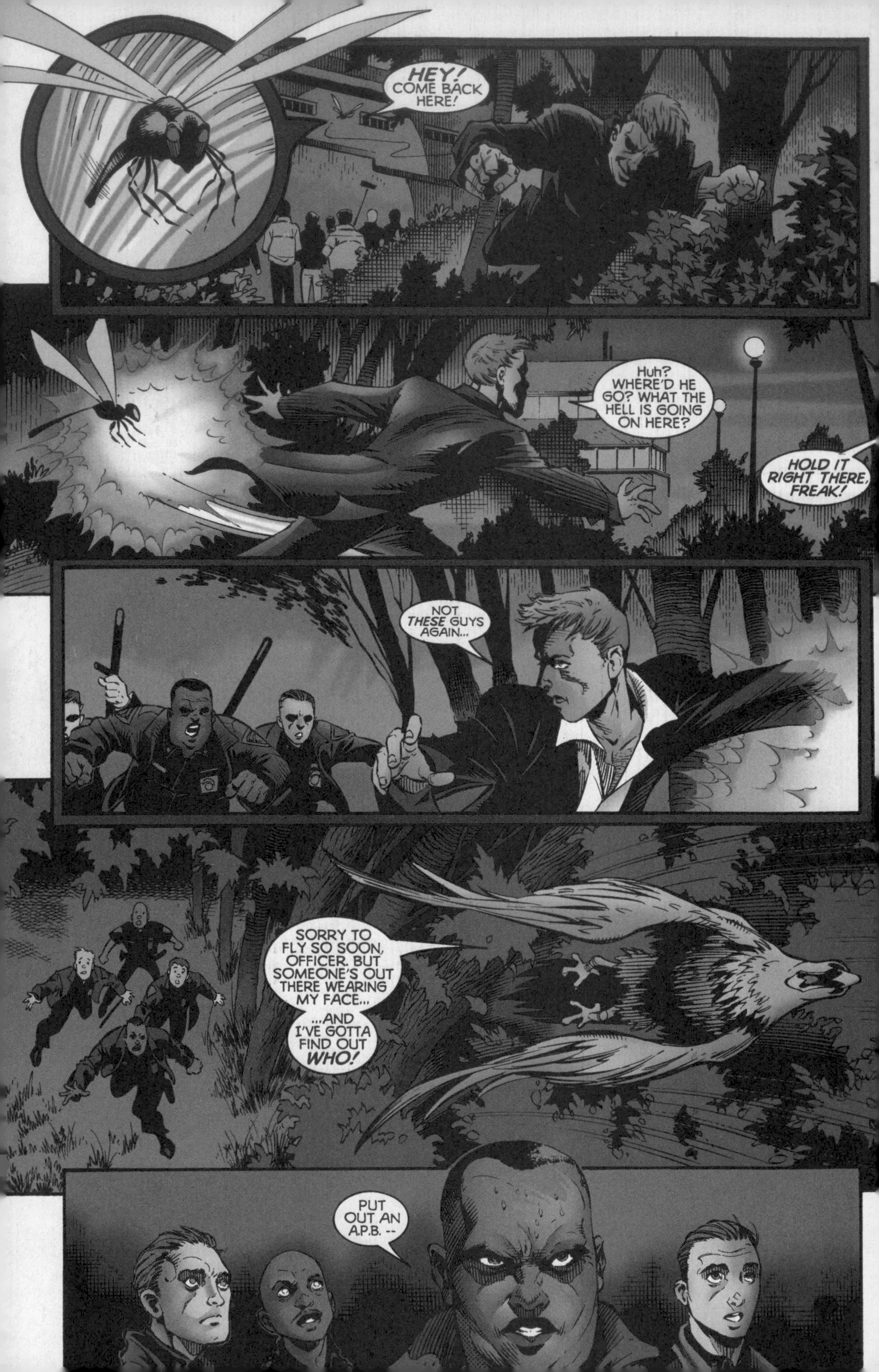
HEY! COME BACK HERE!
Huh? WHERE'D HE GO? WHAT THE HELL IS GOING ON HERE?
HOLD IT RIGHT THERE, FREAK!
NOT THESE GUYS AGAIN...
SORRY TO FLY SO SOON, OFFICER. BUT SOMEONE'S OUT THERE WEARING MY FACE...
...AND I'VE GOTTA FIND OUT WHO!
PUT OUT AN A.P.B. --

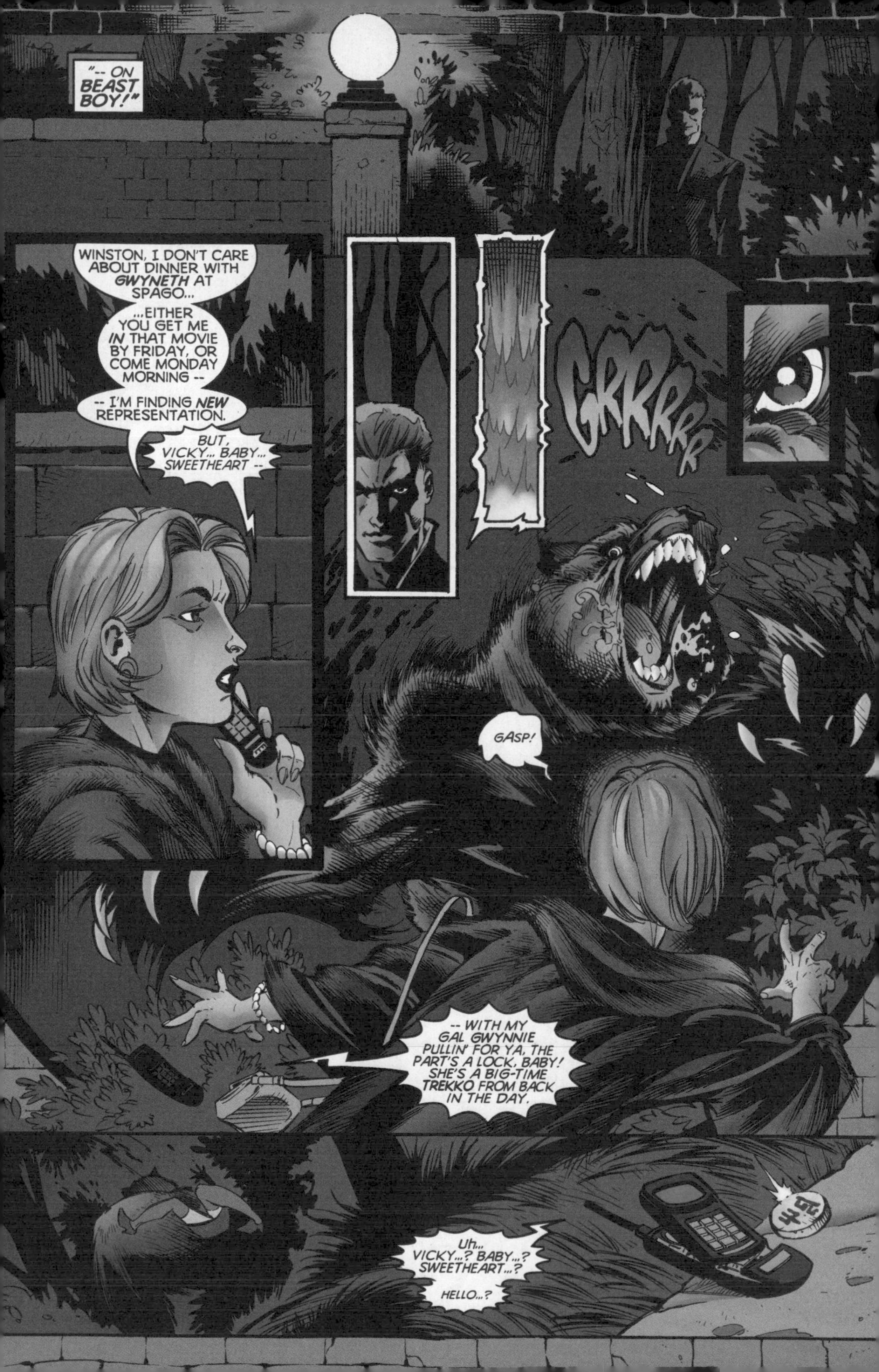
"-- ON BEAST BOY!"
WINSTON, I DON'T CARE ABOUT DINNER WITH GWYNETH AT SPAGO...
...EITHER YOU GET ME IN THAT MOVIE BY FRIDAY, OR COME MONDAY MORNING --
-- I'M FINDING NEW REPRESENTATION.
BUT, VICKY... BABY... SWEETHEART --
GRRRRR
GASP!
-- WITH MY GAL GWYNNIE PULLIN' FOR YA, THE PART'S A LOCK, BABY! SHE'S A BIG-TIME TREKKO FROM BACK IN THE DAY.
Uh... VICKY...? BABY...? SWEETHEART...?
HELLO...?

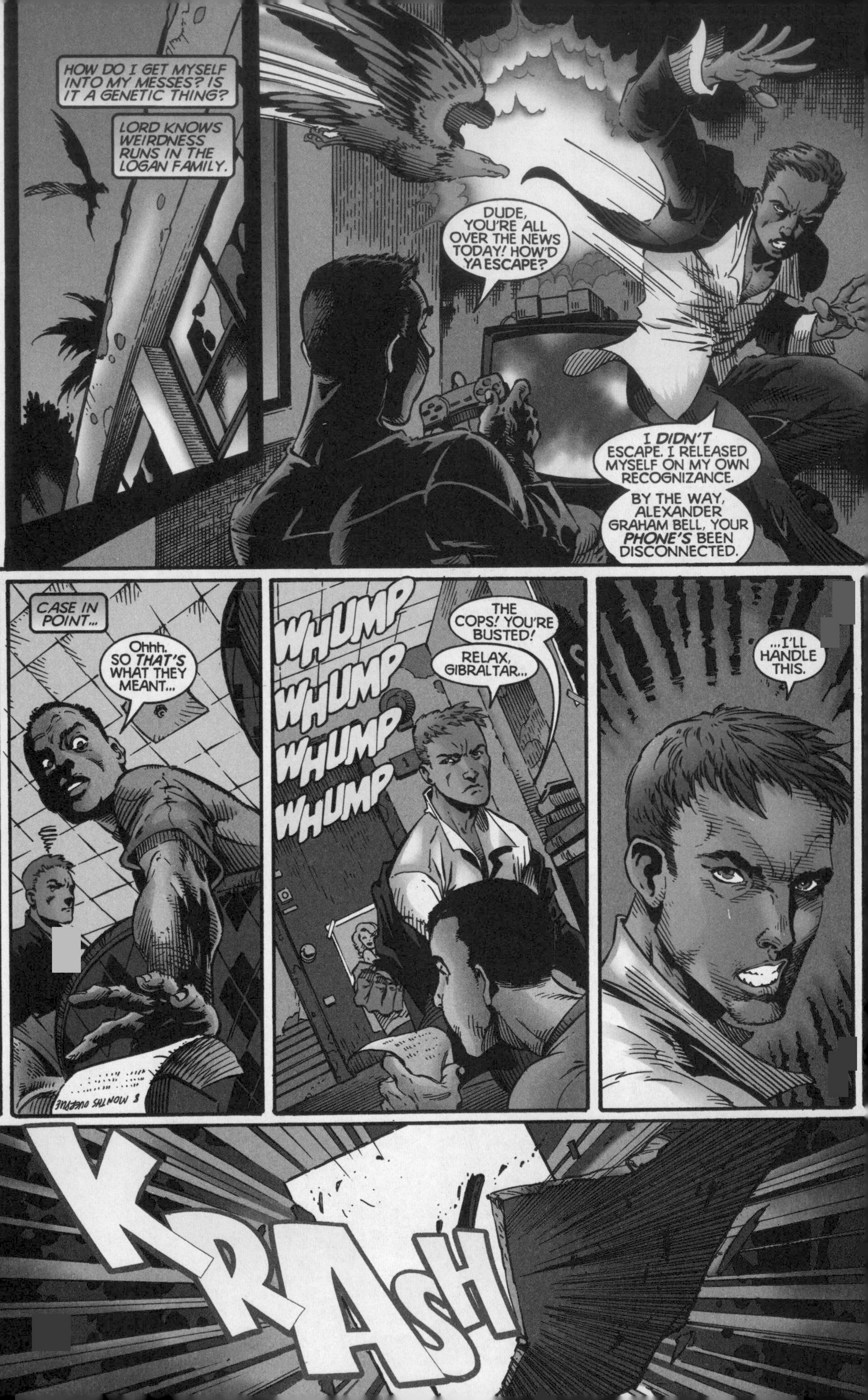
HOW DO I GET MYSELF INTO MY MESSES? IS IT A GENETIC THING?
LORD KNOWS WEIRDNESS RUNS IN THE LOGAN FAMILY.
DUDE, YOU'RE ALL OVER THE NEWS TODAY! HOW'D YA ESCAPE?
I DIDN'T ESCAPE. I RELEASED MYSELF ON MY OWN RECOGNIZANCE.
BY THE WAY, ALEXANDER GRAHAM BELL, YOUR PHONE'S BEEN DISCONNECTED.
CASE IN POINT...
Ohhh. SO THAT'S WHAT THEY MEANT...
WHUMP
WHUMP
WHUMP
WHUMP
THE COPS! YOU'RE BUSTED!
RELAX, GIBRALTAR...
...I'LL HANDLE THIS.
KRASH

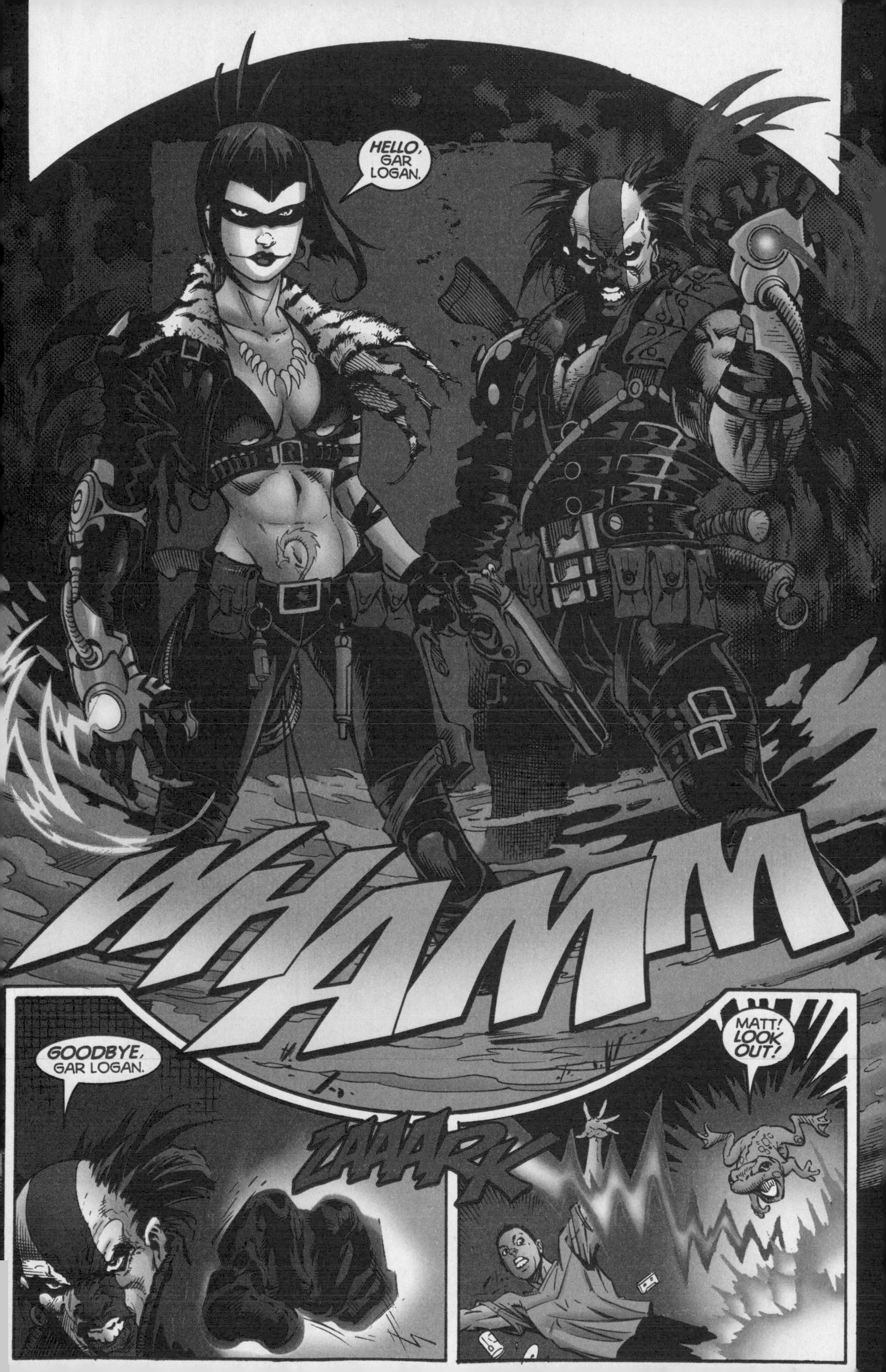
HELLO, GAR LOGAN.
WHAMM
GOODBYE, GAR LOGAN.
ZAAARK
MATT! LOOK OUT!

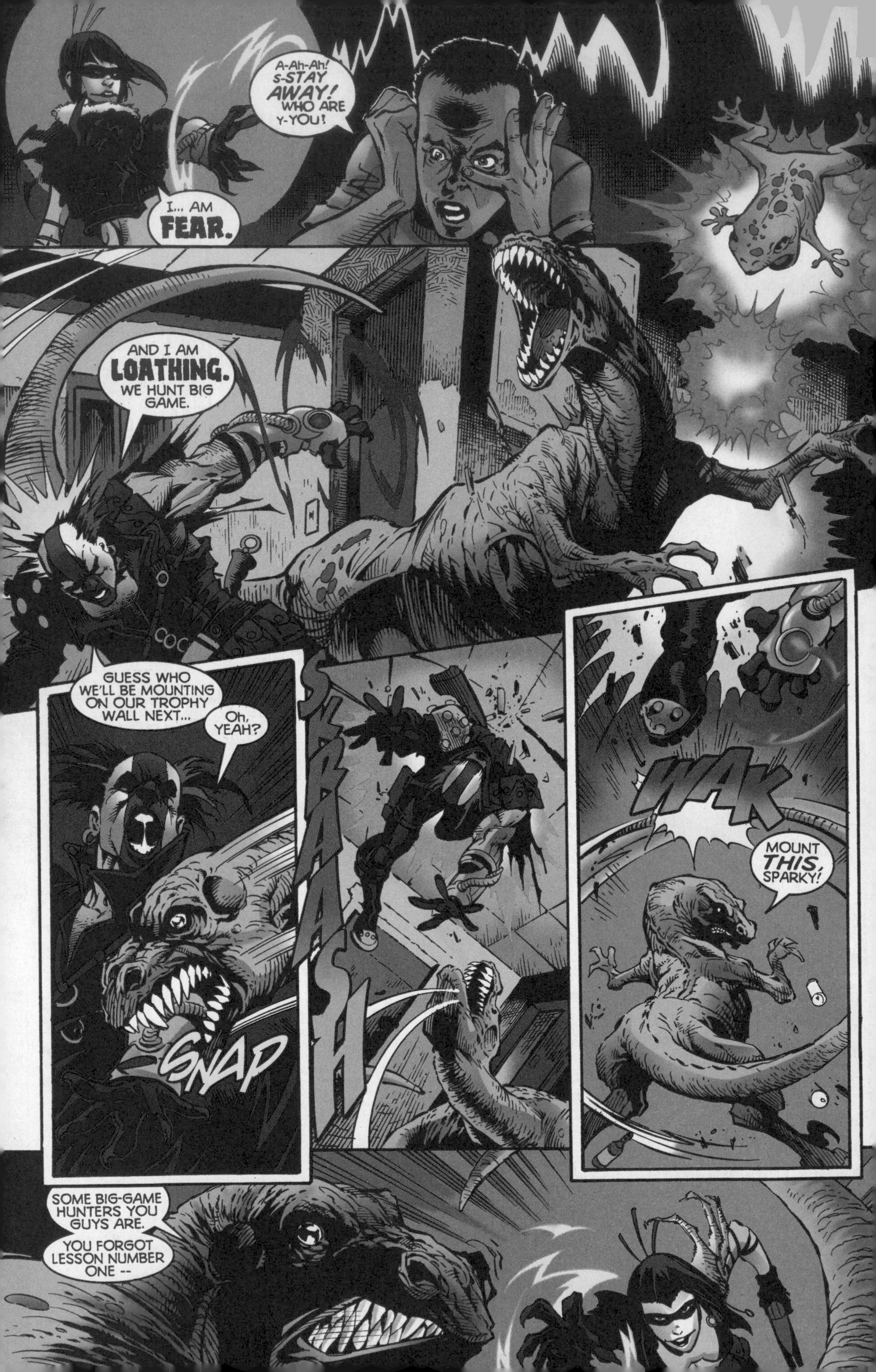
A-Ah-Ah! S-STAY AWAY! WHO ARE Y-YOU!
I... AM FEAR.
AND I AM LOATHING. WE HUNT BIG GAME.
GUESS WHO WE'LL BE MOUNTING ON OUR TROPHY WALL NEXT...
Oh, YEAH?
SNAP
SKRAAAH
WAK
MOUNT THIS, SPARKY!
SOME BIG-GAME HUNTERS YOU GUYS ARE.
YOU FORGOT LESSON NUMBER ONE --

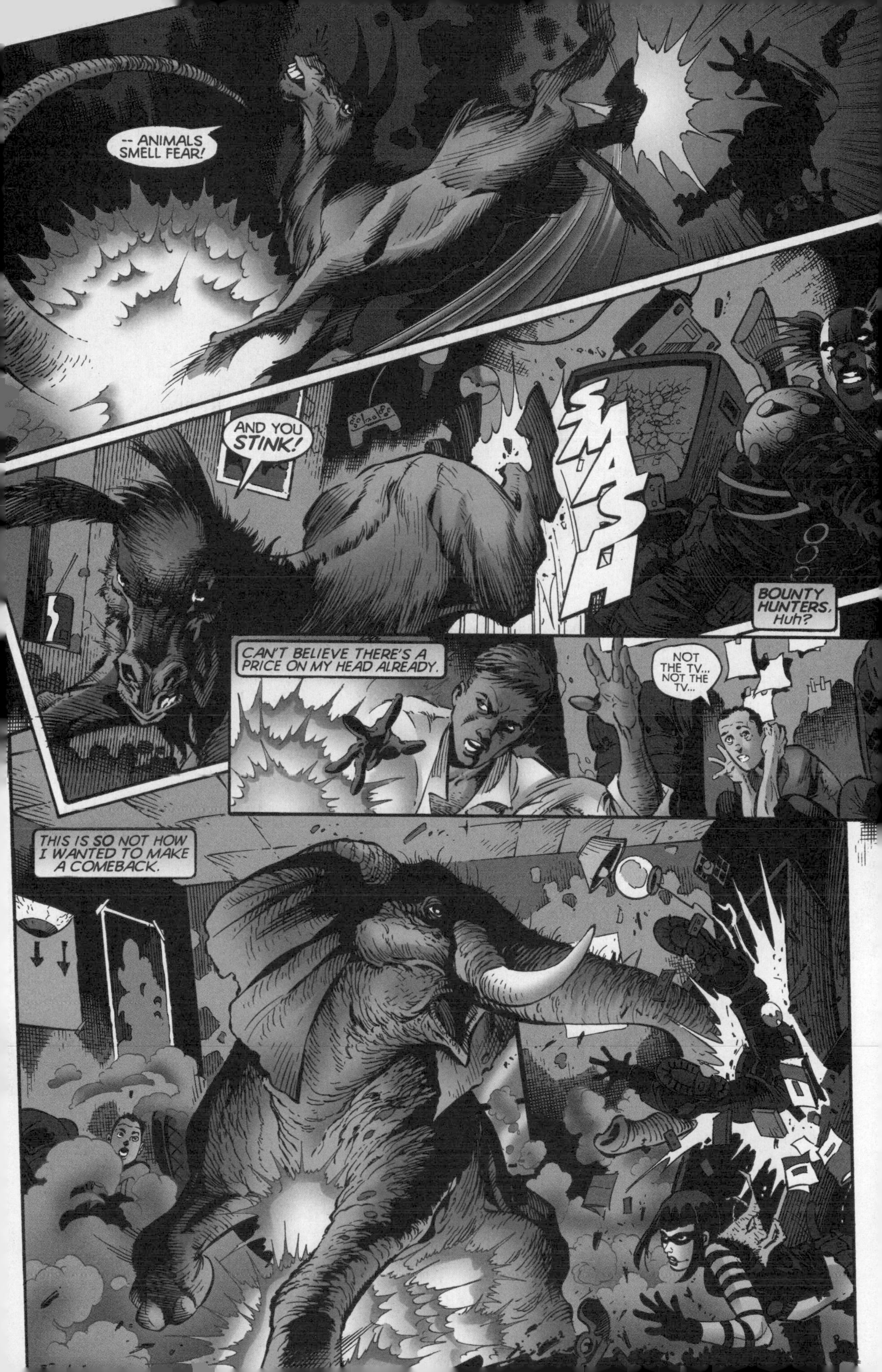
-- ANIMALS SMELL FEAR!
AND YOU STINK!
SMASH
BOUNTY HUNTERS, Huh?
CAN'T BELIEVE THERE'S A PRICE ON MY HEAD ALREADY.
NOT THE TV... NOT THE TV...
THIS IS SO NOT HOW I WANTED TO MAKE A COMEBACK.

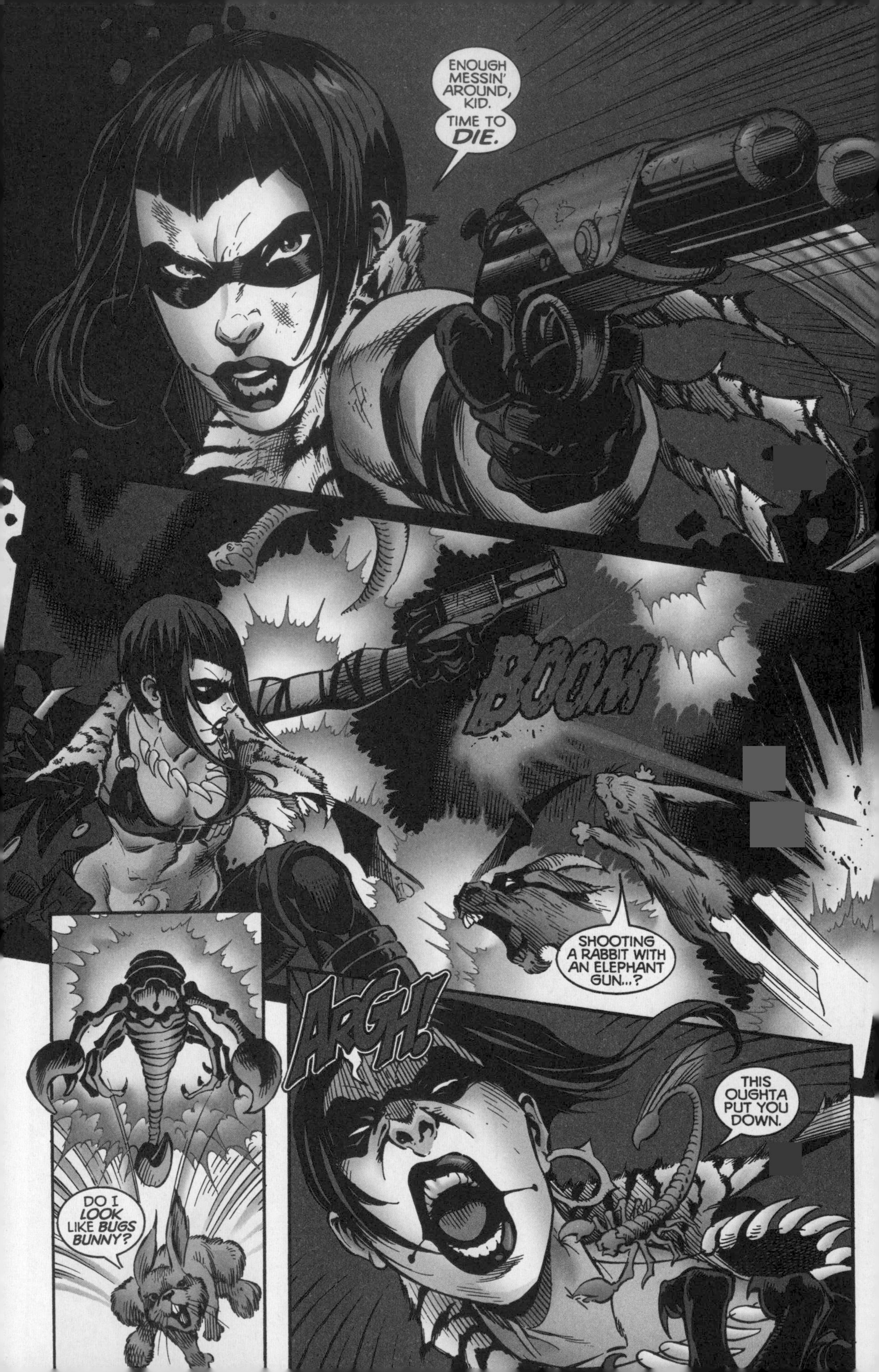
ENOUGH MESSIN' AROUND, KID. TIME TO DIE.
BOOM
SHOOTING A RABBIT WITH AN ELEPHANT GUN...?
DO I LOOK LIKE BUGS BUNNY?
ARGH!
THIS OUGHTA PUT YOU DOWN.

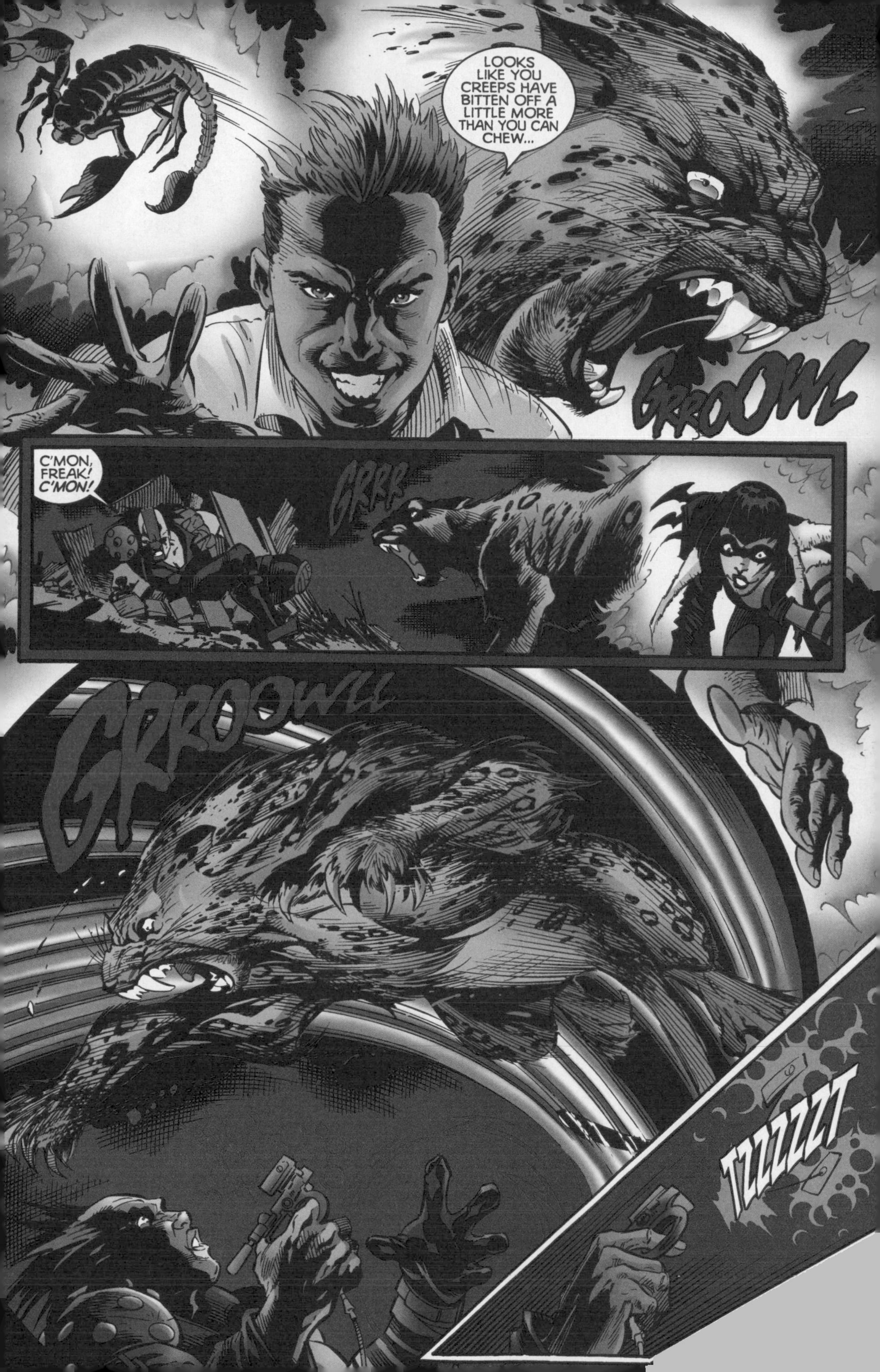
LOOKS LIKE YOU CREEPS HAVE BITTEN OFF A LITTLE MORE THAN YOU CAN CHEW...
GRROOWL
C'MON, FREAK! C'MON!
GRRR
GRROOWLL
TZZZZZZT

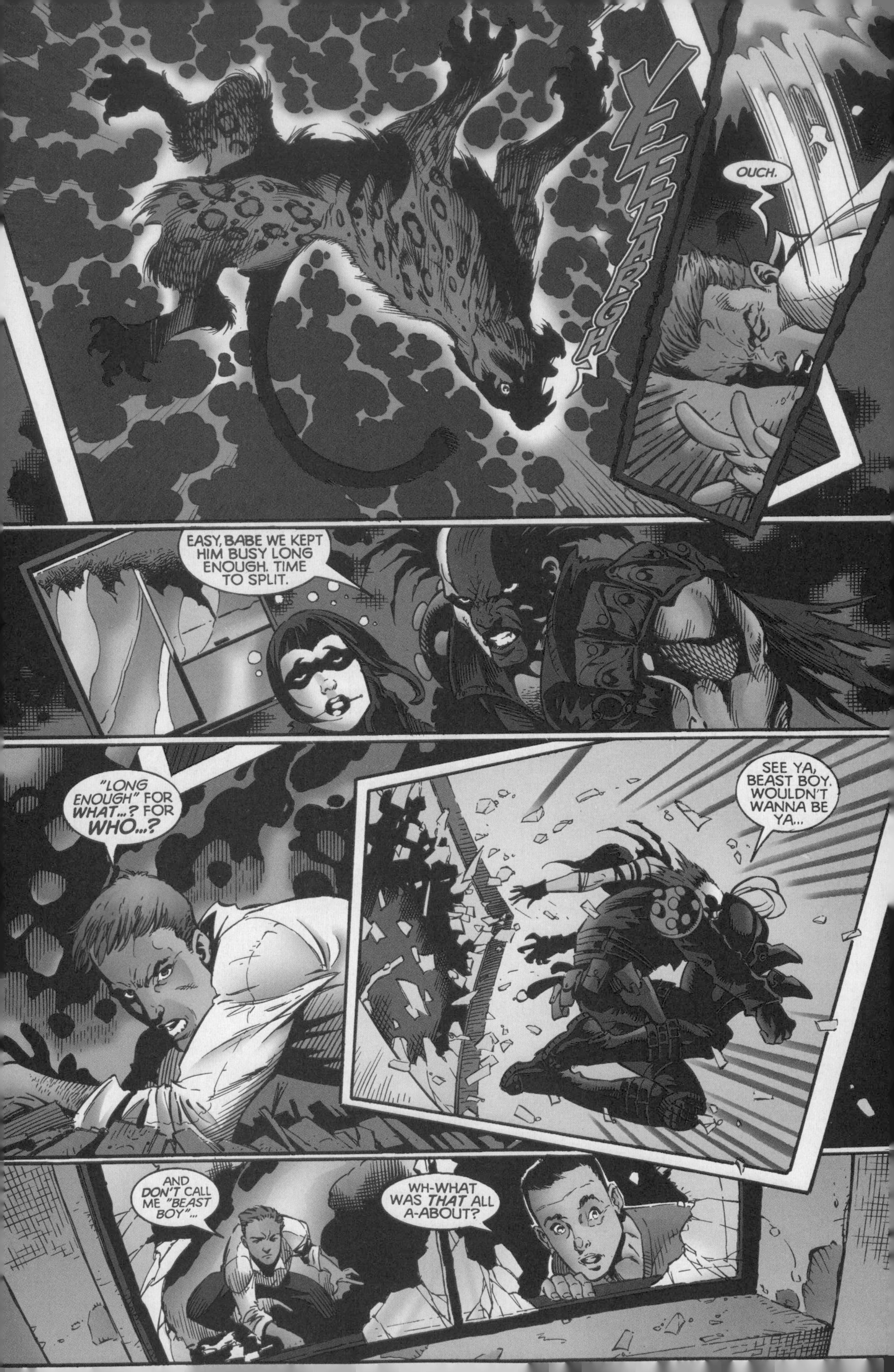
YEEEARGH
OUCH.
EASY, BABE WE KEPT HIM BUSY LONG ENOUGH. TIME TO SPLIT.
"LONG ENOUGH" FOR WHAT...? FOR WHO...?
SEE YA, BEAST BOY. WOULDN'T WANNA BE YA...
AND DON'T CALL ME "BEAST BOY"...
WH-WHAT WAS THAT ALL A-ABOUT?

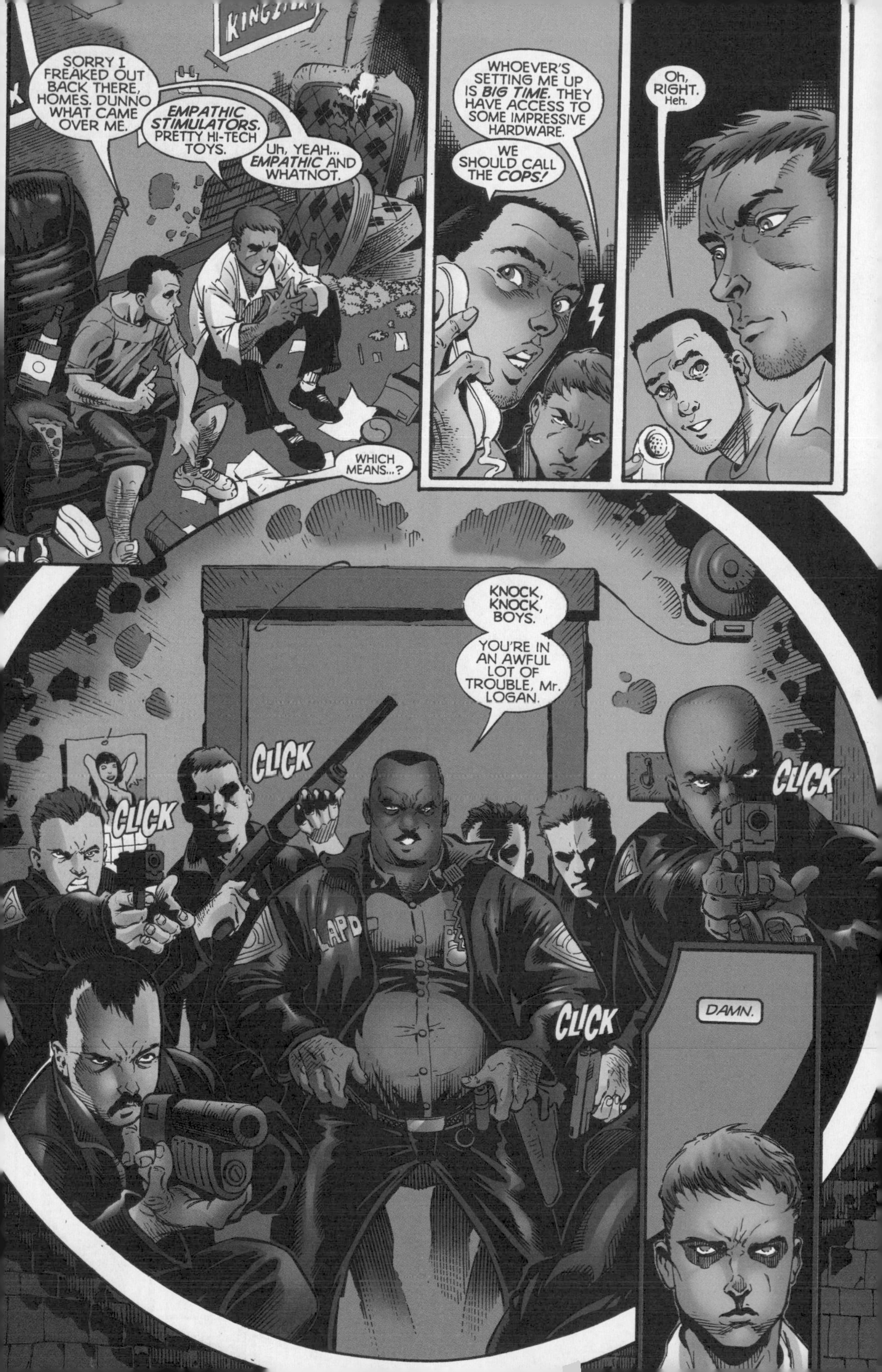
KINGZILLA
SORRY I FREAKED OUT BACK THERE, HOMES. DUNNO WHAT CAME OVER ME.
EMPATHIC STIMULATORS. PRETTY HI-TECH TOYS.
Uh, YEAH... *EMPATHIC* AND WHATNOT.
WHICH MEANS...?
WHOEVER'S SETTING ME UP IS *BIG TIME.* THEY HAVE ACCESS TO SOME IMPRESSIVE HARDWARE.
WE SHOULD CALL THE *COPS!*
Oh, RIGHT. Heh.
KNOCK, KNOCK, BOYS.
YOU'RE IN AN AWFUL LOT OF TROUBLE, Mr. LOGAN.
CLICK
CLICK
CLICK
LAPD
CLICK
DAMN.

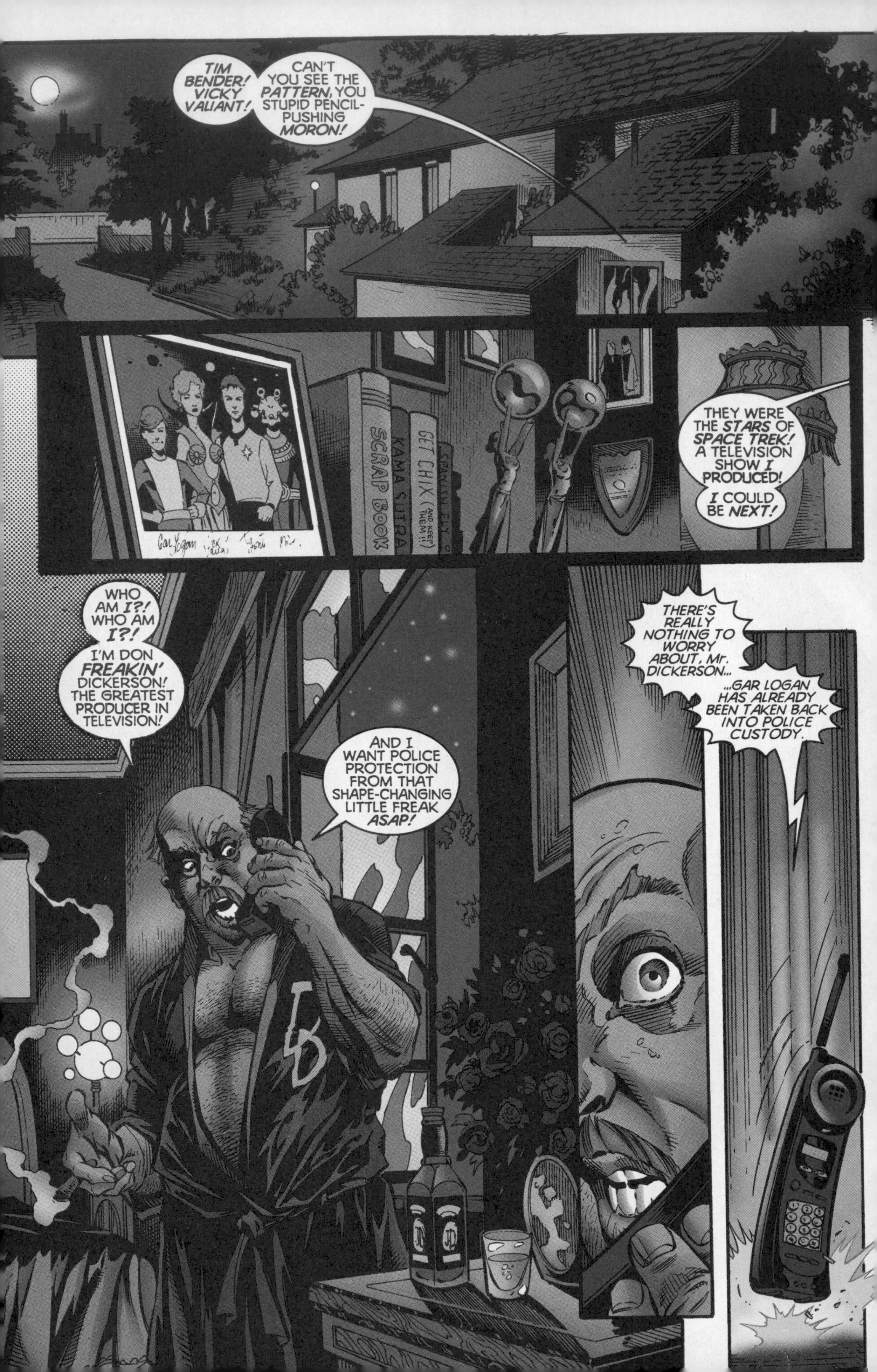
TIM BENDER! VICKY VALIANT!
CAN'T YOU SEE THE PATTERN, YOU STUPID PENCIL-PUSHING MORON!
SCRAP BOOK
KAMA SUTRA
GET CHIX (AND KEEP THEM!!)
SPANISH FLY
THEY WERE THE STARS OF SPACE TREK! A TELEVISION SHOW I PRODUCED!
I COULD BE NEXT!
WHO AM I?! WHO AM I?!
I'M DON FREAKIN' DICKERSON! THE GREATEST PRODUCER IN TELEVISION!
AND I WANT POLICE PROTECTION FROM THAT SHAPE-CHANGING LITTLE FREAK ASAP!
THERE'S REALLY NOTHING TO WORRY ABOUT, Mr. DICKERSON...
...GAR LOGAN HAS ALREADY BEEN TAKEN BACK INTO POLICE CUSTODY.

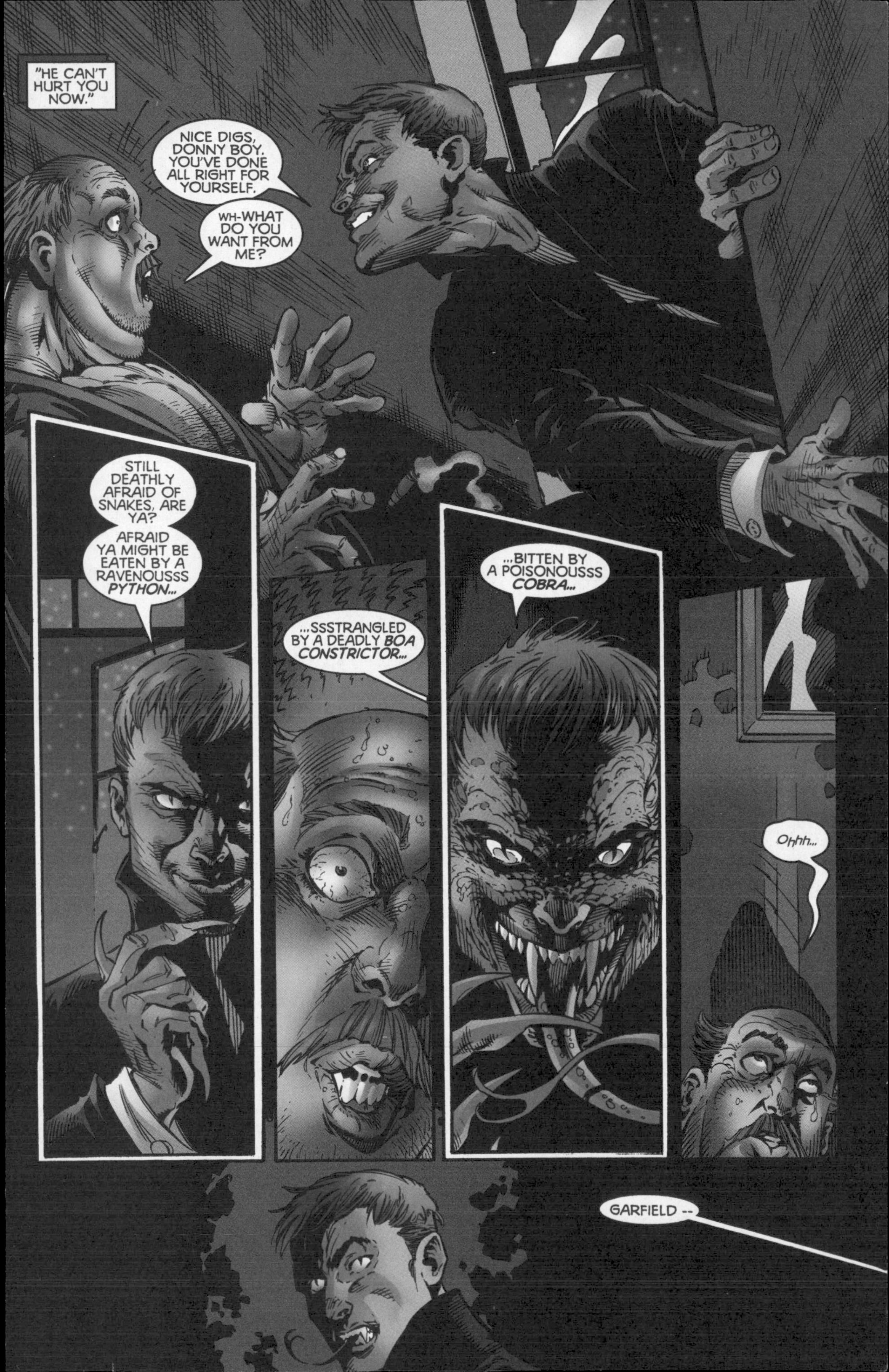
"HE CAN'T HURT YOU NOW."
NICE DIGS, DONNY BOY. YOU'VE DONE ALL RIGHT FOR YOURSELF.
WH-WHAT DO YOU WANT FROM ME?
STILL DEATHLY AFRAID OF SNAKES, ARE YA?
AFRAID YA MIGHT BE EATEN BY A RAVENOUSSS PYTHON...
...SSSTRANGLED BY A DEADLY BOA CONSTRICTOR...
...BITTEN BY A POISONOUSSS COBRA...
Ohhh...
GARFIELD --

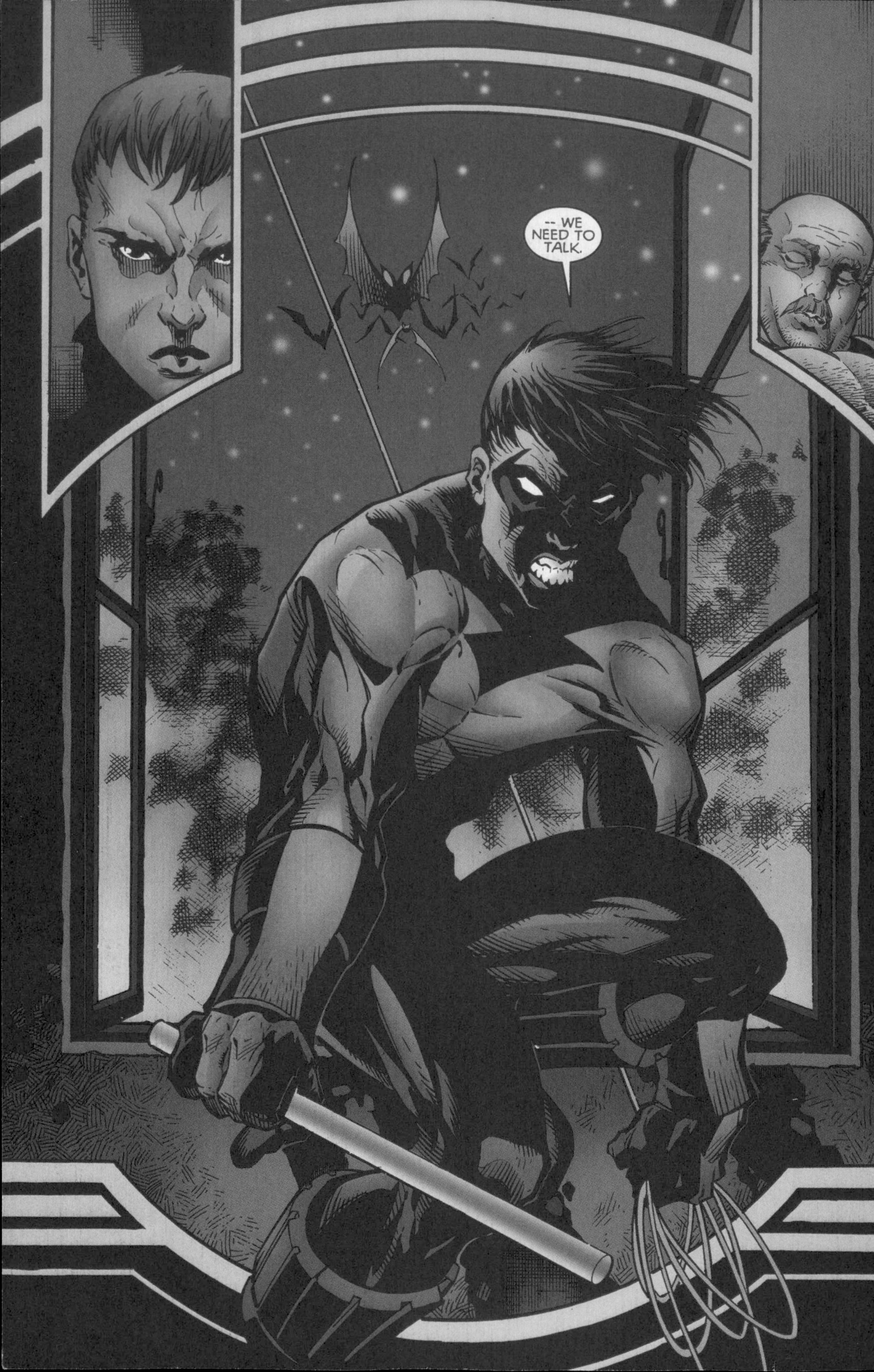
-- WE NEED TO TALK.

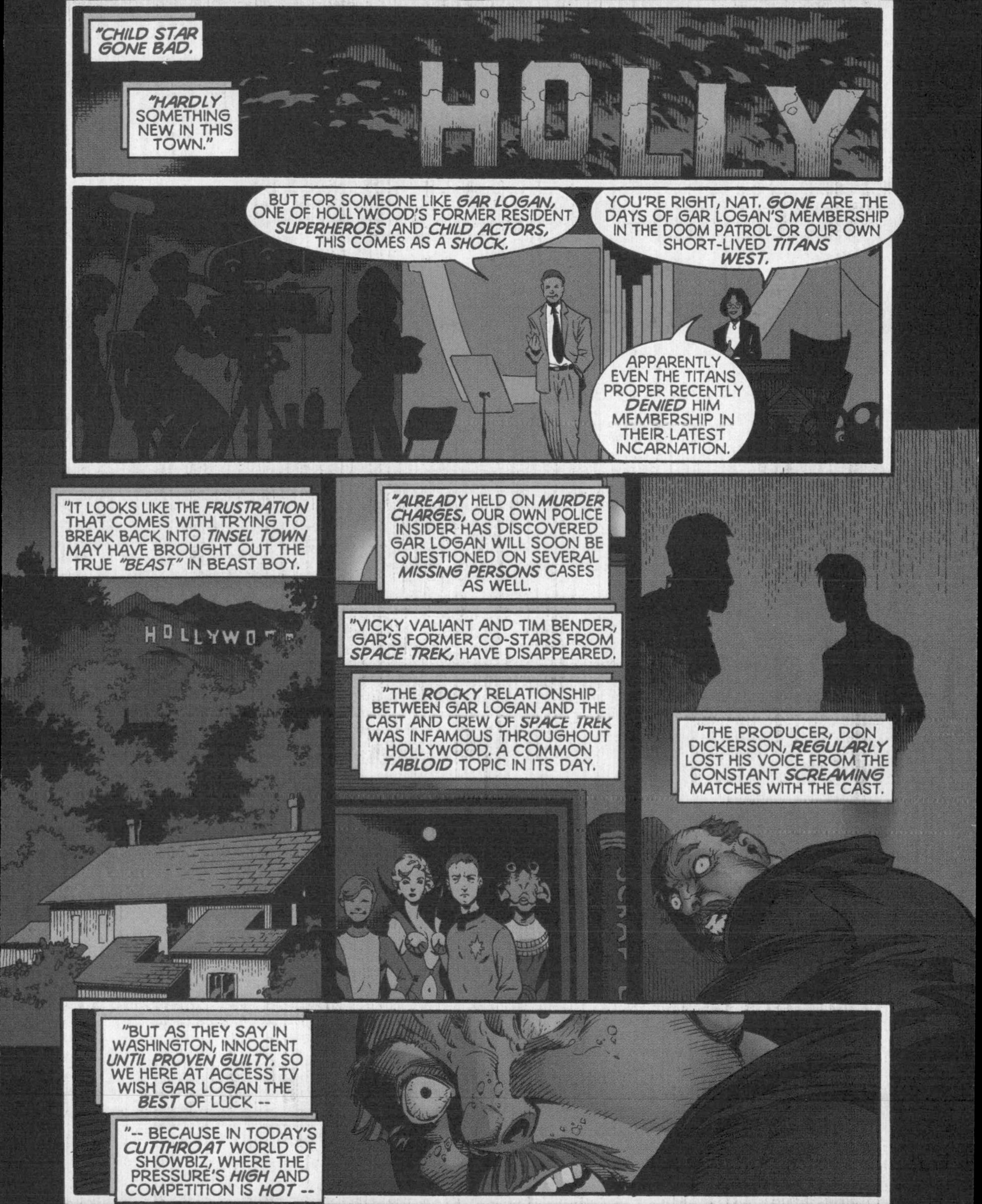
"CHILD STAR GONE BAD.
"HARDLY SOMETHING NEW IN THIS TOWN."
HOLLY
BUT FOR SOMEONE LIKE GAR LOGAN, ONE OF HOLLYWOOD'S FORMER RESIDENT SUPERHEROES AND CHILD ACTORS, THIS COMES AS A SHOCK.
YOU'RE RIGHT, NAT. GONE ARE THE DAYS OF GAR LOGAN'S MEMBERSHIP IN THE DOOM PATROL OR OUR OWN SHORT-LIVED TITANS WEST.
APPARENTLY EVEN THE TITANS PROPER RECENTLY DENIED HIM MEMBERSHIP IN THEIR LATEST INCARNATION.
"IT LOOKS LIKE THE FRUSTRATION THAT COMES WITH TRYING TO BREAK BACK INTO TINSEL TOWN MAY HAVE BROUGHT OUT THE TRUE "BEAST" IN BEAST BOY.
"ALREADY HELD ON MURDER CHARGES, OUR OWN POLICE INSIDER HAS DISCOVERED GAR LOGAN WILL SOON BE QUESTIONED ON SEVERAL MISSING PERSONS CASES AS WELL.
"VICKY VALIANT AND TIM BENDER, GAR'S FORMER CO-STARS FROM SPACE TREK, HAVE DISAPPEARED.
"THE ROCKY RELATIONSHIP BETWEEN GAR LOGAN AND THE CAST AND CREW OF SPACE TREK WAS INFAMOUS THROUGHOUT HOLLYWOOD. A COMMON TABLOID TOPIC IN ITS DAY.
"THE PRODUCER, DON DICKERSON, REGULARLY LOST HIS VOICE FROM THE CONSTANT SCREAMING MATCHES WITH THE CAST.
"BUT AS THEY SAY IN WASHINGTON, INNOCENT UNTIL PROVEN GUILTY. SO WE HERE AT ACCESS TV WISH GAR LOGAN THE BEST OF LUCK --
"-- BECAUSE IN TODAY'S CUTTHROAT WORLD OF SHOWBIZ, WHERE THE PRESSURE'S HIGH AND COMPETITION IS HOT --

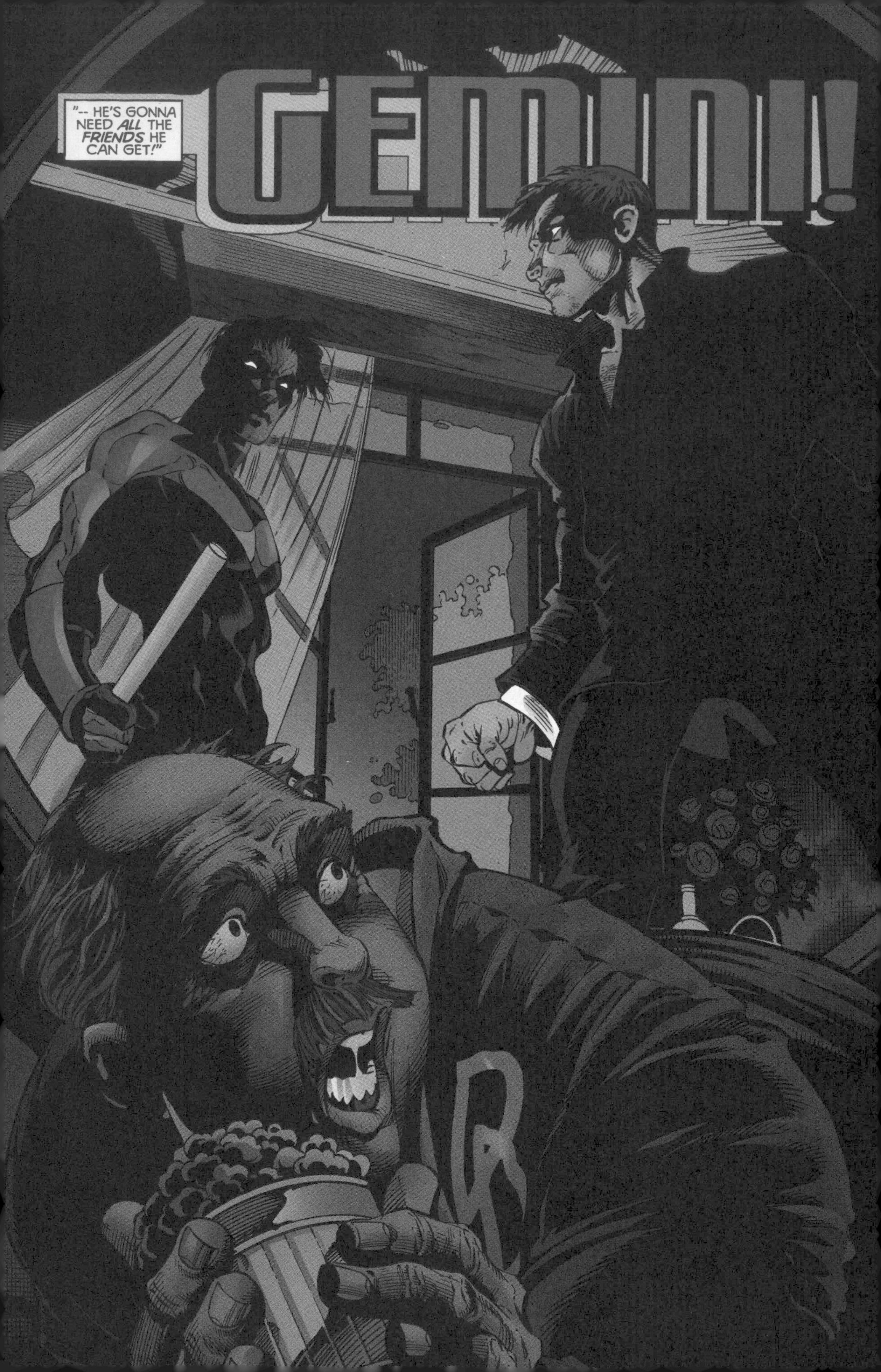
"-- HE'S GONNA NEED ALL THE FRIENDS HE CAN GET!"
GEMINI!

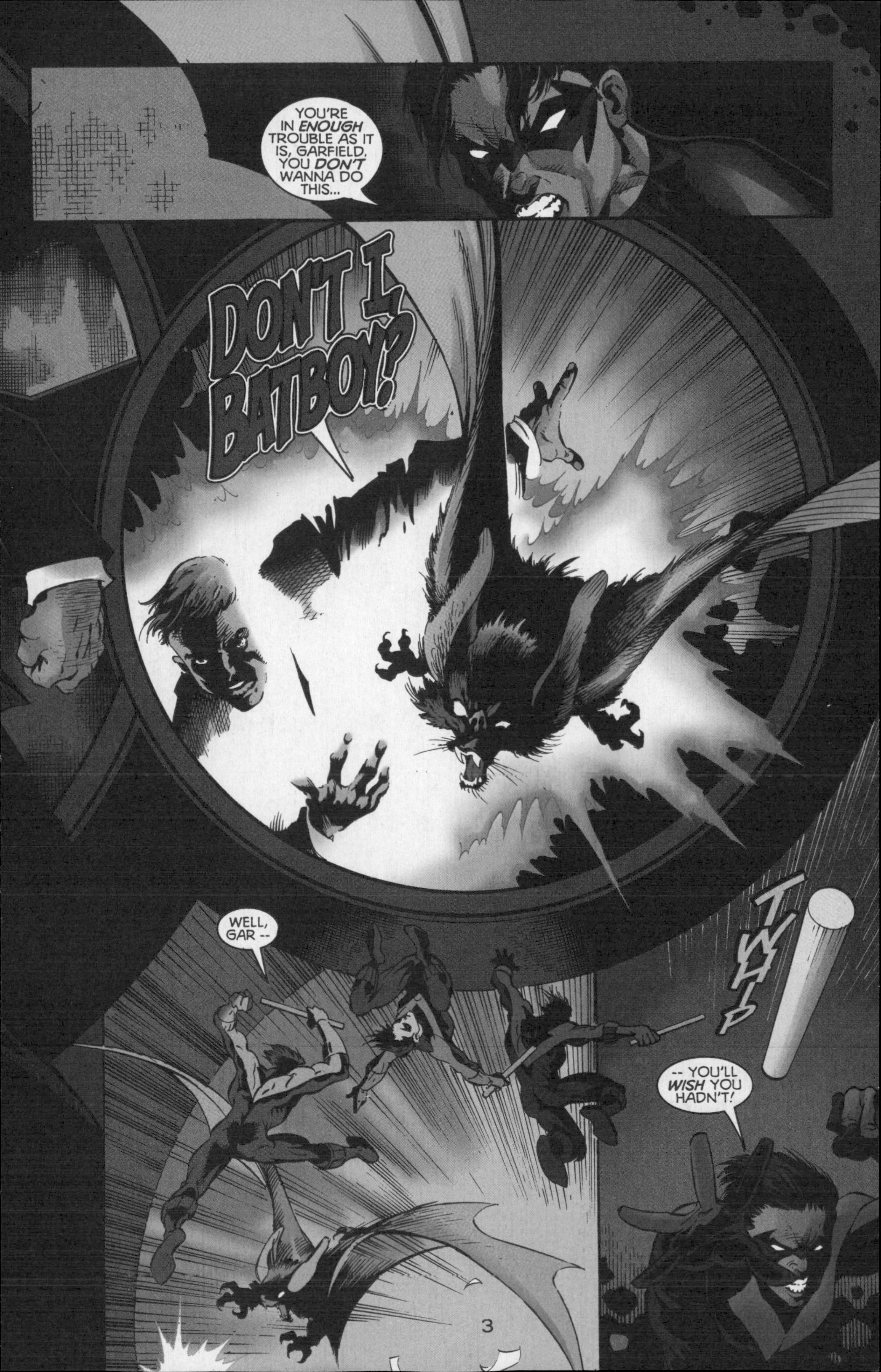
YOU'RE IN ENOUGH TROUBLE AS IT IS, GARFIELD. YOU DON'T WANNA DO THIS...
DON'T I, BATBOY?
WELL, GAR --
TWHIP
-- YOU'LL WISH YOU HADN'T!

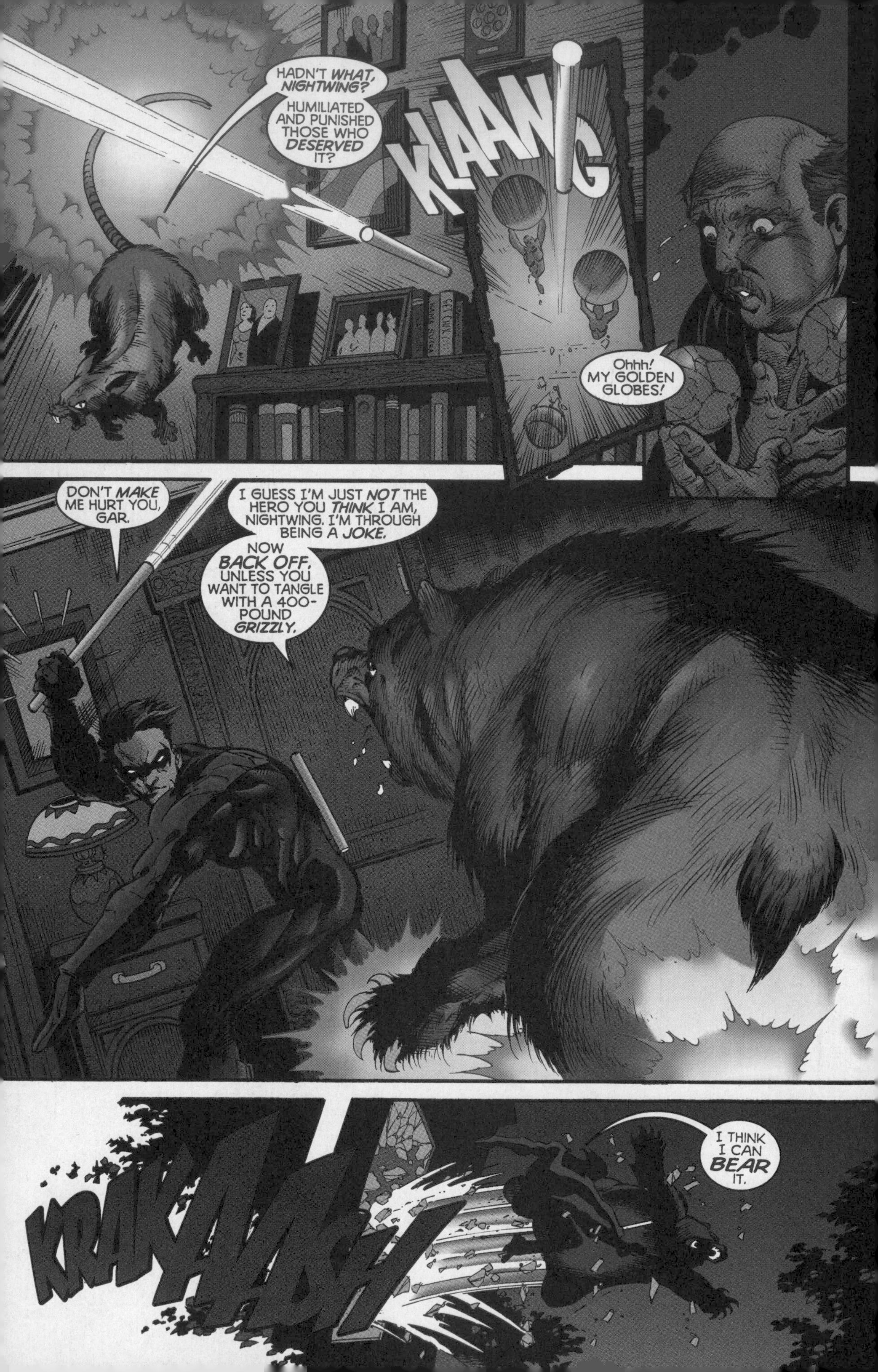
HADN'T WHAT, NIGHTWING?
HUMILIATED AND PUNISHED THOSE WHO DESERVED IT?
KLAANG
Ohhh! MY GOLDEN GLOBES!
DON'T MAKE ME HURT YOU, GAR.
I GUESS I'M JUST NOT THE HERO YOU THINK I AM, NIGHTWING. I'M THROUGH BEING A JOKE.
NOW BACK OFF, UNLESS YOU WANT TO TANGLE WITH A 400-POUND GRIZZLY.
KRAKADOOSH
I THINK I CAN BEAR IT.

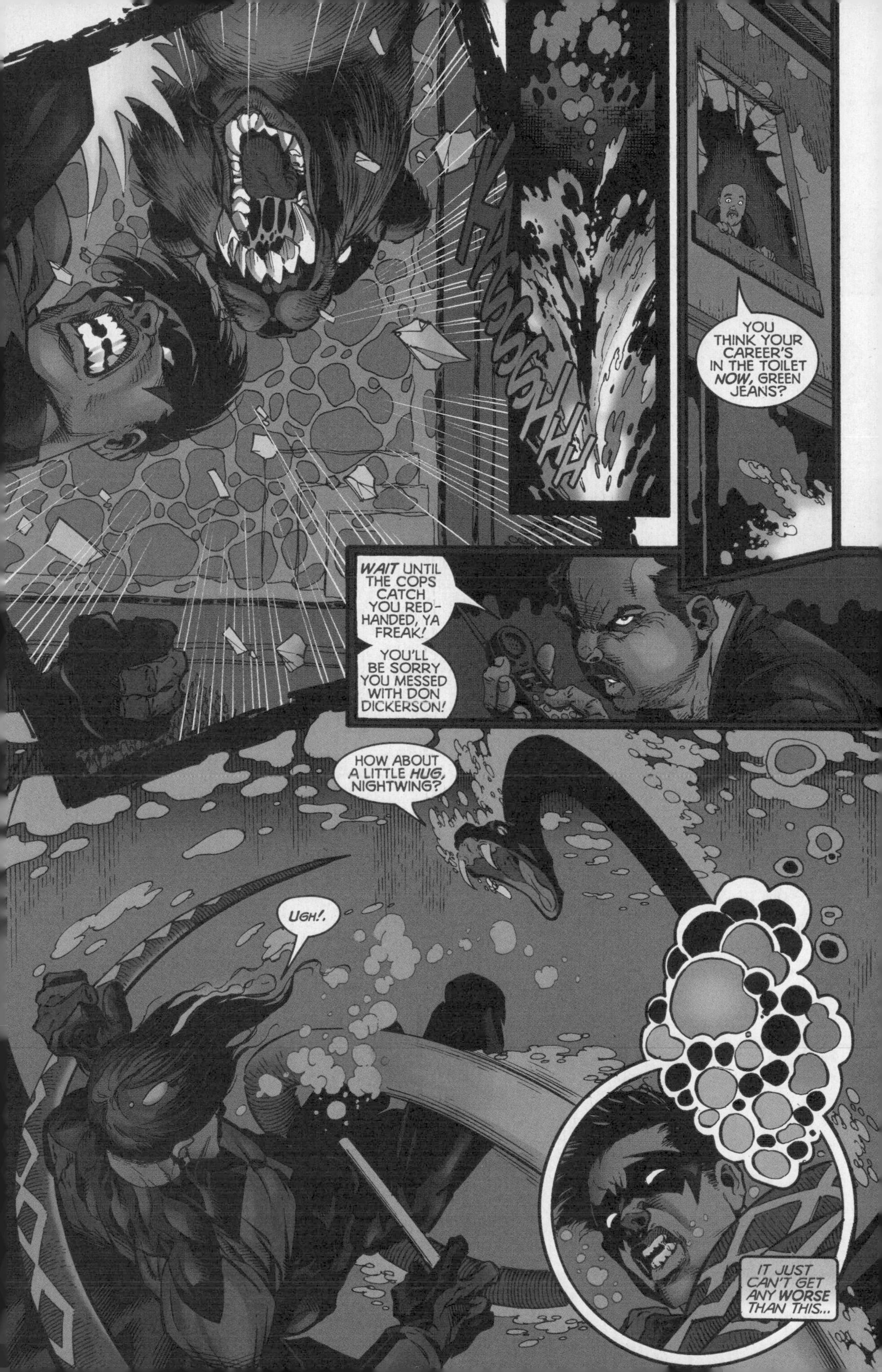
HHOOSSSHHHH
YOU THINK YOUR CAREER'S IN THE TOILET *NOW,* GREEN JEANS?
WAIT UNTIL THE COPS CATCH YOU RED-HANDED, YA FREAK!
YOU'LL BE SORRY YOU MESSED WITH DON DICKERSON!
HOW ABOUT A LITTLE *HUG,* NIGHTWING?
UGH!.
IT JUST CAN'T GET ANY *WORSE* THAN THIS...

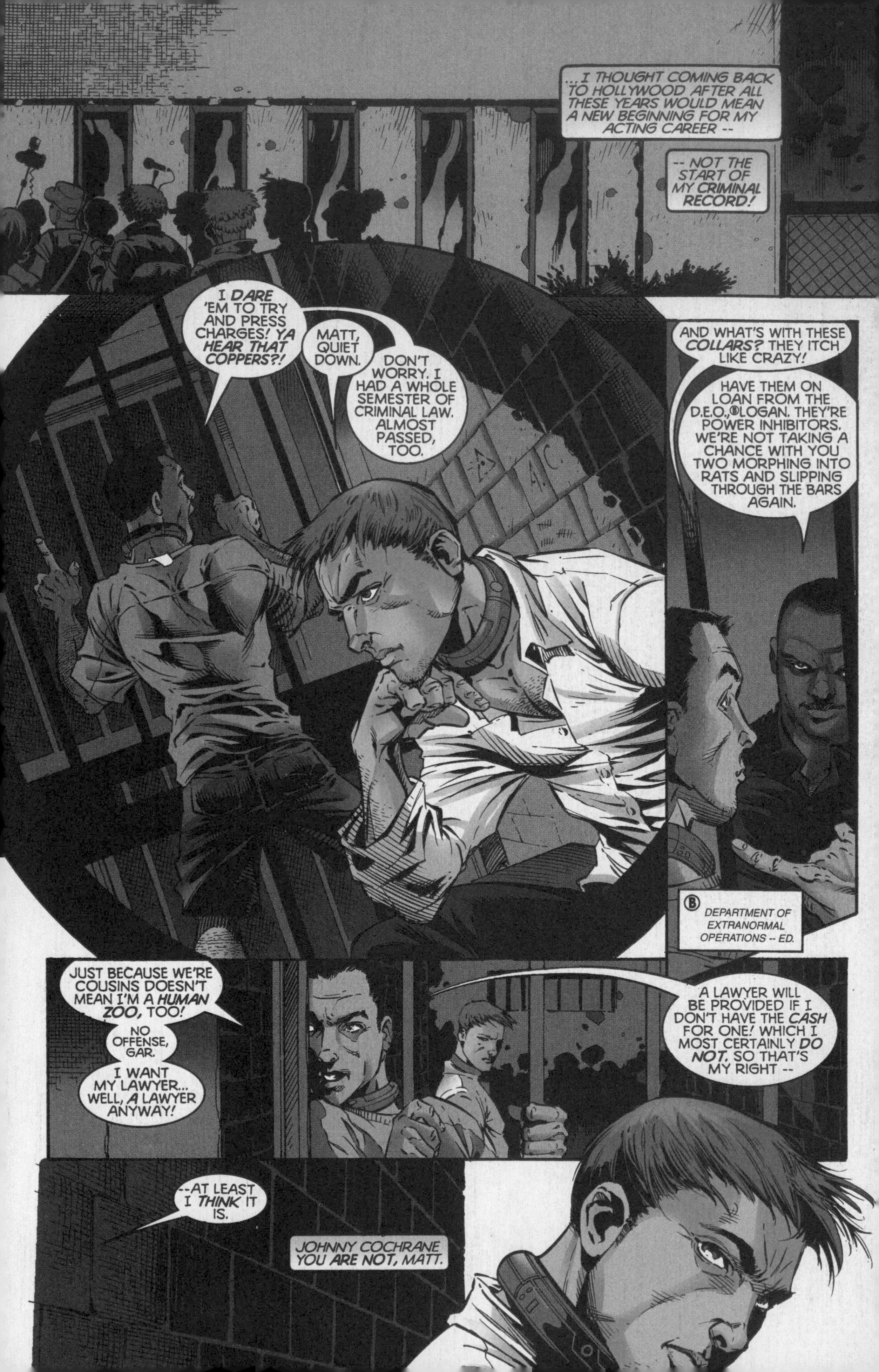
...I THOUGHT COMING BACK TO HOLLYWOOD AFTER ALL THESE YEARS WOULD MEAN A NEW BEGINNING FOR MY ACTING CAREER --
-- NOT THE START OF MY CRIMINAL RECORD!
I DARE 'EM TO TRY AND PRESS CHARGES! YA HEAR THAT COPPERS?!
MATT, QUIET DOWN.
DON'T WORRY. I HAD A WHOLE SEMESTER OF CRIMINAL LAW. ALMOST PASSED, TOO.
AND WHAT'S WITH THESE COLLARS? THEY ITCH LIKE CRAZY!
HAVE THEM ON LOAN FROM THE D.E.O.,(B) LOGAN. THEY'RE POWER INHIBITORS. WE'RE NOT TAKING A CHANCE WITH YOU TWO MORPHING INTO RATS AND SLIPPING THROUGH THE BARS AGAIN.
(B) DEPARTMENT OF EXTRANORMAL OPERATIONS -- ED.
JUST BECAUSE WE'RE COUSINS DOESN'T MEAN I'M A HUMAN ZOO, TOO!
NO OFFENSE, GAR.
I WANT MY LAWYER... WELL, A LAWYER ANYWAY!
A LAWYER WILL BE PROVIDED IF I DON'T HAVE THE CASH FOR ONE! WHICH I MOST CERTAINLY DO NOT, SO THAT'S MY RIGHT --
--AT LEAST I THINK IT IS.
JOHNNY COCHRANE YOU ARE NOT, MATT.

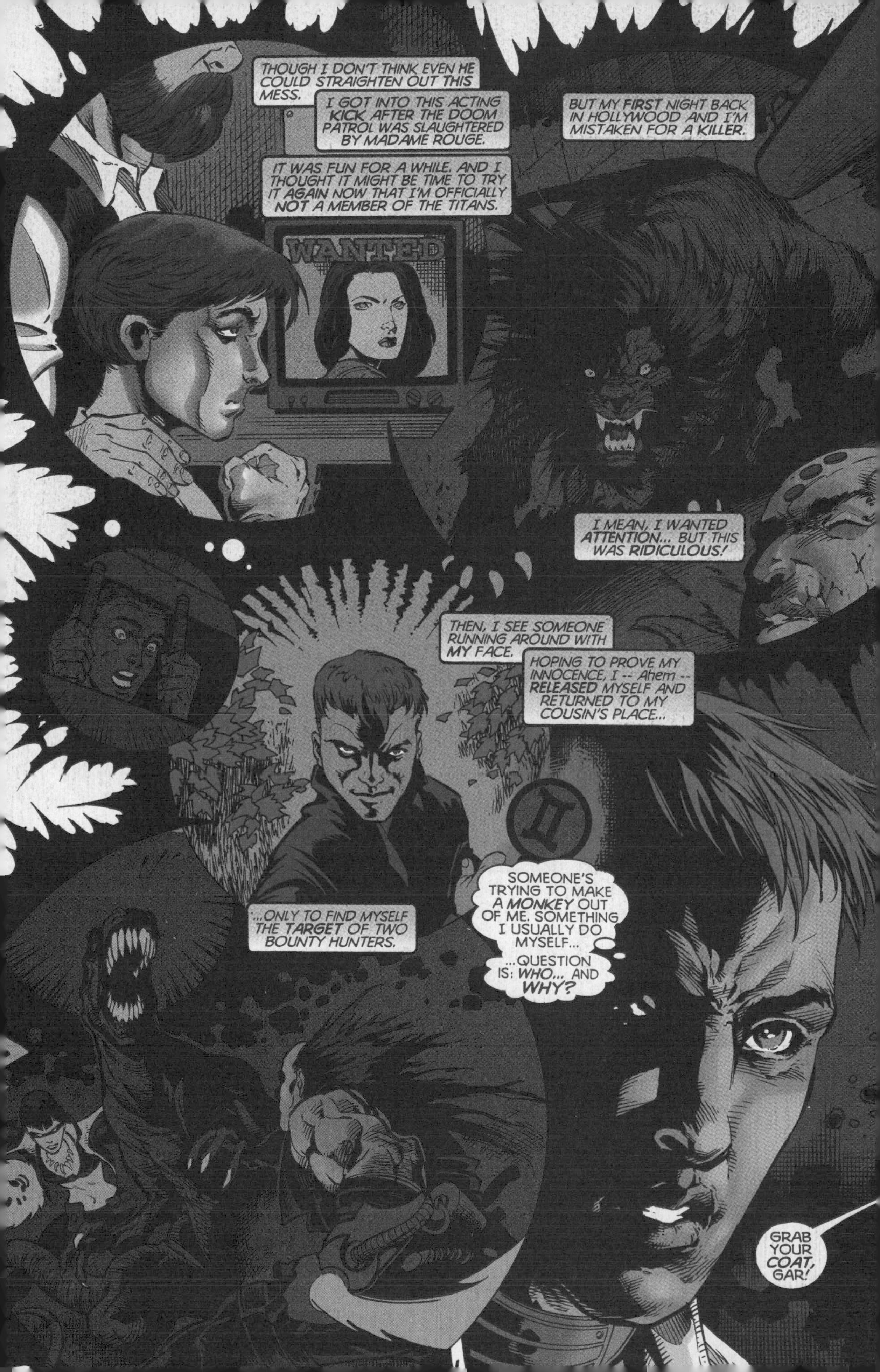
THOUGH I DON'T THINK EVEN HE COULD STRAIGHTEN OUT THIS MESS.
I GOT INTO THIS ACTING KICK AFTER THE DOOM PATROL WAS SLAUGHTERED BY MADAME ROUGE.
IT WAS FUN FOR A WHILE. AND I THOUGHT IT MIGHT BE TIME TO TRY IT AGAIN NOW THAT I'M OFFICIALLY NOT A MEMBER OF THE TITANS.
WANTED
BUT MY FIRST NIGHT BACK IN HOLLYWOOD AND I'M MISTAKEN FOR A KILLER.
I MEAN, I WANTED ATTENTION... BUT THIS WAS RIDICULOUS!
THEN, I SEE SOMEONE RUNNING AROUND WITH MY FACE.
HOPING TO PROVE MY INNOCENCE, I -- Ahem -- RELEASED MYSELF AND RETURNED TO MY COUSIN'S PLACE...
...ONLY TO FIND MYSELF THE TARGET OF TWO BOUNTY HUNTERS.
SOMEONE'S TRYING TO MAKE A MONKEY OUT OF ME. SOMETHING I USUALLY DO MYSELF...
...QUESTION IS: WHO... AND WHY?
GRAB YOUR COAT, GAR!

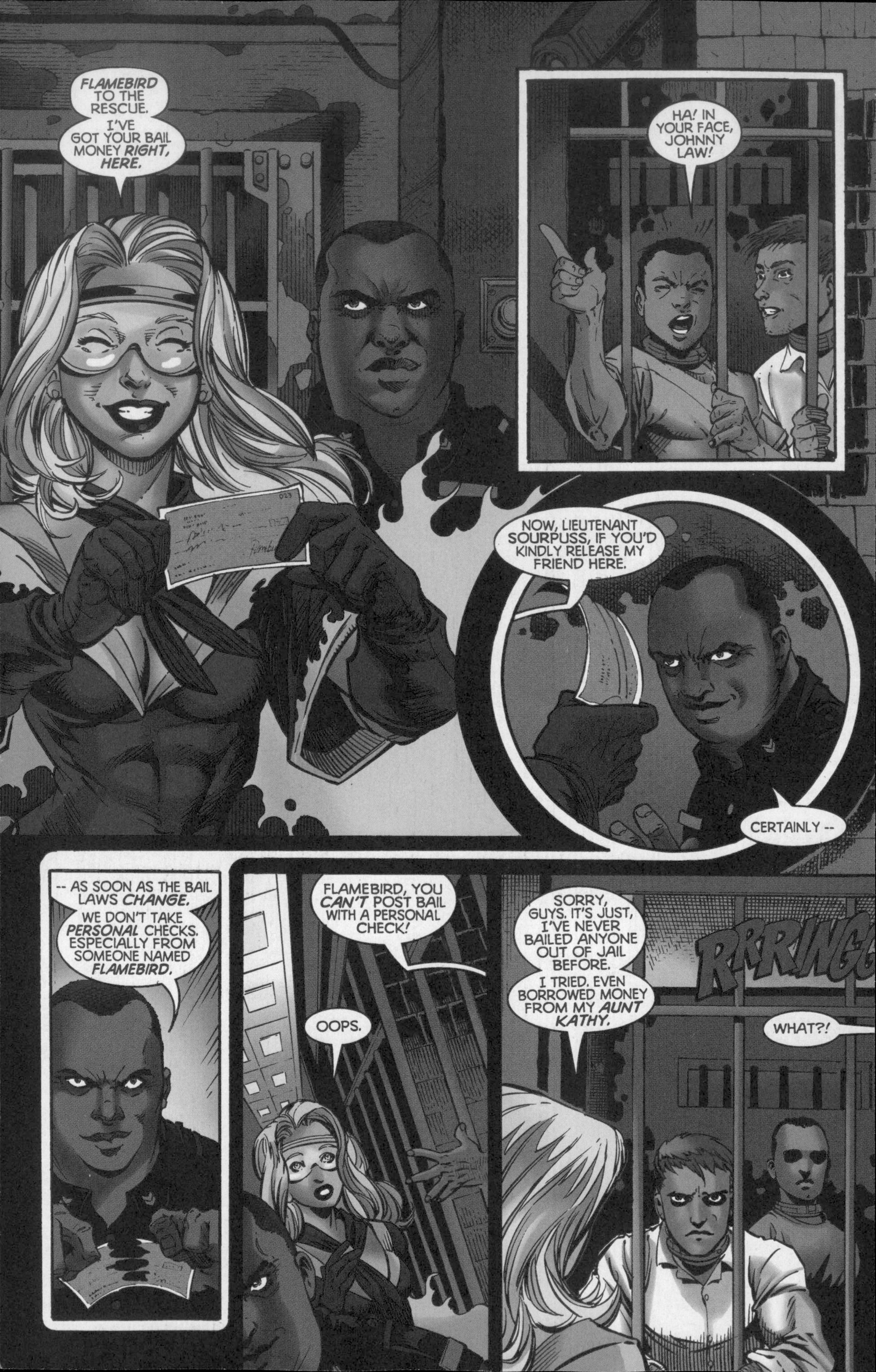
FLAMEBIRD TO THE RESCUE. I'VE GOT YOUR BAIL MONEY RIGHT, HERE.
HA! IN YOUR FACE, JOHNNY LAW!
NOW, LIEUTENANT SOURPUSS, IF YOU'D KINDLY RELEASE MY FRIEND HERE.
CERTAINLY --
-- AS SOON AS THE BAIL LAWS CHANGE.
WE DON'T TAKE PERSONAL CHECKS. ESPECIALLY FROM SOMEONE NAMED FLAMEBIRD.
FLAMEBIRD, YOU CAN'T POST BAIL WITH A PERSONAL CHECK!
OOPS.
SORRY, GUYS. IT'S JUST, I'VE NEVER BAILED ANYONE OUT OF JAIL BEFORE.
I TRIED. EVEN BORROWED MONEY FROM MY AUNT KATHY.
WHAT?!

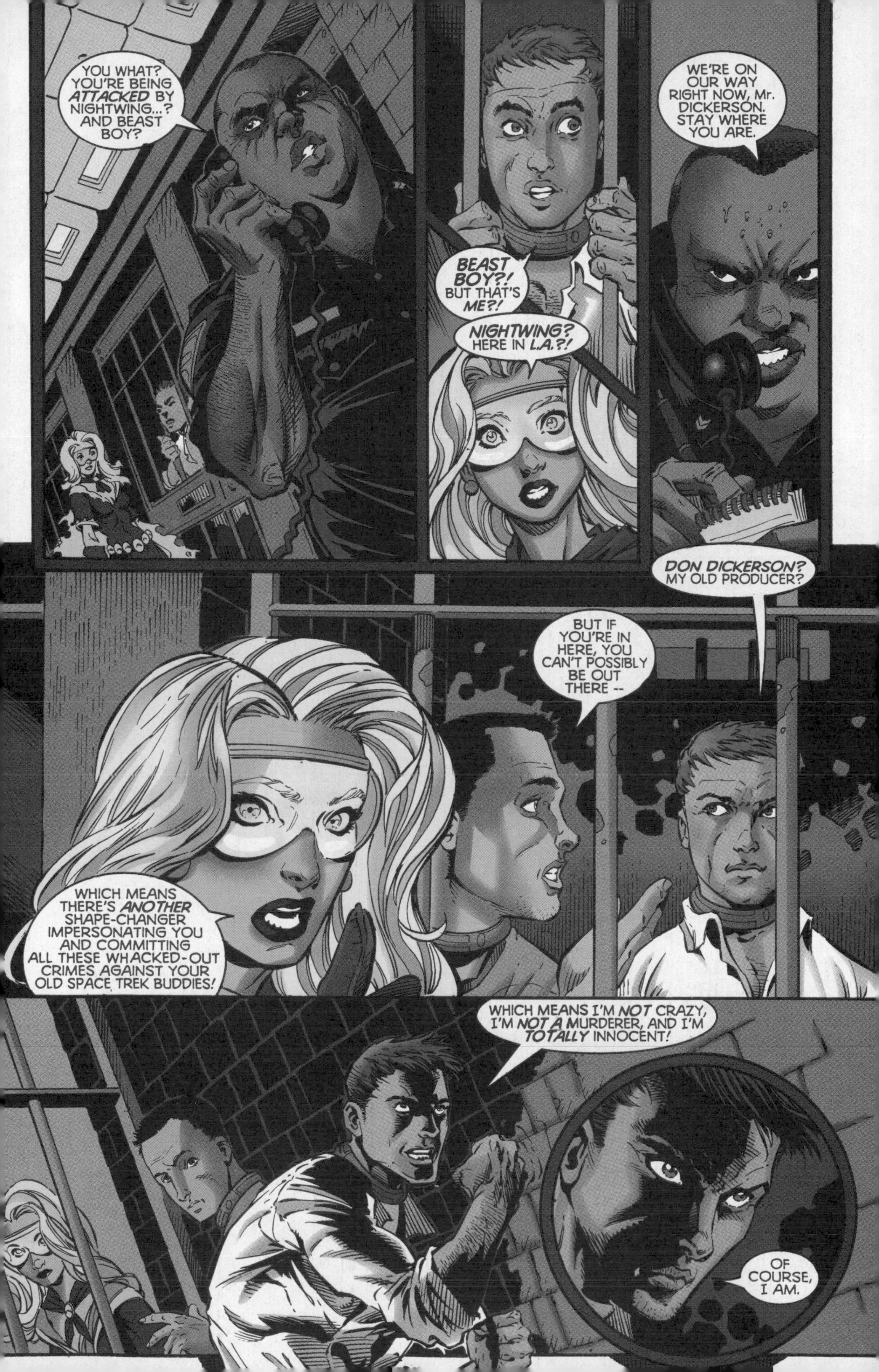
YOU WHAT? YOU'RE BEING *ATTACKED* BY NIGHTWING...? AND BEAST BOY?
BEAST BOY?! BUT THAT'S *ME?!*
NIGHTWING? HERE IN *L.A.?!*
WE'RE ON OUR WAY RIGHT NOW, Mr. DICKERSON. STAY WHERE YOU ARE.
DON DICKERSON? MY OLD PRODUCER?
BUT IF YOU'RE IN HERE, YOU CAN'T POSSIBLY BE OUT THERE --
WHICH MEANS THERE'S *ANOTHER* SHAPE-CHANGER IMPERSONATING YOU AND COMMITTING ALL THESE WHACKED-OUT CRIMES AGAINST YOUR OLD SPACE TREK BUDDIES!
WHICH MEANS I'M *NOT* CRAZY, I'M *NOT A* MURDERER, AND I'M *TOTALLY* INNOCENT!
OF COURSE, I AM.

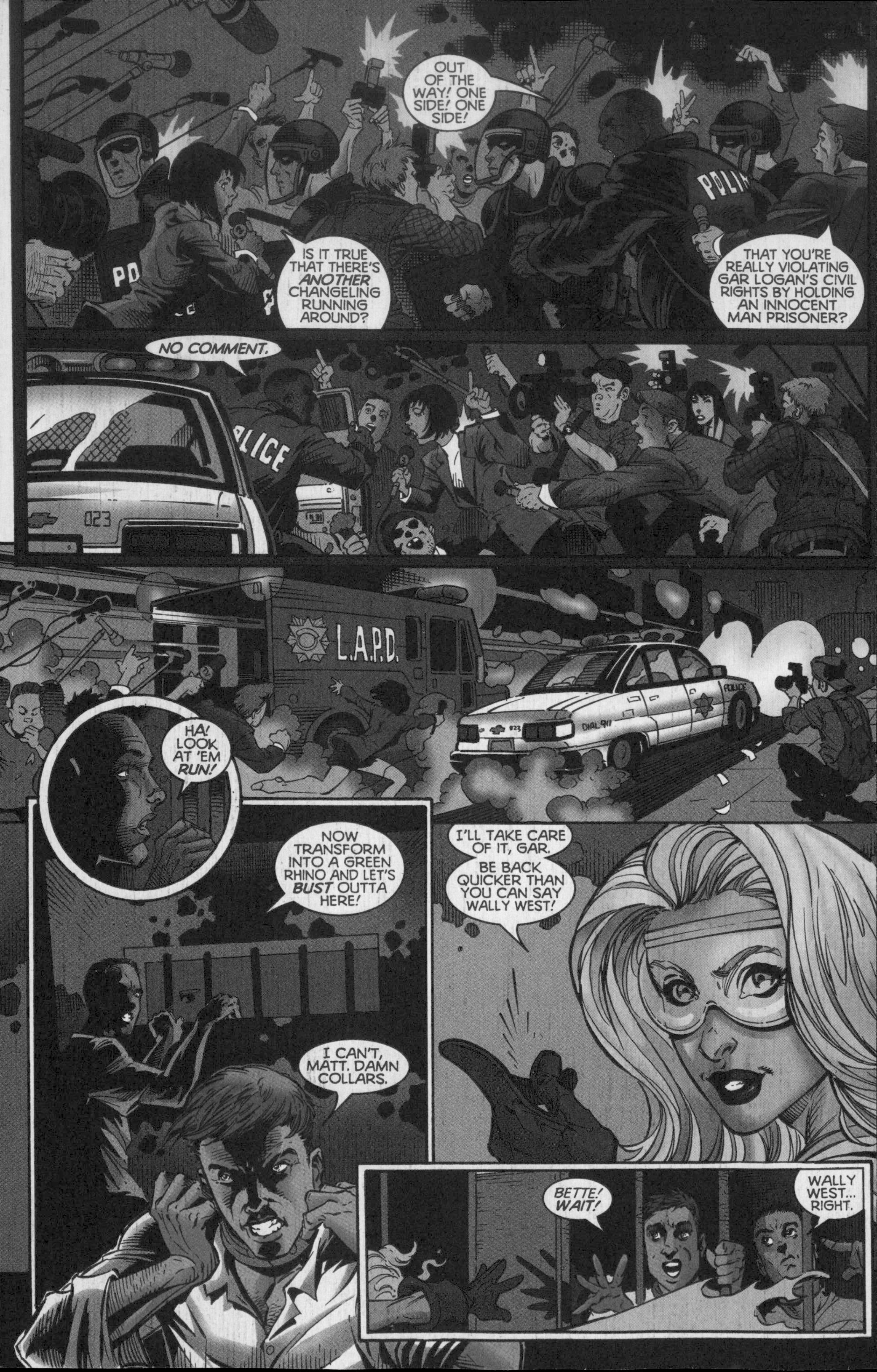
OUT OF THE WAY! ONE SIDE! ONE SIDE!
IS IT TRUE THAT THERE'S ANOTHER CHANGELING RUNNING AROUND?
THAT YOU'RE REALLY VIOLATING GAR LOGAN'S CIVIL RIGHTS BY HOLDING AN INNOCENT MAN PRISONER?
NO COMMENT.
POLICE
023
L.A.P.D.
HA! LOOK AT 'EM RUN!
NOW TRANSFORM INTO A GREEN RHINO AND LET'S BUST OUTTA HERE!
I CAN'T, MATT. DAMN COLLARS.
I'LL TAKE CARE OF IT, GAR.
BE BACK QUICKER THAN YOU CAN SAY WALLY WEST!
BETTE! WAIT!
WALLY WEST... RIGHT.

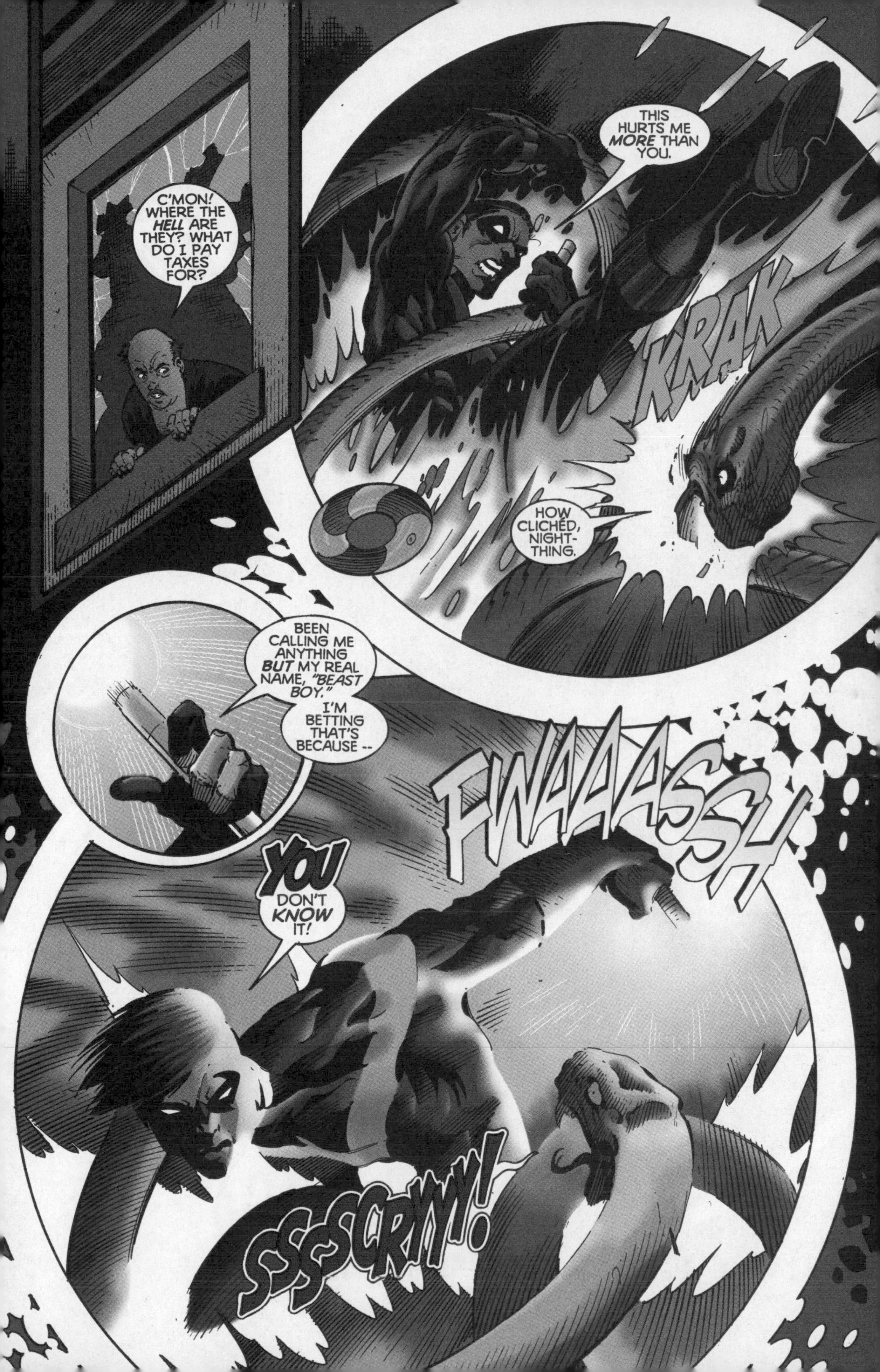
C'MON! WHERE THE HELL ARE THEY? WHAT DO I PAY TAXES FOR?
THIS HURTS ME MORE THAN YOU.
KRAK
HOW CLICHÉD, NIGHT-THING.
BEEN CALLING ME ANYTHING BUT MY REAL NAME, "BEAST BOY."
I'M BETTING THAT'S BECAUSE --
FWAAASH
YOU DON'T KNOW IT!
SSSSCRIYYY!

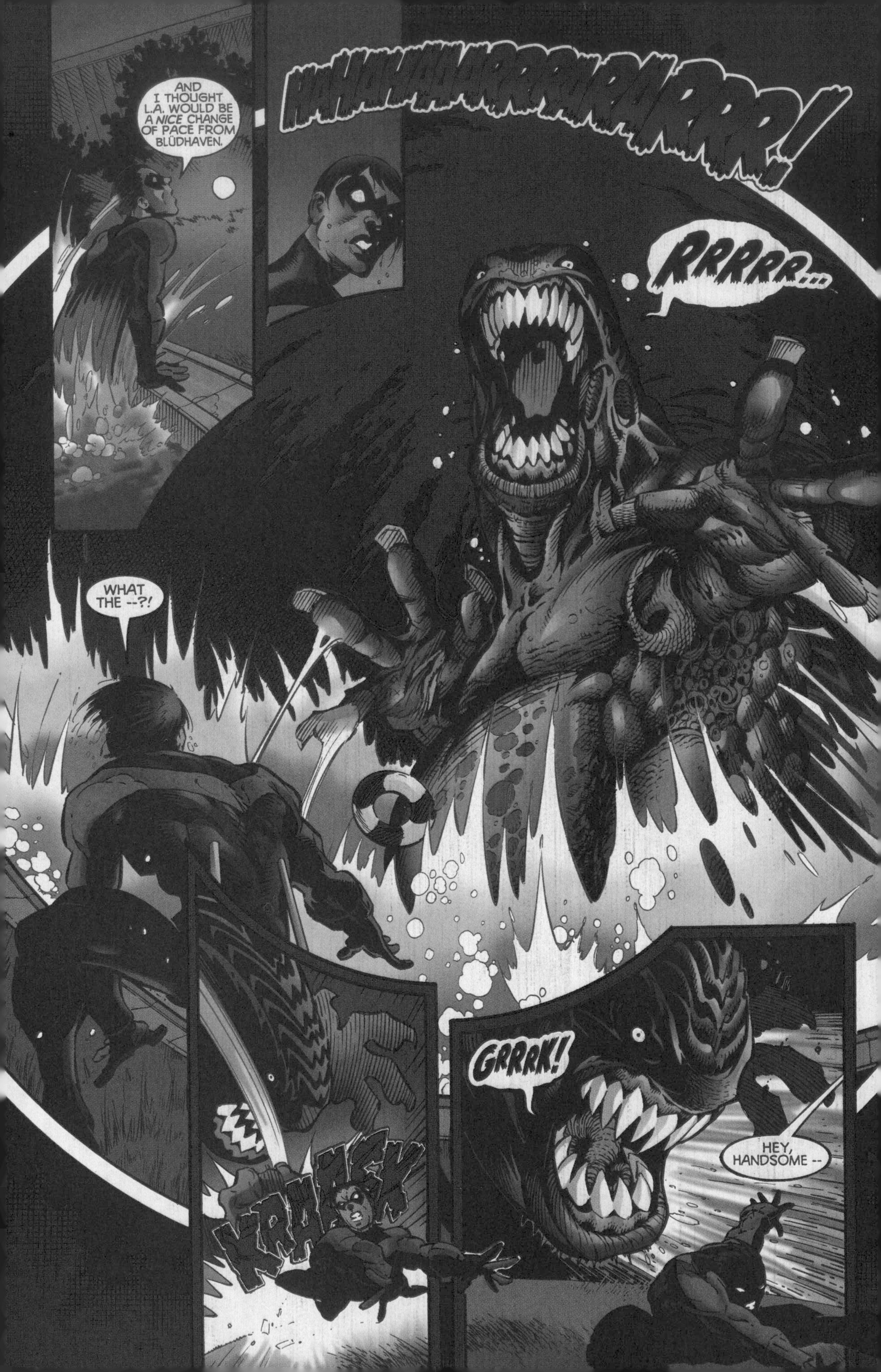
AND I THOUGHT L.A. WOULD BE A NICE CHANGE OF PACE FROM BLÜDHAVEN.
WHAHHAHAARRRGHRAHRRRR!
RRRRR...
WHAT THE --?!
KRAKK
GRRRK!
HEY, HANDSOME --

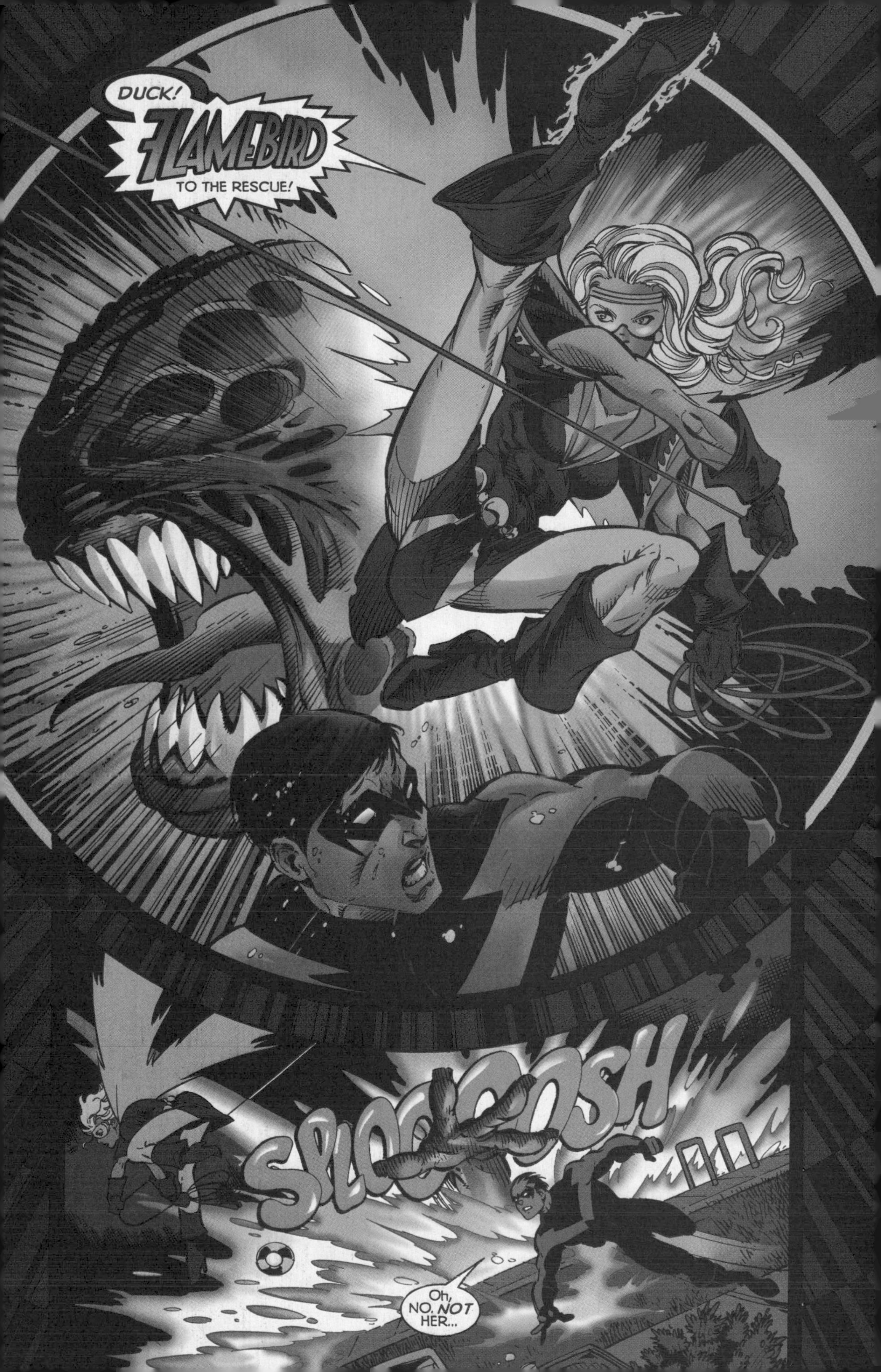
DUCK!
FLAMEBIRD
TO THE RESCUE!
SPLOOOOOSH
Oh, NO. NOT HER...

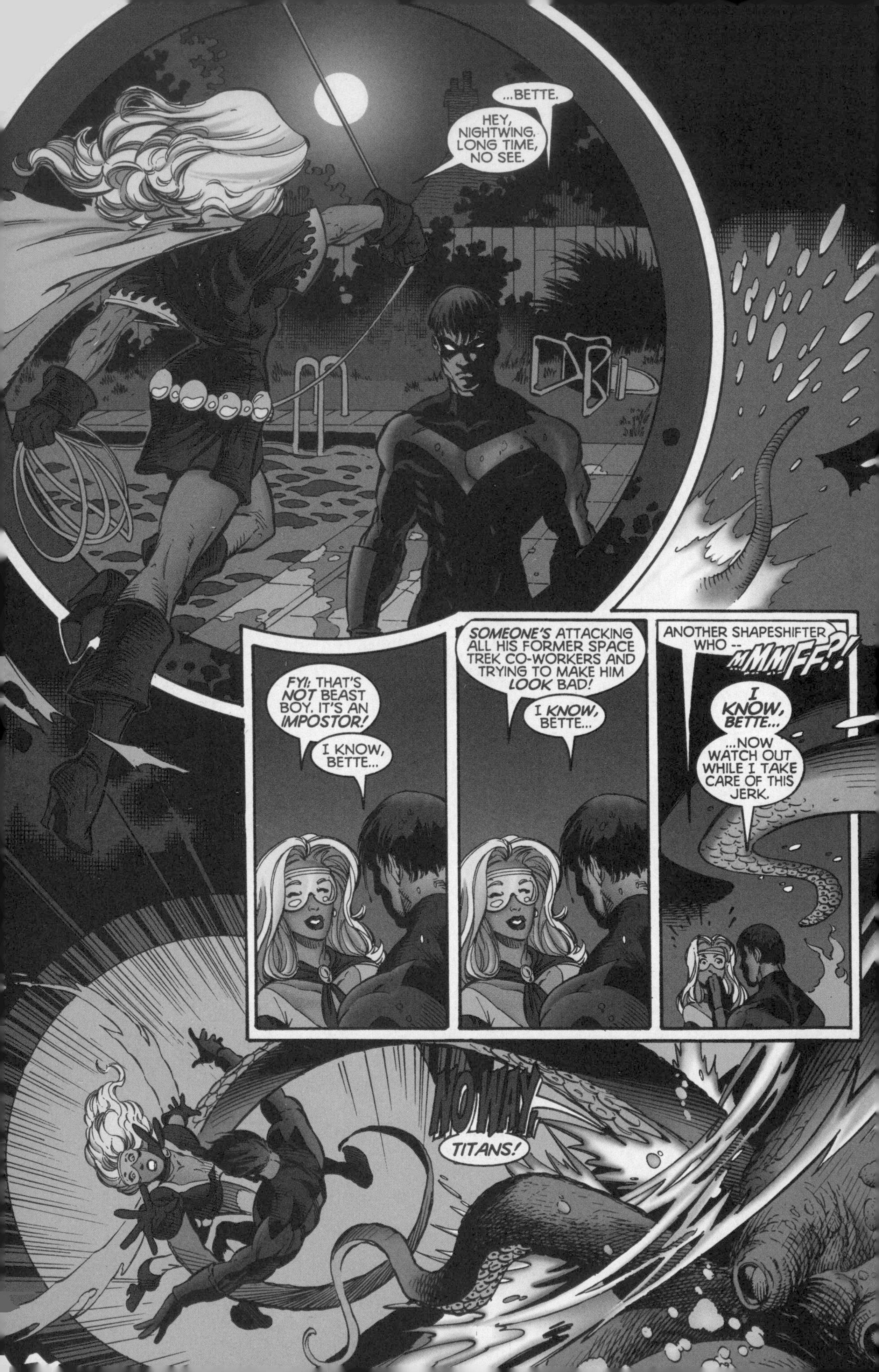
...BETTE.
HEY, NIGHTWING. LONG TIME, NO SEE.
FYI: THAT'S NOT BEAST BOY. IT'S AN IMPOSTOR!
I KNOW, BETTE...
SOMEONE'S ATTACKING ALL HIS FORMER SPACE TREK CO-WORKERS AND TRYING TO MAKE HIM LOOK BAD!
I KNOW, BETTE...
ANOTHER SHAPESHIFTER WHO --
MMMFF?!
I KNOW, BETTE...
...NOW WATCH OUT WHILE I TAKE CARE OF THIS JERK.
NO WAY,
TITANS!

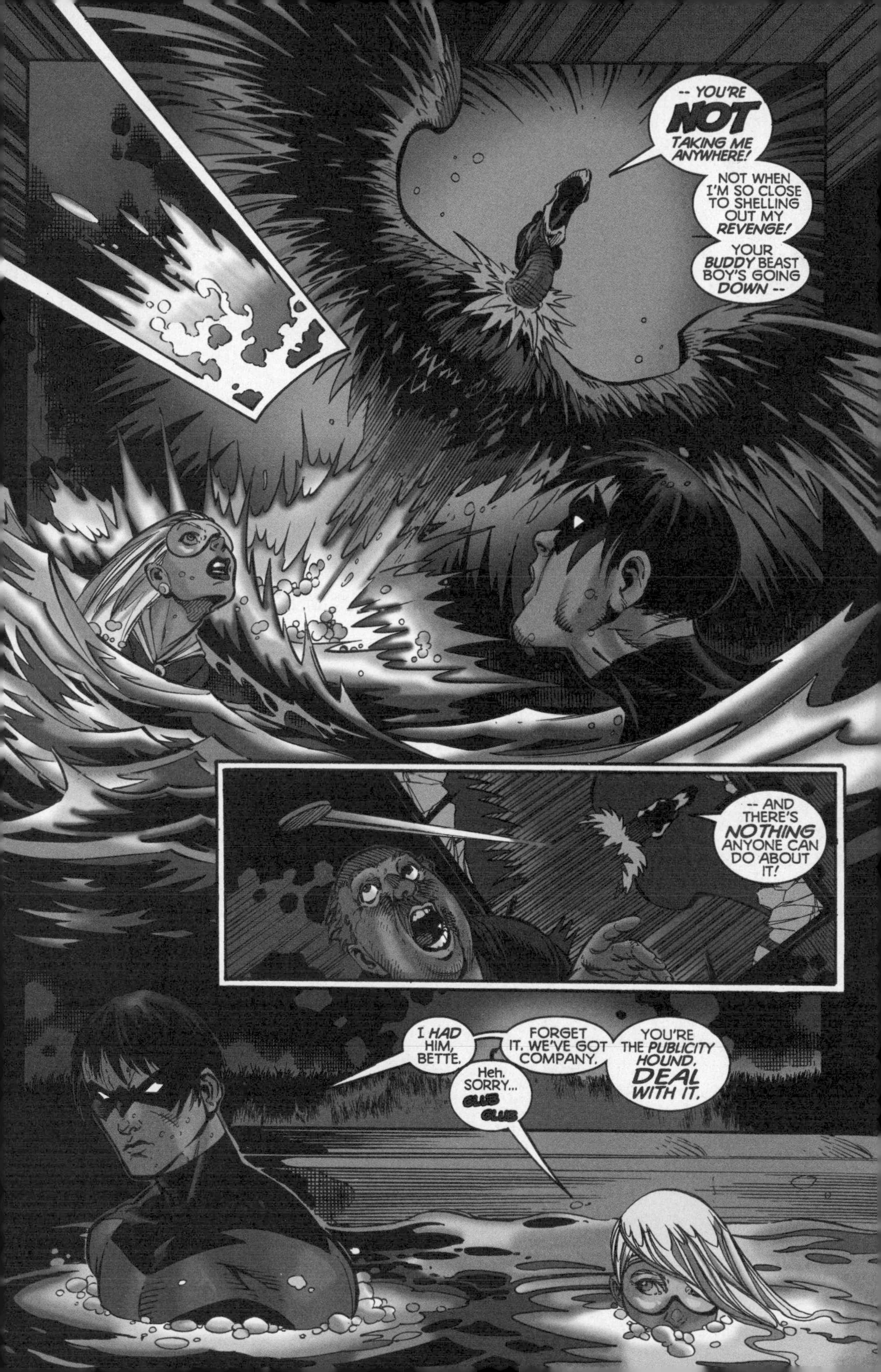

-- YOU'RE NOT TAKING ME ANYWHERE!
NOT WHEN I'M SO CLOSE TO SHELLING OUT MY REVENGE!
YOUR BUDDY BEAST BOY'S GOING DOWN --
-- AND THERE'S NOTHING ANYONE CAN DO ABOUT IT!
I HAD HIM, BETTE.
FORGET IT. WE'VE GOT COMPANY.
YOU'RE THE PUBLICITY HOUND. DEAL WITH IT.
Heh. SORRY... GLUB GLUB

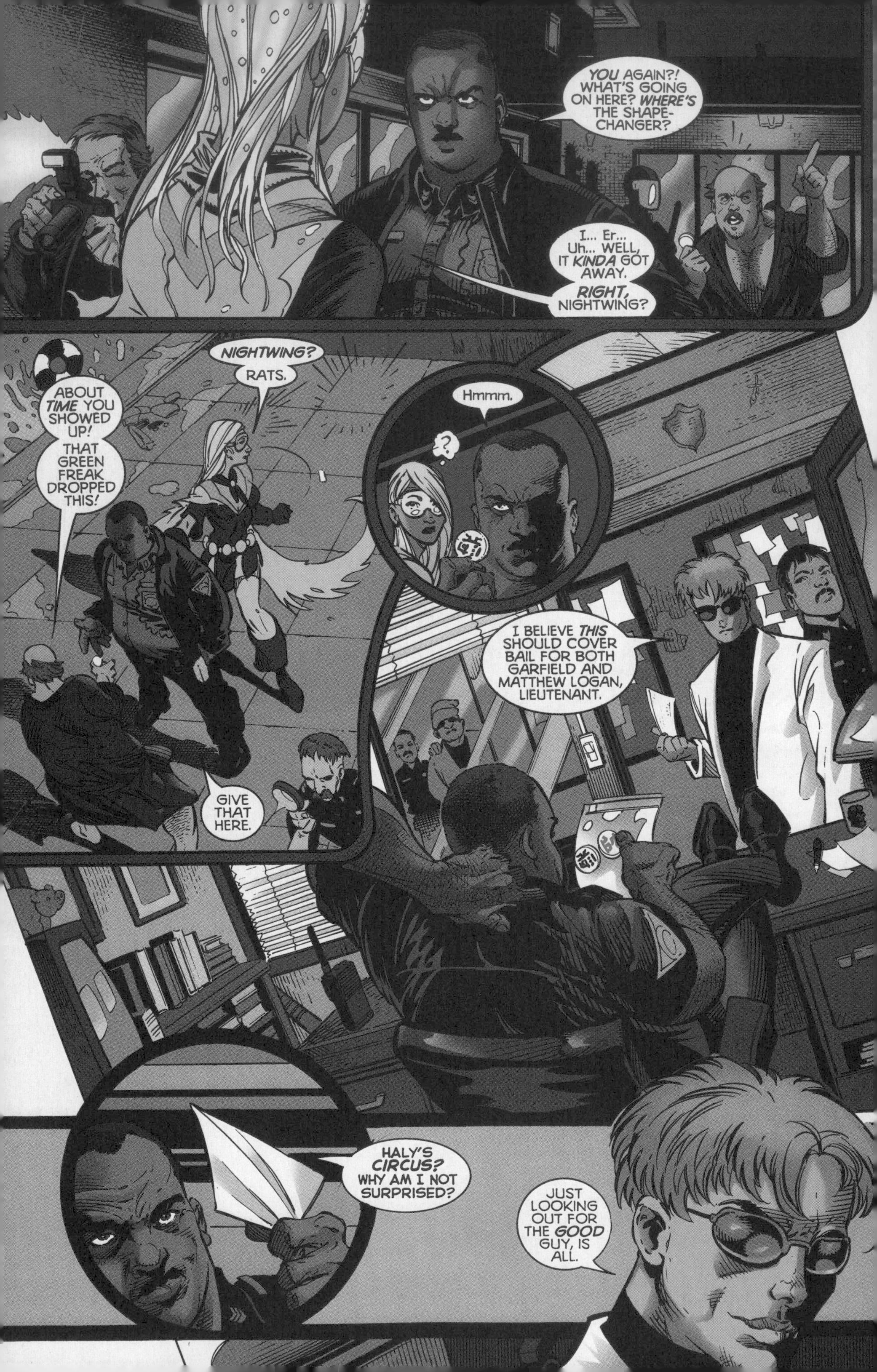
YOU AGAIN?! WHAT'S GOING ON HERE? WHERE'S THE SHAPE-CHANGER?
I... Er... Uh... WELL, IT KINDA GOT AWAY. RIGHT, NIGHTWING?
NIGHTWING? RATS.
ABOUT TIME YOU SHOWED UP! THAT GREEN FREAK DROPPED THIS!
GIVE THAT HERE.
Hmmm.
?
I BELIEVE THIS SHOULD COVER BAIL FOR BOTH GARFIELD AND MATTHEW LOGAN, LIEUTENANT.
HALY'S CIRCUS? WHY AM I NOT SURPRISED?
JUST LOOKING OUT FOR THE GOOD GUY, IS ALL.

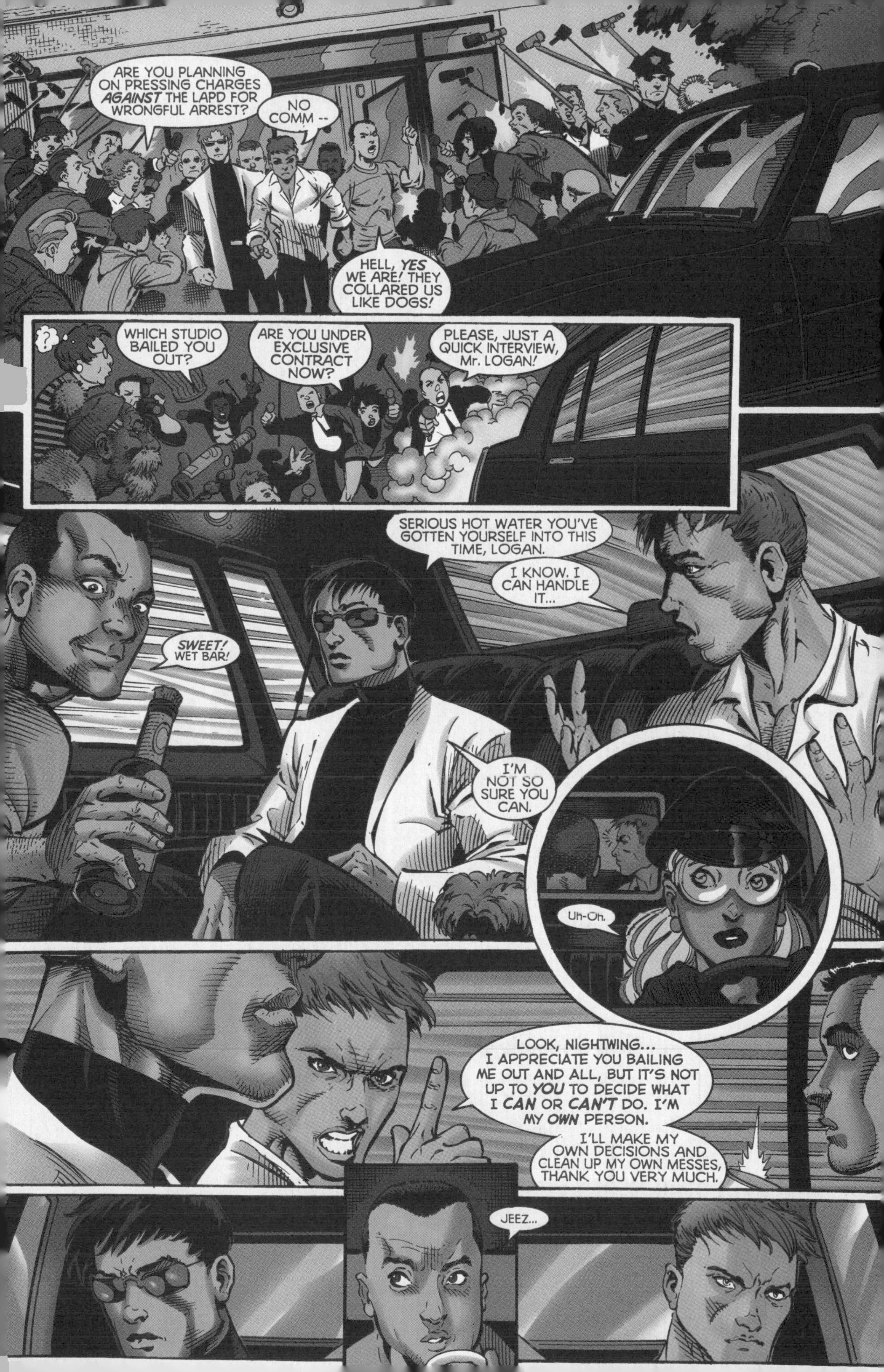
ARE YOU PLANNING ON PRESSING CHARGES AGAINST THE LAPD FOR WRONGFUL ARREST?
NO COMM --
HELL, YES WE ARE! THEY COLLARED US LIKE DOGS!
WHICH STUDIO BAILED YOU OUT?
ARE YOU UNDER EXCLUSIVE CONTRACT NOW?
PLEASE, JUST A QUICK INTERVIEW, Mr. LOGAN!
SERIOUS HOT WATER YOU'VE GOTTEN YOURSELF INTO THIS TIME, LOGAN.
I KNOW. I CAN HANDLE IT...
SWEET! WET BAR!
I'M NOT SO SURE YOU CAN.
Uh-Oh.
LOOK, NIGHTWING... I APPRECIATE YOU BAILING ME OUT AND ALL, BUT IT'S NOT UP TO YOU TO DECIDE WHAT I CAN OR CAN'T DO. I'M MY OWN PERSON.
I'LL MAKE MY OWN DECISIONS AND CLEAN UP MY OWN MESSES, THANK YOU VERY MUCH.
JEEZ...

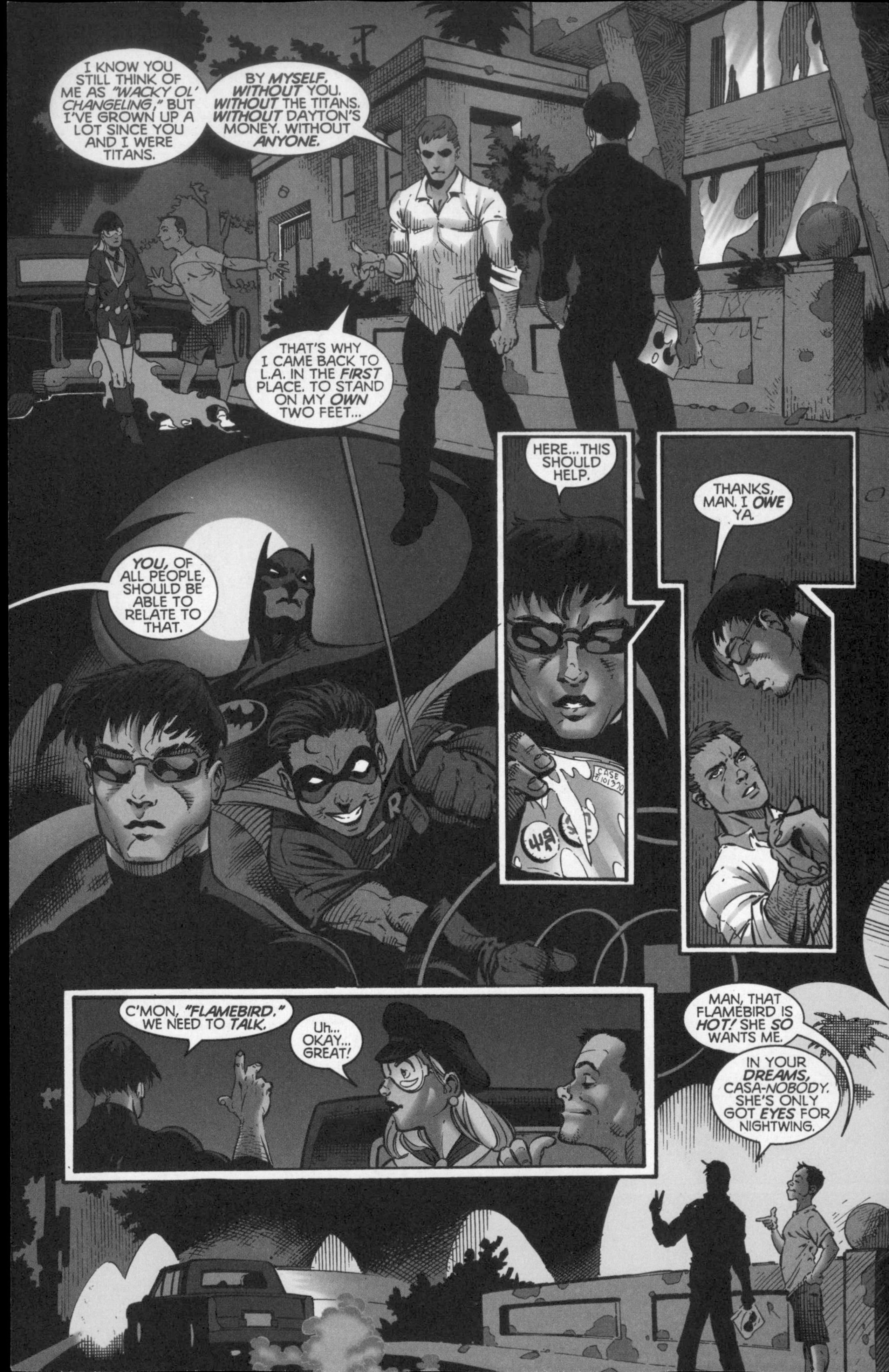
I KNOW YOU STILL THINK OF ME AS "WACKY OL' CHANGELING," BUT I'VE GROWN UP A LOT SINCE YOU AND I WERE TITANS.
BY MYSELF. WITHOUT YOU. WITHOUT THE TITANS. WITHOUT DAYTON'S MONEY. WITHOUT ANYONE.
THAT'S WHY I CAME BACK TO L.A. IN THE FIRST PLACE. TO STAND ON MY OWN TWO FEET...
YOU, OF ALL PEOPLE, SHOULD BE ABLE TO RELATE TO THAT.
HERE...THIS SHOULD HELP.
CASE #101970
THANKS, MAN. I OWE YA.
C'MON, "FLAMEBIRD." WE NEED TO TALK.
Uh... OKAY... GREAT!
MAN, THAT FLAMEBIRD IS HOT! SHE SO WANTS ME.
IN YOUR DREAMS, CASA-NOBODY. SHE'S ONLY GOT EYES FOR NIGHTWING.

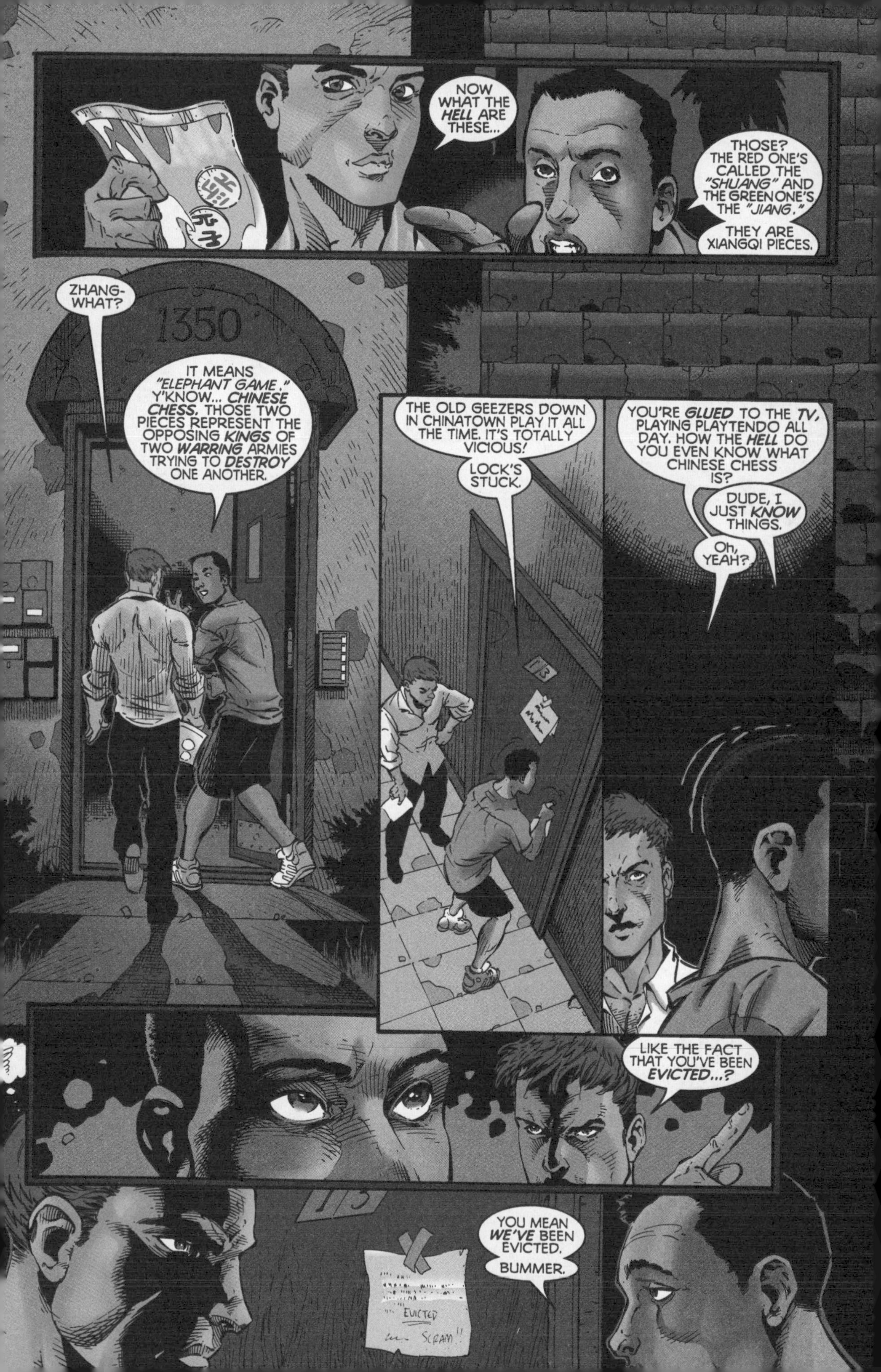
NOW WHAT THE HELL ARE THESE...
THOSE? THE RED ONE'S CALLED THE "SHUANG" AND THE GREEN ONE'S THE "JIANG."
THEY ARE XIANGQI PIECES.
ZHANG-WHAT?
1350
IT MEANS "ELEPHANT GAME." Y'KNOW... CHINESE CHESS. THOSE TWO PIECES REPRESENT THE OPPOSING KINGS OF TWO WARRING ARMIES TRYING TO DESTROY ONE ANOTHER.
THE OLD GEEZERS DOWN IN CHINATOWN PLAY IT ALL THE TIME. IT'S TOTALLY VICIOUS!
LOCK'S STUCK.
YOU'RE GLUED TO THE TV, PLAYING PLAYTENDO ALL DAY. HOW THE HELL DO YOU EVEN KNOW WHAT CHINESE CHESS IS?
DUDE, I JUST KNOW THINGS.
Oh, YEAH?
LIKE THE FACT THAT YOU'VE BEEN EVICTED...?
YOU MEAN WE'VE BEEN EVICTED.
BUMMER.
EVICTED
SCRAM!!

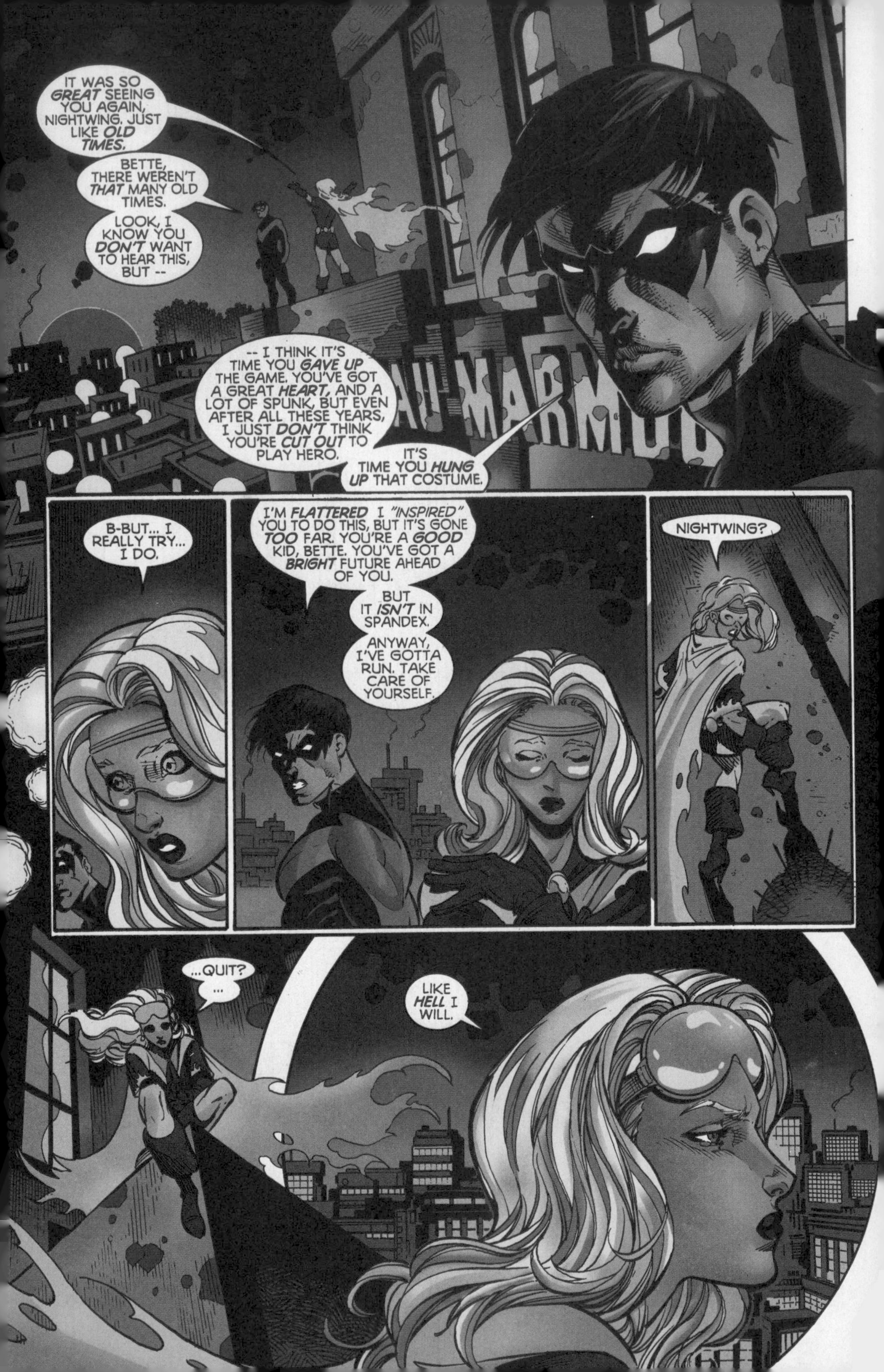
IT WAS SO GREAT SEEING YOU AGAIN, NIGHTWING. JUST LIKE OLD TIMES.
BETTE, THERE WEREN'T THAT MANY OLD TIMES.
LOOK, I KNOW YOU DON'T WANT TO HEAR THIS, BUT --
-- I THINK IT'S TIME YOU GAVE UP THE GAME. YOU'VE GOT A GREAT HEART, AND A LOT OF SPUNK, BUT EVEN AFTER ALL THESE YEARS, I JUST DON'T THINK YOU'RE CUT OUT TO PLAY HERO.
IT'S TIME YOU HUNG UP THAT COSTUME.
AU MARMOU
B-BUT... I REALLY TRY... I DO.
I'M FLATTERED I "INSPIRED" YOU TO DO THIS, BUT IT'S GONE TOO FAR. YOU'RE A GOOD KID, BETTE. YOU'VE GOT A BRIGHT FUTURE AHEAD OF YOU.
BUT IT ISN'T IN SPANDEX.
ANYWAY, I'VE GOTTA RUN. TAKE CARE OF YOURSELF.
NIGHTWING?
...QUIT? ...
LIKE HELL I WILL.

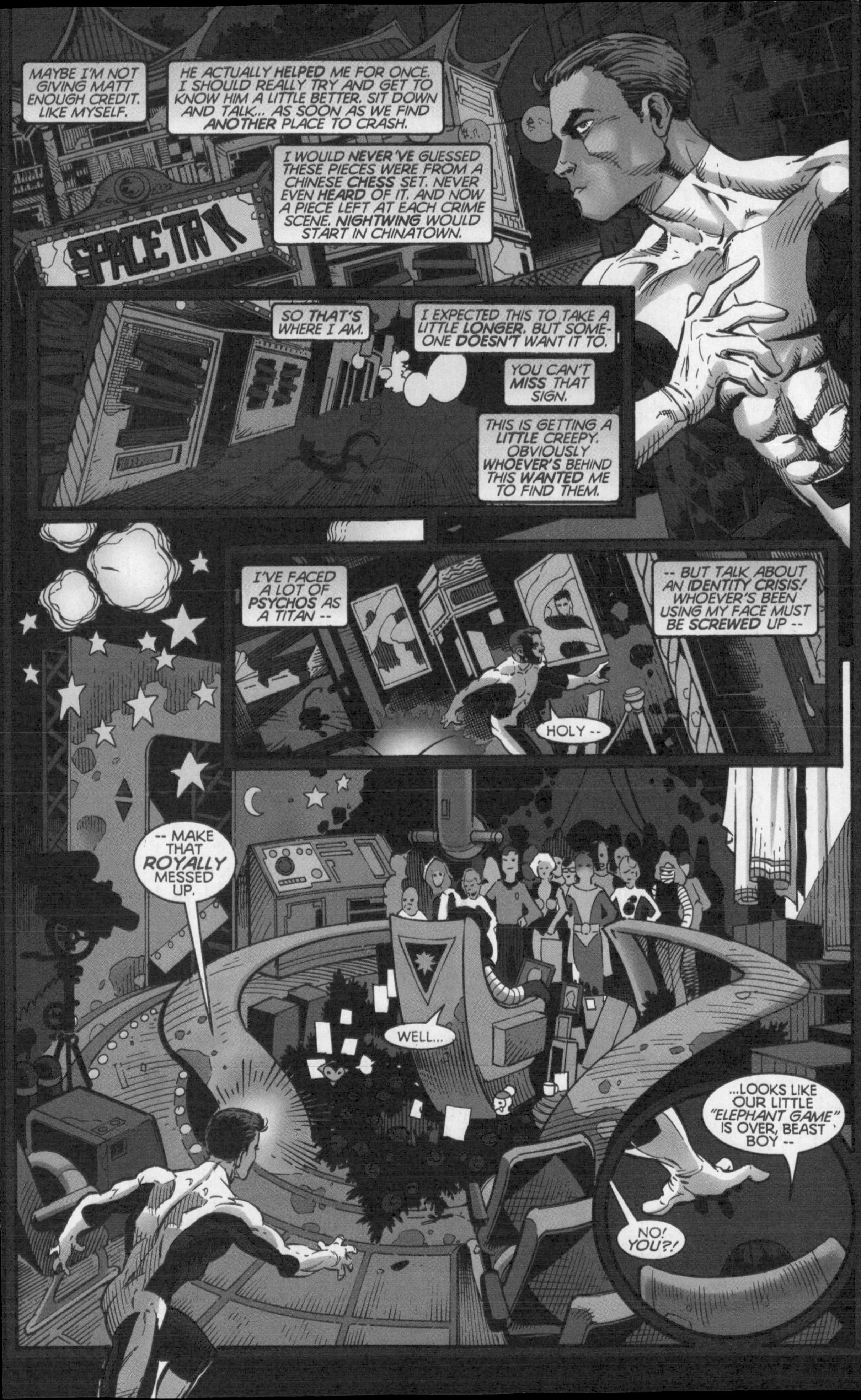

MAYBE I'M NOT GIVING MATT ENOUGH CREDIT. LIKE MYSELF.
HE ACTUALLY HELPED ME FOR ONCE. I SHOULD REALLY TRY AND GET TO KNOW HIM A LITTLE BETTER. SIT DOWN AND TALK... AS SOON AS WE FIND ANOTHER PLACE TO CRASH.
I WOULD NEVER'VE GUESSED THESE PIECES WERE FROM A CHINESE CHESS SET. NEVER EVEN HEARD OF IT. AND NOW A PIECE LEFT AT EACH CRIME SCENE. NIGHTWING WOULD START IN CHINATOWN.
SPACE TRIX
SO THAT'S WHERE I AM.
I EXPECTED THIS TO TAKE A LITTLE LONGER. BUT SOMEONE DOESN'T WANT IT TO.
YOU CAN'T MISS THAT SIGN.
THIS IS GETTING A LITTLE CREEPY. OBVIOUSLY WHOEVER'S BEHIND THIS WANTED ME TO FIND THEM.
I'VE FACED A LOT OF PSYCHOS AS A TITAN --
-- BUT TALK ABOUT AN IDENTITY CRISIS! WHOEVER'S BEEN USING MY FACE MUST BE SCREWED UP --
HOLY --
-- MAKE THAT ROYALLY MESSED UP.
WELL...
...LOOKS LIKE OUR LITTLE "ELEPHANT GAME" IS OVER, BEAST BOY --
NO! YOU?!

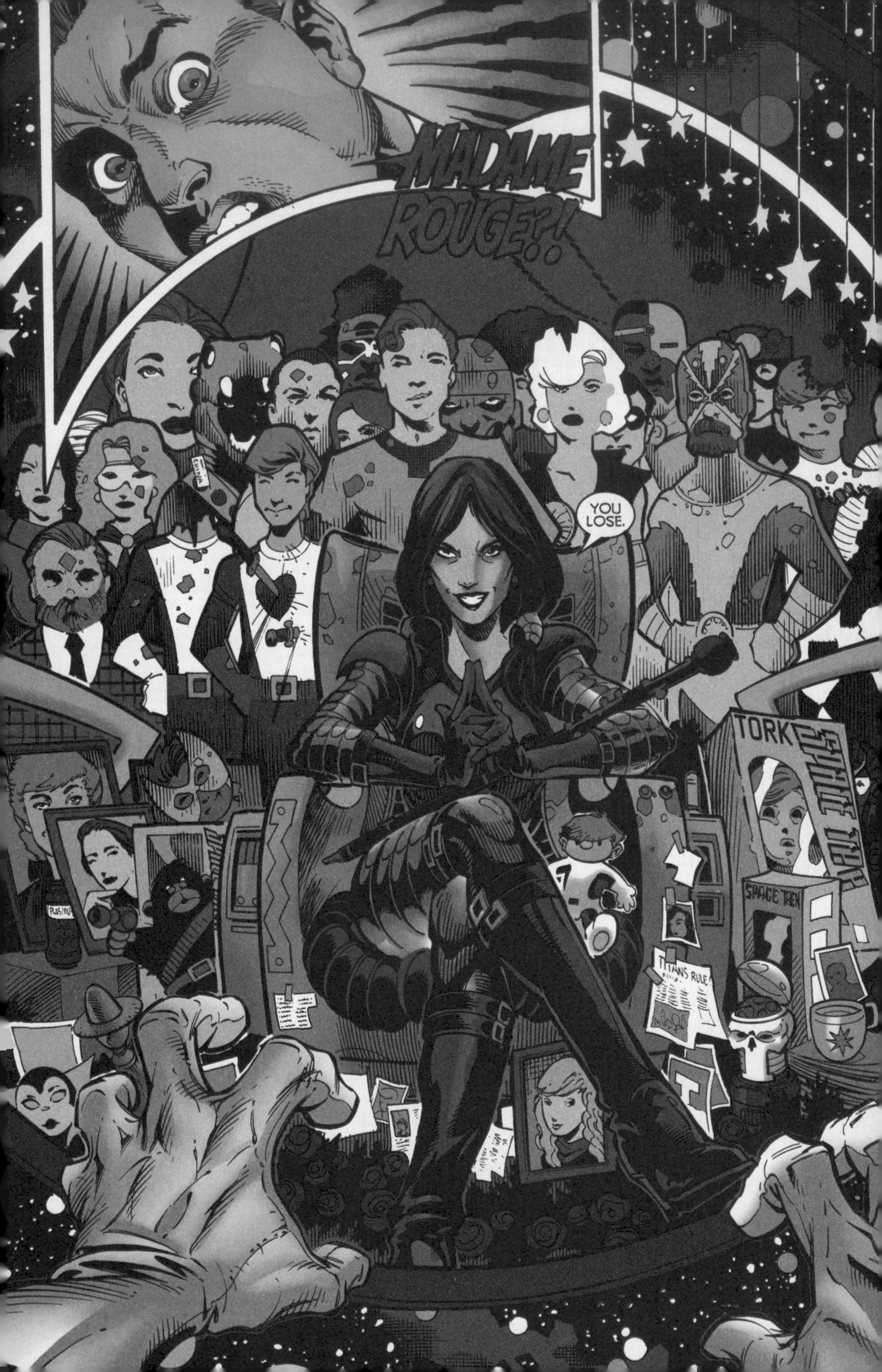
MADAME ROUGE?!
YOU LOSE.
TORK
SPACE TREK
TITANS RULE!

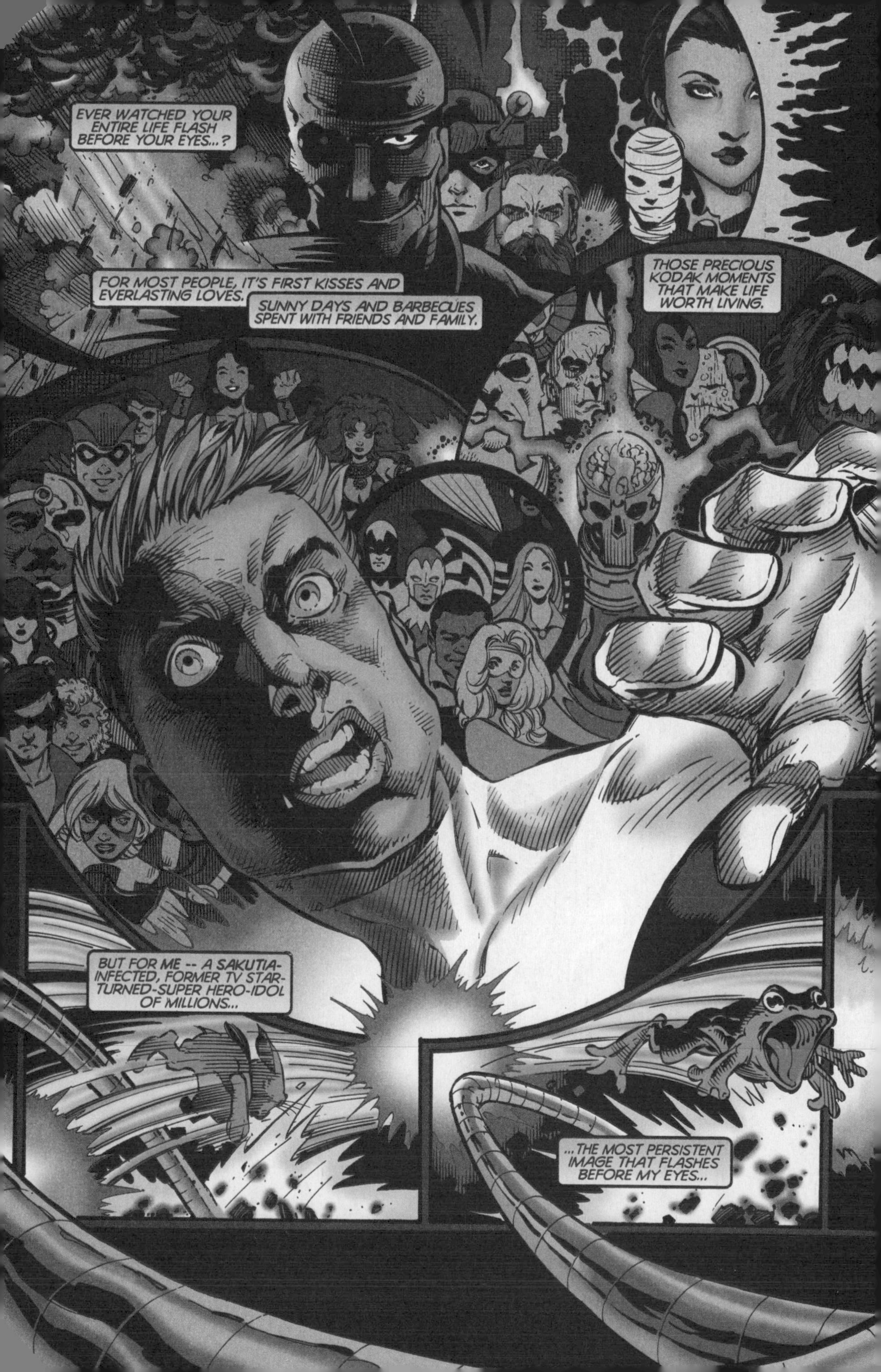
EVER WATCHED YOUR ENTIRE LIFE FLASH BEFORE YOUR EYES...?
FOR MOST PEOPLE, IT'S FIRST KISSES AND EVERLASTING LOVES.
SUNNY DAYS AND BARBECUES SPENT WITH FRIENDS AND FAMILY.
THOSE PRECIOUS KODAK MOMENTS THAT MAKE LIFE WORTH LIVING.
BUT FOR ME -- A SAKUTIA-INFECTED, FORMER TV STAR-TURNED-SUPER HERO-IDOL OF MILLIONS...
...THE MOST PERSISTENT IMAGE THAT FLASHES BEFORE MY EYES...

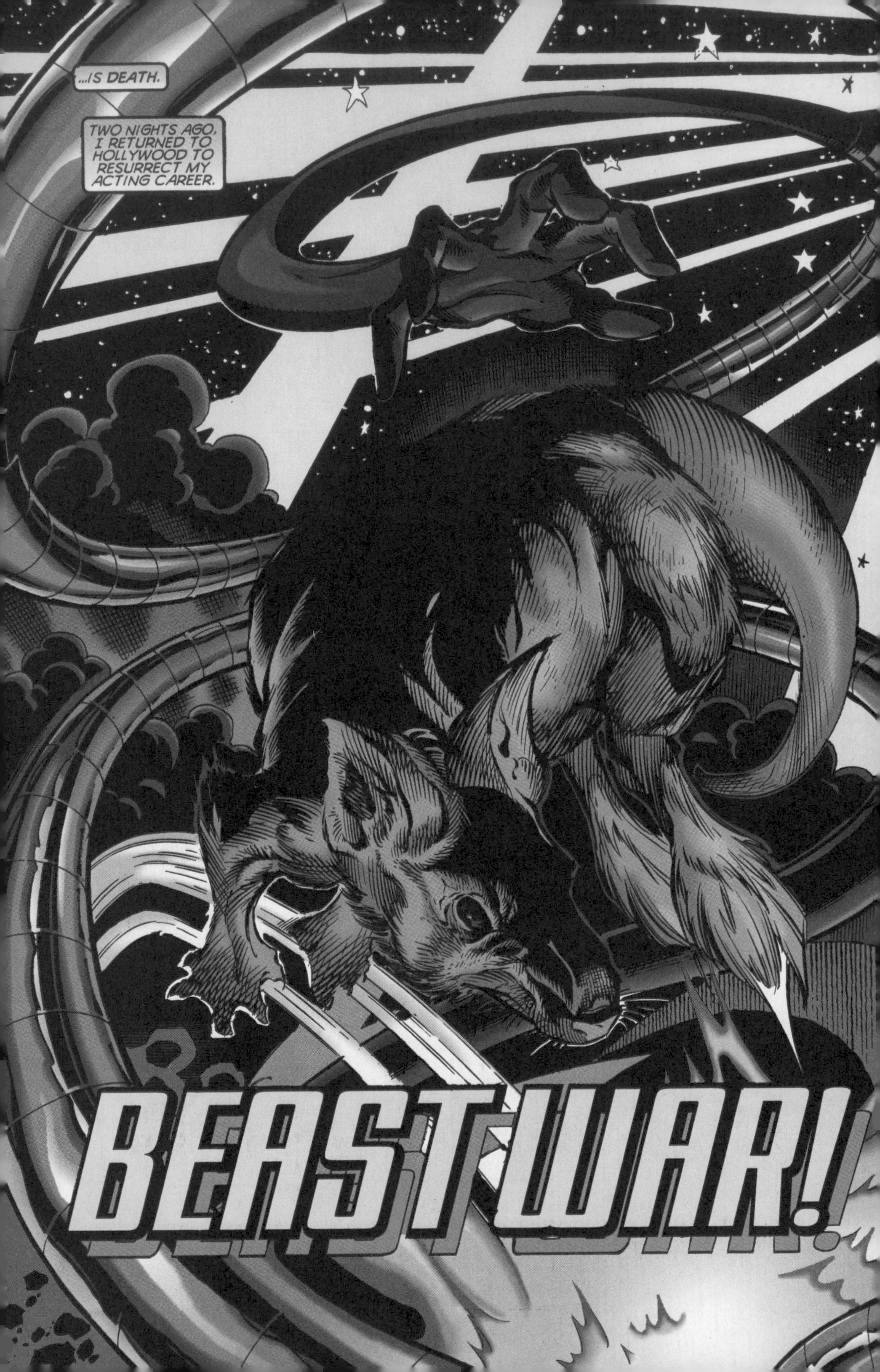
...IS DEATH.
TWO NIGHTS AGO, I RETURNED TO HOLLYWOOD TO RESURRECT MY ACTING CAREER.
BEAST WAR!

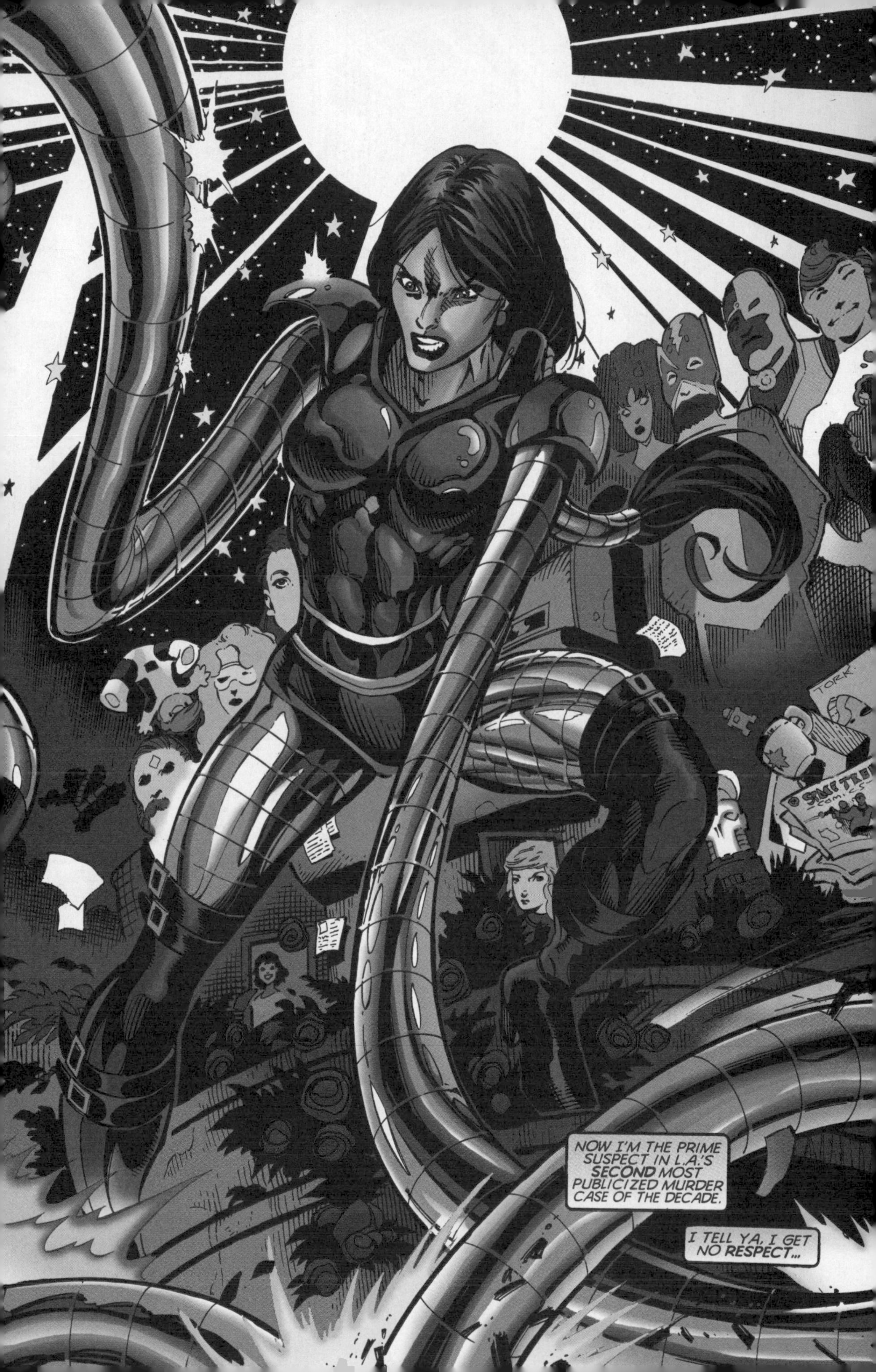
NOW I'M THE PRIME SUSPECT IN L.A.'S SECOND MOST PUBLICIZED MURDER CASE OF THE DECADE.
I TELL YA, I GET NO RESPECT...
TORK

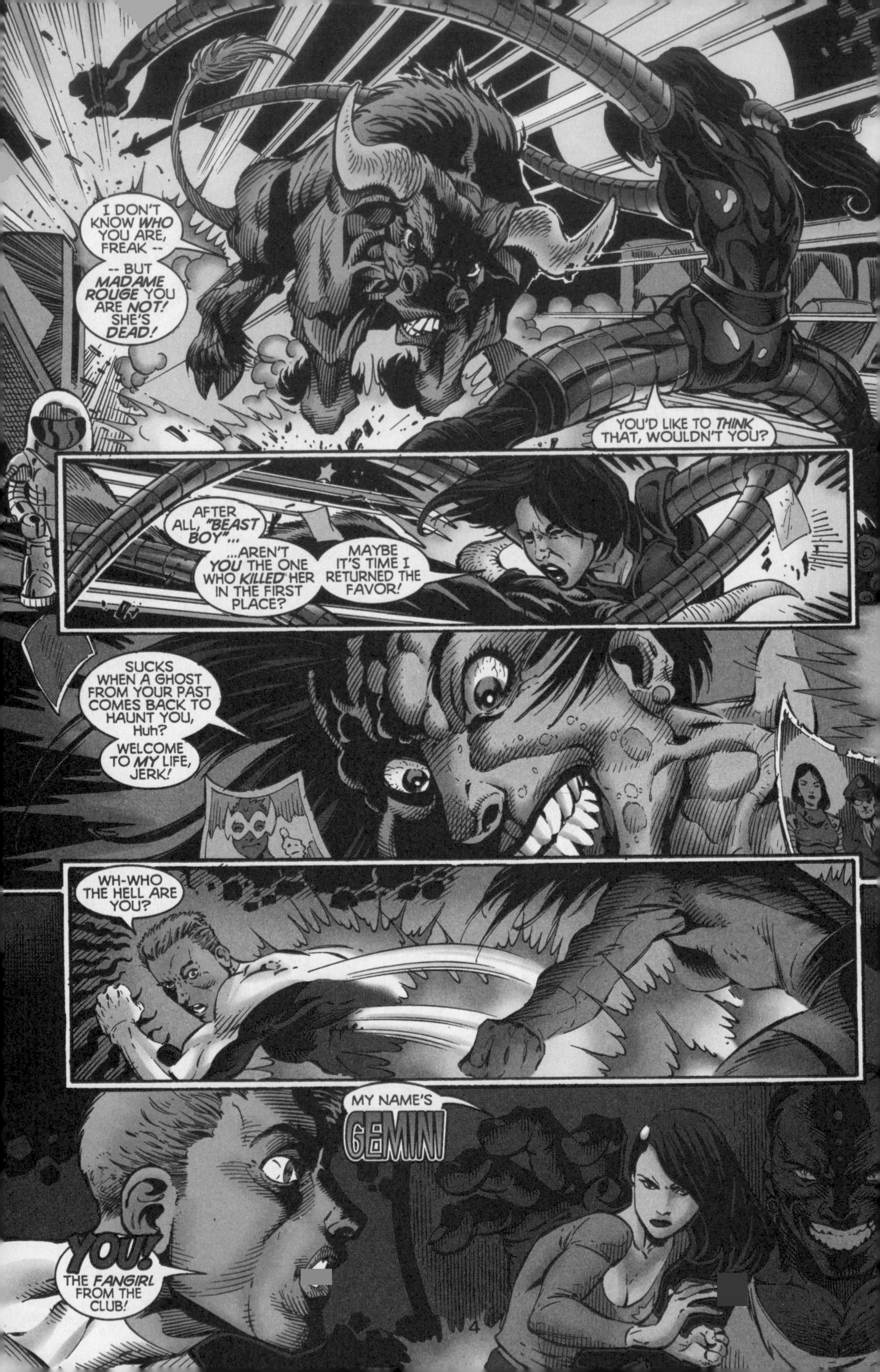
I DON'T KNOW WHO YOU ARE, FREAK --
-- BUT MADAME ROUGE YOU ARE NOT! SHE'S DEAD!
YOU'D LIKE TO THINK THAT, WOULDN'T YOU?
AFTER ALL, "BEAST BOY"...
...AREN'T YOU THE ONE WHO KILLED HER IN THE FIRST PLACE?
MAYBE IT'S TIME I RETURNED THE FAVOR!
SUCKS WHEN A GHOST FROM YOUR PAST COMES BACK TO HAUNT YOU, Huh?
WELCOME TO MY LIFE, JERK!
WH-WHO THE HELL ARE YOU?
MY NAME'S
GEMINI
YOU! THE FANGIRL FROM THE CLUB!

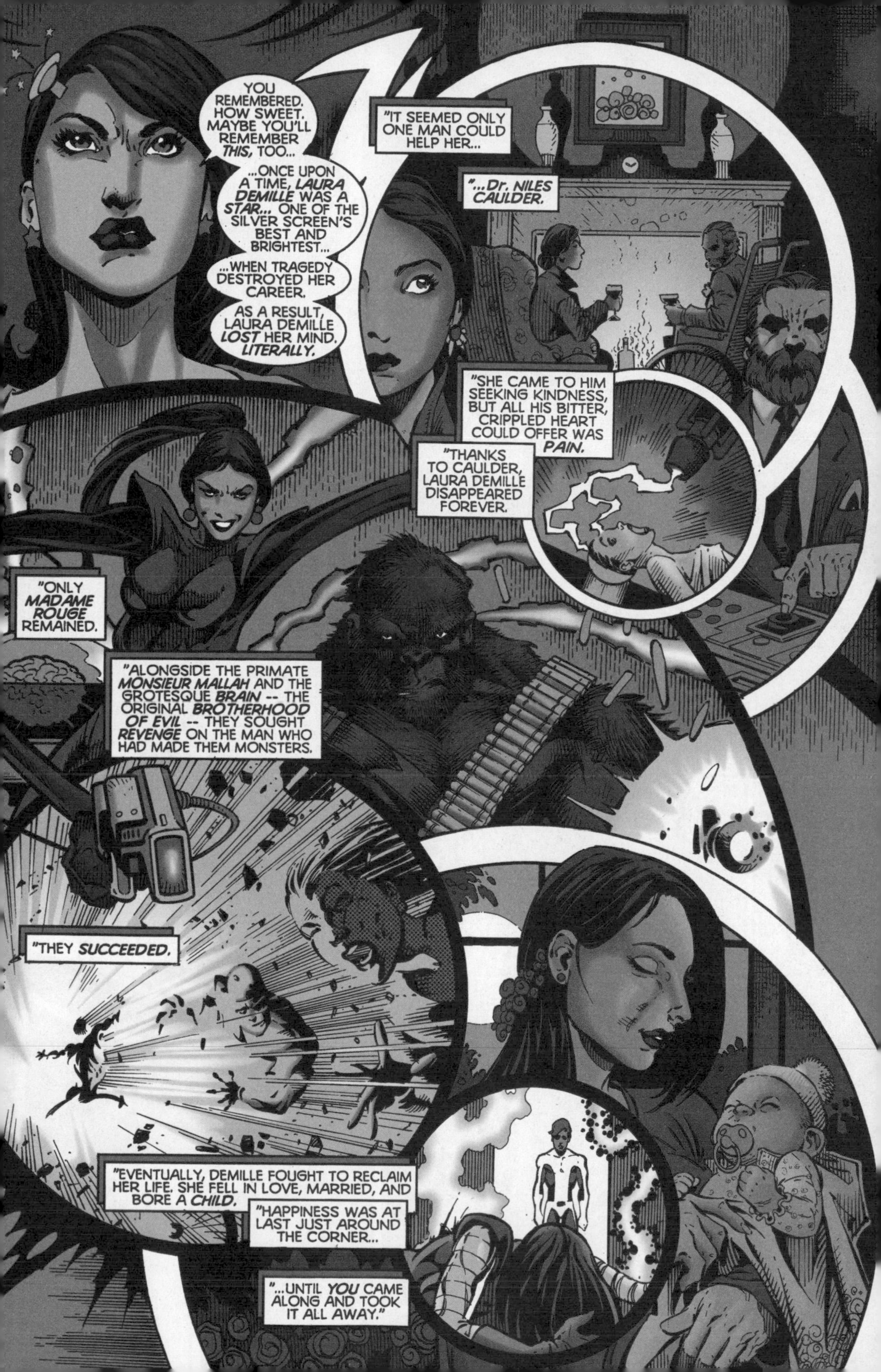
YOU REMEMBERED. HOW SWEET. MAYBE YOU'LL REMEMBER THIS, TOO...
...ONCE UPON A TIME, LAURA DEMILLE WAS A STAR... ONE OF THE SILVER SCREEN'S BEST AND BRIGHTEST...
...WHEN TRAGEDY DESTROYED HER CAREER.
AS A RESULT, LAURA DEMILLE LOST HER MIND. LITERALLY.
"IT SEEMED ONLY ONE MAN COULD HELP HER...
"...Dr. NILES CAULDER.
"SHE CAME TO HIM SEEKING KINDNESS, BUT ALL HIS BITTER, CRIPPLED HEART COULD OFFER WAS PAIN.
"THANKS TO CAULDER, LAURA DEMILLE DISAPPEARED FOREVER.
"ONLY MADAME ROUGE REMAINED.
"ALONGSIDE THE PRIMATE MONSIEUR MALLAH AND THE GROTESQUE BRAIN -- THE ORIGINAL BROTHERHOOD OF EVIL -- THEY SOUGHT REVENGE ON THE MAN WHO HAD MADE THEM MONSTERS.
"THEY SUCCEEDED.
"EVENTUALLY, DEMILLE FOUGHT TO RECLAIM HER LIFE. SHE FELL IN LOVE, MARRIED, AND BORE A CHILD.
"HAPPINESS WAS AT LAST JUST AROUND THE CORNER...
"...UNTIL YOU CAME ALONG AND TOOK IT ALL AWAY."

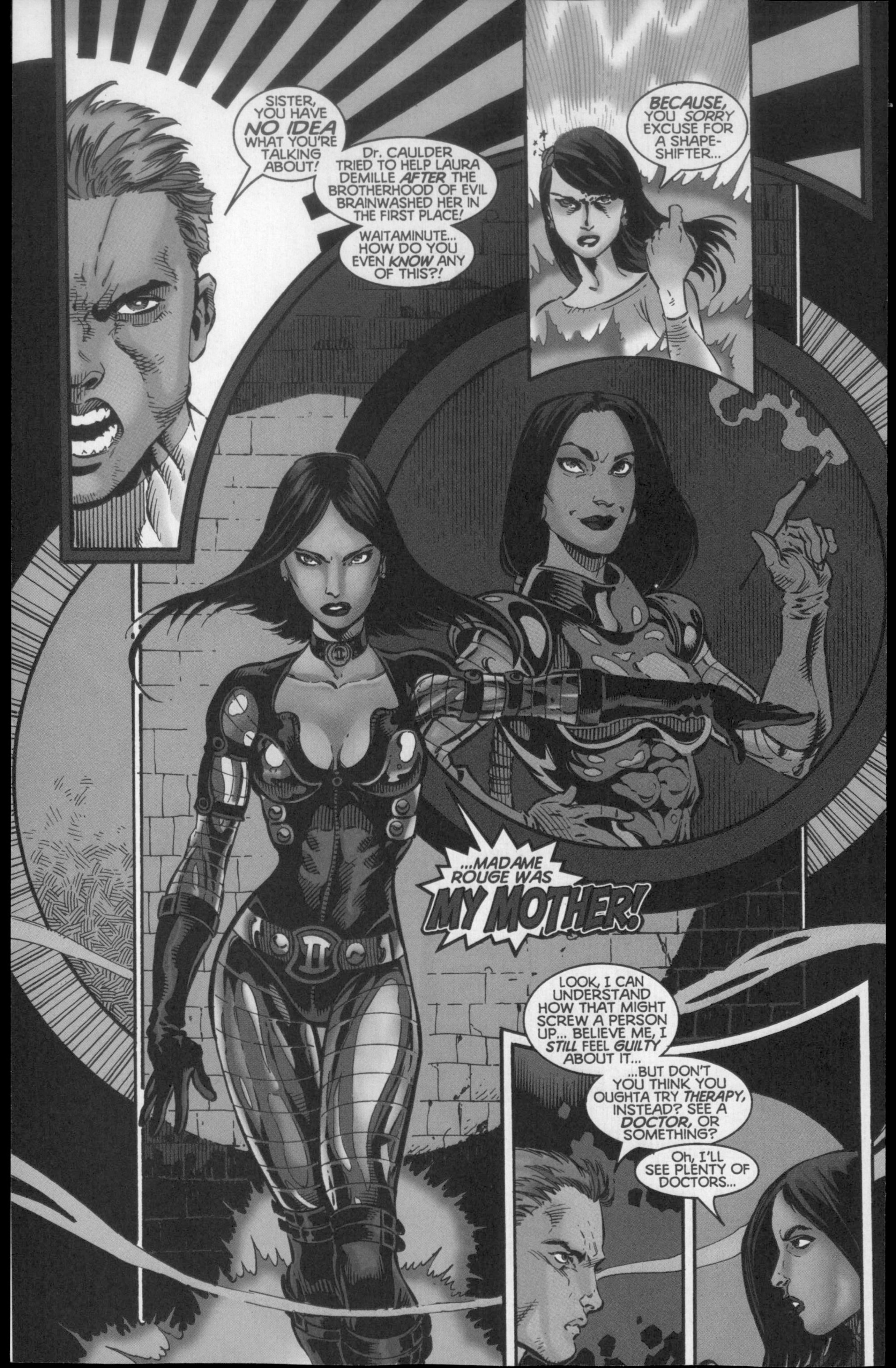
SISTER, YOU HAVE NO IDEA WHAT YOU'RE TALKING ABOUT!
Dr. CAULDER TRIED TO HELP LAURA DEMILLE AFTER THE BROTHERHOOD OF EVIL BRAINWASHED HER IN THE FIRST PLACE!
WAITAMINUTE... HOW DO YOU EVEN KNOW ANY OF THIS?!
BECAUSE, YOU SORRY EXCUSE FOR A SHAPE-SHIFTER...
...MADAME ROUGE WAS MY MOTHER!
LOOK, I CAN UNDERSTAND HOW THAT MIGHT SCREW A PERSON UP... BELIEVE ME, I STILL FEEL GUILTY ABOUT IT...
...BUT DON'T YOU THINK YOU OUGHTA TRY THERAPY, INSTEAD? SEE A DOCTOR, OR SOMETHING?
Oh, I'LL SEE PLENTY OF DOCTORS...

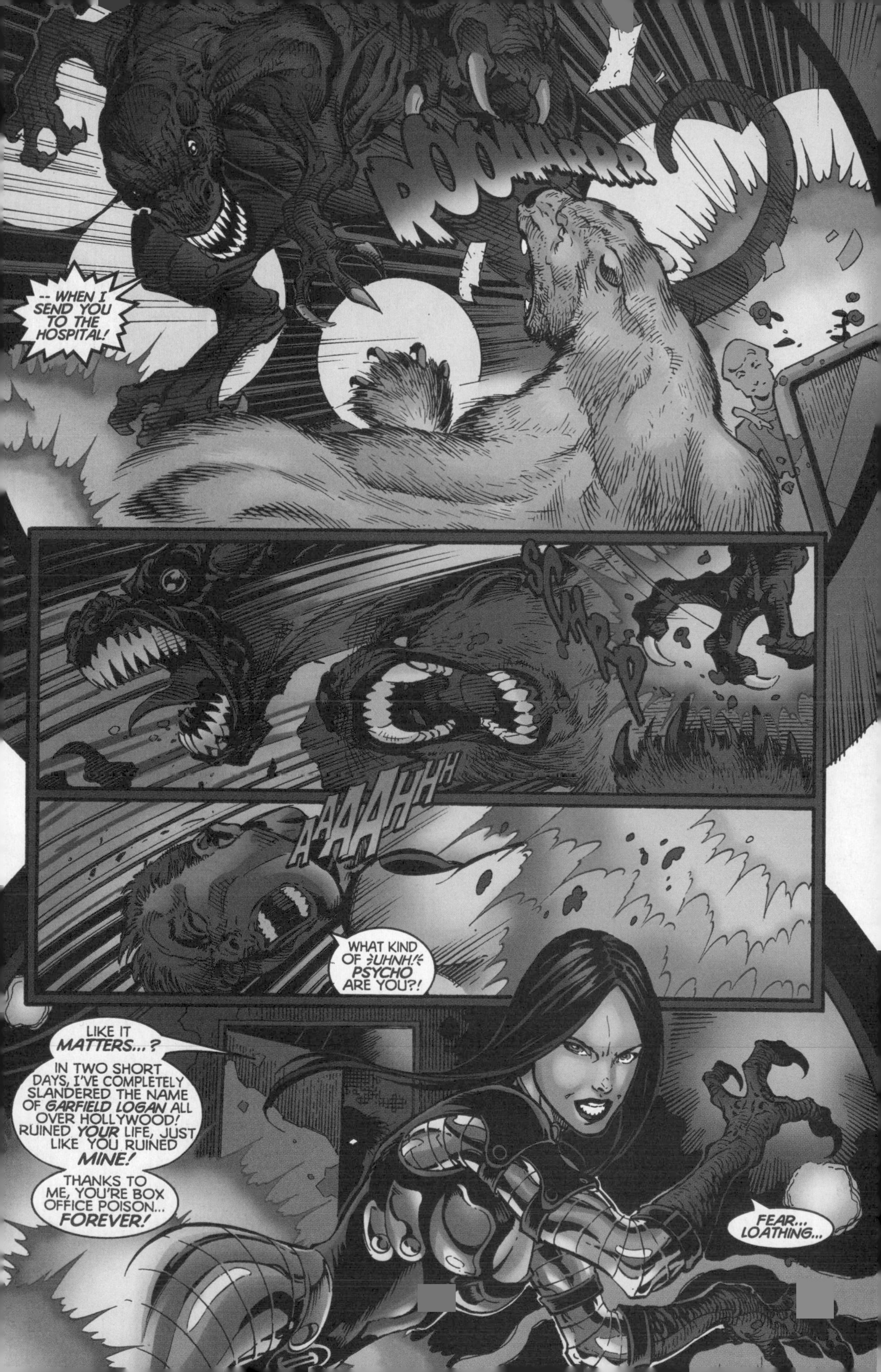

ROOOAARRR
-- WHEN I SEND YOU TO THE HOSPITAL!
SCHRP
AAAAHHH
WHAT KIND OF -UHNH!- PSYCHO ARE YOU?!
LIKE IT MATTERS...?
IN TWO SHORT DAYS, I'VE COMPLETELY SLANDERED THE NAME OF GARFIELD LOGAN ALL OVER HOLLYWOOD! RUINED YOUR LIFE, JUST LIKE YOU RUINED MINE!
THANKS TO ME, YOU'RE BOX OFFICE POISON... FOREVER!
FEAR... LOATHING...

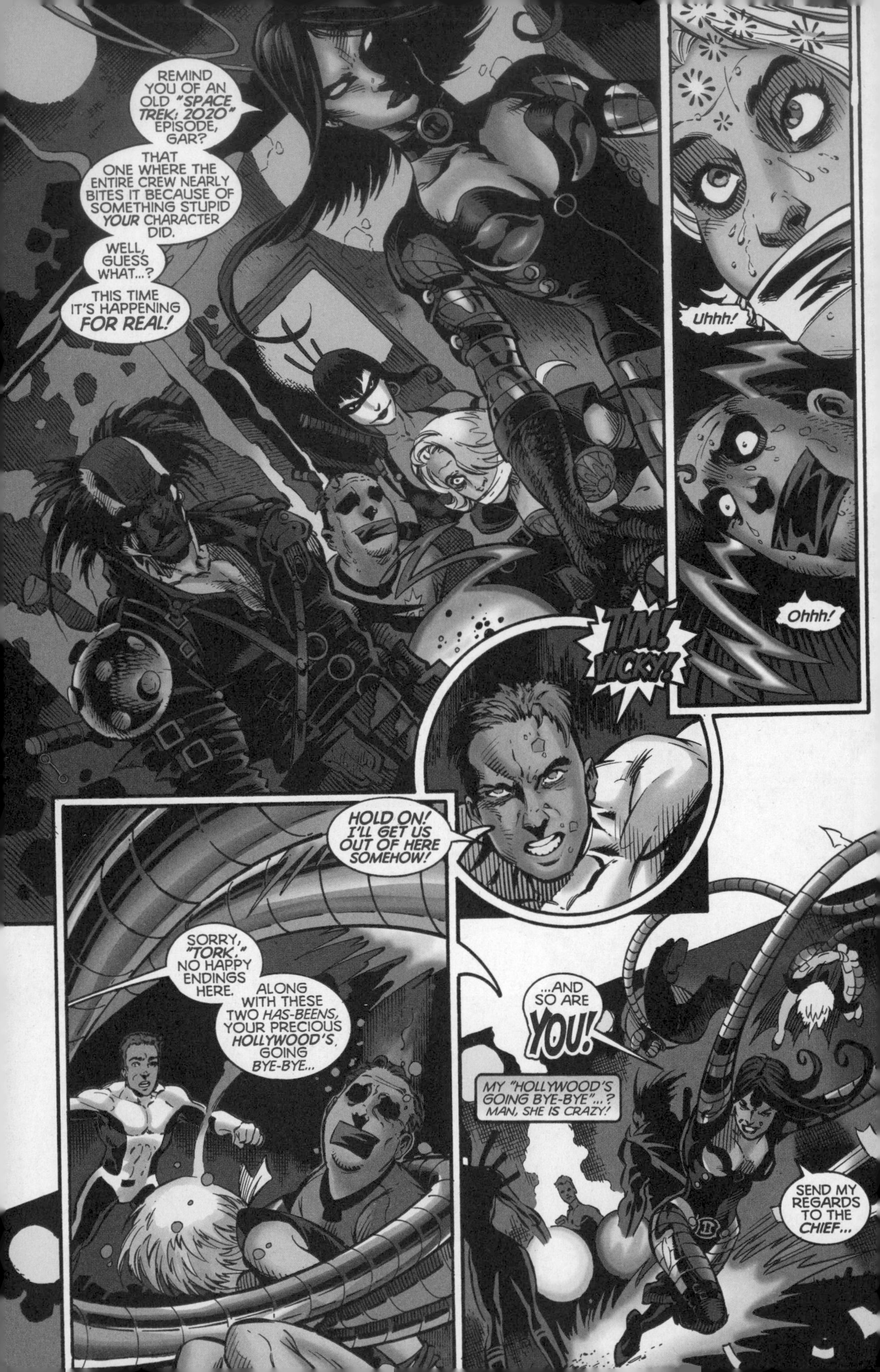
REMIND YOU OF AN OLD "SPACE TREK: 2020" EPISODE, GAR?
THAT ONE WHERE THE ENTIRE CREW NEARLY BITES IT BECAUSE OF SOMETHING STUPID YOUR CHARACTER DID.
WELL, GUESS WHAT...?
THIS TIME IT'S HAPPENING FOR REAL!
Uhhh!
Ohhh!
TIM! VICKY!
HOLD ON! I'LL GET US OUT OF HERE SOMEHOW!
SORRY, "TORK." NO HAPPY ENDINGS HERE.
ALONG WITH THESE TWO HAS-BEENS, YOUR PRECIOUS HOLLYWOOD'S GOING BYE-BYE...
...AND SO ARE YOU!
MY "HOLLYWOOD'S GOING BYE-BYE"...? MAN, SHE IS CRAZY!
SEND MY REGARDS TO THE CHIEF...

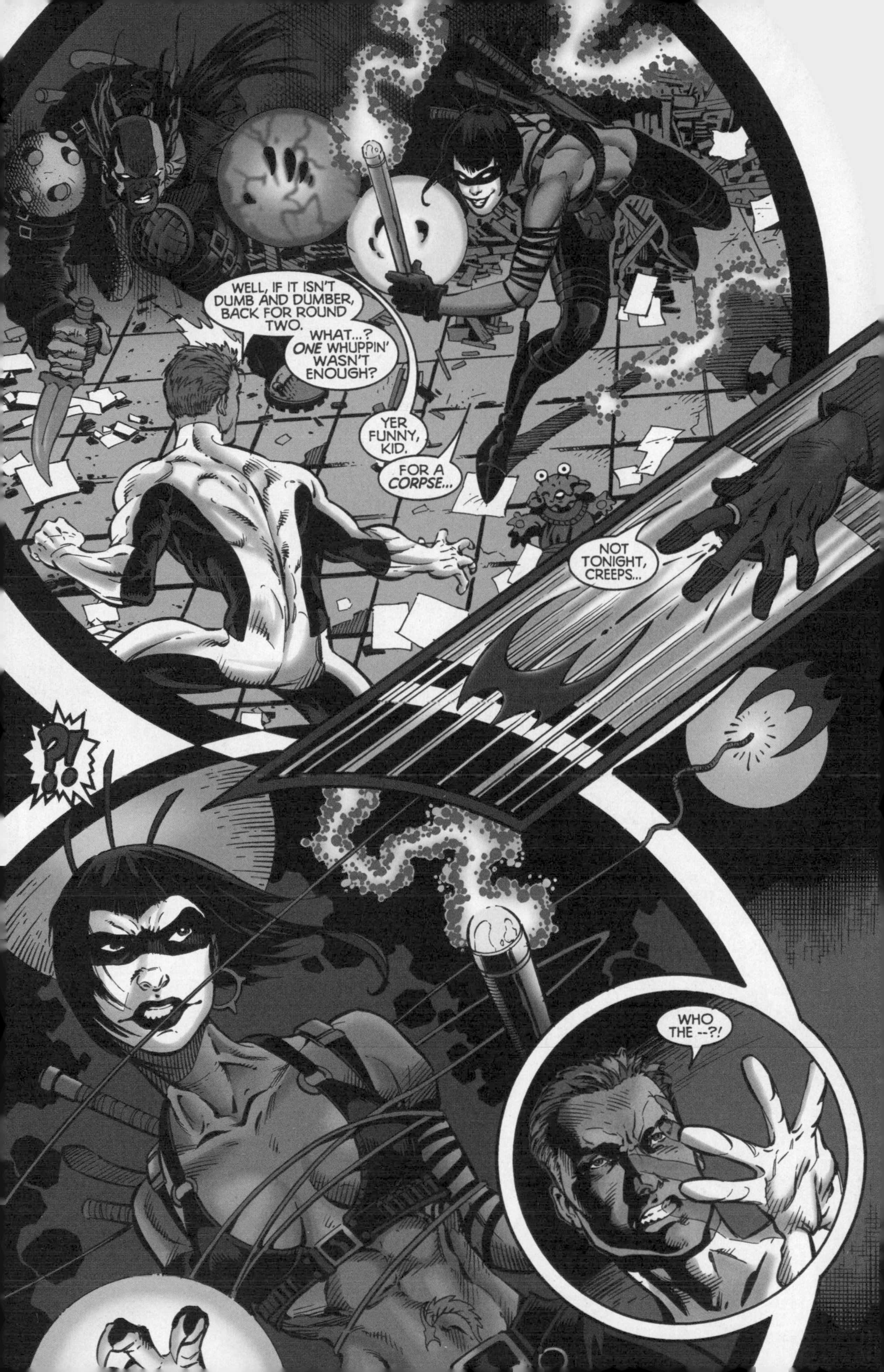
WELL, IF IT ISN'T DUMB AND DUMBER, BACK FOR ROUND TWO.
WHAT...? *ONE* WHUPPIN' WASN'T ENOUGH?
YER FUNNY, KID.
FOR A *CORPSE*...
NOT TONIGHT, CREEPS...
?!
WHO THE --?!

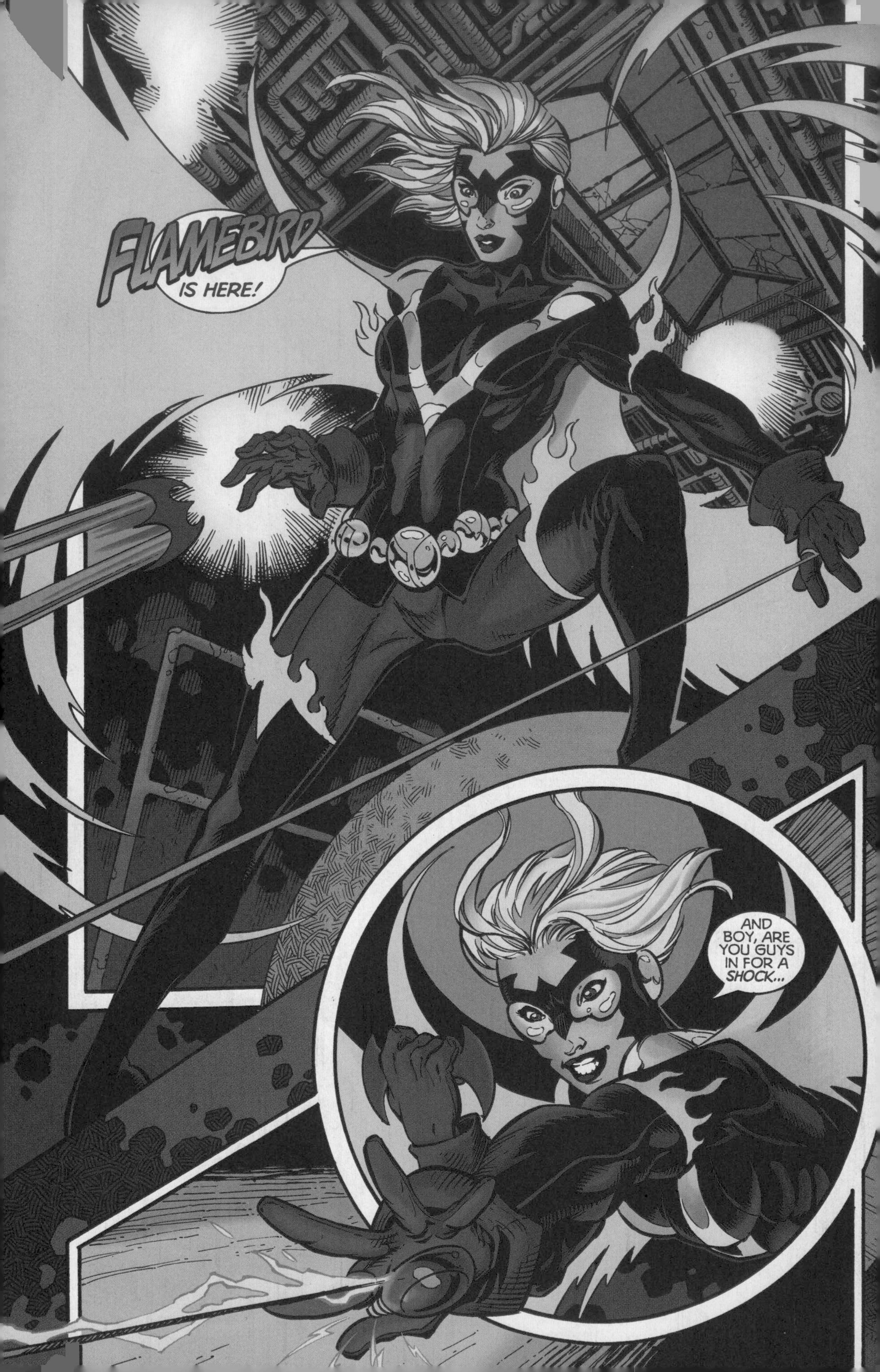
FLAMEBIRD IS HERE!
AND BOY, ARE YOU GUYS IN FOR A SHOCK...

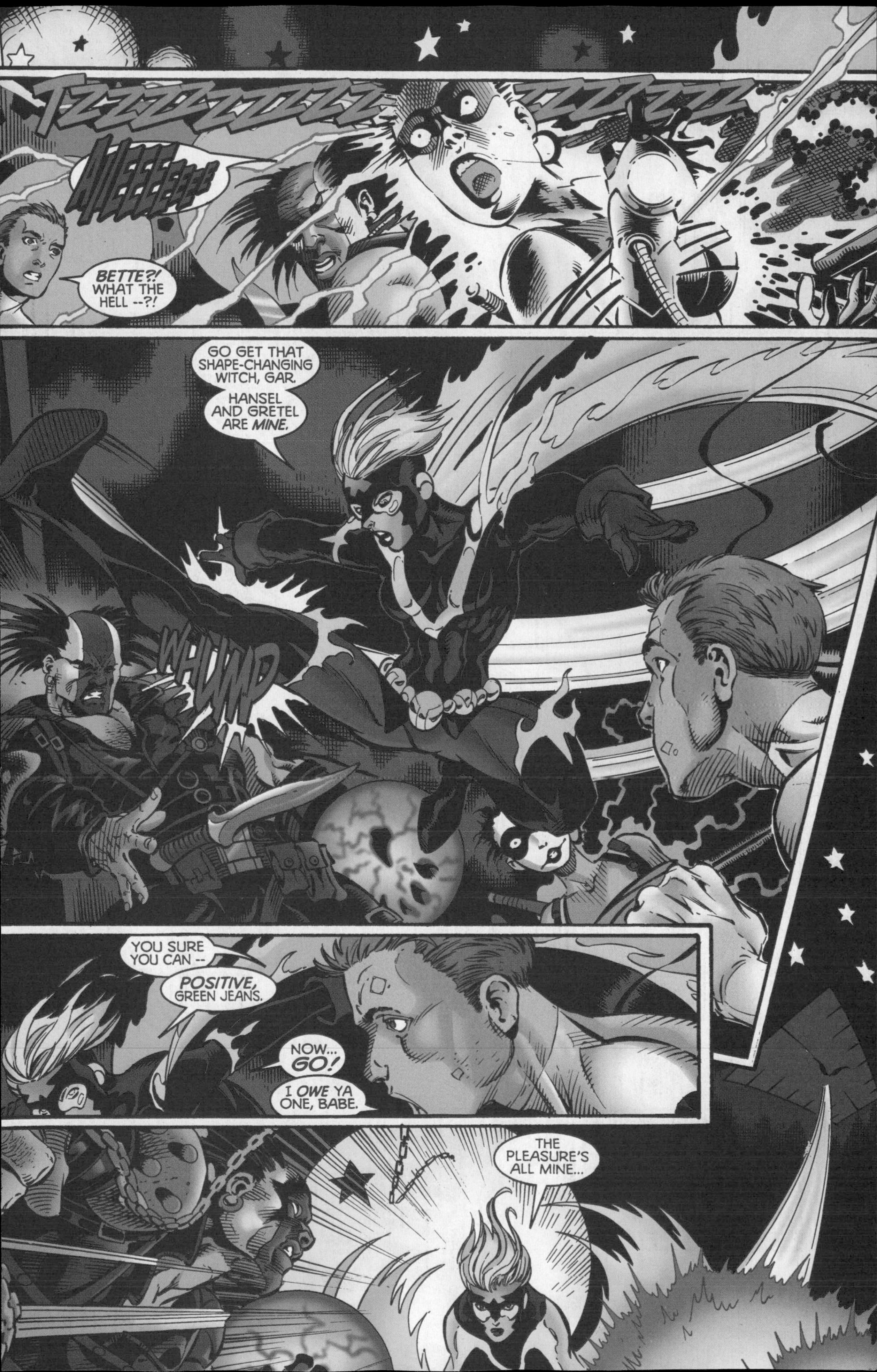
TZZZZZZZZZZZ ZZZZZZ
AIIEEEEEEEE
BETTE?! WHAT THE HELL --?!
GO GET THAT SHAPE-CHANGING WITCH, GAR.
HANSEL AND GRETEL ARE MINE.
WHUMP
YOU SURE YOU CAN --
POSITIVE, GREEN JEANS.
NOW... GO!
I OWE YA ONE, BABE.
THE PLEASURE'S ALL MINE...

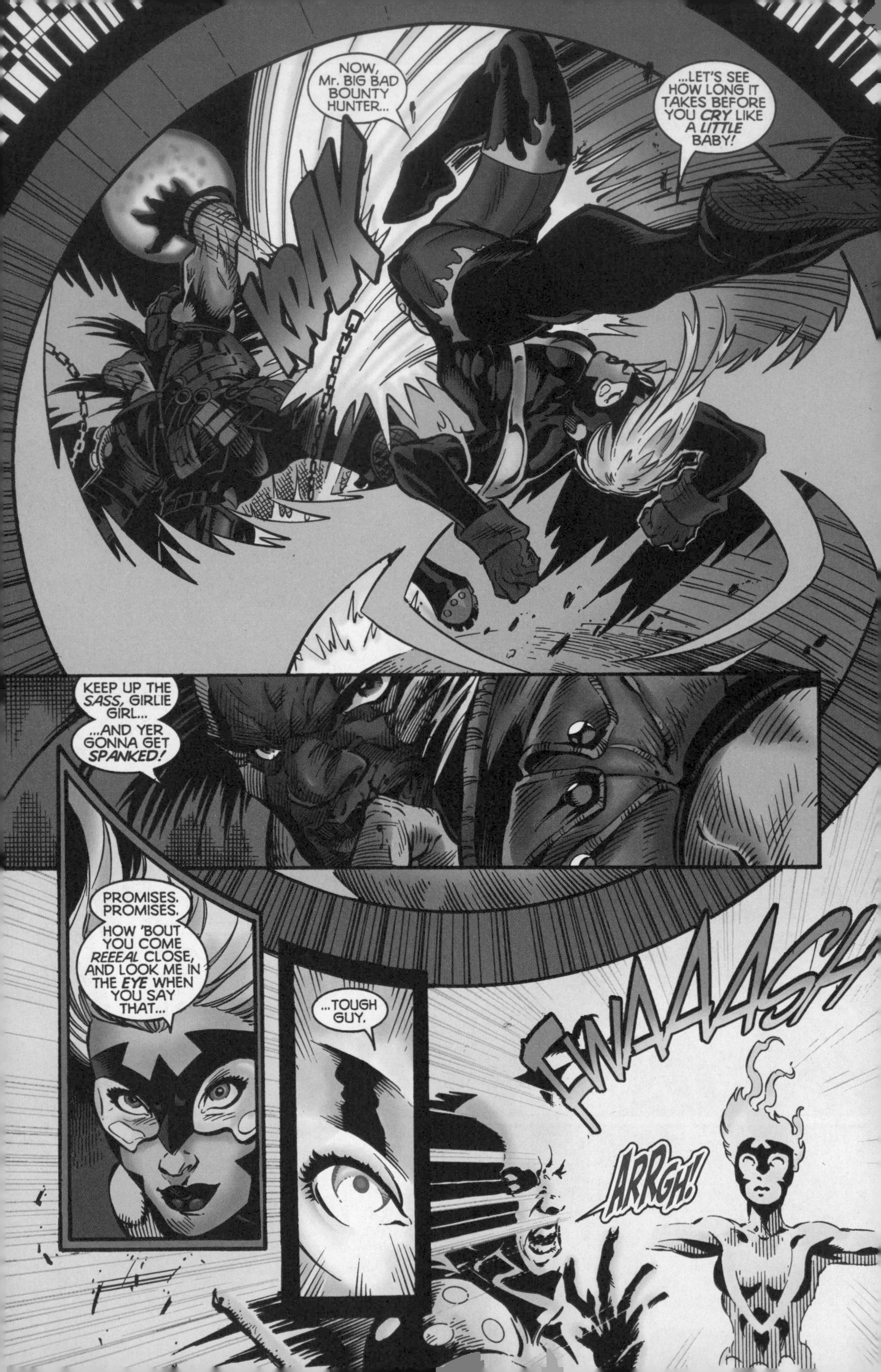
NOW, Mr. BIG BAD BOUNTY HUNTER...
...LET'S SEE HOW LONG IT TAKES BEFORE YOU CRY LIKE A LITTLE BABY!
KRAK
KEEP UP THE SASS, GIRLIE GIRL...
...AND YER GONNA GET SPANKED!
PROMISES, PROMISES.
HOW 'BOUT YOU COME REEEAL CLOSE, AND LOOK ME IN THE EYE WHEN YOU SAY THAT...
...TOUGH GUY.
FWAAASH
ARRGH!

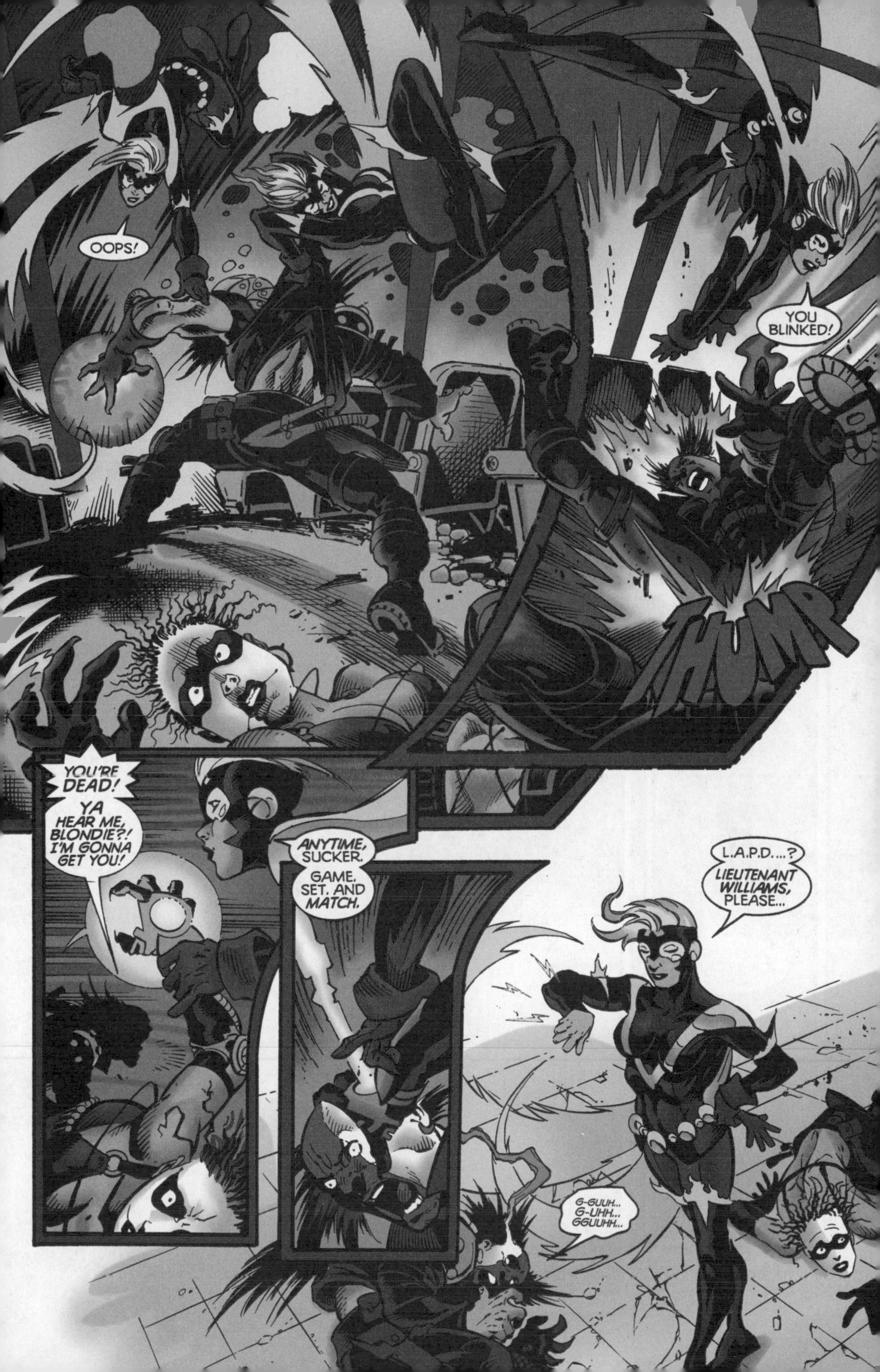

OOPS!
YOU BLINKED!
THUMP
YOU'RE DEAD!
YA HEAR ME, BLONDIE?! I'M GONNA GET YOU!
ANYTIME, SUCKER.
GAME. SET. AND MATCH.
L.A.P.D. ...?
LIEUTENANT WILLIAMS, PLEASE...
G-GUUH... G-UHH... GGUUHH...

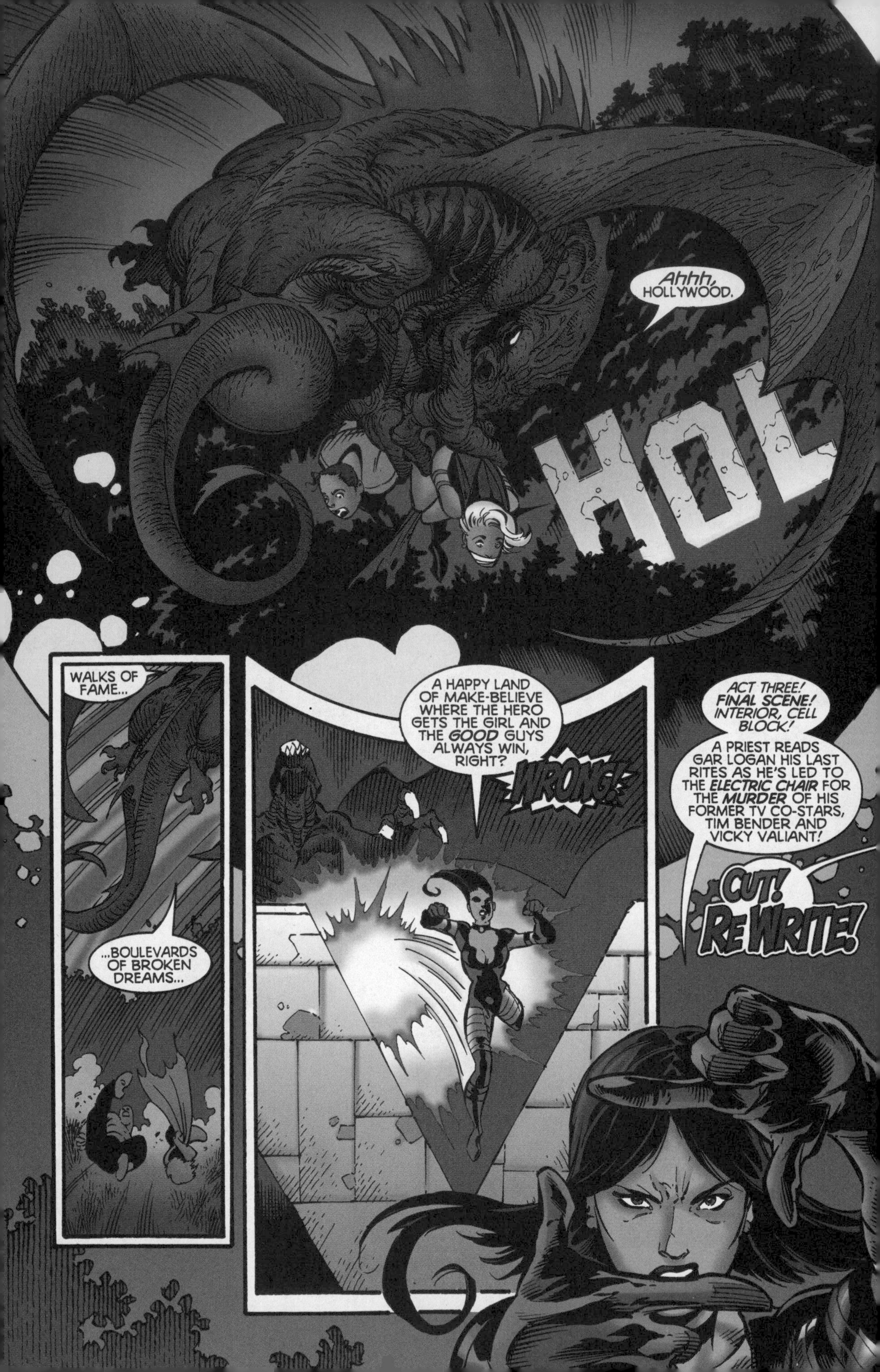
Ahhh, HOLLYWOOD.
HOL
WALKS OF FAME...
...BOULEVARDS OF BROKEN DREAMS...
A HAPPY LAND OF MAKE-BELIEVE WHERE THE HERO GETS THE GIRL AND THE GOOD GUYS ALWAYS WIN, RIGHT?
WRONG!
ACT THREE! FINAL SCENE! INTERIOR, CELL BLOCK!
A PRIEST READS GAR LOGAN HIS LAST RITES AS HE'S LED TO THE ELECTRIC CHAIR FOR THE MURDER OF HIS FORMER TV CO-STARS, TIM BENDER AND VICKY VALIANT!
CUT! RE WRITE!

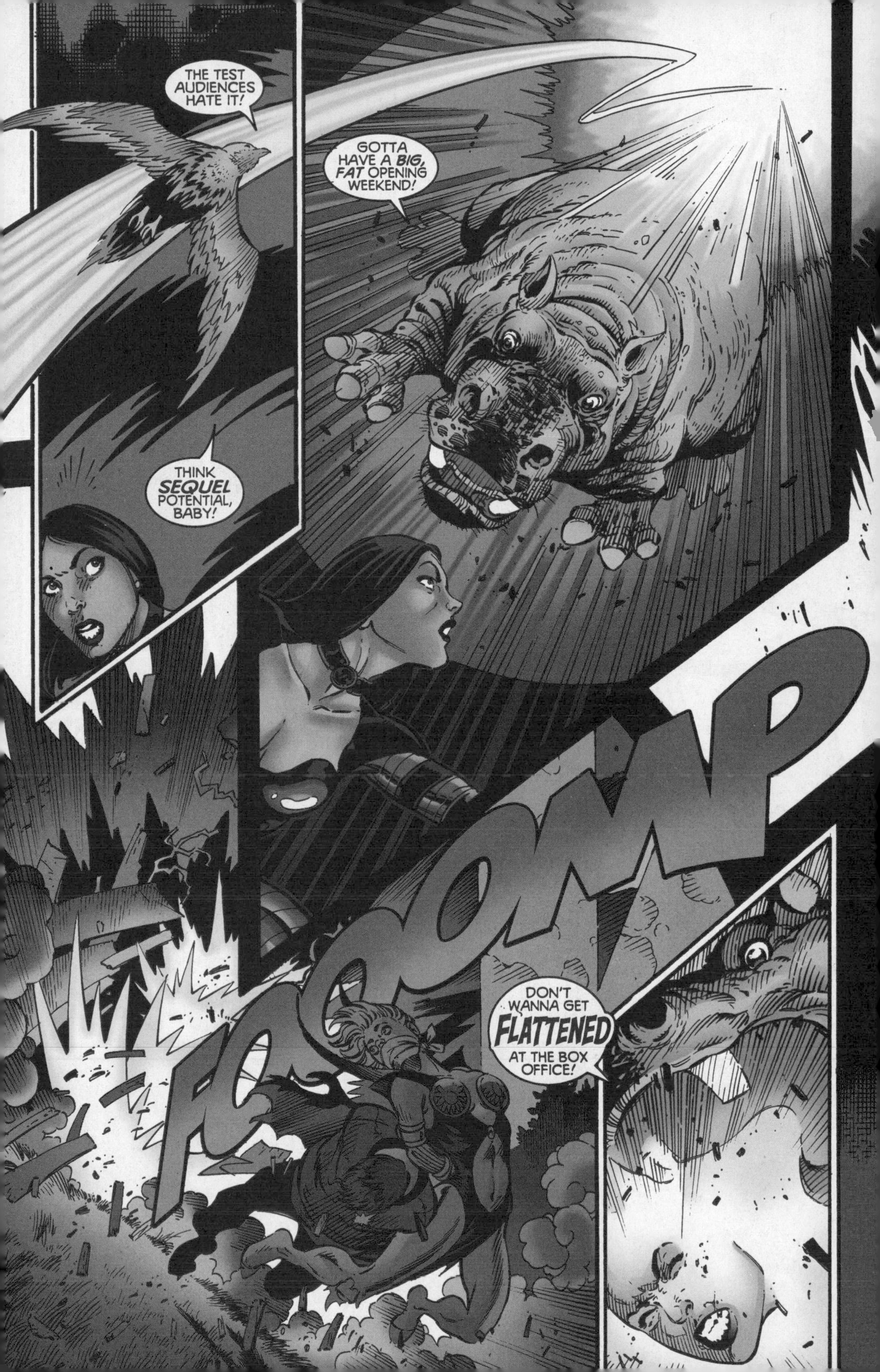
THE TEST AUDIENCES HATE IT!
GOTTA HAVE A BIG, FAT OPENING WEEKEND!
THINK SEQUEL POTENTIAL, BABY!
FOOMP
DON'T WANNA GET FLATTENED AT THE BOX OFFICE!

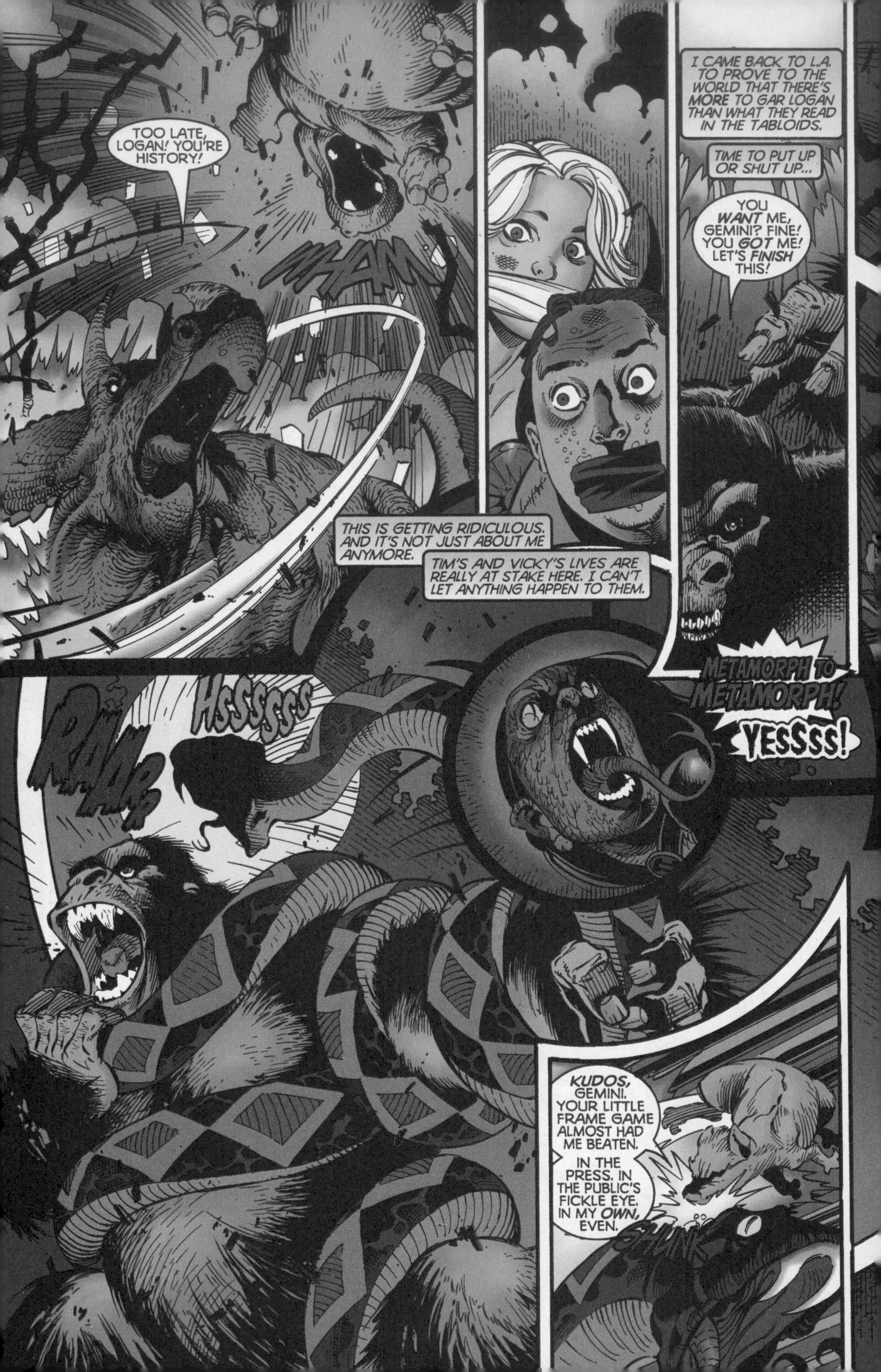
TOO LATE, LOGAN! YOU'RE HISTORY!
WHAM
I CAME BACK TO L.A. TO PROVE TO THE WORLD THAT THERE'S MORE TO GAR LOGAN THAN WHAT THEY READ IN THE TABLOIDS.
TIME TO PUT UP OR SHUT UP...
YOU WANT ME, GEMINI!? FINE! YOU GOT ME! LET'S FINISH THIS!
THIS IS GETTING RIDICULOUS. AND IT'S NOT JUST ABOUT ME ANYMORE.
TIM'S AND VICKY'S LIVES ARE REALLY AT STAKE HERE. I CAN'T LET ANYTHING HAPPEN TO THEM.
METAMORPH TO METAMORPH!
YESSSS!
RAAAR
HSSSSSS
KUDOS, GEMINI. YOUR LITTLE FRAME GAME ALMOST HAD ME BEATEN.
IN THE PRESS. IN THE PUBLIC'S FICKLE EYE. IN MY OWN, EVEN.
SHUNK

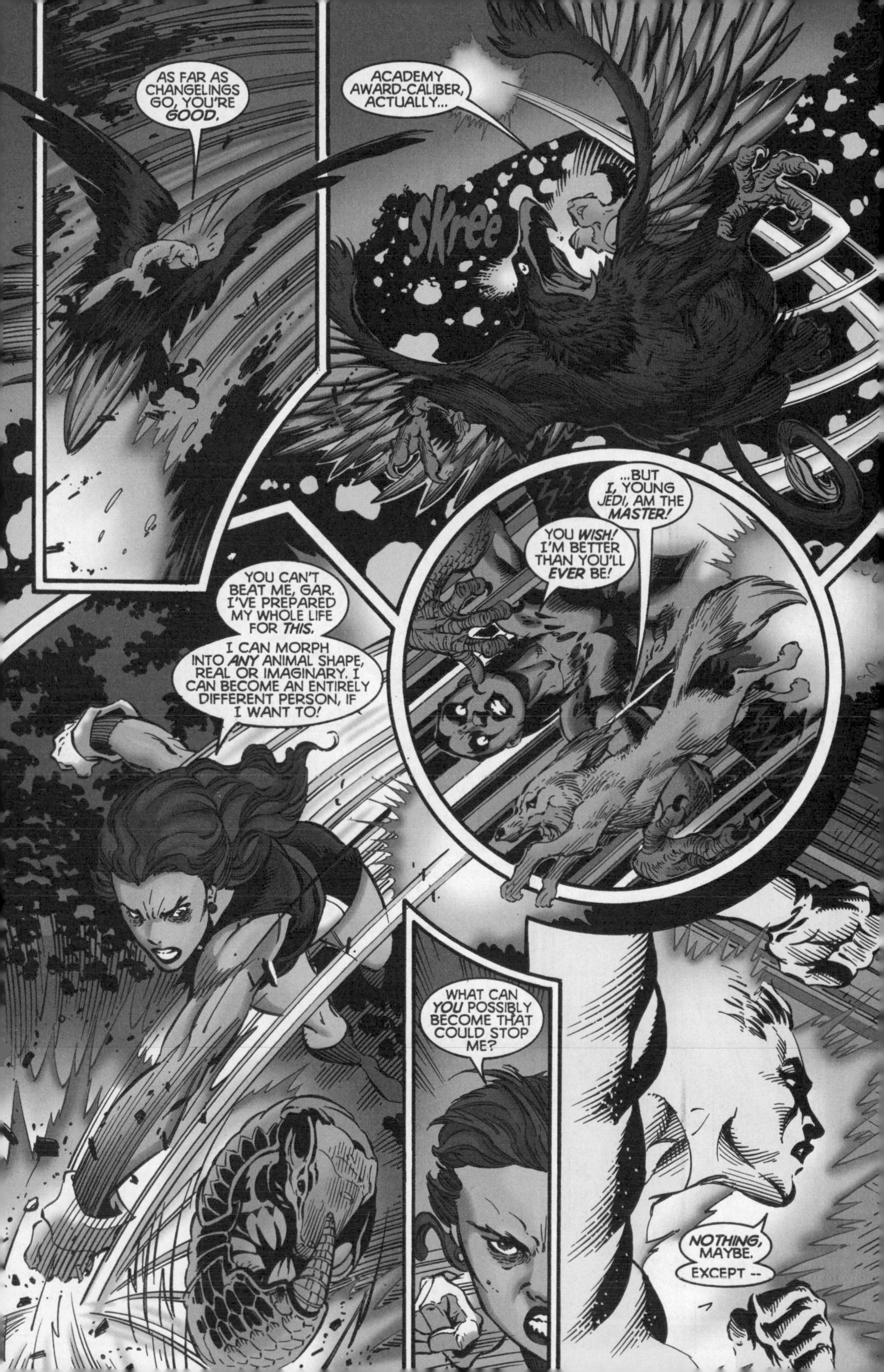

AS FAR AS CHANGELINGS GO, YOU'RE *GOOD.*
ACADEMY AWARD-CALIBER, ACTUALLY...
SKREE
...BUT *I*, YOUNG *JEDI*, AM THE *MASTER!*
YOU *WISH!* I'M BETTER THAN YOU'LL *EVER* BE!
YOU CAN'T BEAT ME, GAR. I'VE PREPARED MY WHOLE LIFE FOR *THIS.*
I CAN MORPH INTO *ANY* ANIMAL SHAPE, REAL OR IMAGINARY. I CAN BECOME AN ENTIRELY DIFFERENT PERSON, IF I WANT TO!
WHAT CAN *YOU* POSSIBLY BECOME THAT COULD STOP ME?
NOTHING, MAYBE.
EXCEPT --

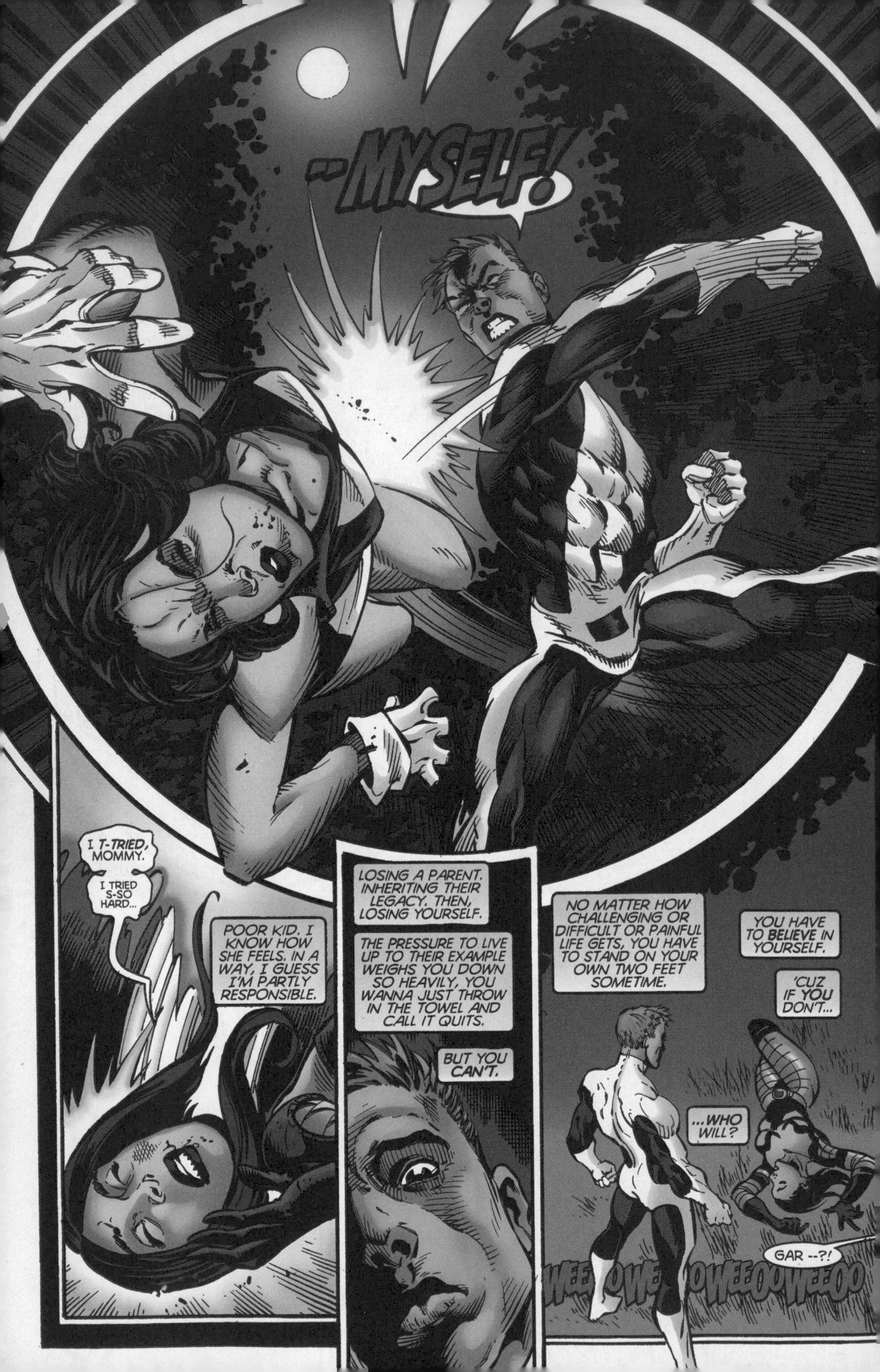
--MYSELF!
I T-TRIED, MOMMY.
I TRIED S-SO HARD...
POOR KID. I KNOW HOW SHE FEELS. IN A WAY, I GUESS I'M PARTLY RESPONSIBLE.
LOSING A PARENT. INHERITING THEIR LEGACY. THEN, LOSING YOURSELF.
THE PRESSURE TO LIVE UP TO THEIR EXAMPLE WEIGHS YOU DOWN SO HEAVILY, YOU WANNA JUST THROW IN THE TOWEL AND CALL IT QUITS.
BUT YOU CAN'T.
NO MATTER HOW CHALLENGING OR DIFFICULT OR PAINFUL LIFE GETS, YOU HAVE TO STAND ON YOUR OWN TWO FEET SOMETIME.
YOU HAVE TO BELIEVE IN YOURSELF.
'CUZ IF YOU DON'T...
...WHO WILL?
GAR --?!
WEEOOWEEOOWEEOOWEEOO

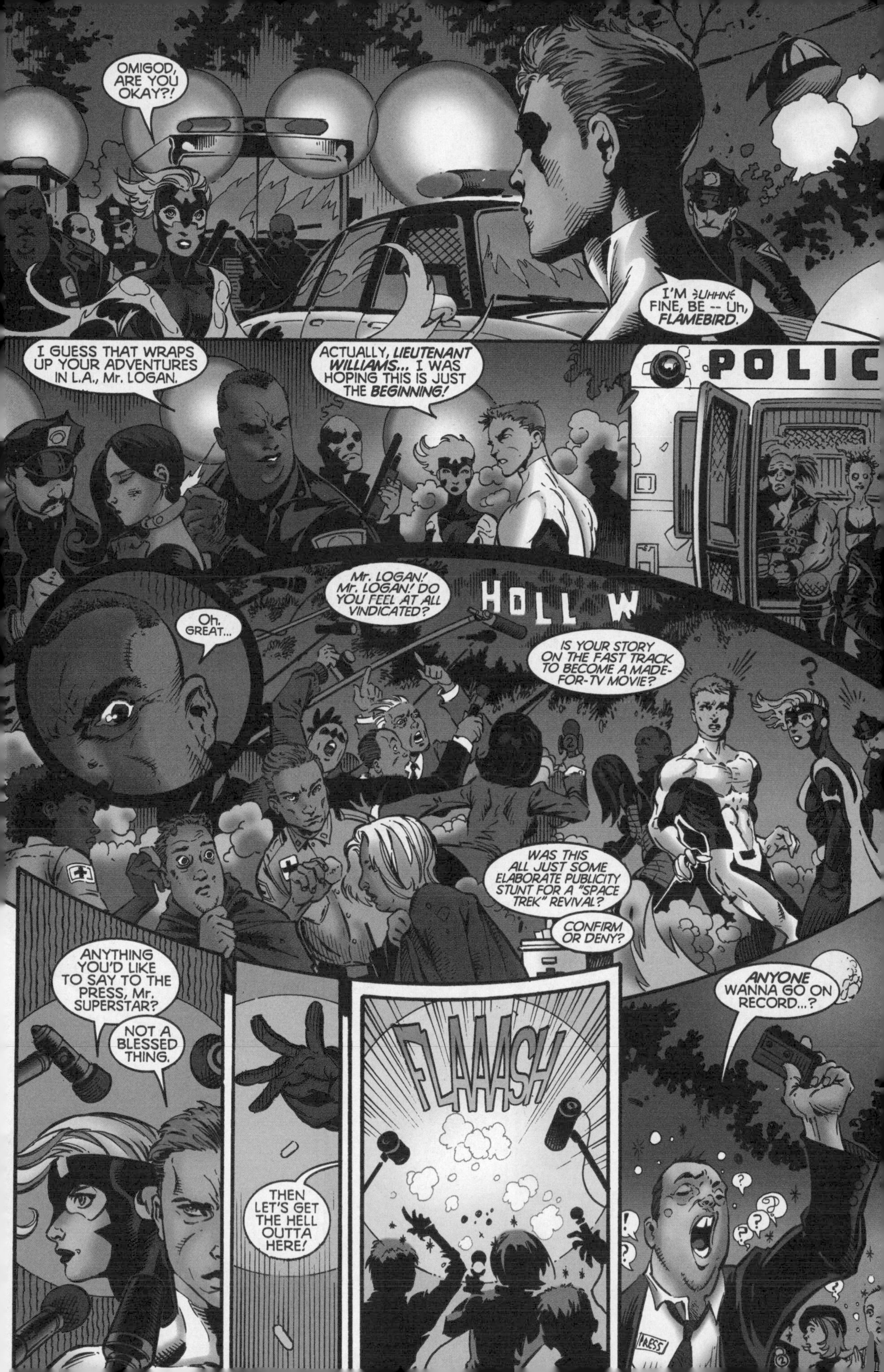
OMIGOD, ARE YOU OKAY?!
I'M ≷UHHN≶ FINE, BE -- Uh, FLAMEBIRD.
I GUESS THAT WRAPS UP YOUR ADVENTURES IN L.A., Mr. LOGAN.
ACTUALLY, LIEUTENANT WILLIAMS... I WAS HOPING THIS IS JUST THE BEGINNING!
POLIC
Oh. GREAT...
Mr. LOGAN! Mr. LOGAN! DO YOU FEEL AT ALL VINDICATED?
HOLL W
IS YOUR STORY ON THE FAST TRACK TO BECOME A MADE-FOR-TV MOVIE?
WAS THIS ALL JUST SOME ELABORATE PUBLICITY STUNT FOR A "SPACE TREK" REVIVAL?
CONFIRM OR DENY?
ANYTHING YOU'D LIKE TO SAY TO THE PRESS, Mr. SUPERSTAR?
NOT A BLESSED THING.
THEN LET'S GET THE HELL OUTTA HERE!
FLAAASH
ANYONE WANNA GO ON RECORD...?
PRESS

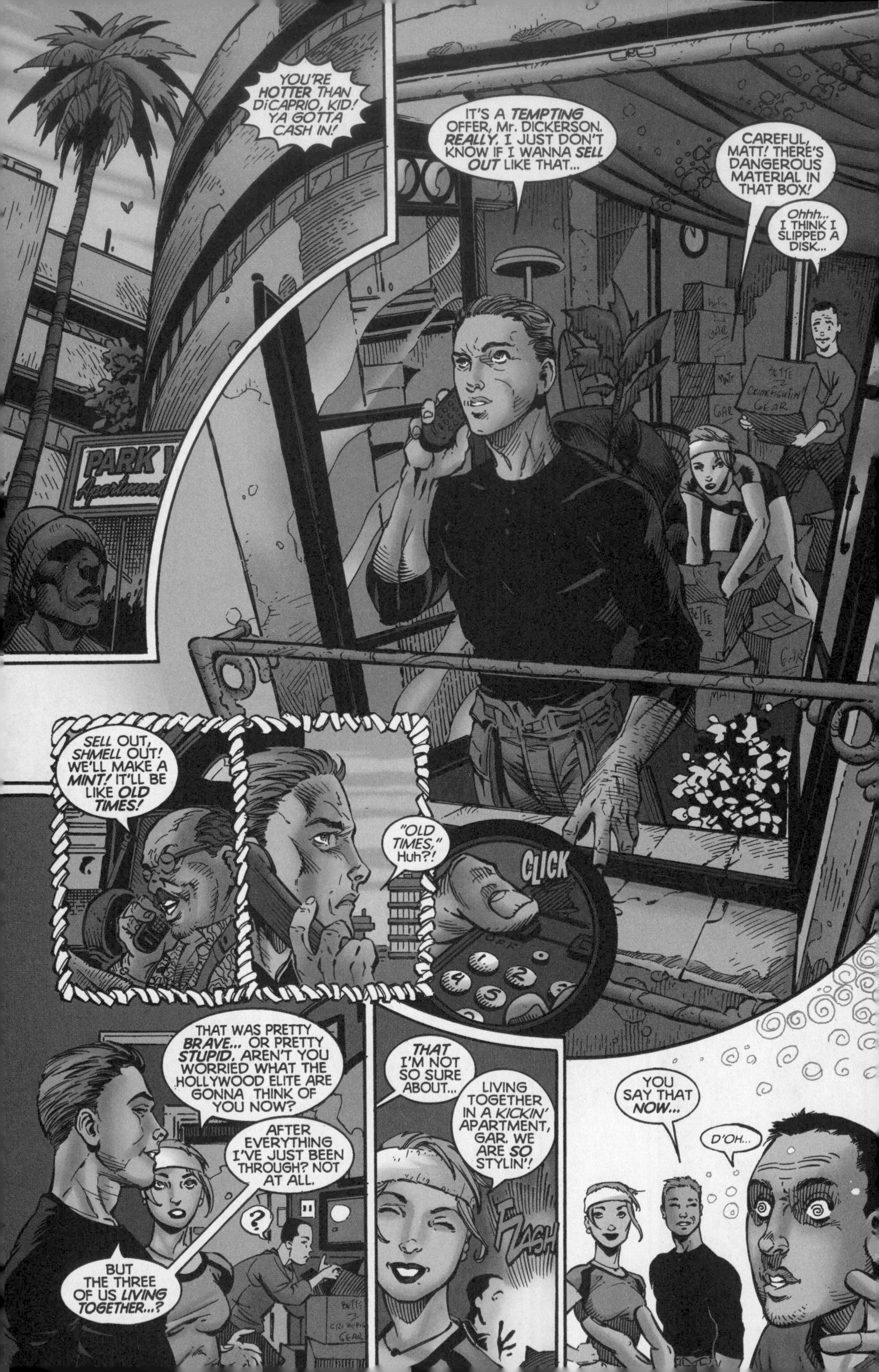

YOU'RE HOTTER THAN DiCAPRIO, KID! YA GOTTA CASH IN!
IT'S A TEMPTING OFFER, Mr. DICKERSON. REALLY. I JUST DON'T KNOW IF I WANNA SELL OUT LIKE THAT...
CAREFUL, MATT! THERE'S DANGEROUS MATERIAL IN THAT BOX!
Ohhh... I THINK I SLIPPED A DISK...
PARK
Apartment
SELL OUT, SHMELL OUT! WE'LL MAKE A MINT! IT'LL BE LIKE OLD TIMES!
"OLD TIMES," Huh?!
CLICK
THAT WAS PRETTY BRAVE... OR PRETTY STUPID. AREN'T YOU WORRIED WHAT THE HOLLYWOOD ELITE ARE GONNA THINK OF YOU NOW?
AFTER EVERYTHING I'VE JUST BEEN THROUGH? NOT AT ALL.
?
BUT THE THREE OF US LIVING TOGETHER...?
THAT I'M NOT SO SURE ABOUT...
LIVING TOGETHER IN A KICKIN' APARTMENT, GAR. WE ARE SO STYLIN'!
FLASH
YOU SAY THAT NOW...
D'OH...

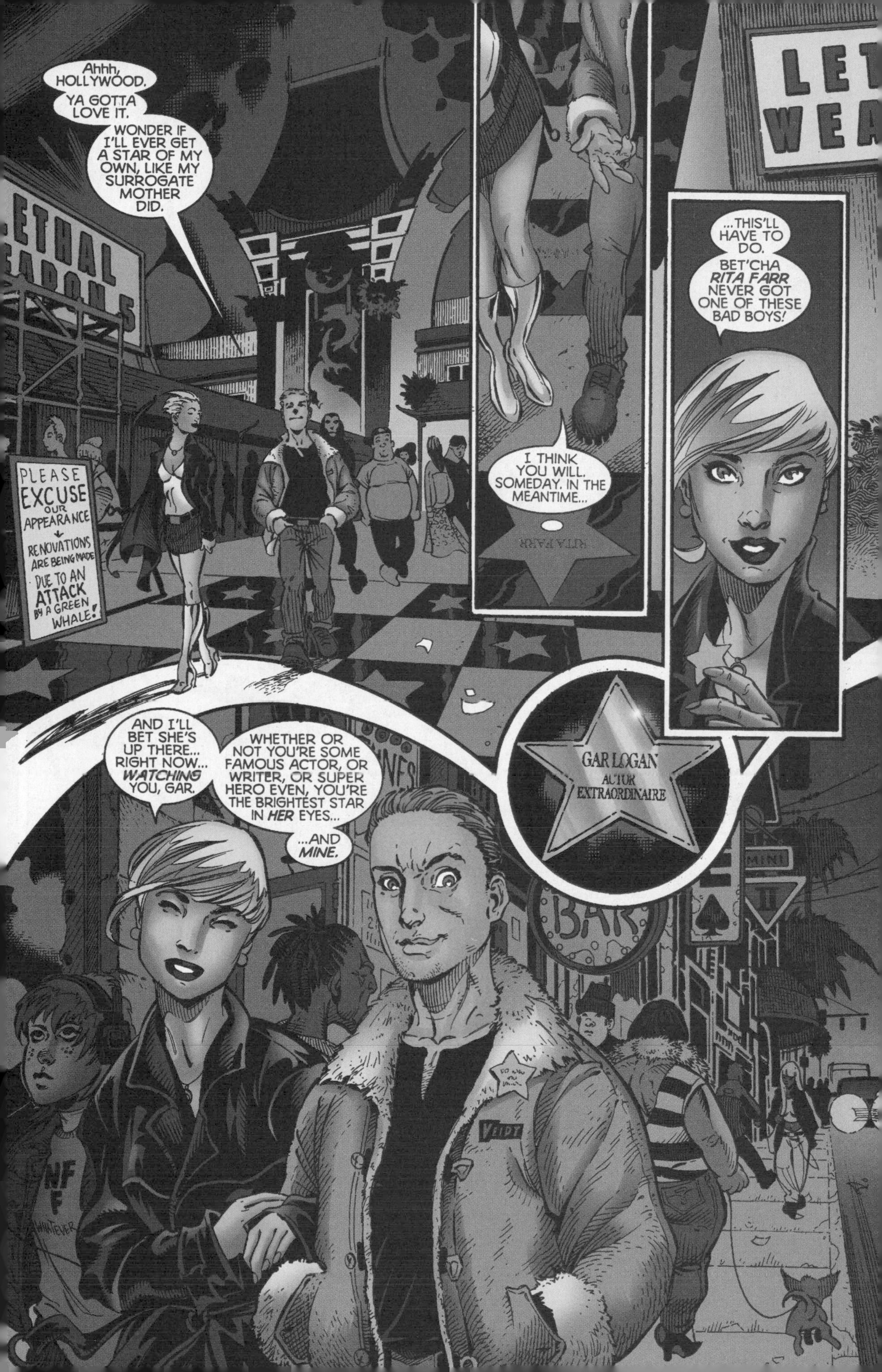

LET
WEA
Ahhh, HOLLYWOOD.
YA GOTTA LOVE IT.
WONDER IF I'LL EVER GET A STAR OF MY OWN, LIKE MY SURROGATE MOTHER DID.
LETHAL WEAPON 5
PLEASE EXCUSE OUR APPEARANCE
RENOVATIONS ARE BEING MADE DUE TO AN ATTACK BY A GREEN WHALE!
I THINK YOU WILL. SOMEDAY. IN THE MEANTIME...
RITA FARR
...THIS'LL HAVE TO DO.
BET'CHA RITA FARR NEVER GOT ONE OF THESE BAD BOYS!
GAR LOGAN
ACTOR EXTRAORDINAIRE
AND I'LL BET SHE'S UP THERE... RIGHT NOW... WATCHING YOU, GAR.
WHETHER OR NOT YOU'RE SOME FAMOUS ACTOR, OR WRITER, OR SUPER HERO EVEN, YOU'RE THE BRIGHTEST STAR IN HER EYES...
...AND MINE.
BAR

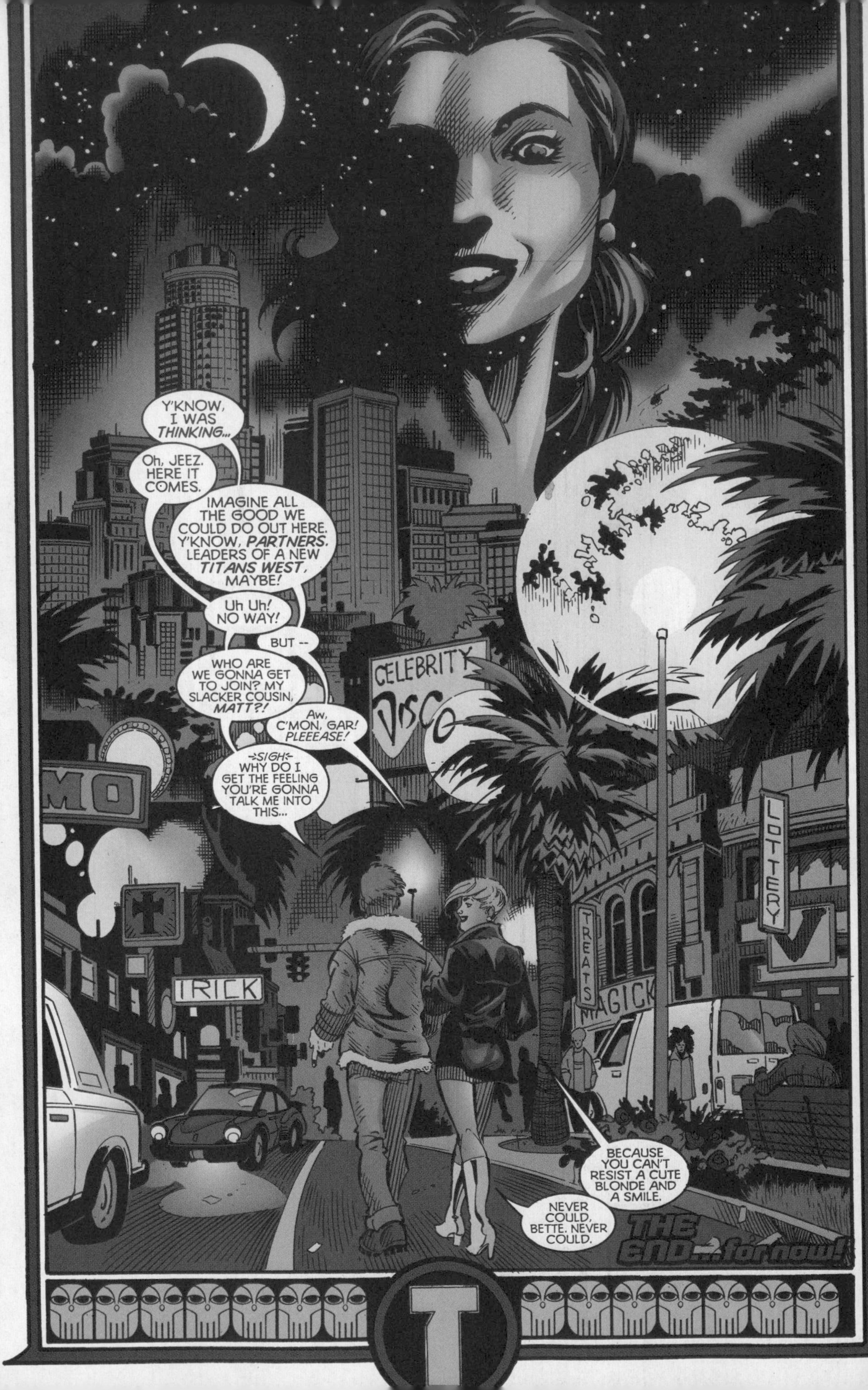

Y'KNOW, I WAS *THINKING*...
Oh, JEEZ. HERE IT COMES.
IMAGINE ALL THE GOOD WE COULD DO OUT HERE. Y'KNOW, ***PARTNERS***. LEADERS OF A NEW ***TITANS WEST***, MAYBE!
Uh Uh! NO WAY!
BUT --
WHO ARE WE GONNA GET TO JOIN? MY SLACKER COUSIN, ***MATT***?!
AW, C'MON, GAR! *PLEEEASE!*
-SIGH- WHY DO I GET THE FEELING YOU'RE GONNA TALK ME INTO THIS...
CELEBRITY DISCO
MO
TRICK
TREATS
MAGICK
LOTTERY
BECAUSE YOU CAN'T RESIST A CUTE BLONDE AND A SMILE.
NEVER COULD, BETTE. NEVER COULD.
THE END... for now!

There has
always been a
next generation
of hero to be
trained. As
much can be
learned from
fellow novices as
from a mentor,
so were born
the Teen Titans.
Over the years
the lineup has
changed, but the
need for guidance
remains as does
the spirit of
comradery and
friendship.

Teen Titans

BEAST BOYS & GIRLS

Geoff Johns Writer

Tom Grummett Penciller

Lary Stucker Inker

Comicraft Letterer

Jeromy Cox Colorist

Ed McGuinness & Dexter Vines Original Covers

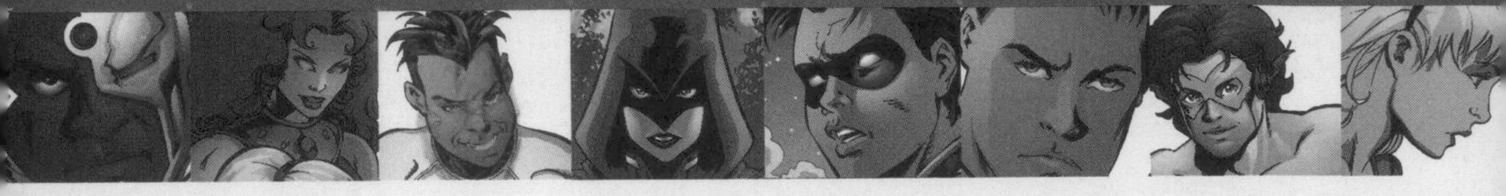

WHO'S WHO

CYBORG
Victor Stone's parents were research scientists for S.T.A.R. Labs, and during an experiment his mother accidentally unleashed a destructive force, killing her and destroying most of Vic's body. His father saved the youth's life with cybernetic components, making Vic feel like an outsider. He only came to accept his fate when he joined the Titans. Through many changes, Vic remains committed to the team. Currently, Cyborg has taken it upon himself to re-form the Titans and usher in today's teenaged super-heroes at the new Titans Tower in San Francisco.

STARFIRE
Princess Koriand'r of Tamaran was sacrificed by her father to save their world. Subjected to horrendous experiments, she gained the ability to generate energy bolts in addition to her natural gift of flight. Escaping her tormentors, she made her way to Earth and found a new life as Starfire. Her world is now gone, a victim of Imperiex. Starfire tends to be impatient, and that, combined with her disinterest in being anyone's teacher, has made her uncomfortable about her role on the new team.

BEAST BOY
Garfield Logan was poisoned with Sakutia, a rare African toxin. His geneticist parents used an experimental treatment to save his life, and in so doing imbued him with green skin and the ability to transform himself into any animal life form. When his parents died in an accident, he was adopted by Rita Farr and Steve Dayton of the Doom Patrol. Gar desperately wants to be an actor but is most comfortable serving with the various incarnations of the Titans. At age 19, Beast Boy finds himself acting as the mediator between the older and younger Titans, a role he readily accepts.

RAVEN
The daughter of a human and the demon Trigon, she has spent much of her life trying to escape her father's influence. Raven was warned to always keep her anger and frustrations in check, else she might give in to her father's demonic influence. When Trigon wanted to invade Earth, she preceded him, helping form one version of the Titans to stop him. Since then, she has opposed Trigon frequently, losing her mortal body in the process. Without a body to inhabit, Raven's soul-self wandered the world aimlessly until recently.

ROBIN
Perhaps the best prepared of the younger heroes, Tim Drake has been trained by the best – Batman and the first Robin, Dick Grayson. Tim wants to fight crime, but not forever, and uses his quick mind and strong body in addition to a veritable arsenal to stop crime. He has hated lying to his father about his costumed exploits and recently suffered the crushing dissolution of Young Justice, a team he led. Robin remains a mystery to those around him. Even when the Titans began to believe they could predict his next move, they found out they were mistaken.

SUPERBOY
In the wake of Superman's death, a clone was formed using DNA drawn from not only Superman, but from Lex Luthor. Being a hybrid human/Kryptonian, Superboy has a different set of abilities including flight, strength, speed, limited invulnerability and something he calls tactile telekinesis. Impulsive, the clone strives to do the right thing but acts without thinking. Superman recently asked his adoptive parents, the Kents, to help raise the teen. He also entrusted the youth, now called Conner, with Krypto's safekeeping.

KID FLASH
Bart Allen has quite a legacy to live up to. His grandfather was Barry Allen, the second Flash. Born in the 30th century, Bart was brought to the 21st century by his grandmother to be properly schooled in the use of his natural super-speed. For a time, he operated as Impulse, under the tutelage of Max Mercury, Zen master of speed. After recent events, Bart decided it was time to grow up, and toward that goal he has speed-read and memorized the contents of the San Francisco Public Library. He has the facts but now needs the experience to be worthy of the Flash mantle. Changing his name to Kid Flash was the first step in the process.

WONDER GIRL
Cassie Sandsmark was thrilled to befriend Diana, the Themysciran princess known as Wonder Woman, so much so that during a crisis, she borrowed the Sandals of Hermes and the Gauntlet of Atlas to aid Diana. She then boldly asked Zeus for additional powers. Amused, he granted her strength and flight and she adventured as Wonder Girl. She began training under Artemis until the death of Donna Troy, the first Wonder Girl. Cassie's secret identity was exposed, and she now attends a private school. Cassie continues to grow into her heroic role, discovering new limits to her powers and finding new allies and enemies lurking among Ancient Myth, such as the war god Ares who recently gave her a golden lasso.

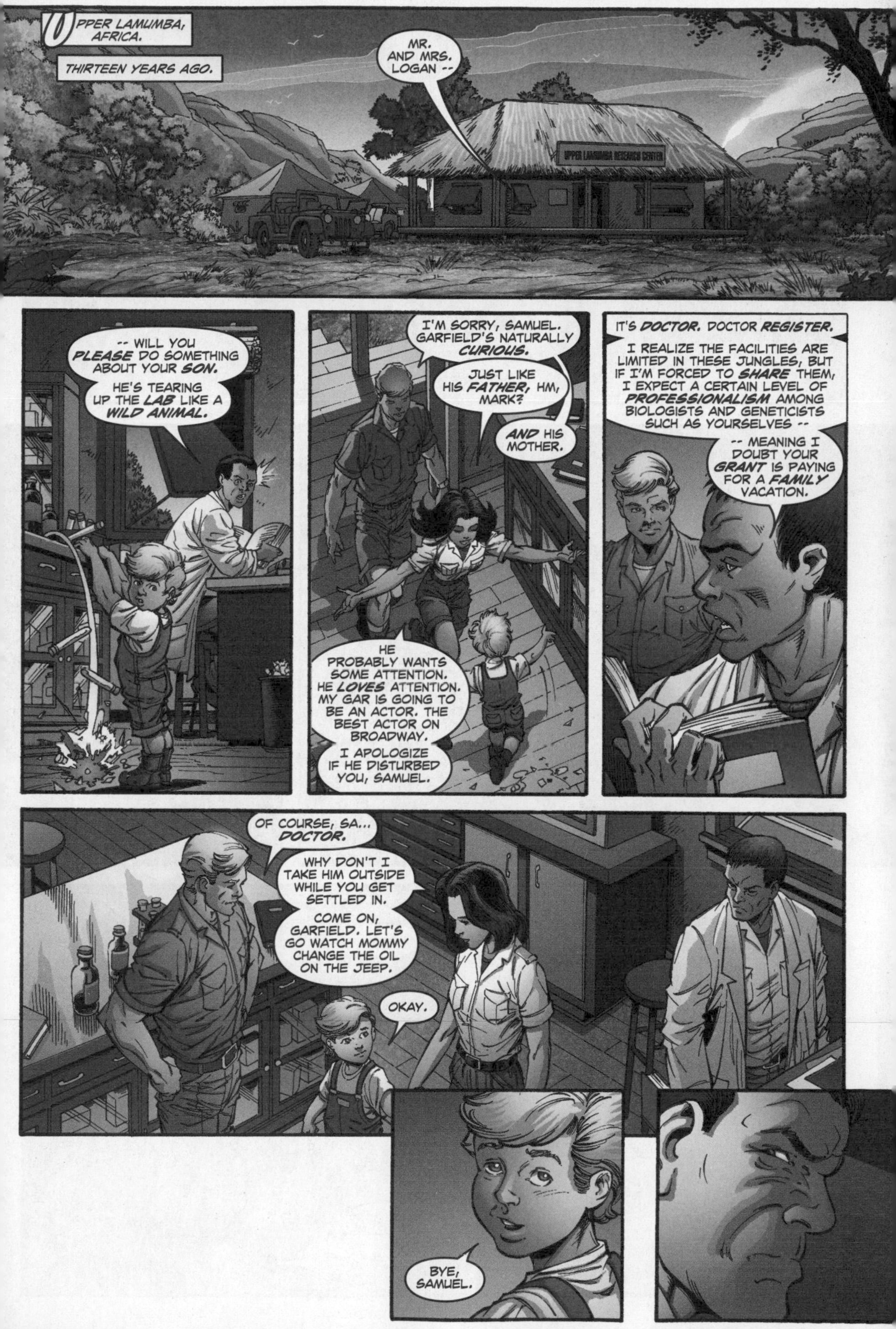
UPPER LAMUMBA, AFRICA.
THIRTEEN YEARS AGO.
MR. AND MRS. LOGAN --
UPPER LAMUMBA RESEARCH CENTER
-- WILL YOU PLEASE DO SOMETHING ABOUT YOUR SON.
HE'S TEARING UP THE LAB LIKE A WILD ANIMAL.
I'M SORRY, SAMUEL. GARFIELD'S NATURALLY CURIOUS.
JUST LIKE HIS FATHER, HM, MARK?
AND HIS MOTHER.
HE PROBABLY WANTS SOME ATTENTION. HE LOVES ATTENTION. MY GAR IS GOING TO BE AN ACTOR. THE BEST ACTOR ON BROADWAY.
I APOLOGIZE IF HE DISTURBED YOU, SAMUEL.
IT'S DOCTOR. DOCTOR REGISTER.
I REALIZE THE FACILITIES ARE LIMITED IN THESE JUNGLES, BUT IF I'M FORCED TO SHARE THEM, I EXPECT A CERTAIN LEVEL OF PROFESSIONALISM AMONG BIOLOGISTS AND GENETICISTS SUCH AS YOURSELVES --
-- MEANING I DOUBT YOUR GRANT IS PAYING FOR A FAMILY VACATION.
OF COURSE, SA... DOCTOR.
WHY DON'T I TAKE HIM OUTSIDE WHILE YOU GET SETTLED IN.
COME ON, GARFIELD. LET'S GO WATCH MOMMY CHANGE THE OIL ON THE JEEP.
OKAY.
BYE, SAMUEL.

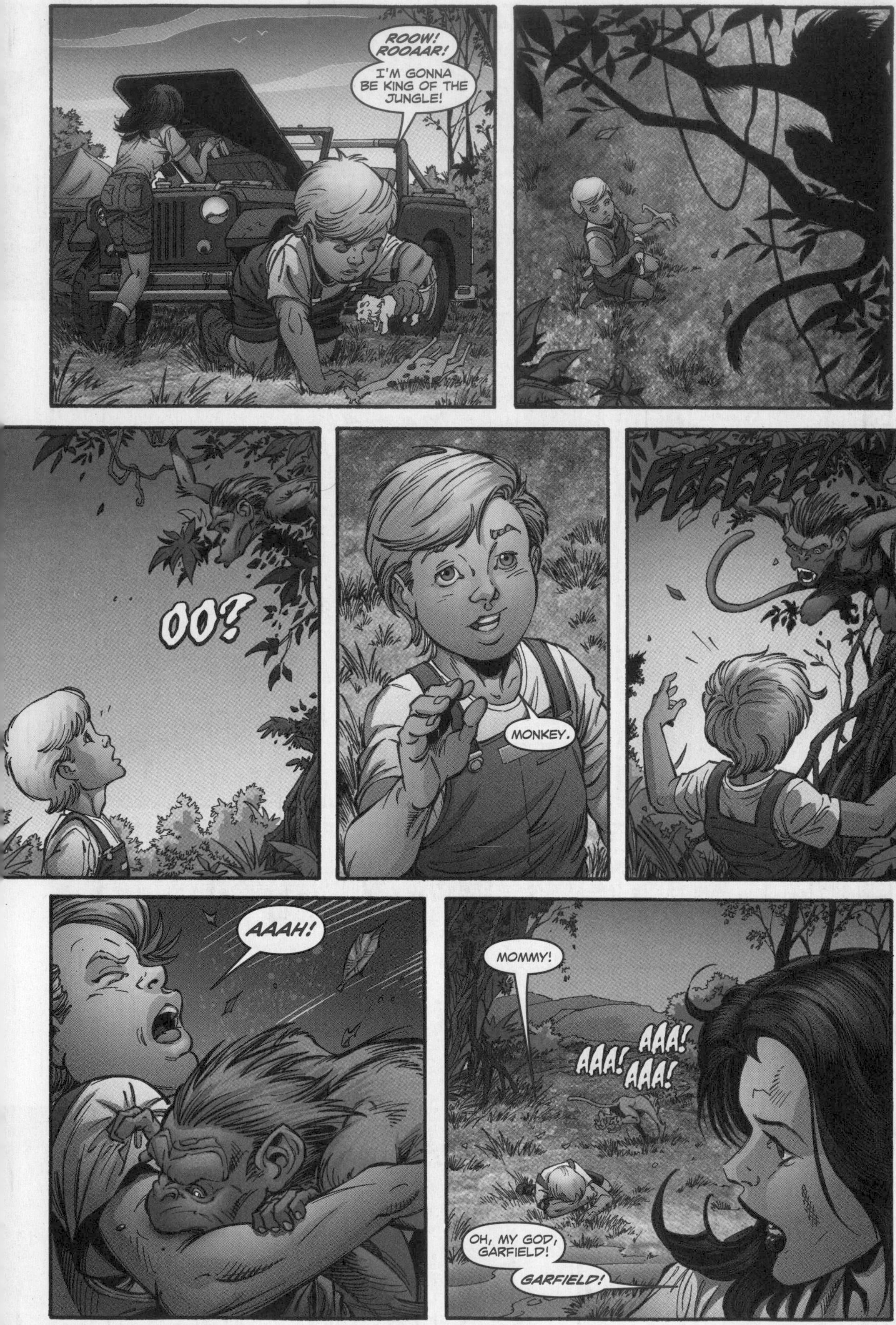
ROOW! ROOAAR!
I'M GONNA BE KING OF THE JUNGLE!
OO?
MONKEY.
EEEEEE!
AAAH!
MOMMY!
AAA! AAA! AAA! AAA!
OH, MY GOD, GARFIELD!
GARFIELD!

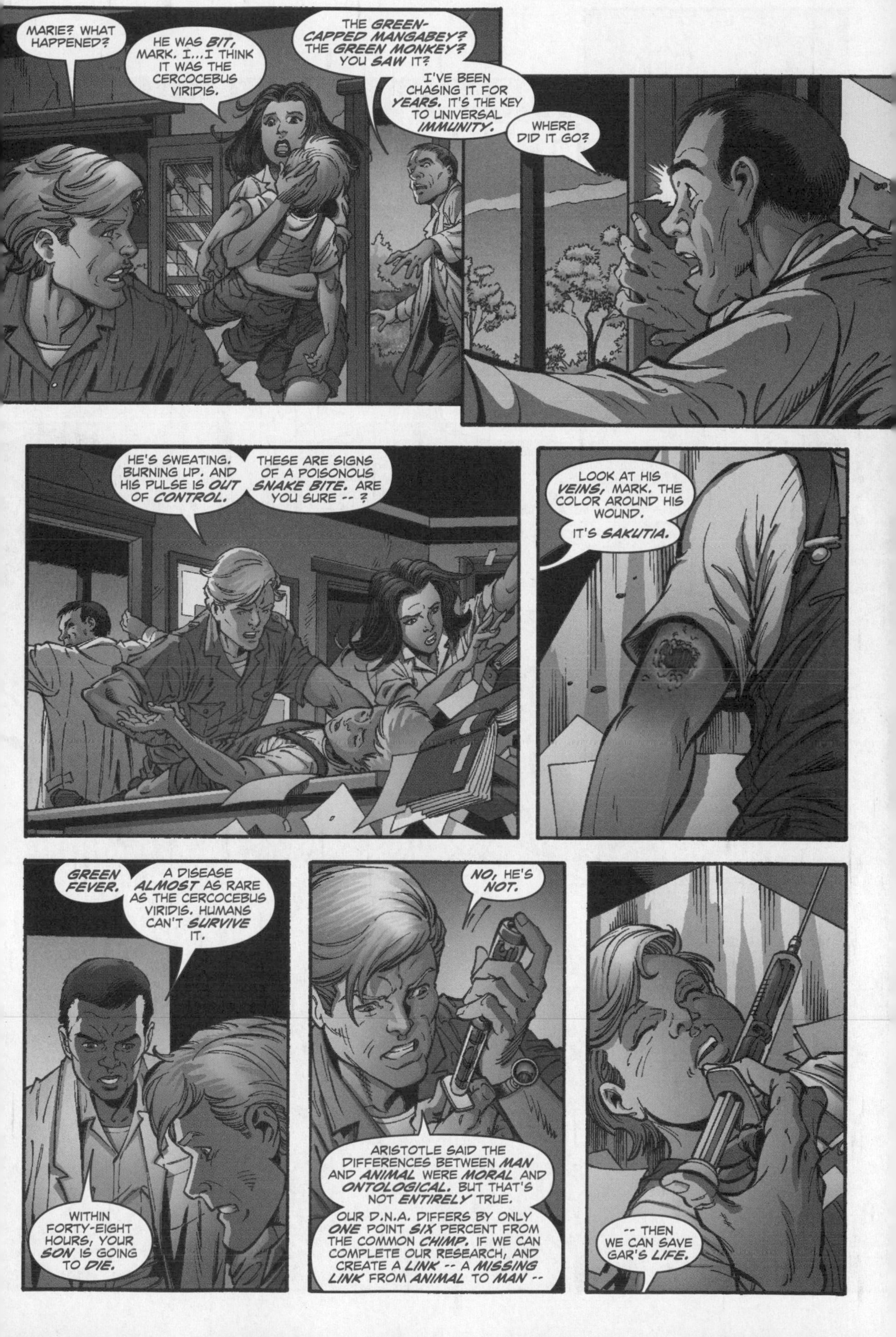
MARIE? WHAT HAPPENED?
HE WAS BIT, MARK. I...I THINK IT WAS THE CERCOCEBUS VIRIDIS.
THE GREEN-CAPPED MANGABEY? THE GREEN MONKEY? YOU SAW IT?
I'VE BEEN CHASING IT FOR YEARS. IT'S THE KEY TO UNIVERSAL IMMUNITY.
WHERE DID IT GO?
HE'S SWEATING. BURNING UP. AND HIS PULSE IS OUT OF CONTROL.
THESE ARE SIGNS OF A POISONOUS SNAKE BITE. ARE YOU SURE -- ?
LOOK AT HIS VEINS, MARK. THE COLOR AROUND HIS WOUND.
IT'S SAKUTIA.
GREEN FEVER.
A DISEASE ALMOST AS RARE AS THE CERCOCEBUS VIRIDIS. HUMANS CAN'T SURVIVE IT.
WITHIN FORTY-EIGHT HOURS, YOUR SON IS GOING TO DIE.
NO, HE'S NOT.
ARISTOTLE SAID THE DIFFERENCES BETWEEN MAN AND ANIMAL WERE MORAL AND ONTOLOGICAL. BUT THAT'S NOT ENTIRELY TRUE.
OUR D.N.A. DIFFERS BY ONLY ONE POINT SIX PERCENT FROM THE COMMON CHIMP. IF WE CAN COMPLETE OUR RESEARCH, AND CREATE A LINK -- A MISSING LINK FROM ANIMAL TO MAN --
-- THEN WE CAN SAVE GAR'S LIFE.

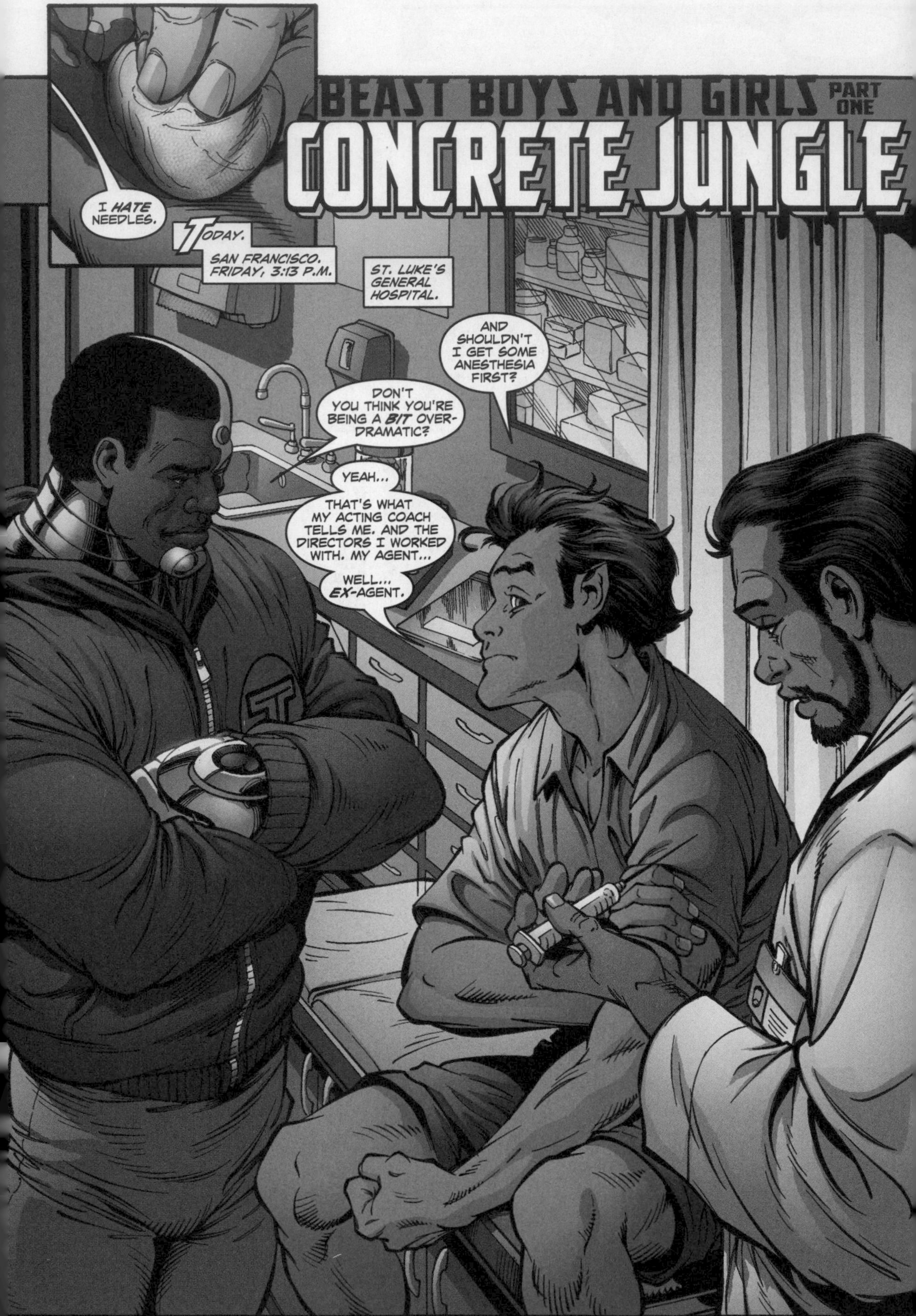
BEAST BOYS AND GIRLS PART ONE
CONCRETE JUNGLE
I HATE NEEDLES.
TODAY.
SAN FRANCISCO. FRIDAY, 3:13 P.M.
ST. LUKE'S GENERAL HOSPITAL.
AND SHOULDN'T I GET SOME ANESTHESIA FIRST?
DON'T YOU THINK YOU'RE BEING A BIT OVER-DRAMATIC?
YEAH...
THAT'S WHAT MY ACTING COACH TELLS ME. AND THE DIRECTORS I WORKED WITH. MY AGENT...
WELL... EX-AGENT.

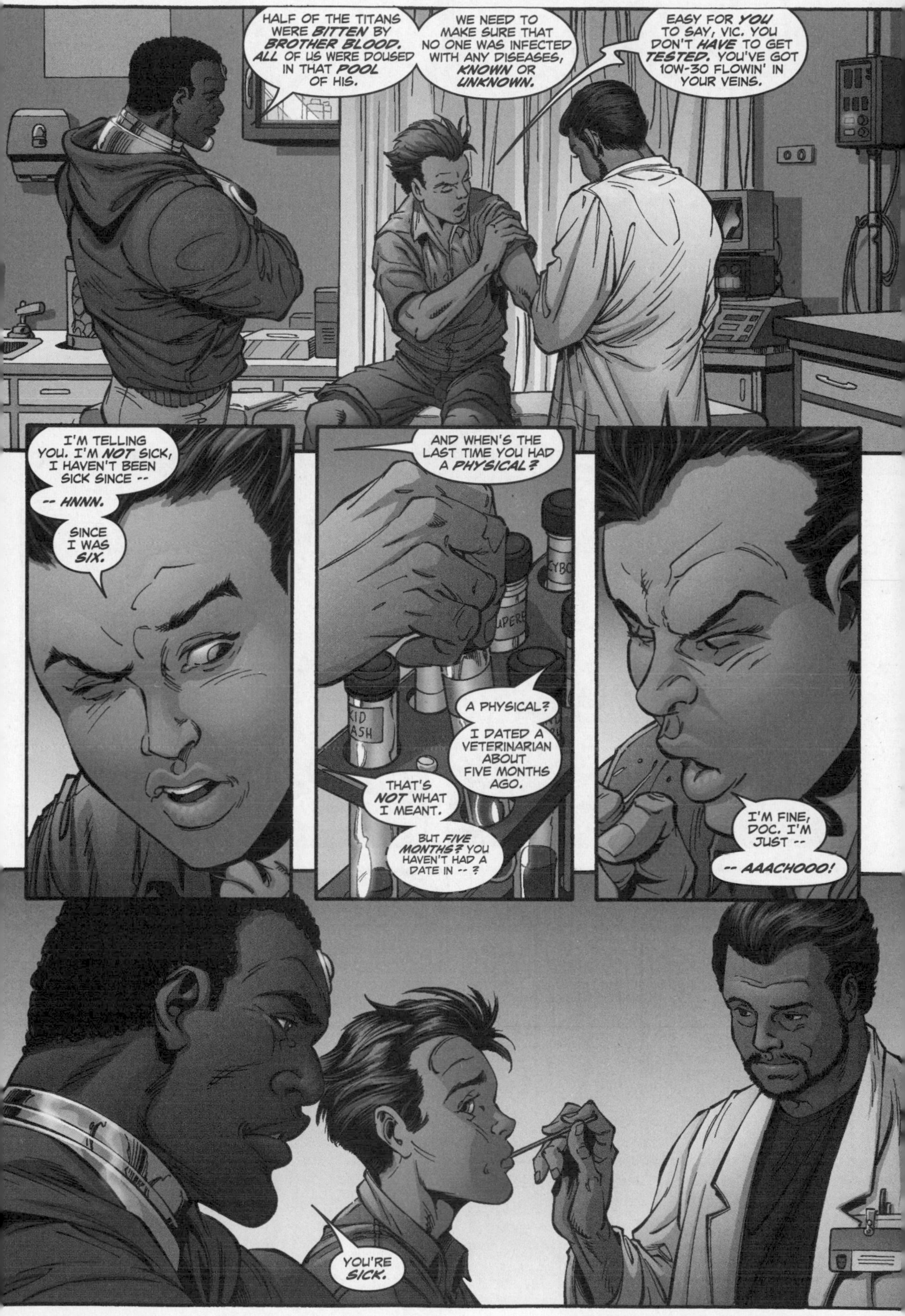
HALF OF THE TITANS WERE BITTEN BY BROTHER BLOOD. ALL OF US WERE DOUSED IN THAT POOL OF HIS.
WE NEED TO MAKE SURE THAT NO ONE WAS INFECTED WITH ANY DISEASES, KNOWN OR UNKNOWN.
EASY FOR YOU TO SAY, VIC. YOU DON'T HAVE TO GET TESTED. YOU'VE GOT 10W-30 FLOWIN' IN YOUR VEINS.
I'M TELLING YOU. I'M NOT SICK, I HAVEN'T BEEN SICK SINCE --
-- HNNN.
SINCE I WAS SIX.
AND WHEN'S THE LAST TIME YOU HAD A PHYSICAL?
A PHYSICAL?
I DATED A VETERINARIAN ABOUT FIVE MONTHS AGO.
THAT'S NOT WHAT I MEANT.
BUT FIVE MONTHS? YOU HAVEN'T HAD A DATE IN -- ?
I'M FINE, DOC. I'M JUST --
-- AAACHOOO!
YOU'RE SICK.

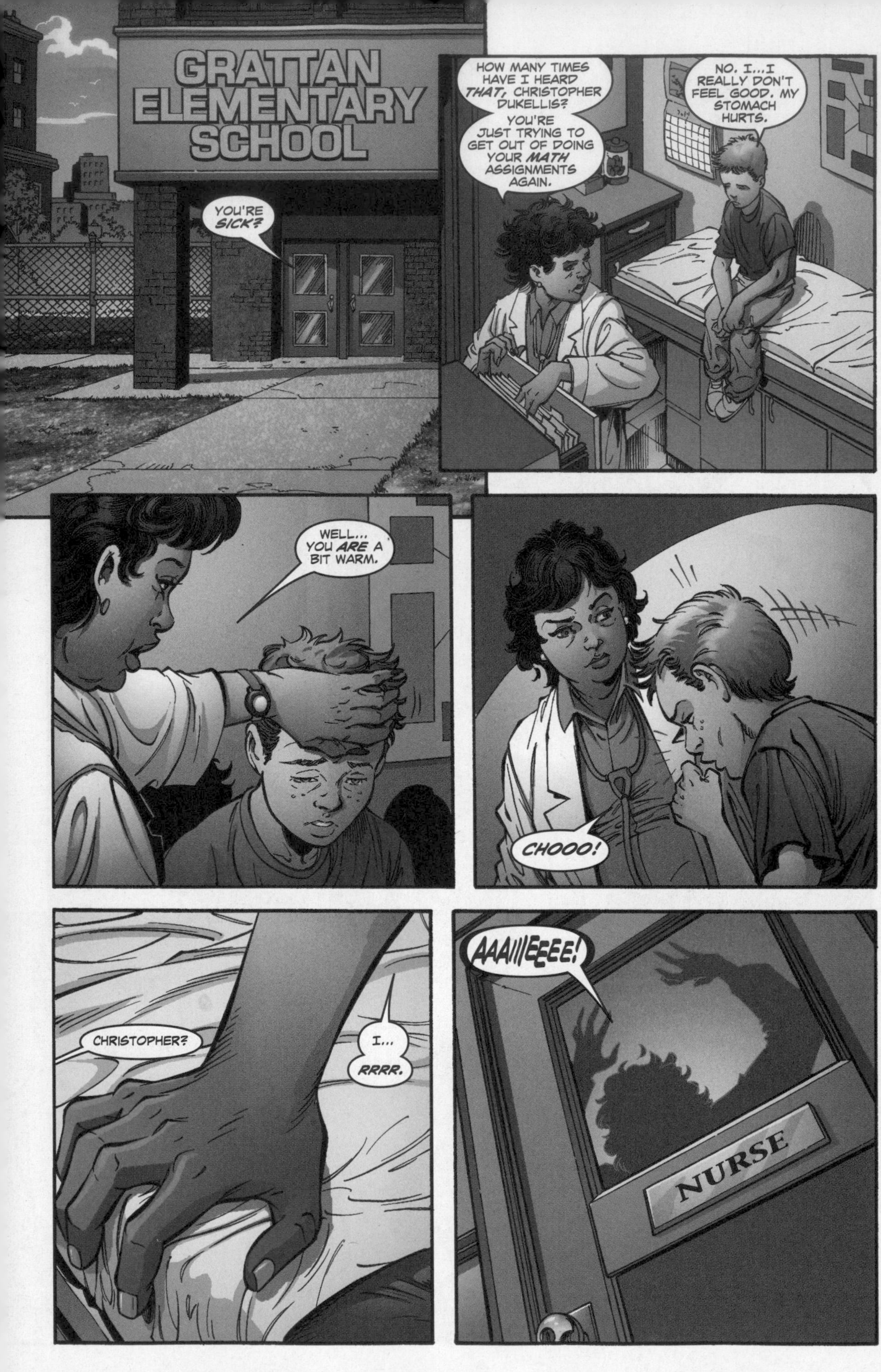
GRATTAN ELEMENTARY SCHOOL
YOU'RE *SICK?*
HOW MANY TIMES HAVE I HEARD *THAT,* CHRISTOPHER DUKELLIS?
YOU'RE JUST TRYING TO GET OUT OF DOING YOUR *MATH* ASSIGNMENTS AGAIN.
NO. I...I REALLY DON'T FEEL GOOD. MY STOMACH HURTS.
WELL... YOU *ARE* A BIT WARM.
CHOOO!
CHRISTOPHER?
I... *RRRR.*
AAAIIIEEEEE!
NURSE

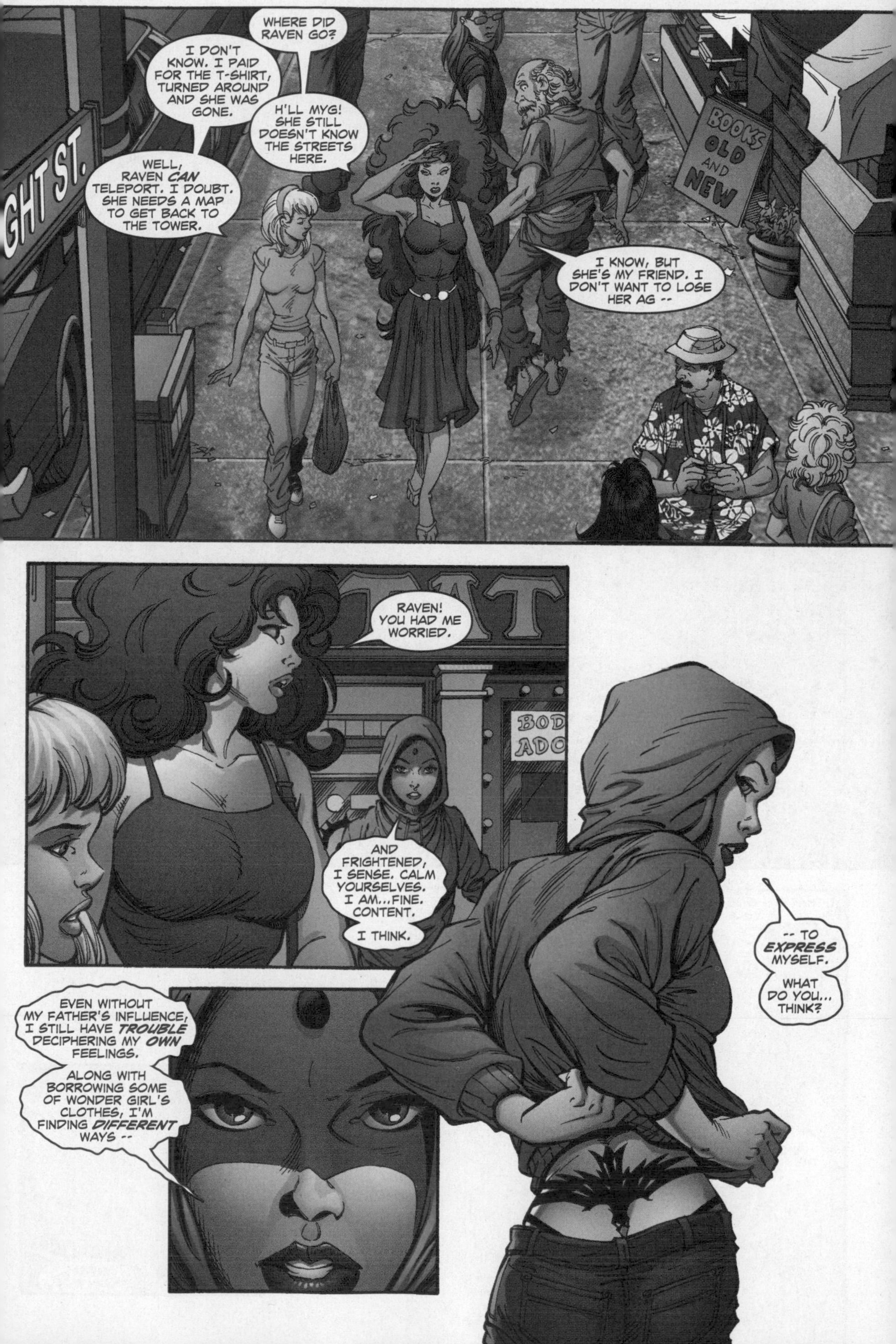
GHT ST.
I DON'T KNOW. I PAID FOR THE T-SHIRT, TURNED AROUND AND SHE WAS GONE.
WHERE DID RAVEN GO?
H'LL MYG! SHE STILL DOESN'T KNOW THE STREETS HERE.
WELL, RAVEN *CAN* TELEPORT. I DOUBT. SHE NEEDS A MAP TO GET BACK TO THE TOWER.
BOOKS OLD AND NEW
I KNOW, BUT SHE'S MY FRIEND. I DON'T WANT TO LOSE HER AG --
RAVEN! YOU HAD ME WORRIED.
AND FRIGHTENED, I SENSE. CALM YOURSELVES. I AM...FINE. CONTENT.
I THINK.
EVEN WITHOUT MY FATHER'S INFLUENCE, I STILL HAVE *TROUBLE* DECIPHERING MY *OWN* FEELINGS.
ALONG WITH BORROWING SOME OF WONDER GIRL'S CLOTHES, I'M FINDING *DIFFERENT* WAYS --
-- TO *EXPRESS* MYSELF.
WHAT DO YOU... THINK?

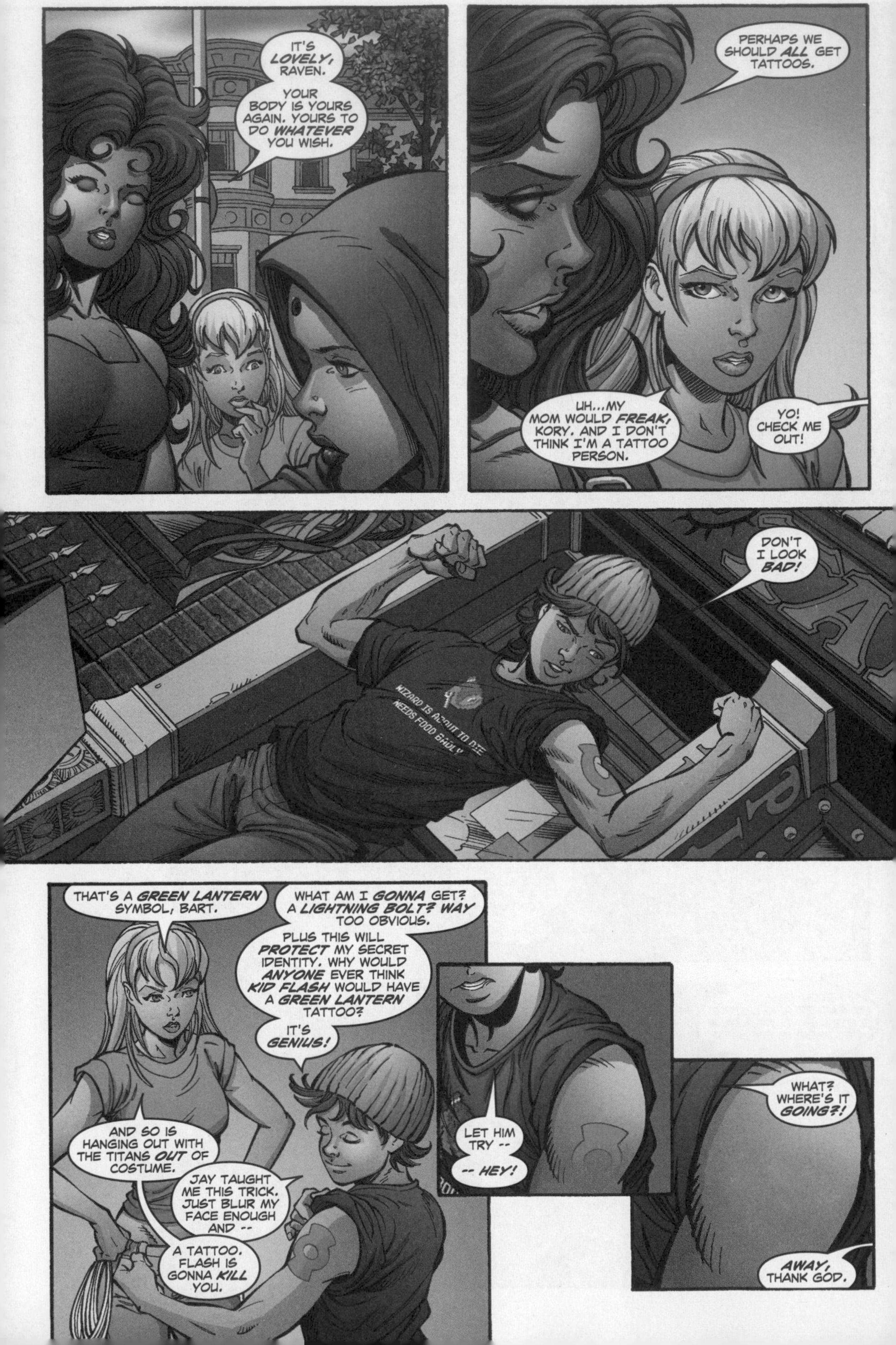
IT'S *LOVELY,* RAVEN.
YOUR BODY IS YOURS AGAIN. YOURS TO DO *WHATEVER* YOU WISH.
PERHAPS WE SHOULD *ALL* GET TATTOOS.
UH...MY MOM WOULD *FREAK,* KORY. AND I DON'T THINK I'M A TATTOO PERSON.
YO! CHECK ME OUT!
DON'T I LOOK *BAD!*
WIZARD IS ABOUT TO DIE
NEEDS FOOD BADLY
THAT'S A *GREEN LANTERN* SYMBOL, BART.
WHAT AM I *GONNA* GET? A *LIGHTNING BOLT? WAY* TOO OBVIOUS.
PLUS THIS WILL *PROTECT* MY SECRET IDENTITY. WHY WOULD *ANYONE* EVER THINK *KID FLASH* WOULD HAVE A *GREEN LANTERN* TATTOO?
IT'S *GENIUS!*
AND SO IS HANGING OUT WITH THE TITANS *OUT* OF COSTUME.
JAY TAUGHT ME THIS TRICK. JUST BLUR MY FACE ENOUGH AND --
A TATTOO. FLASH IS GONNA *KILL* YOU.
LET HIM TRY --
-- *HEY!*
WHAT? WHERE'S IT *GOING?!*
AWAY, THANK GOD.

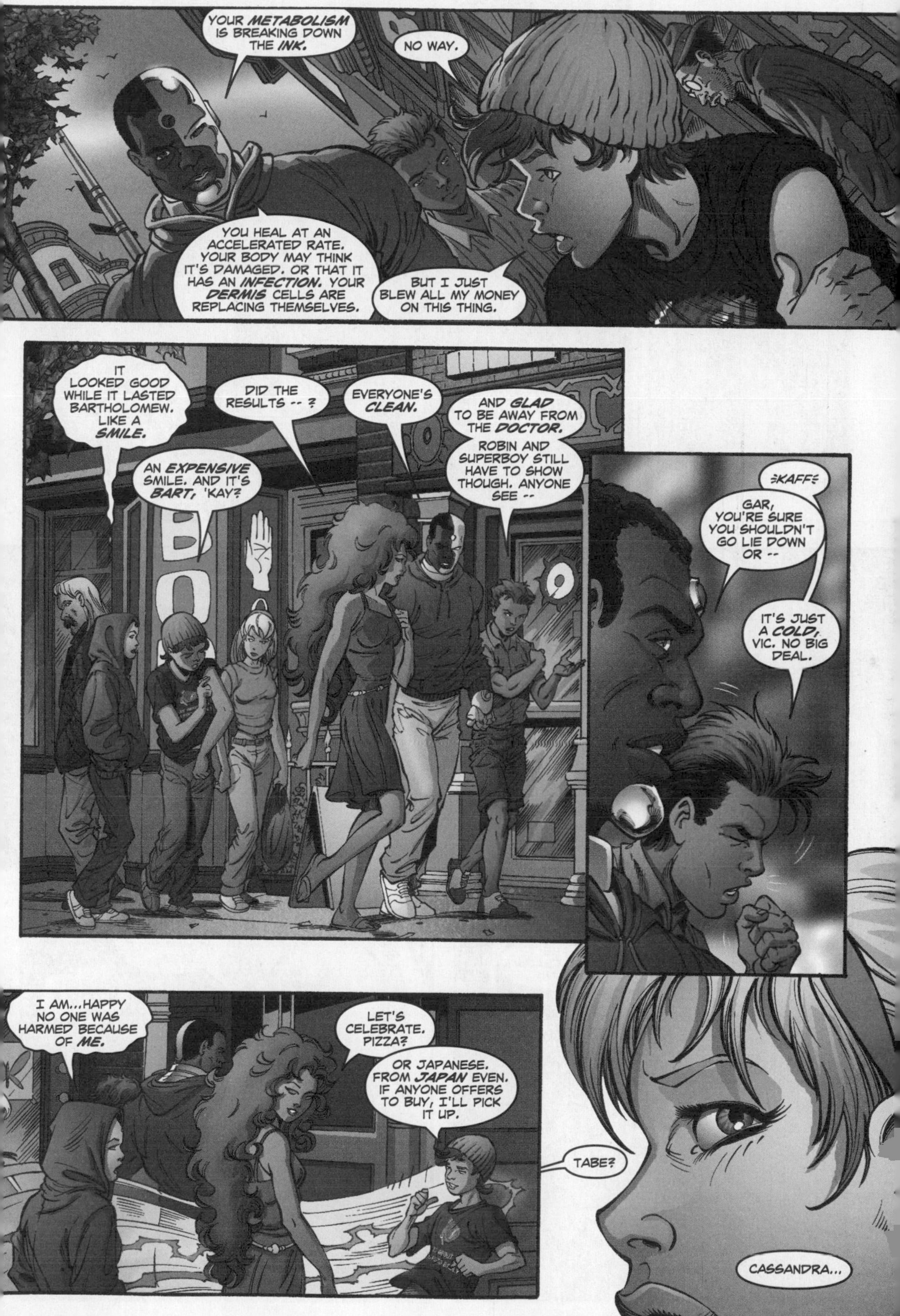
YOUR METABOLISM IS BREAKING DOWN THE INK.
NO WAY.
YOU HEAL AT AN ACCELERATED RATE. YOUR BODY MAY THINK IT'S DAMAGED. OR THAT IT HAS AN INFECTION. YOUR DERMIS CELLS ARE REPLACING THEMSELVES.
BUT I JUST BLEW ALL MY MONEY ON THIS THING.
IT LOOKED GOOD WHILE IT LASTED BARTHOLOMEW. LIKE A SMILE.
AN EXPENSIVE SMILE. AND IT'S BART, 'KAY?
DID THE RESULTS -- ?
EVERYONE'S CLEAN.
AND GLAD TO BE AWAY FROM THE DOCTOR.
ROBIN AND SUPERBOY STILL HAVE TO SHOW THOUGH. ANYONE SEE --
KAFF
GAR, YOU'RE SURE YOU SHOULDN'T GO LIE DOWN OR --
IT'S JUST A COLD, VIC. NO BIG DEAL.
I AM...HAPPY NO ONE WAS HARMED BECAUSE OF ME.
LET'S CELEBRATE. PIZZA?
OR JAPANESE. FROM JAPAN EVEN. IF ANYONE OFFERS TO BUY, I'LL PICK IT UP.
TABE?
CASSANDRA...

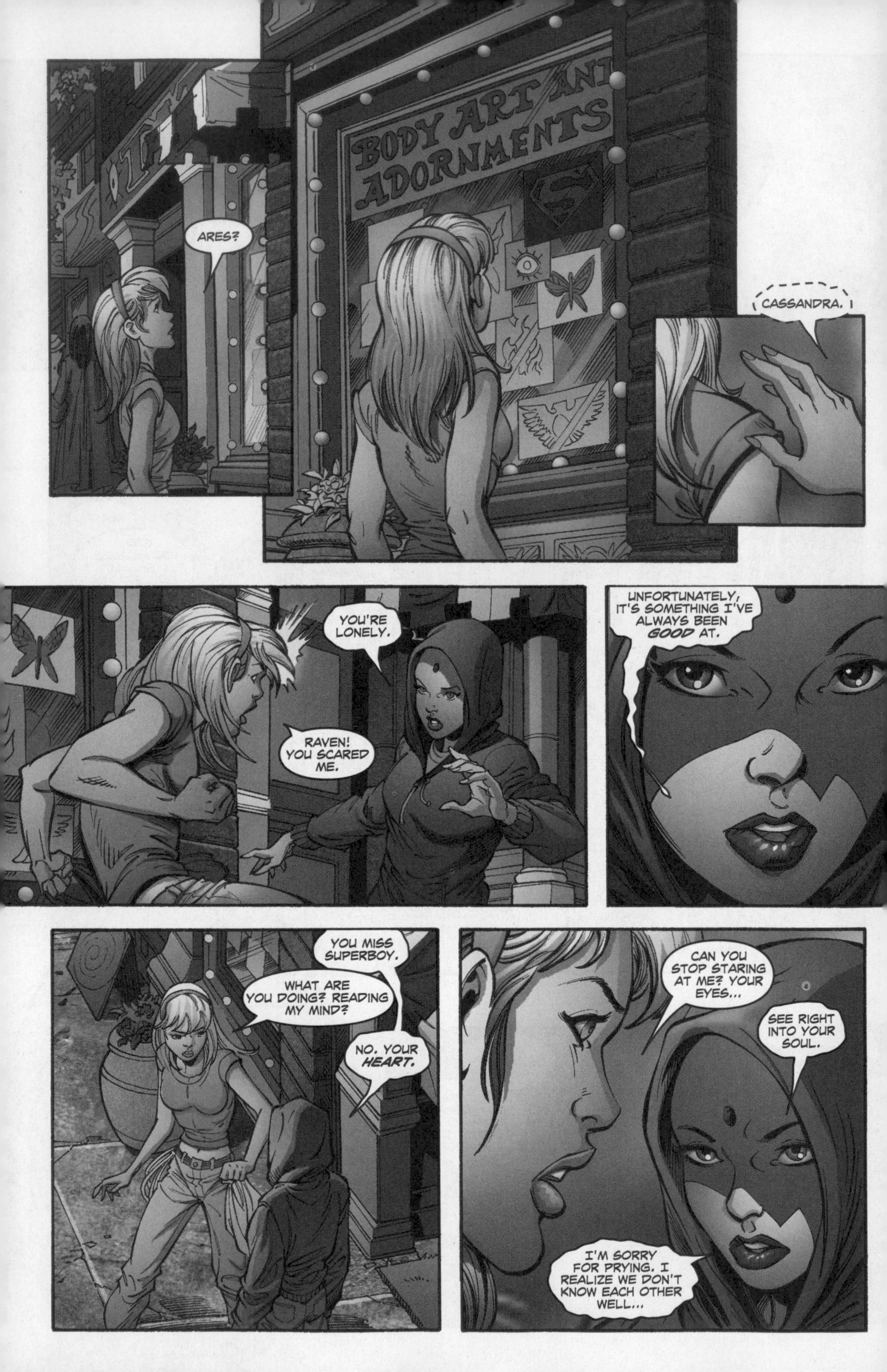
BODY ART ANT
ADORNMENTS
ARES?
CASSANDRA.
YOU'RE LONELY.
RAVEN! YOU SCARED ME.
UNFORTUNATELY, IT'S SOMETHING I'VE ALWAYS BEEN *GOOD* AT.
YOU MISS SUPERBOY.
WHAT ARE YOU DOING? READING MY MIND?
NO. YOUR *HEART*.
CAN YOU STOP STARING AT ME? YOUR EYES...
SEE RIGHT INTO YOUR SOUL.
I'M SORRY FOR PRYING. I REALIZE WE DON'T KNOW EACH OTHER WELL...

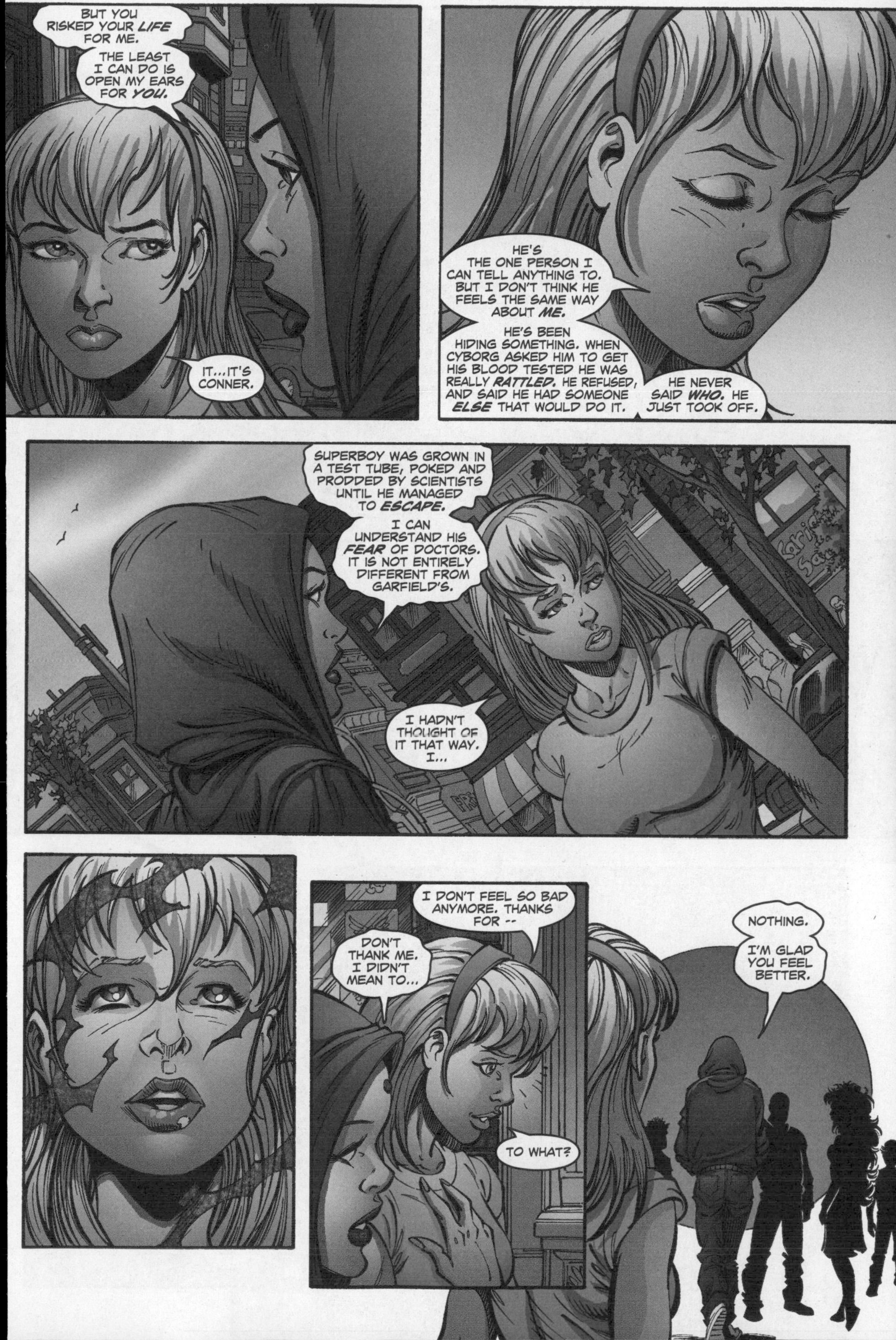
BUT YOU RISKED YOUR LIFE FOR ME.
THE LEAST I CAN DO IS OPEN MY EARS FOR YOU.
IT...IT'S CONNER.
HE'S THE ONE PERSON I CAN TELL ANYTHING TO. BUT I DON'T THINK HE FEELS THE SAME WAY ABOUT ME.
HE'S BEEN HIDING SOMETHING. WHEN CYBORG ASKED HIM TO GET HIS BLOOD TESTED HE WAS REALLY RATTLED. HE REFUSED, AND SAID HE HAD SOMEONE ELSE THAT WOULD DO IT.
HE NEVER SAID WHO. HE JUST TOOK OFF.
SUPERBOY WAS GROWN IN A TEST TUBE, POKED AND PRODDED BY SCIENTISTS UNTIL HE MANAGED TO ESCAPE.
I CAN UNDERSTAND HIS FEAR OF DOCTORS. IT IS NOT ENTIRELY DIFFERENT FROM GARFIELD'S.
I HADN'T THOUGHT OF IT THAT WAY. I...
I DON'T FEEL SO BAD ANYMORE. THANKS FOR --
DON'T THANK ME. I DIDN'T MEAN TO...
TO WHAT?
NOTHING.
I'M GLAD YOU FEEL BETTER.

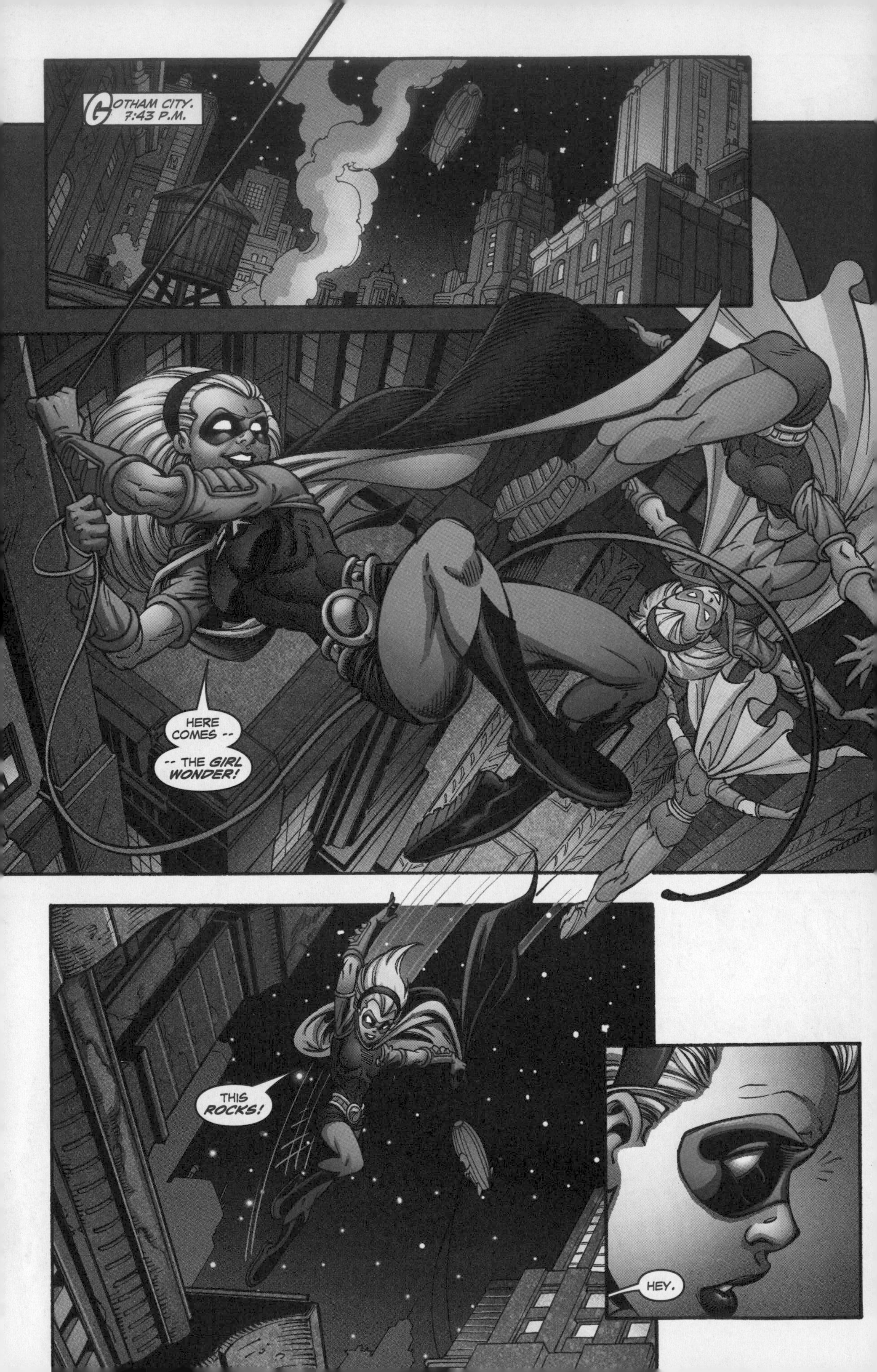
GOTHAM CITY.
7:43 P.M.
HERE COMES --
-- THE GIRL WONDER!
THIS ROCKS!
HEY.

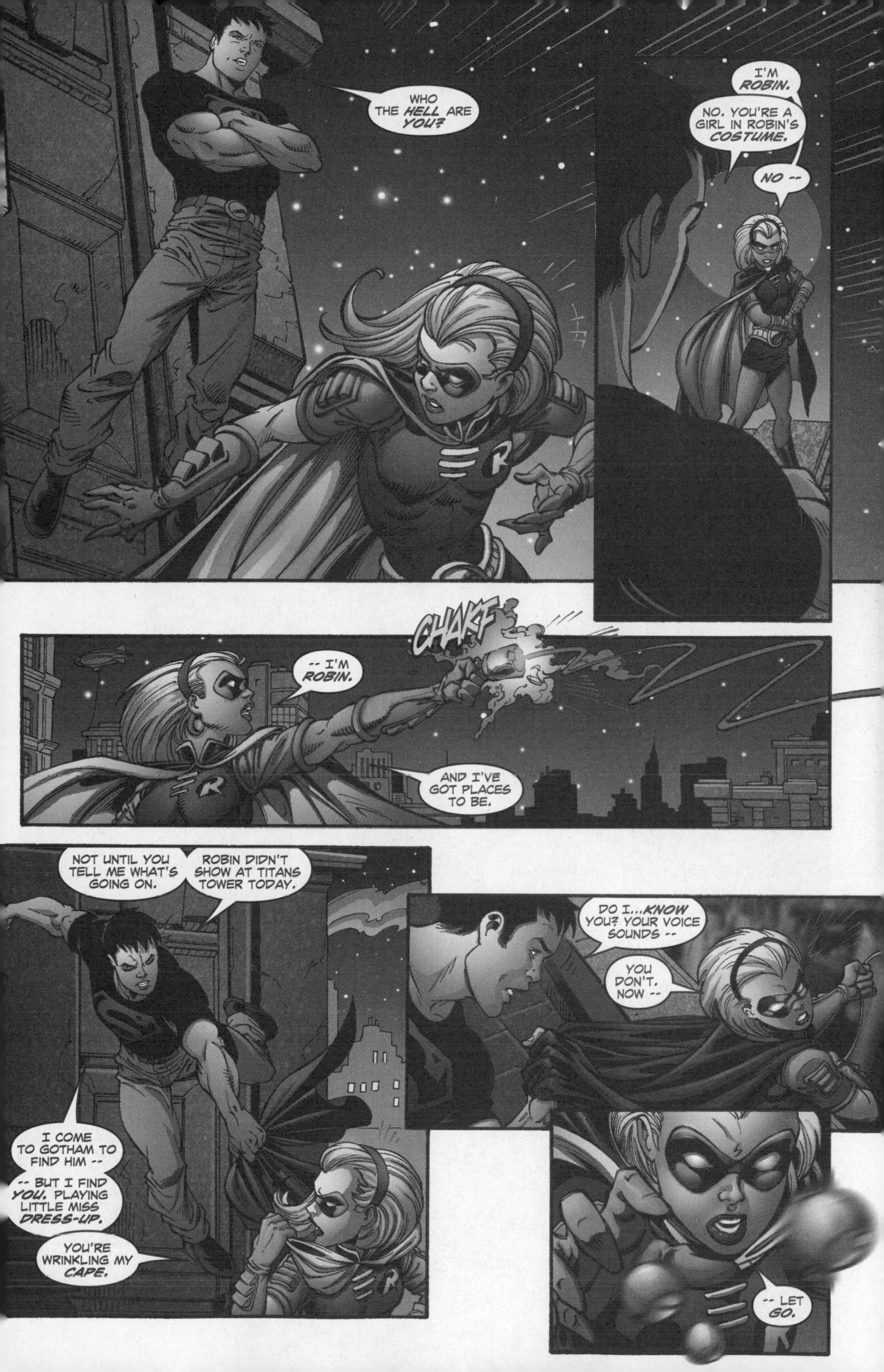
WHO THE HELL ARE YOU?
I'M ROBIN.
NO. YOU'RE A GIRL IN ROBIN'S COSTUME.
NO --
CHAKF
-- I'M ROBIN.
AND I'VE GOT PLACES TO BE.
NOT UNTIL YOU TELL ME WHAT'S GOING ON.
ROBIN DIDN'T SHOW AT TITANS TOWER TODAY.
I COME TO GOTHAM TO FIND HIM --
-- BUT I FIND YOU. PLAYING LITTLE MISS DRESS-UP.
YOU'RE WRINKLING MY CAPE.
DO I...KNOW YOU? YOUR VOICE SOUNDS --
YOU DON'T. NOW --
-- LET GO.

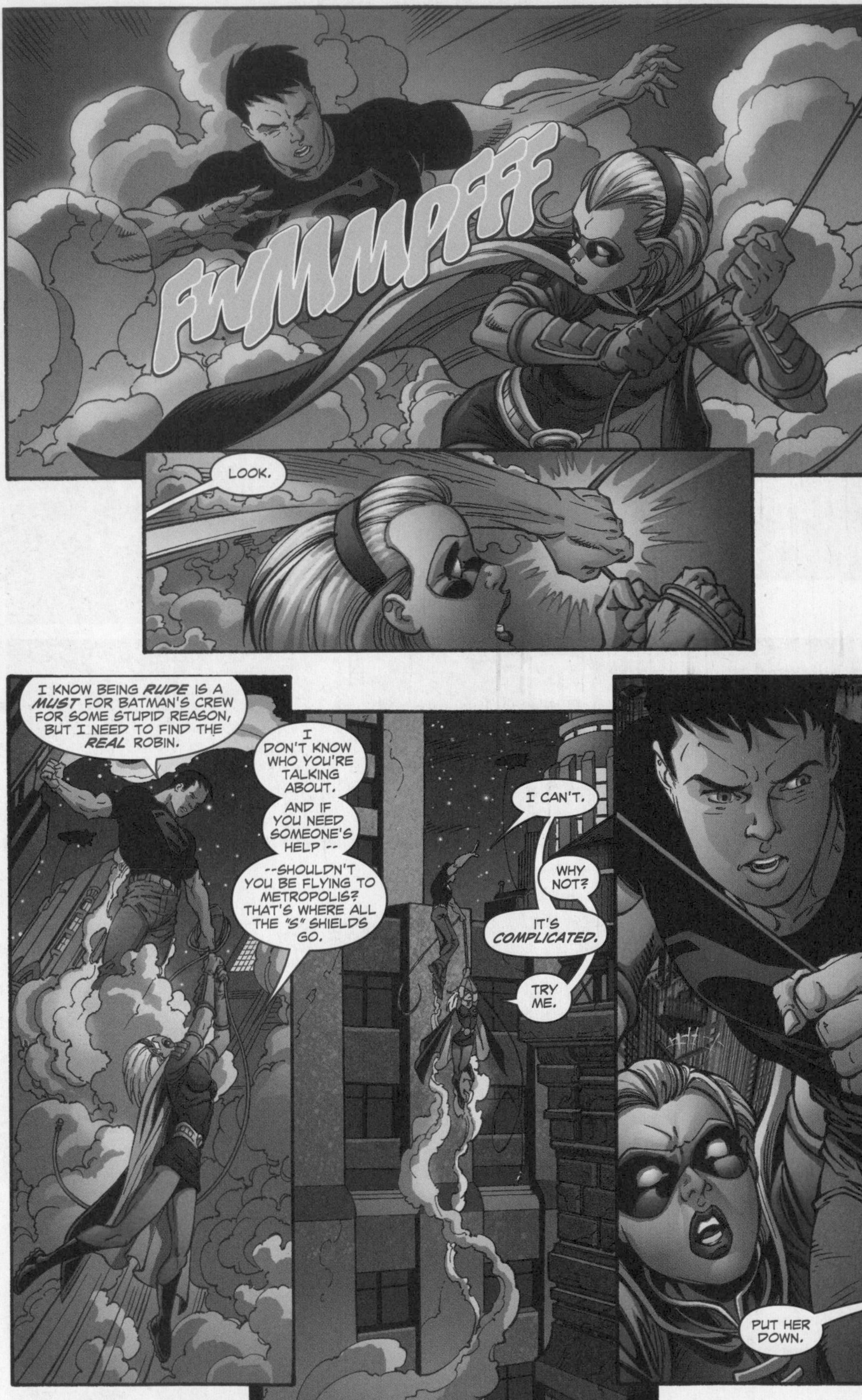
FWMMPFFF
LOOK.
I KNOW BEING RUDE IS A MUST FOR BATMAN'S CREW FOR SOME STUPID REASON, BUT I NEED TO FIND THE REAL ROBIN.
I DON'T KNOW WHO YOU'RE TALKING ABOUT.
AND IF YOU NEED SOMEONE'S HELP --
--SHOULDN'T YOU BE FLYING TO METROPOLIS? THAT'S WHERE ALL THE "S" SHIELDS GO.
I CAN'T.
WHY NOT?
IT'S COMPLICATED.
TRY ME.
PUT HER DOWN.

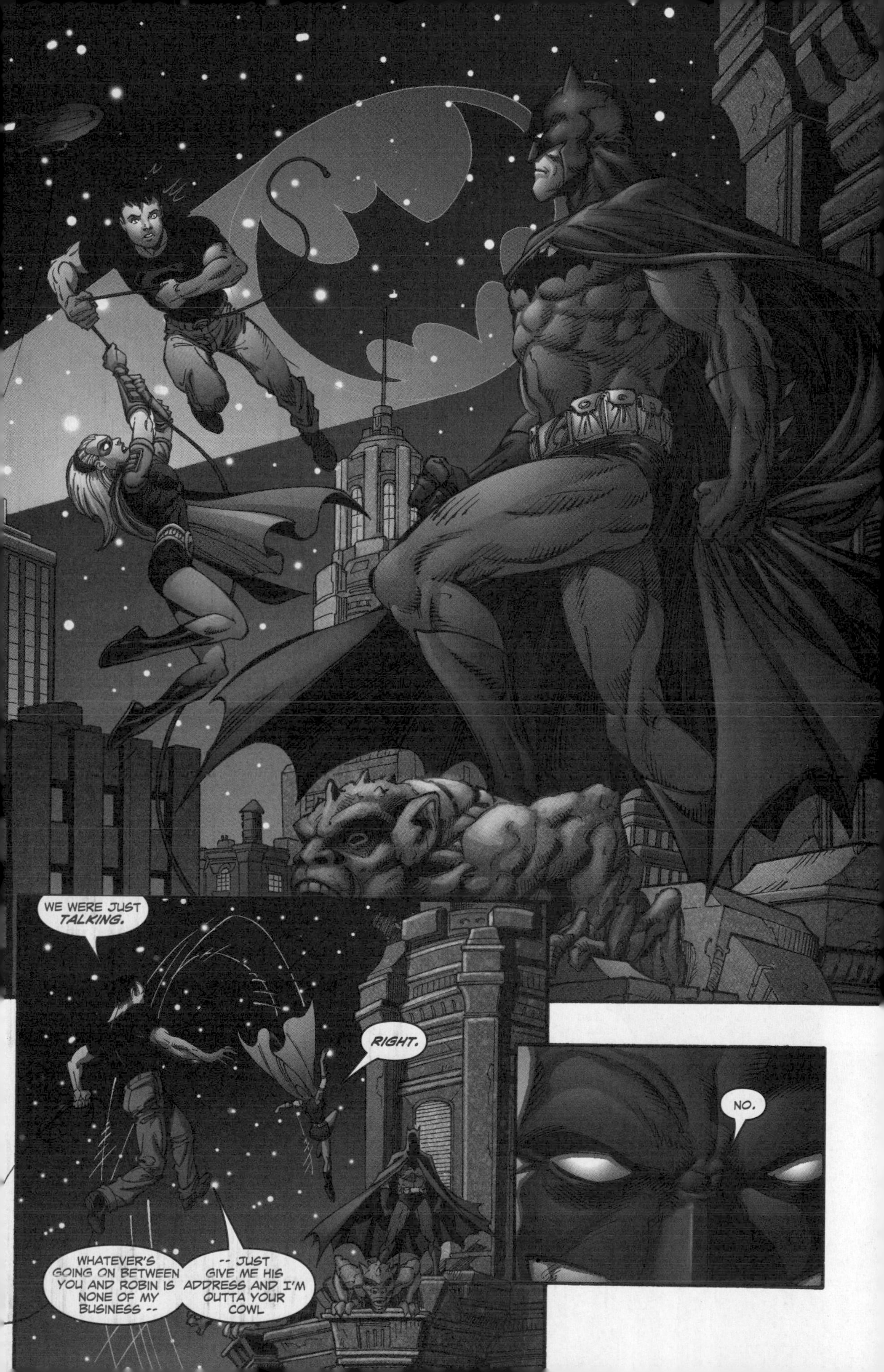
WE WERE JUST TALKING.
RIGHT.
WHATEVER'S GOING ON BETWEEN YOU AND ROBIN IS NONE OF MY BUSINESS --
-- JUST GIVE ME HIS ADDRESS AND I'M OUTTA YOUR COWL
NO.

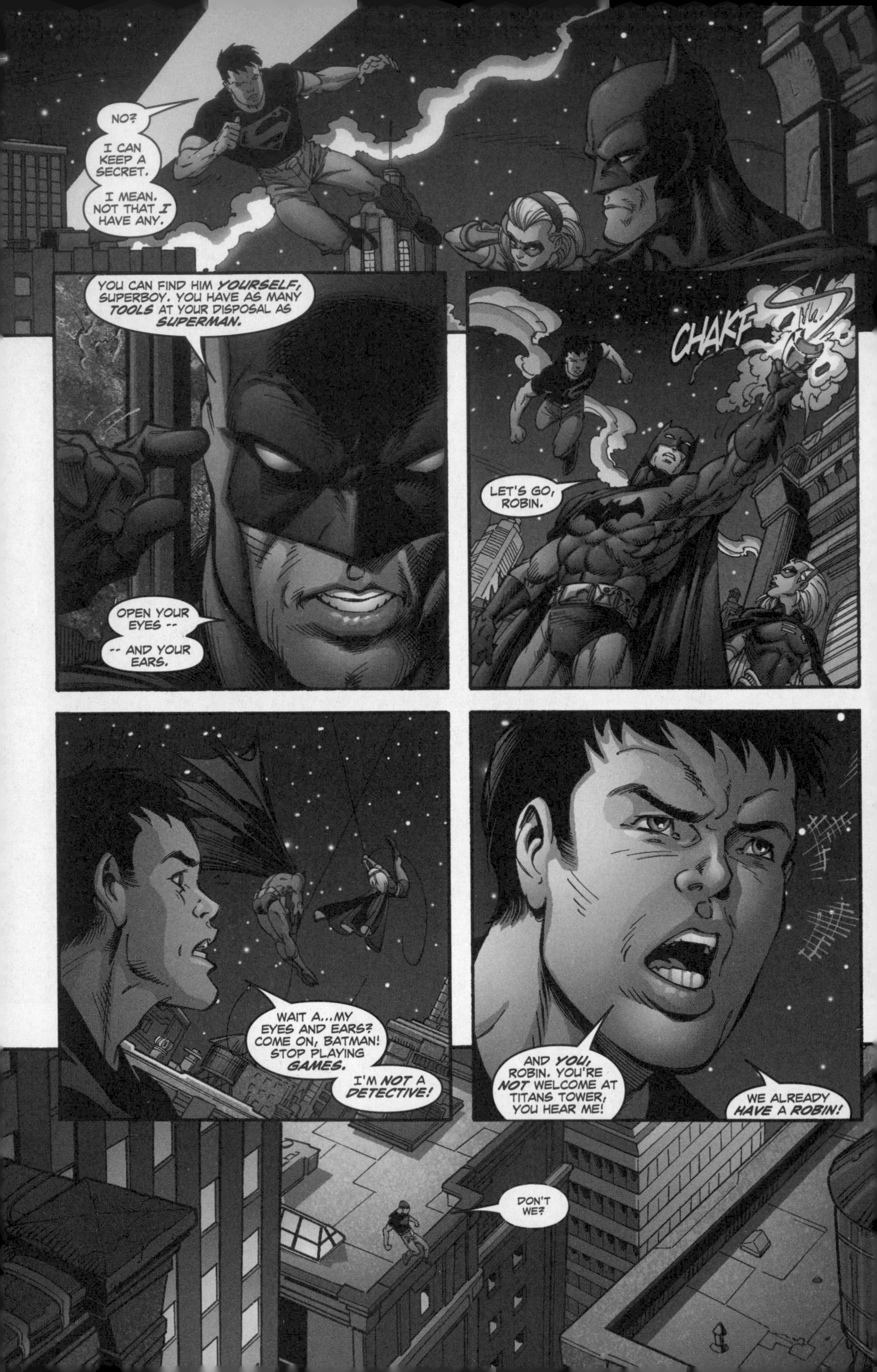
NO?
I CAN KEEP A SECRET.
I MEAN. NOT THAT I HAVE ANY.
YOU CAN FIND HIM YOURSELF, SUPERBOY. YOU HAVE AS MANY TOOLS AT YOUR DISPOSAL AS SUPERMAN.
OPEN YOUR EYES --
-- AND YOUR EARS.
CHAKF
LET'S GO, ROBIN.
WAIT A...MY EYES AND EARS? COME ON, BATMAN! STOP PLAYING GAMES.
I'M NOT A DETECTIVE!
AND YOU, ROBIN. YOU'RE NOT WELCOME AT TITANS TOWER, YOU HEAR ME!
WE ALREADY HAVE A ROBIN!
DON'T WE?

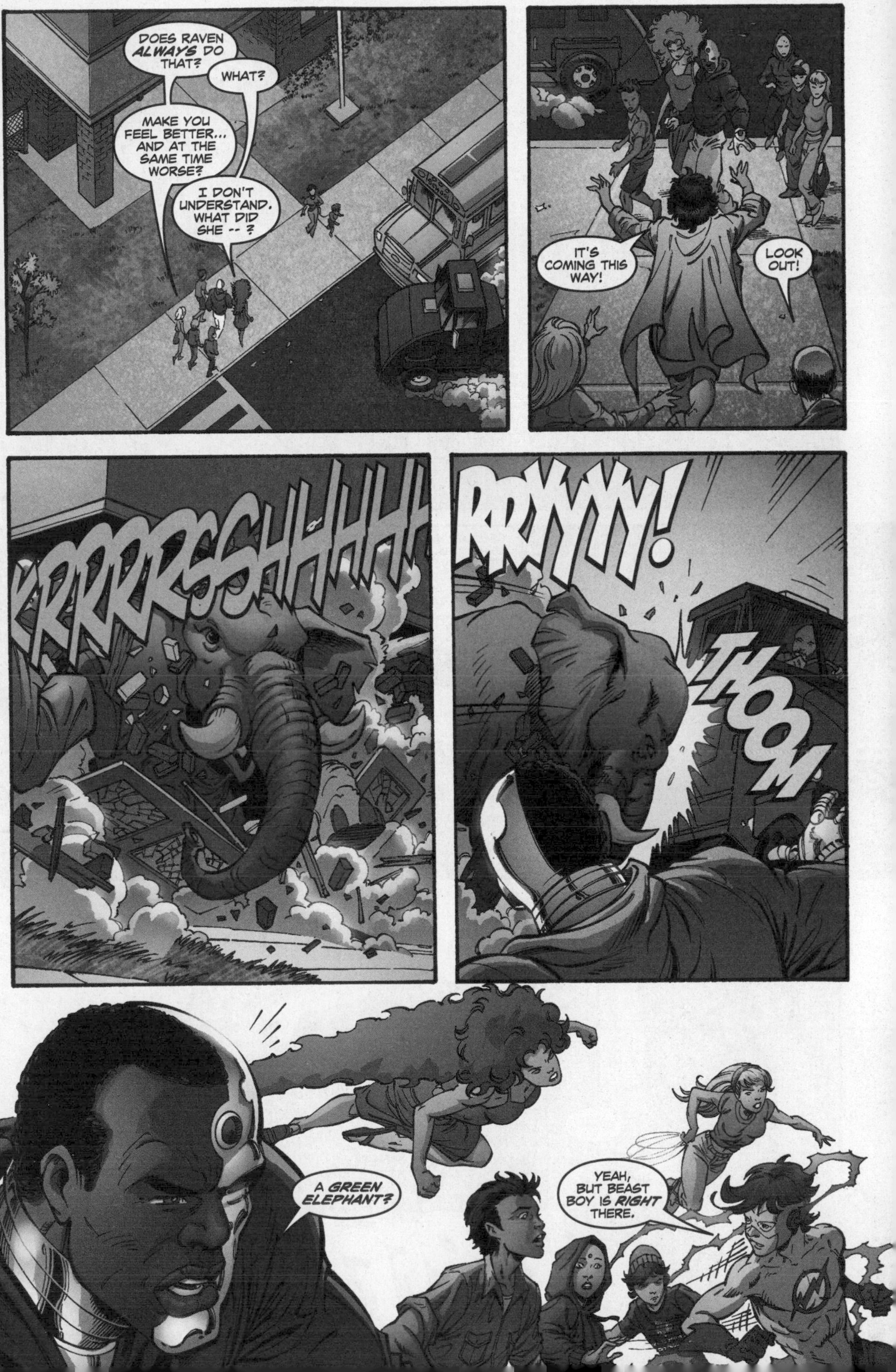
DOES RAVEN ALWAYS DO THAT?
WHAT?
MAKE YOU FEEL BETTER... AND AT THE SAME TIME WORSE?
I DON'T UNDERSTAND. WHAT DID SHE -- ?
IT'S COMING THIS WAY!
LOOK OUT!
KRRRRSHHHH
RRNYYY!
THOOM
A GREEN ELEPHANT?
YEAH, BUT BEAST BOY IS RIGHT THERE.

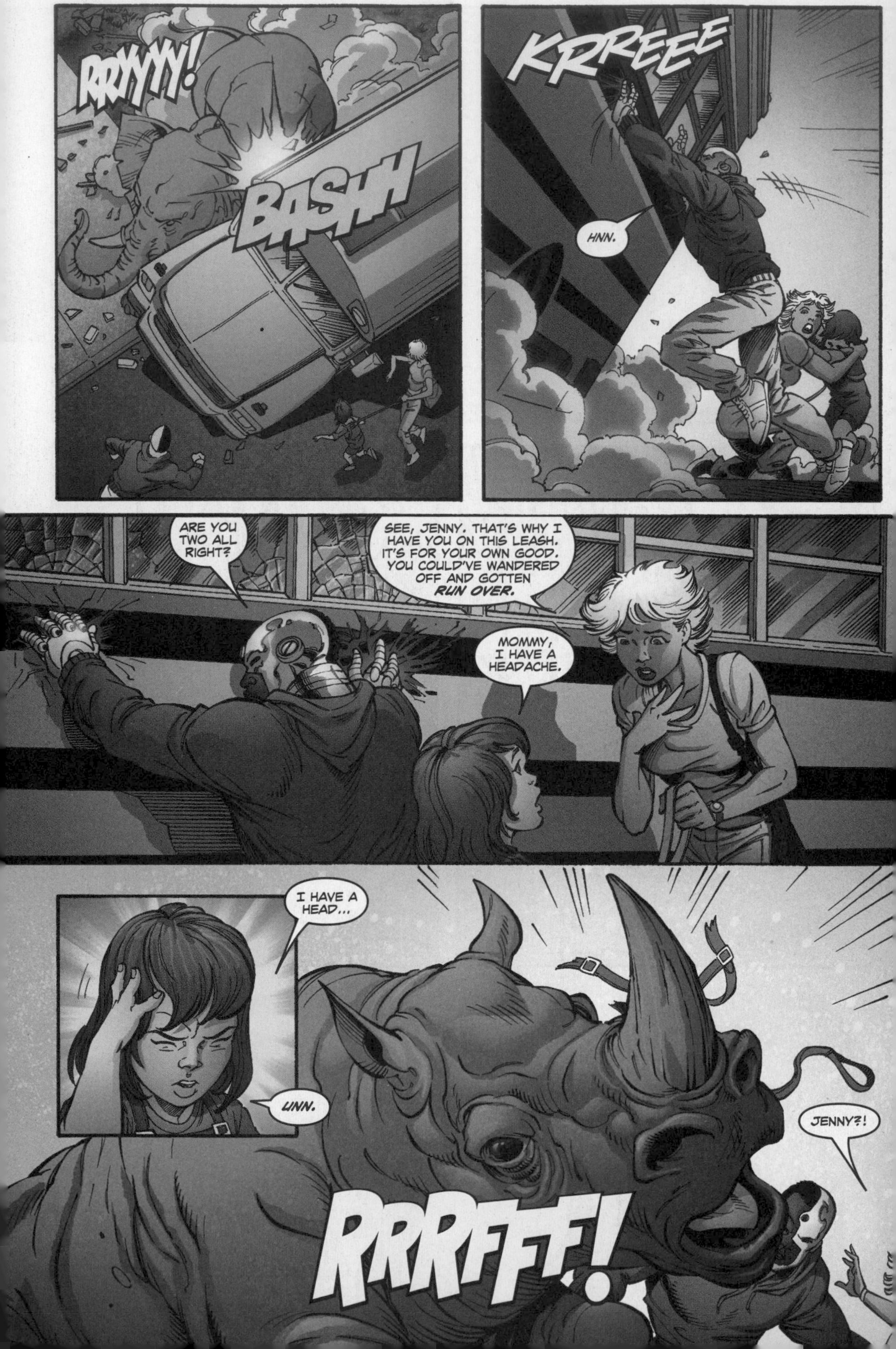
RRYYYY!
BASHH
KRREEE
HNN.
ARE YOU TWO ALL RIGHT?
SEE, JENNY. THAT'S WHY I HAVE YOU ON THIS LEASH. IT'S FOR YOUR OWN GOOD. YOU COULD'VE WANDERED OFF AND GOTTEN RUN OVER.
MOMMY, I HAVE A HEADACHE.
I HAVE A HEAD...
UNN.
JENNY?!
RRRFFF!

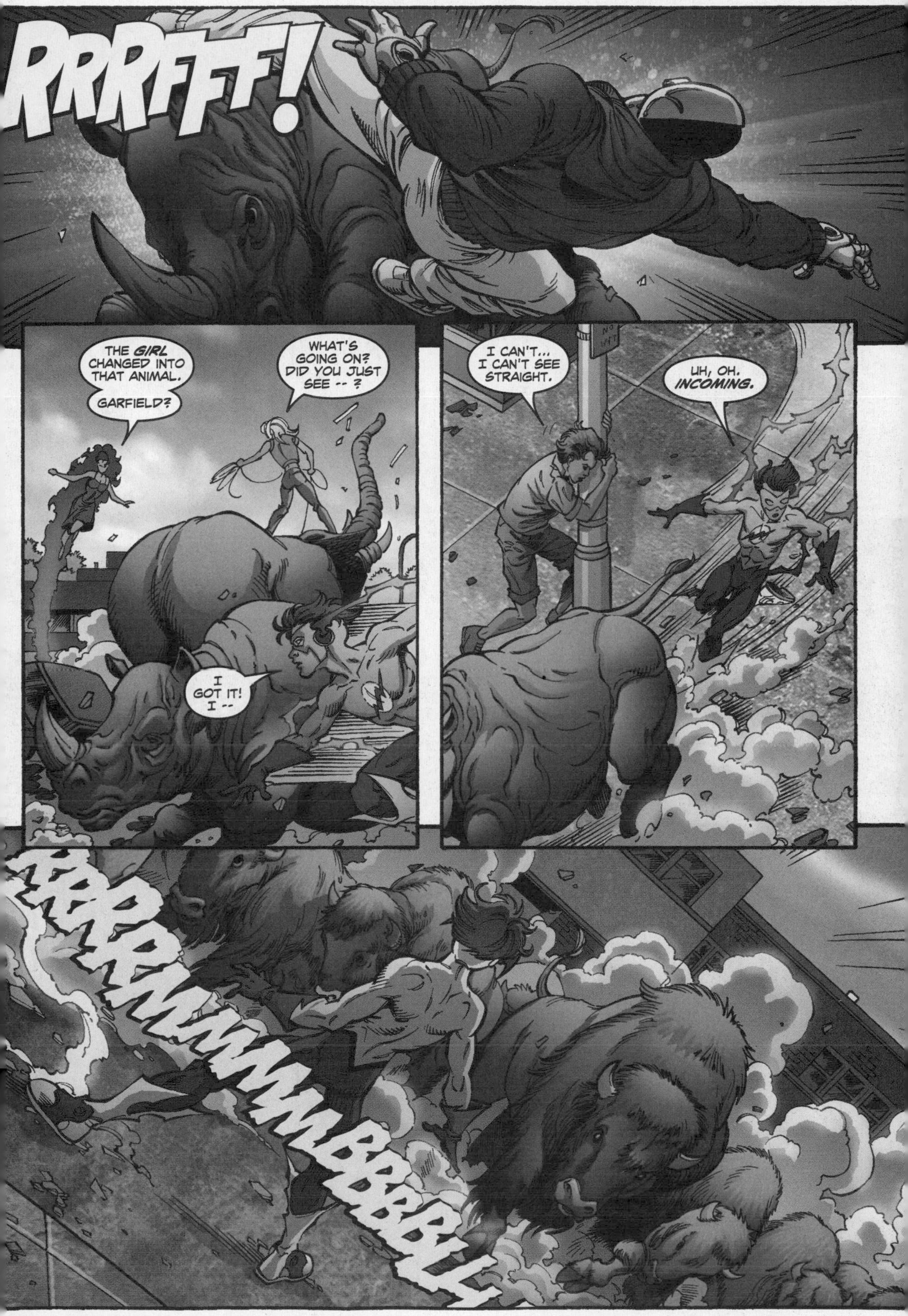
RRRFFF!
THE GIRL CHANGED INTO THAT ANIMAL.
GARFIELD?
WHAT'S GOING ON? DID YOU JUST SEE -- ?
I GOT IT! I --
I CAN'T... I CAN'T SEE STRAIGHT.
UH, OH. INCOMING.
RRRRRUMMMMMBBBBLL

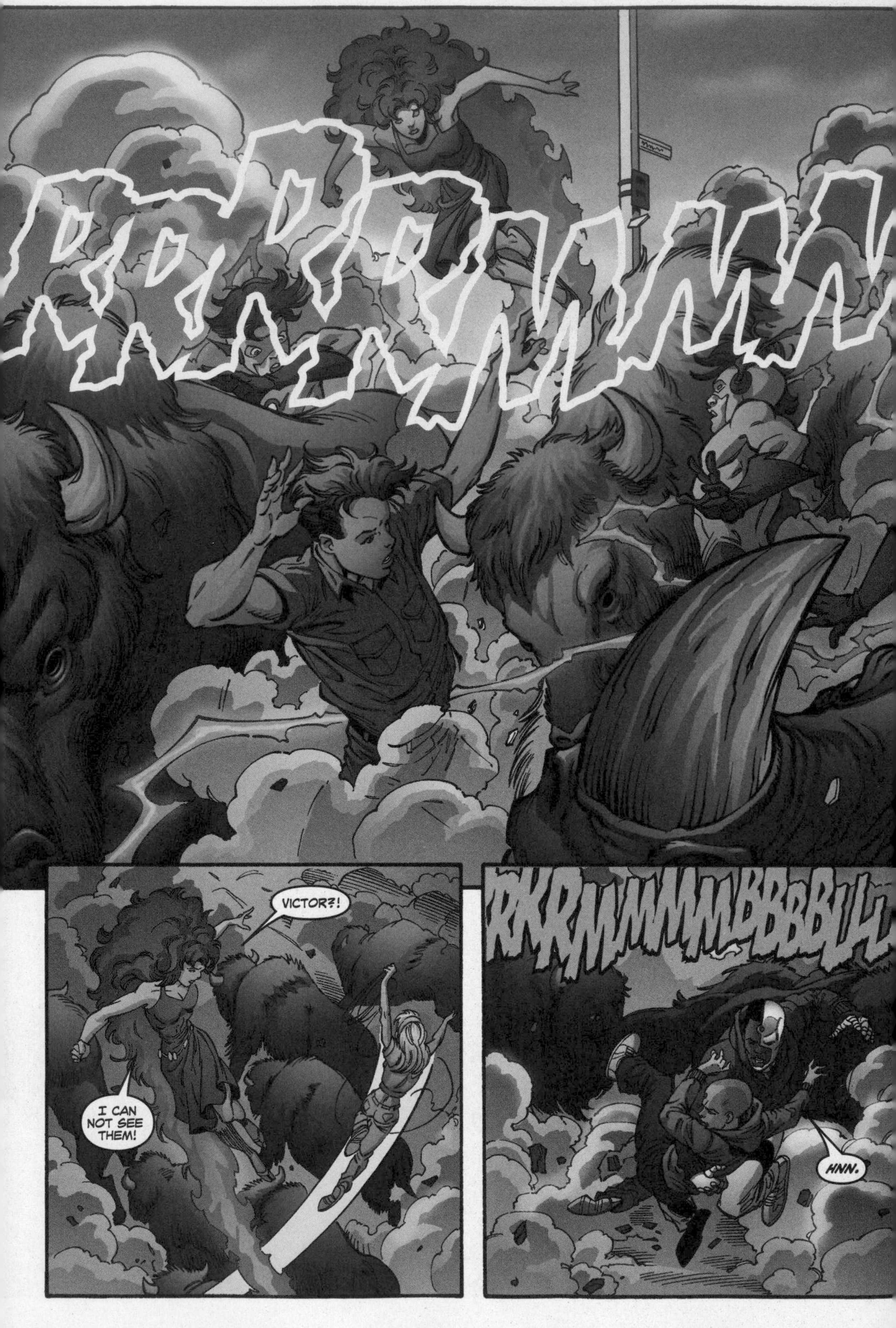
VICTOR?!
I CAN NOT SEE THEM!
HNN.

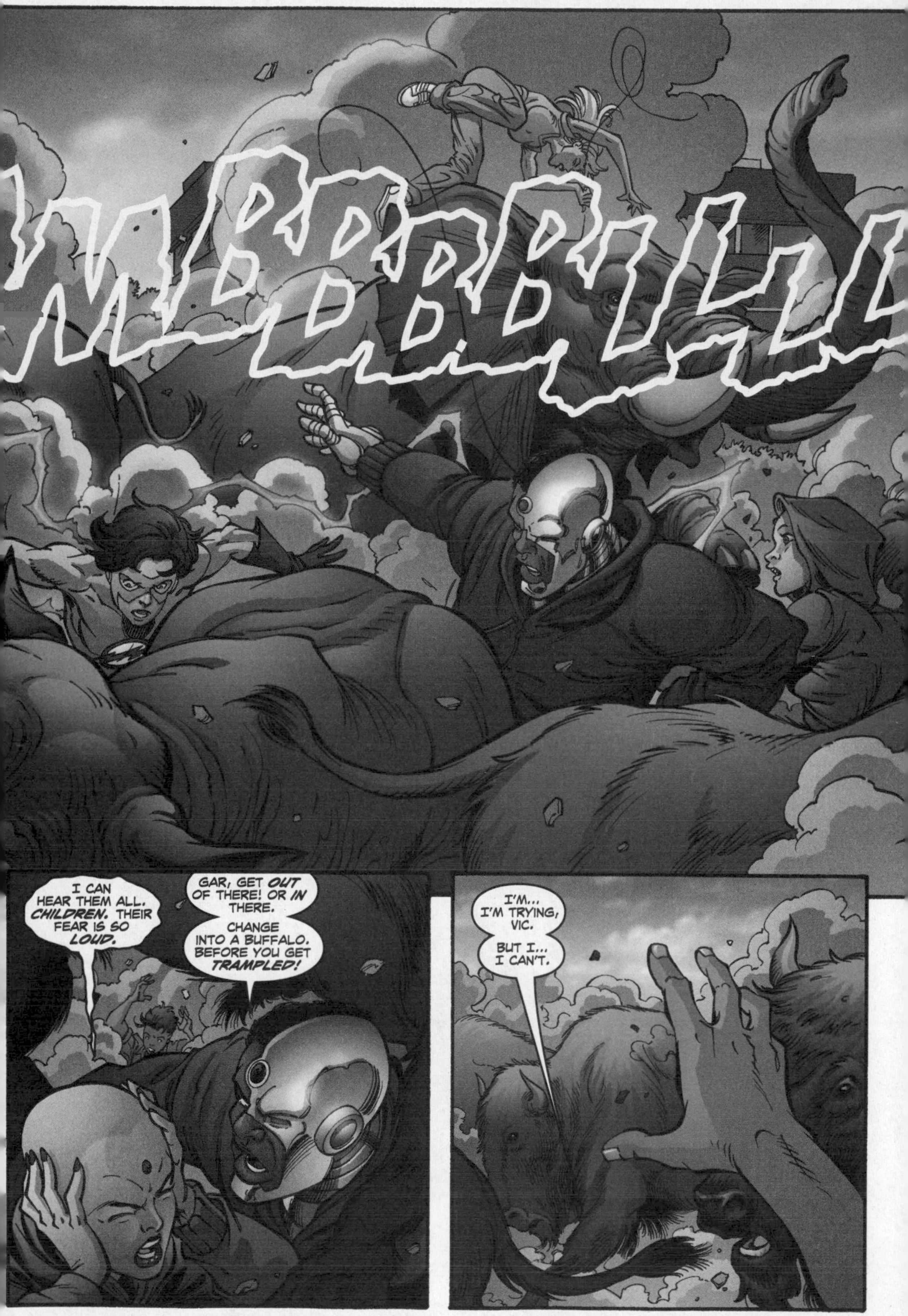
I CAN HEAR THEM ALL. *CHILDREN.* THEIR FEAR IS SO *LOUD.*
GAR, GET *OUT* OF THERE! OR *IN* THERE.
CHANGE INTO A BUFFALO. BEFORE YOU GET *TRAMPLED!*
I'M... I'M TRYING, VIC.
BUT I... I CAN'T.

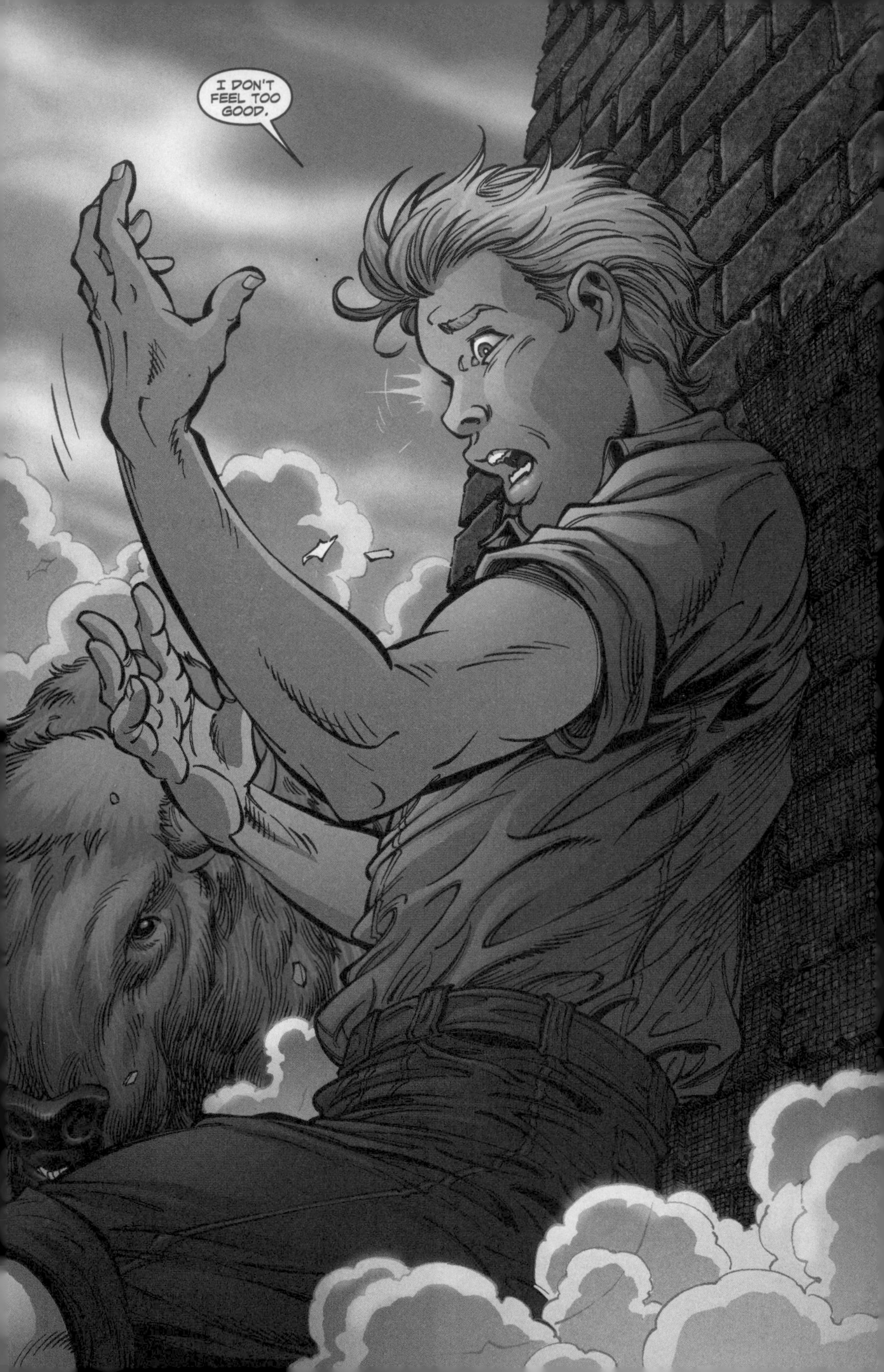
I DON'T FEEL TOO GOOD.

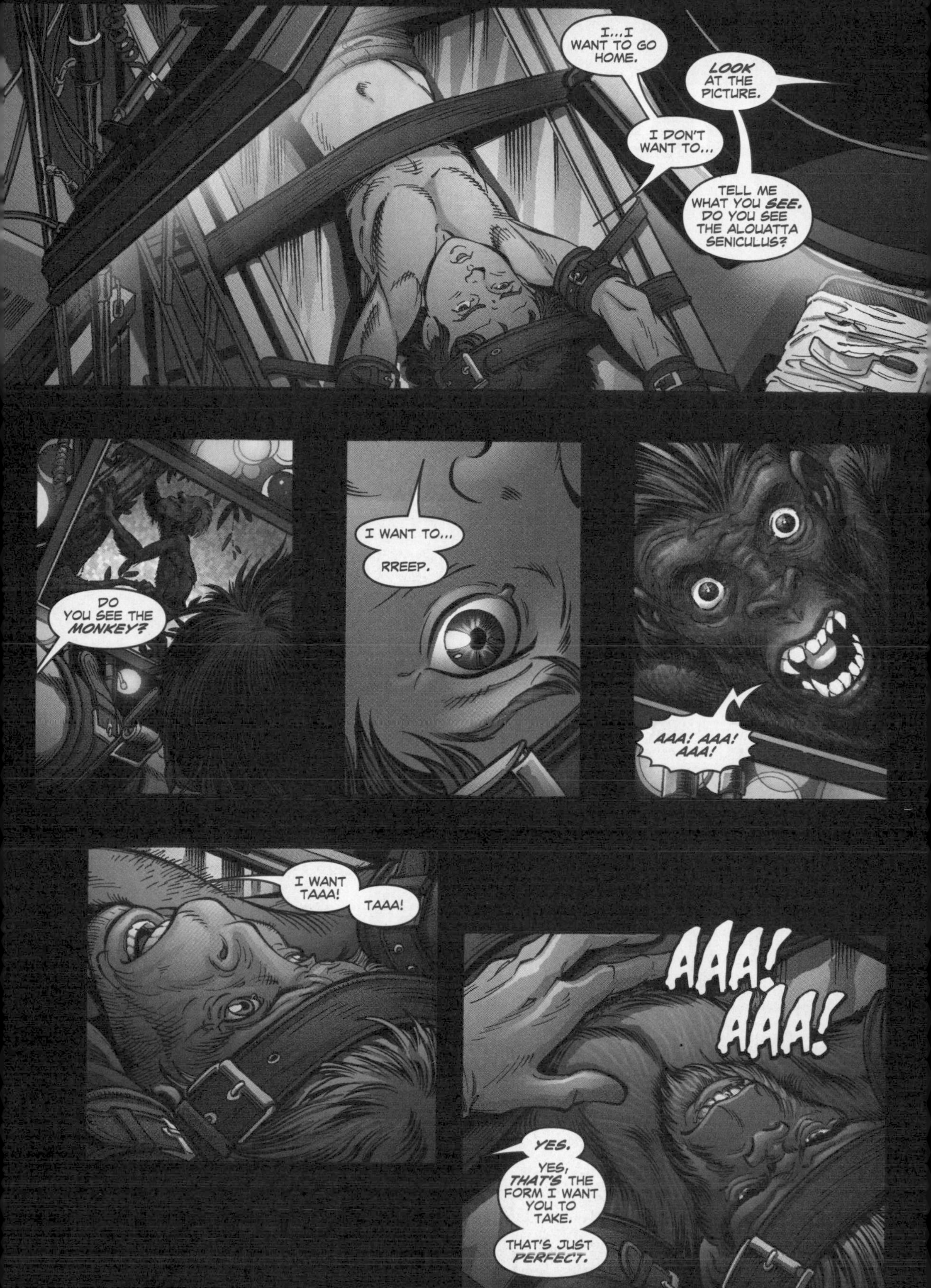
I...I WANT TO GO HOME.
I DON'T WANT TO...
LOOK AT THE PICTURE.
TELL ME WHAT YOU SEE. DO YOU SEE THE ALOUATTA SENICULUS?
DO YOU SEE THE MONKEY?
I WANT TO...
RREEP.
AAA! AAA! AAA!
I WANT TAAA!
TAAA!
AAA! AAA!
YES.
YES, THAT'S THE FORM I WANT YOU TO TAKE.
THAT'S JUST PERFECT.

BEAST BOYS AND GIRLS PART TWO

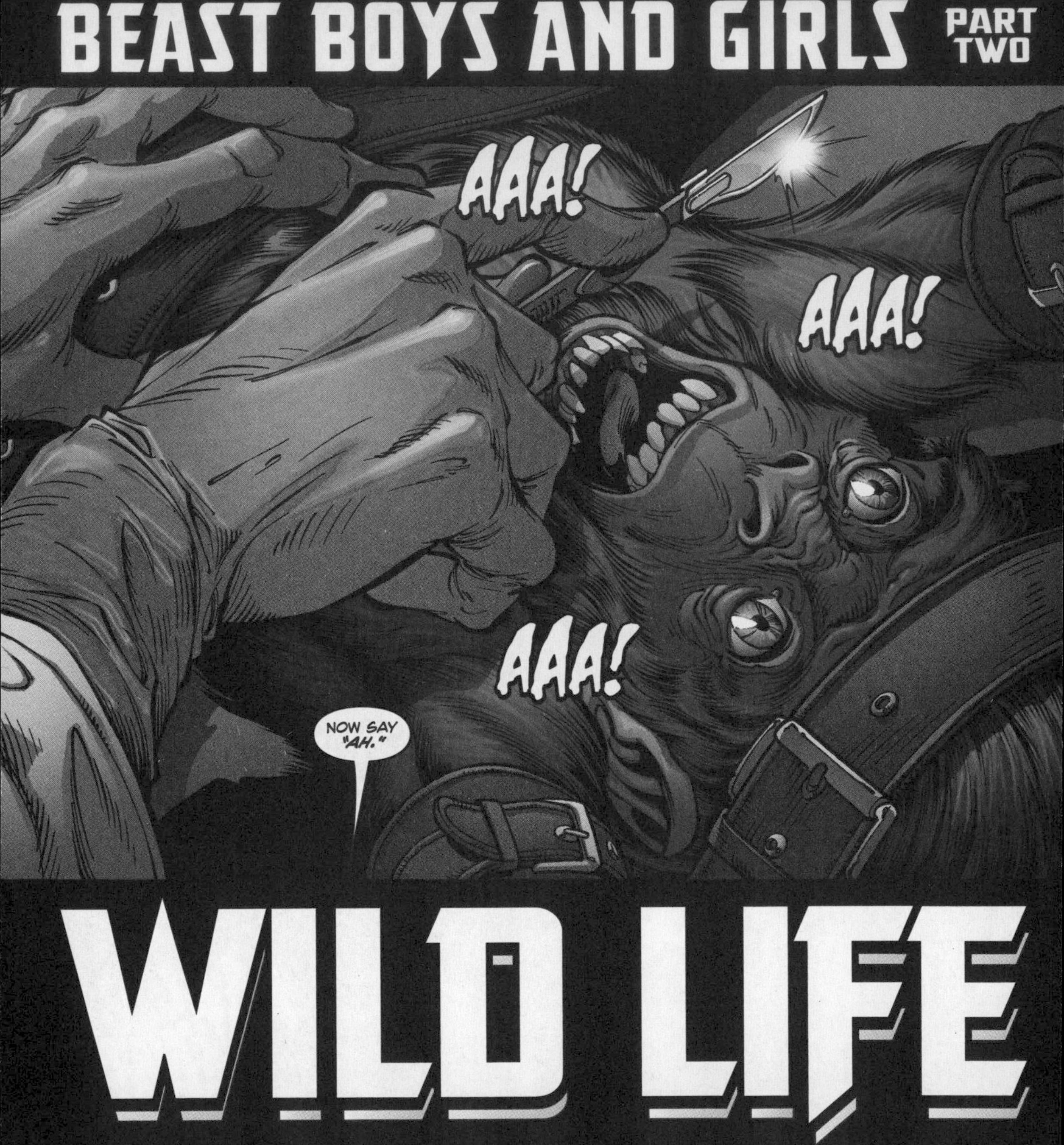
AAA!
AAA!
AAA!
NOW SAY "AH."

WILD LIFE

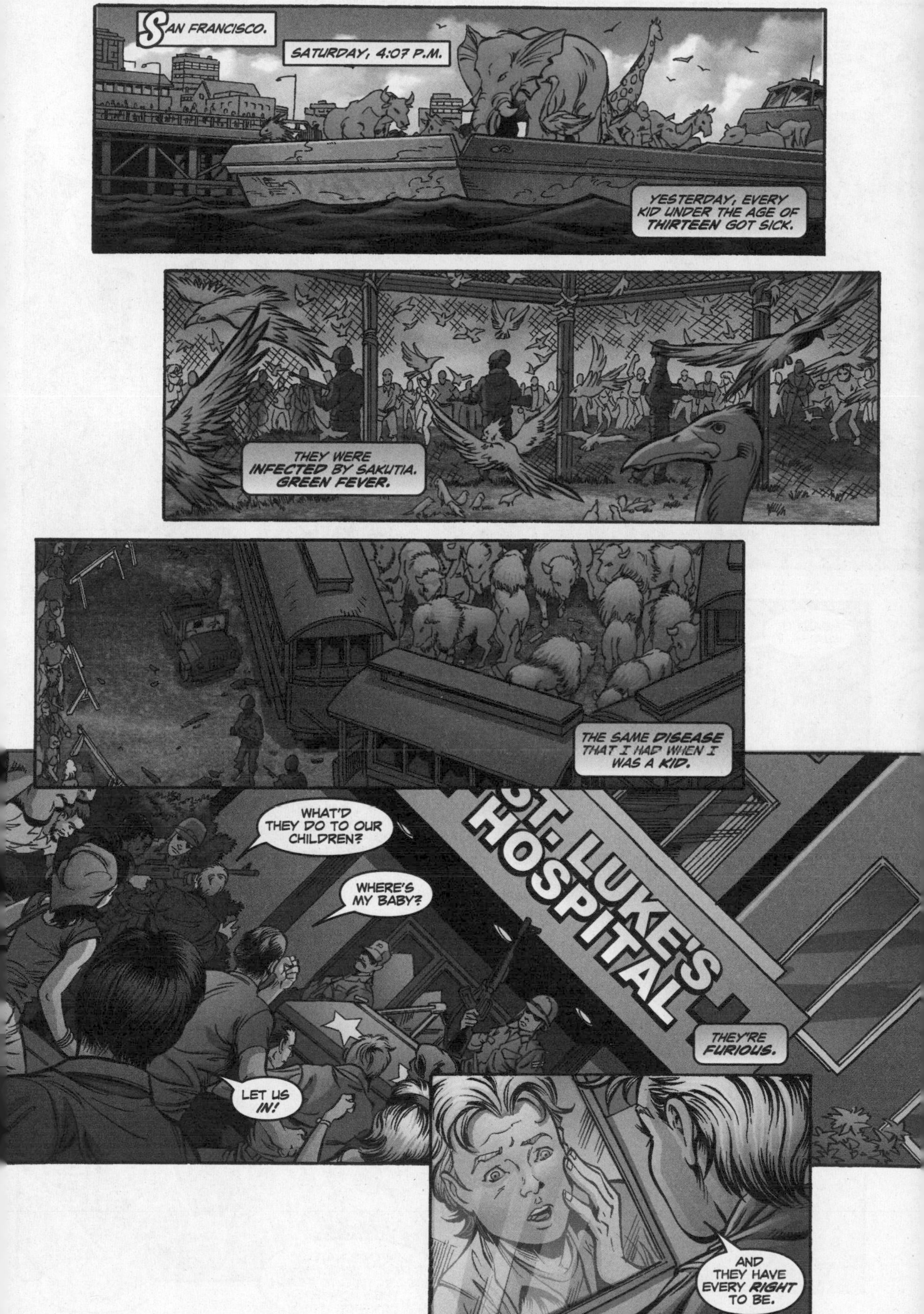
SAN FRANCISCO.
SATURDAY, 4:07 P.M.
YESTERDAY, EVERY KID UNDER THE AGE OF THIRTEEN GOT SICK.
THEY WERE INFECTED BY SAKUTIA. GREEN FEVER.
THE SAME DISEASE THAT I HAD WHEN I WAS A KID.
ST. LUKE'S HOSPITAL
WHAT'D THEY DO TO OUR CHILDREN?
WHERE'S MY BABY?
LET US IN!
THEY'RE FURIOUS.
AND THEY HAVE EVERY RIGHT TO BE.

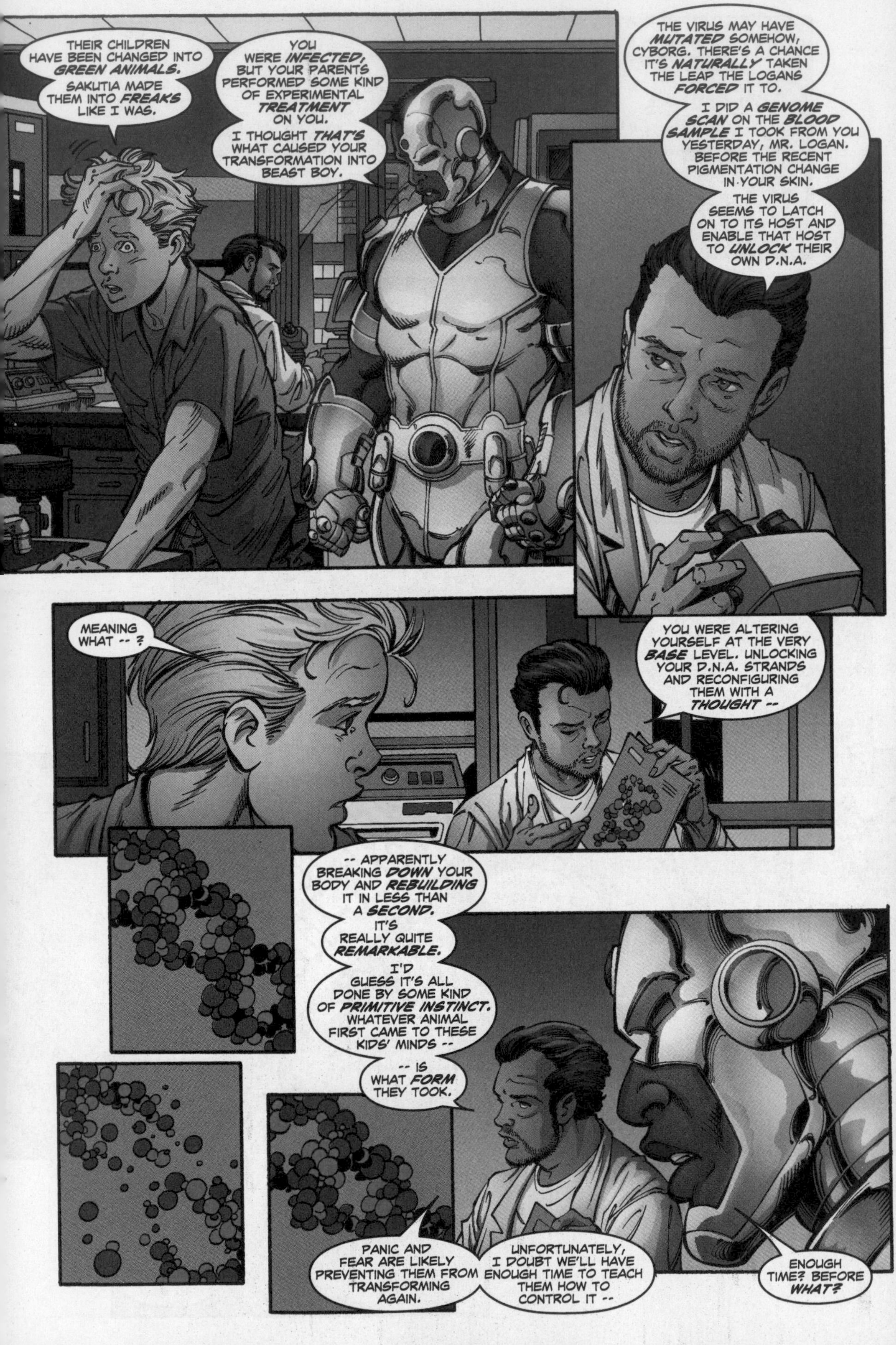

THEIR CHILDREN HAVE BEEN CHANGED INTO GREEN ANIMALS.
SAKUTIA MADE THEM INTO FREAKS LIKE I WAS.
YOU WERE INFECTED, BUT YOUR PARENTS PERFORMED SOME KIND OF EXPERIMENTAL TREATMENT ON YOU.
I THOUGHT THAT'S WHAT CAUSED YOUR TRANSFORMATION INTO BEAST BOY.
THE VIRUS MAY HAVE MUTATED SOMEHOW, CYBORG. THERE'S A CHANCE IT'S NATURALLY TAKEN THE LEAP THE LOGANS FORCED IT TO.
I DID A GENOME SCAN ON THE BLOOD SAMPLE I TOOK FROM YOU YESTERDAY, MR. LOGAN. BEFORE THE RECENT PIGMENTATION CHANGE IN YOUR SKIN.
THE VIRUS SEEMS TO LATCH ON TO ITS HOST AND ENABLE THAT HOST TO UNLOCK THEIR OWN D.N.A.
MEANING WHAT -- ?
YOU WERE ALTERING YOURSELF AT THE VERY BASE LEVEL. UNLOCKING YOUR D.N.A. STRANDS AND RECONFIGURING THEM WITH A THOUGHT --
-- APPARENTLY BREAKING DOWN YOUR BODY AND REBUILDING IT IN LESS THAN A SECOND.
IT'S REALLY QUITE REMARKABLE.
I'D GUESS IT'S ALL DONE BY SOME KIND OF PRIMITIVE INSTINCT. WHATEVER ANIMAL FIRST CAME TO THESE KIDS' MINDS --
-- IS WHAT FORM THEY TOOK.
PANIC AND FEAR ARE LIKELY PREVENTING THEM FROM TRANSFORMING AGAIN.
UNFORTUNATELY, I DOUBT WE'LL HAVE ENOUGH TIME TO TEACH THEM HOW TO CONTROL IT --
ENOUGH TIME? BEFORE WHAT?

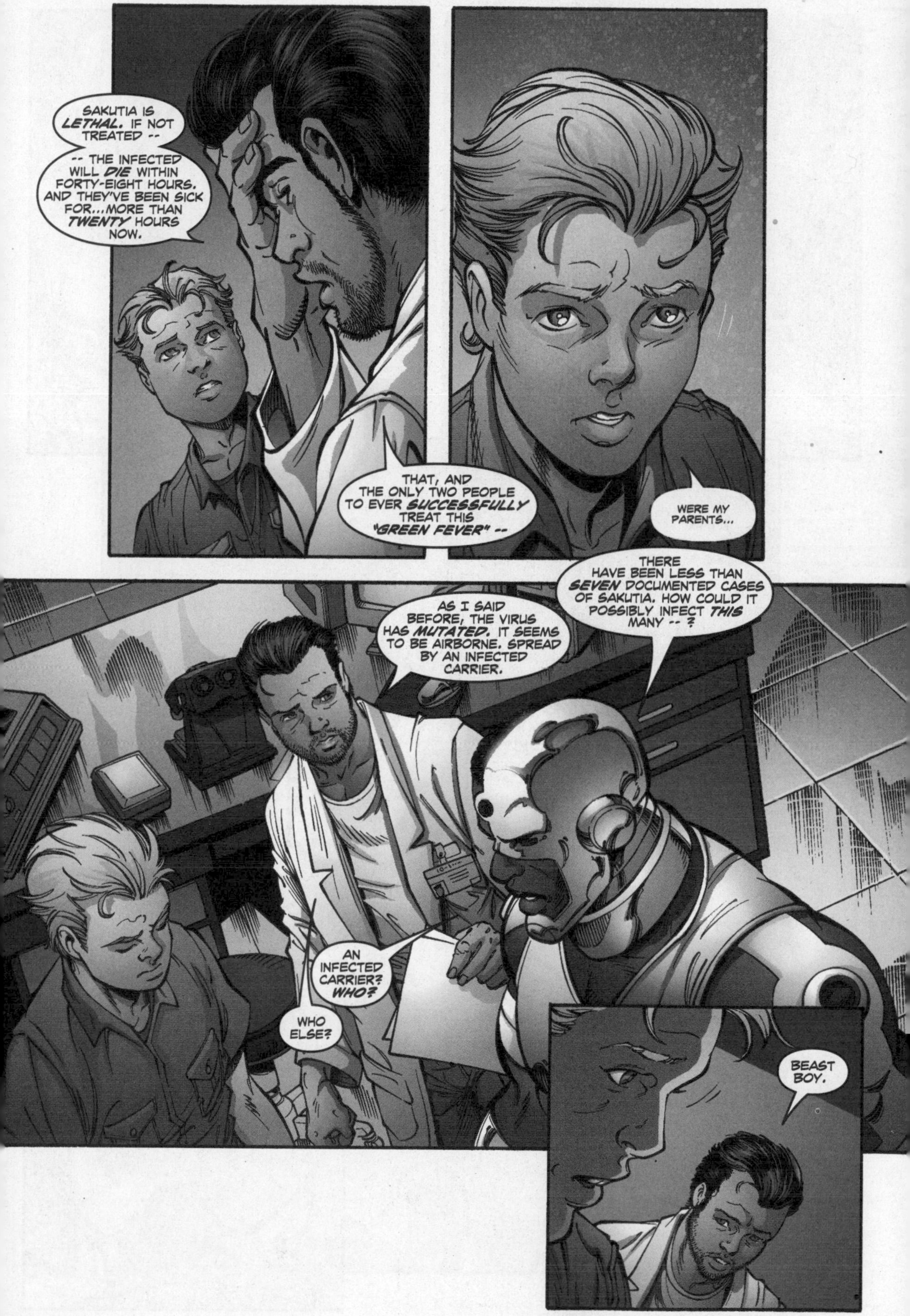

SAKUTIA IS LETHAL. IF NOT TREATED --
-- THE INFECTED WILL DIE WITHIN FORTY-EIGHT HOURS. AND THEY'VE BEEN SICK FOR...MORE THAN TWENTY HOURS NOW.
THAT, AND THE ONLY TWO PEOPLE TO EVER SUCCESSFULLY TREAT THIS "GREEN FEVER" --
WERE MY PARENTS...
THERE HAVE BEEN LESS THAN SEVEN DOCUMENTED CASES OF SAKUTIA. HOW COULD IT POSSIBLY INFECT THIS MANY -- ?
AS I SAID BEFORE, THE VIRUS HAS MUTATED. IT SEEMS TO BE AIRBORNE. SPREAD BY AN INFECTED CARRIER.
AN INFECTED CARRIER? WHO?
WHO ELSE?
BEAST BOY.

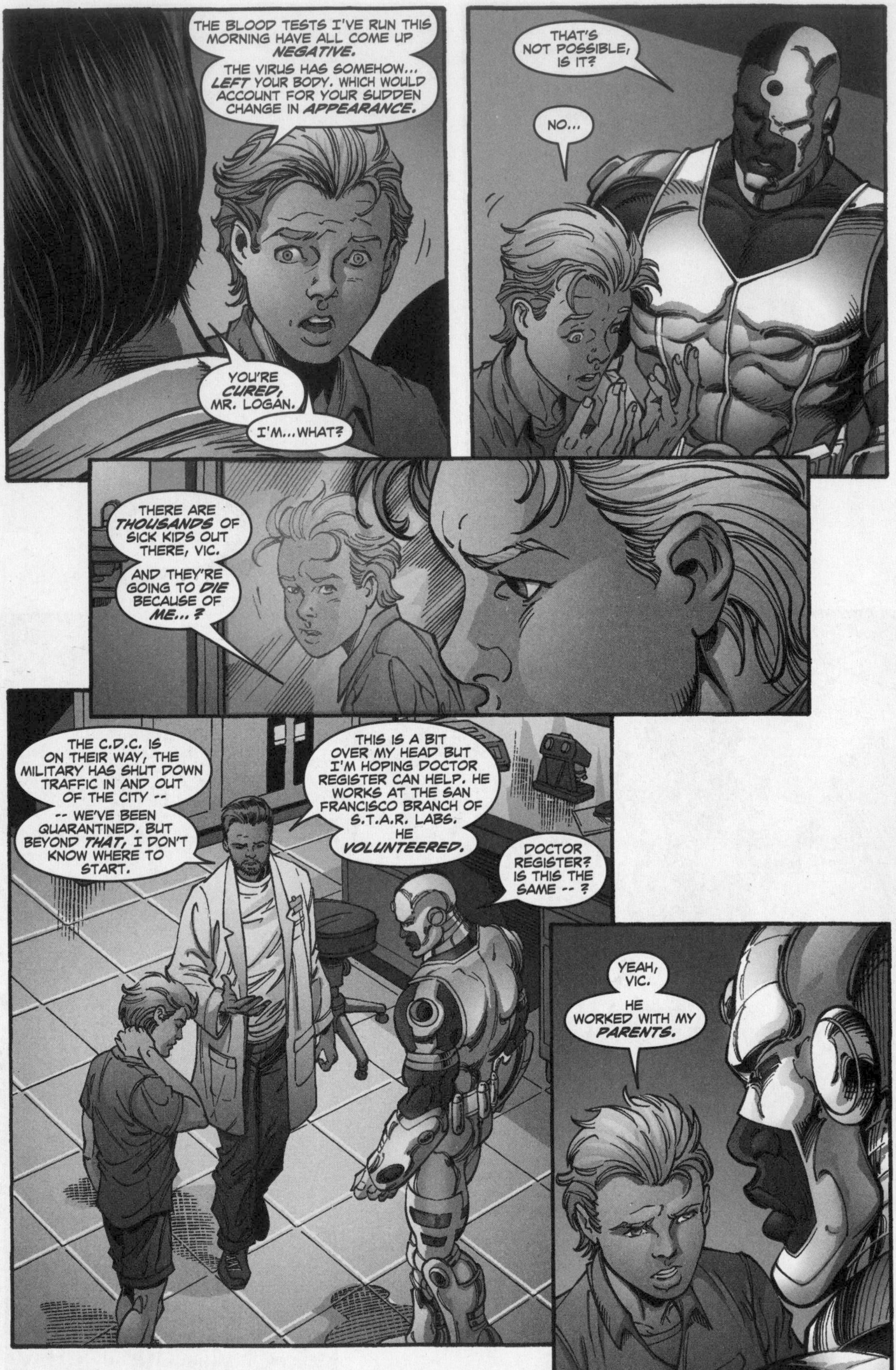

THE BLOOD TESTS I'VE RUN THIS MORNING HAVE ALL COME UP *NEGATIVE.*
THE VIRUS HAS SOMEHOW... *LEFT* YOUR BODY. WHICH WOULD ACCOUNT FOR YOUR SUDDEN CHANGE IN *APPEARANCE.*
YOU'RE *CURED,* MR. LOGAN.
I'M...WHAT?
THAT'S NOT POSSIBLE, IS IT?
NO...
THERE ARE *THOUSANDS* OF SICK KIDS OUT THERE, VIC.
AND THEY'RE GOING TO *DIE* BECAUSE OF *ME...?*
THE C.D.C. IS ON THEIR WAY, THE MILITARY HAS SHUT DOWN TRAFFIC IN AND OUT OF THE CITY --
-- WE'VE BEEN QUARANTINED. BUT BEYOND *THAT,* I DON'T KNOW WHERE TO START.
THIS IS A BIT OVER MY HEAD BUT I'M HOPING DOCTOR REGISTER CAN HELP. HE WORKS AT THE SAN FRANCISCO BRANCH OF S.T.A.R. LABS. HE *VOLUNTEERED.*
DOCTOR REGISTER? IS THIS THE SAME -- ?
YEAH, VIC.
HE WORKED WITH MY *PARENTS.*

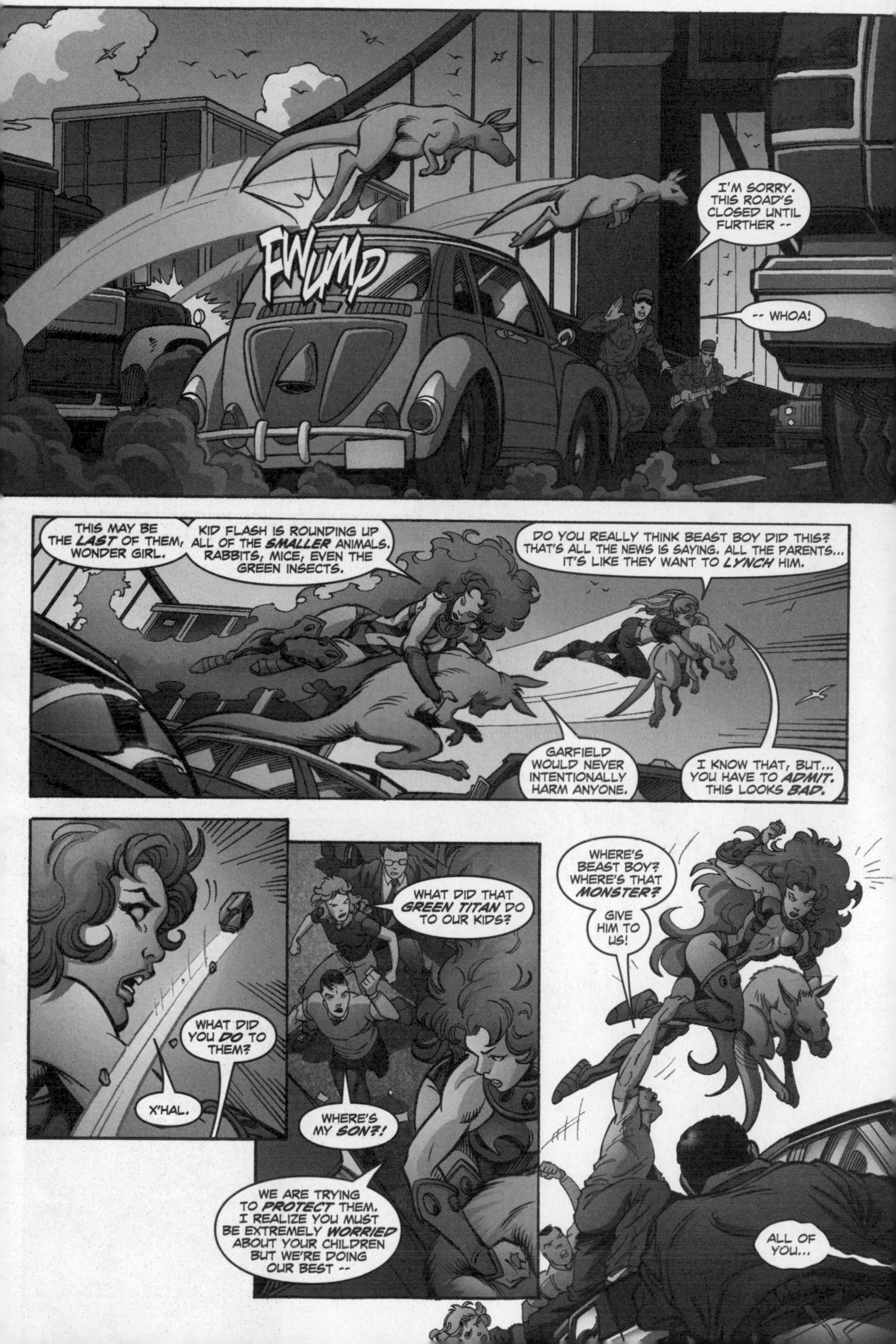
FWUMP
I'M SORRY. THIS ROAD'S CLOSED UNTIL FURTHER --
-- WHOA!
THIS MAY BE THE LAST OF THEM, WONDER GIRL.
KID FLASH IS ROUNDING UP ALL OF THE SMALLER ANIMALS. RABBITS, MICE, EVEN THE GREEN INSECTS.
DO YOU REALLY THINK BEAST BOY DID THIS? THAT'S ALL THE NEWS IS SAYING. ALL THE PARENTS... IT'S LIKE THEY WANT TO LYNCH HIM.
GARFIELD WOULD NEVER INTENTIONALLY HARM ANYONE.
I KNOW THAT, BUT... YOU HAVE TO ADMIT. THIS LOOKS BAD.
WHAT DID YOU DO TO THEM?
X'HAL.
WHAT DID THAT GREEN TITAN DO TO OUR KIDS?
WHERE'S MY SON?!
WE ARE TRYING TO PROTECT THEM. I REALIZE YOU MUST BE EXTREMELY WORRIED ABOUT YOUR CHILDREN BUT WE'RE DOING OUR BEST --
WHERE'S BEAST BOY? WHERE'S THAT MONSTER?
GIVE HIM TO US!
ALL OF YOU...

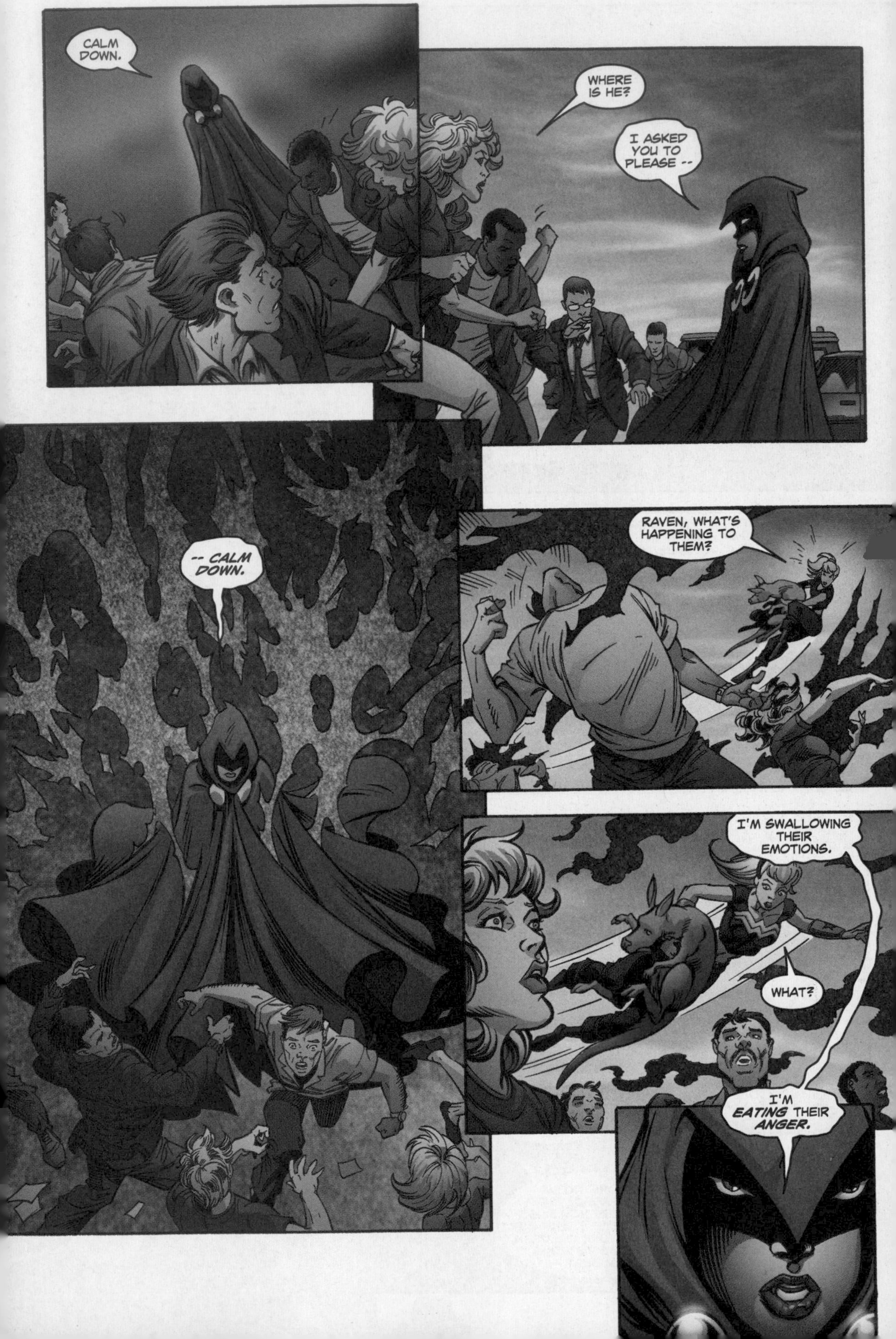
CALM DOWN.
WHERE IS HE?
I ASKED YOU TO PLEASE --
-- CALM DOWN.
RAVEN, WHAT'S HAPPENING TO THEM?
I'M SWALLOWING THEIR EMOTIONS.
WHAT?
I'M EATING THEIR ANGER.

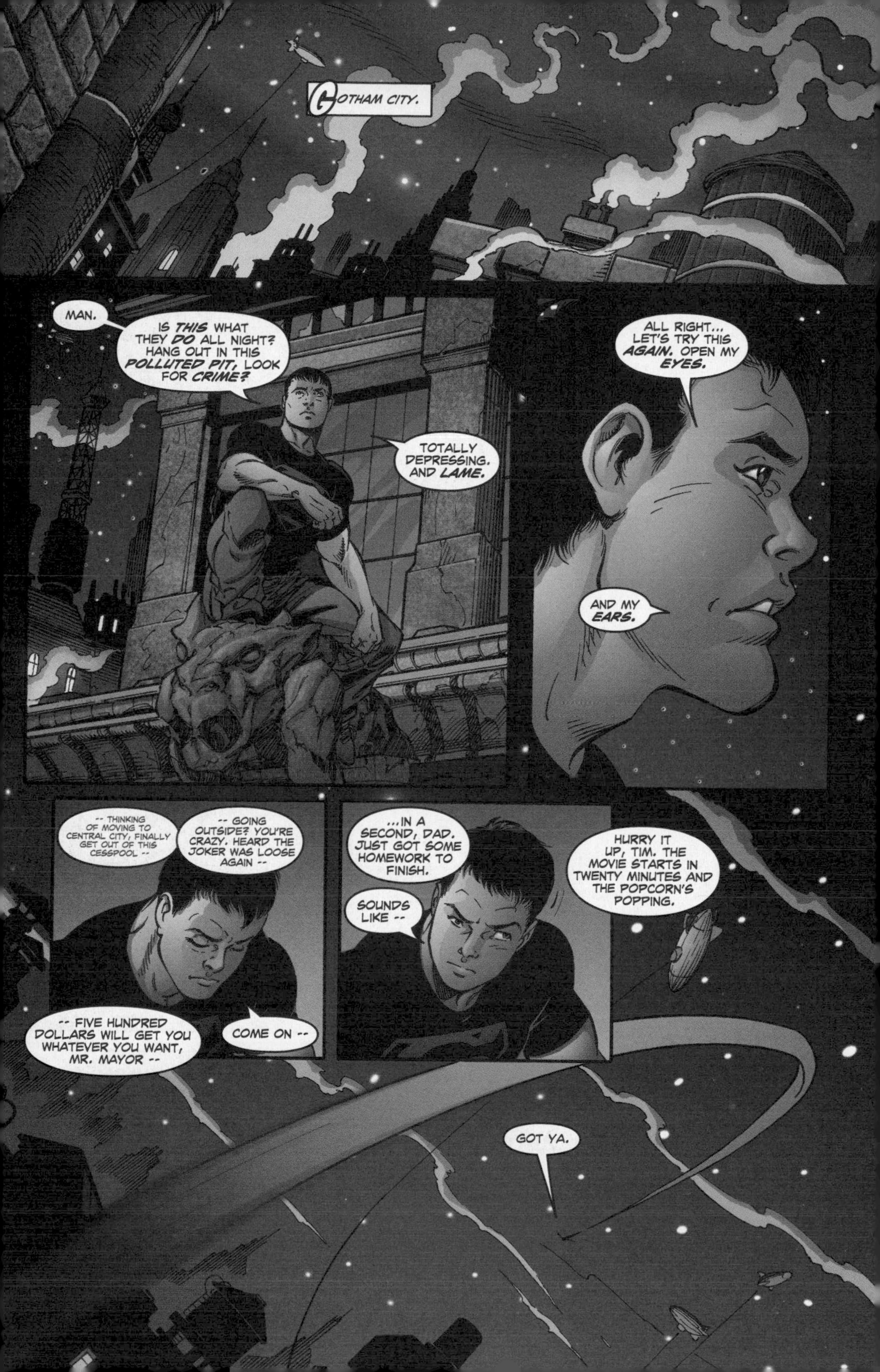
GOTHAM CITY.
MAN.
IS THIS WHAT THEY DO ALL NIGHT? HANG OUT IN THIS POLLUTED PIT, LOOK FOR CRIME?
TOTALLY DEPRESSING. AND LAME.
ALL RIGHT... LET'S TRY THIS AGAIN. OPEN MY EYES.
AND MY EARS.
-- THINKING OF MOVING TO CENTRAL CITY, FINALLY GET OUT OF THIS CESSPOOL --
-- GOING OUTSIDE? YOU'RE CRAZY. HEARD THE JOKER WAS LOOSE AGAIN --
-- FIVE HUNDRED DOLLARS WILL GET YOU WHATEVER YOU WANT, MR. MAYOR --
COME ON --
...IN A SECOND, DAD. JUST GOT SOME HOMEWORK TO FINISH.
SOUNDS LIKE --
HURRY IT UP, TIM. THE MOVIE STARTS IN TWENTY MINUTES AND THE POPCORN'S POPPING.
GOT YA.

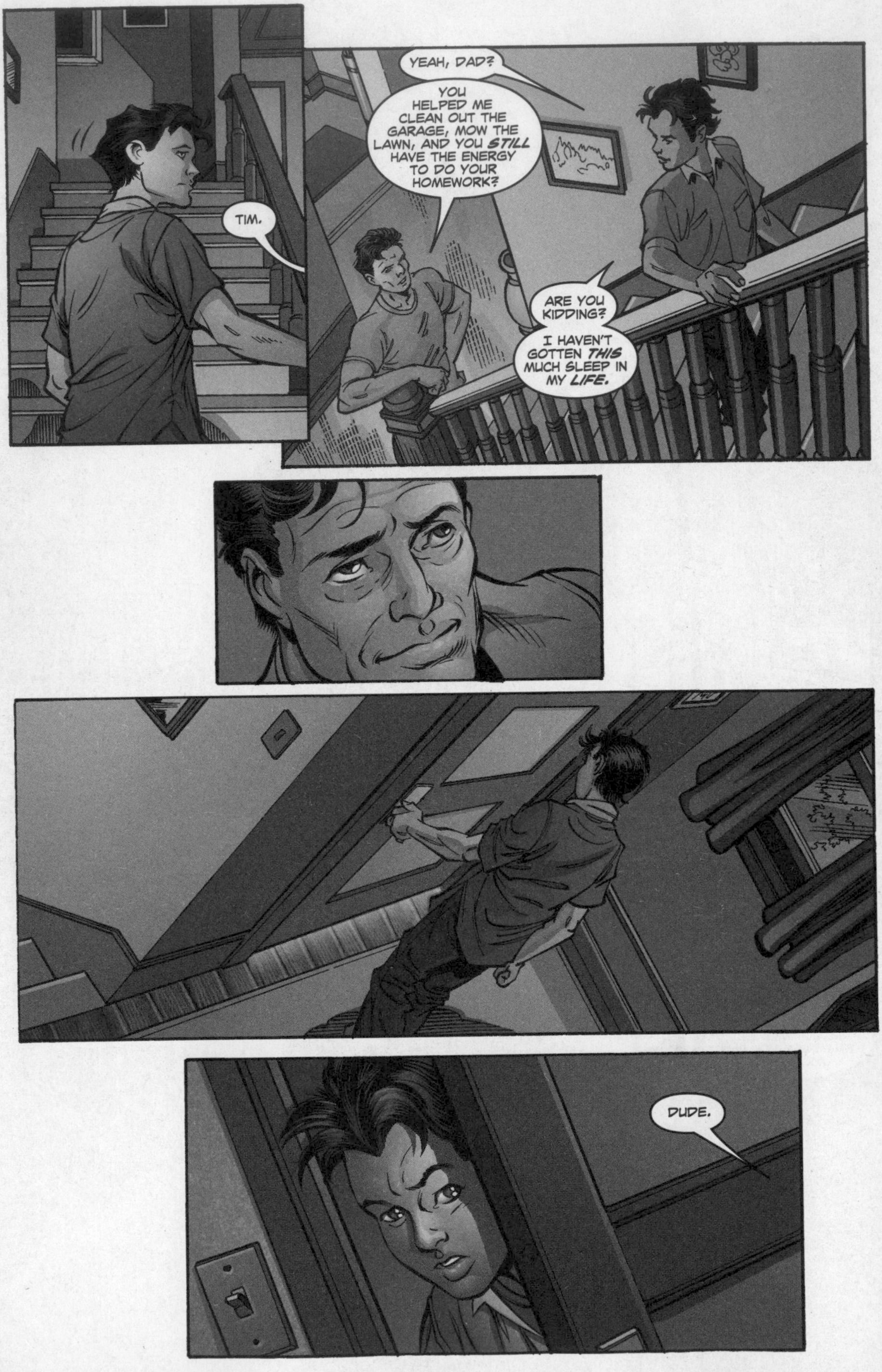
TIM.
YEAH, DAD?
YOU HELPED ME CLEAN OUT THE GARAGE, MOW THE LAWN, AND YOU STILL HAVE THE ENERGY TO DO YOUR HOMEWORK?
ARE YOU KIDDING?
I HAVEN'T GOTTEN THIS MUCH SLEEP IN MY LIFE.
DUDE.

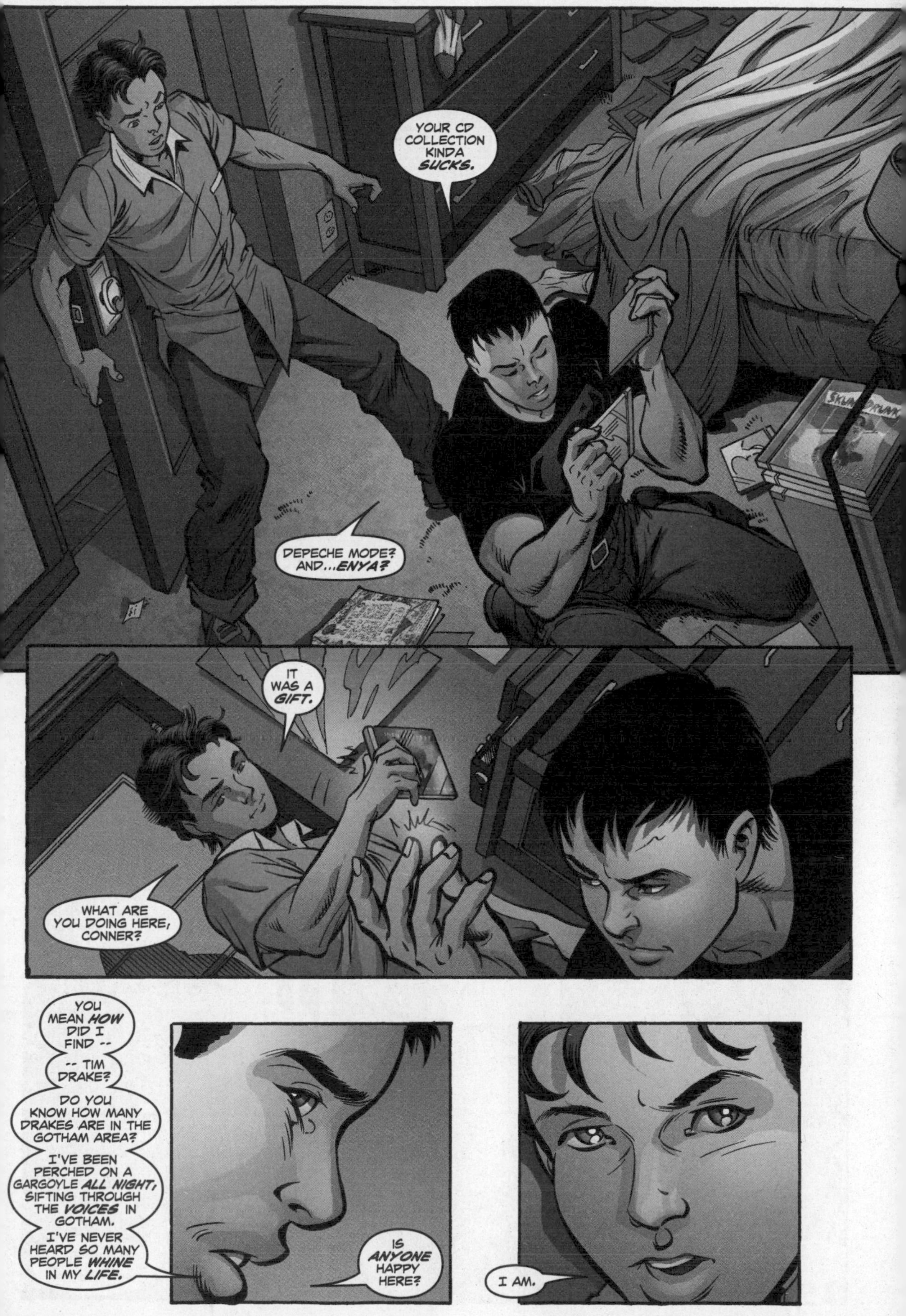

YOUR CD COLLECTION KINDA SUCKS.
DEPECHE MODE? AND...ENYA?
IT WAS A GIFT.
WHAT ARE YOU DOING HERE, CONNER?
YOU MEAN HOW DID I FIND --
-- TIM DRAKE?
DO YOU KNOW HOW MANY DRAKES ARE IN THE GOTHAM AREA?
I'VE BEEN PERCHED ON A GARGOYLE ALL NIGHT, SIFTING THROUGH THE VOICES IN GOTHAM.
I'VE NEVER HEARD SO MANY PEOPLE WHINE IN MY LIFE.
IS ANYONE HAPPY HERE?
I AM.

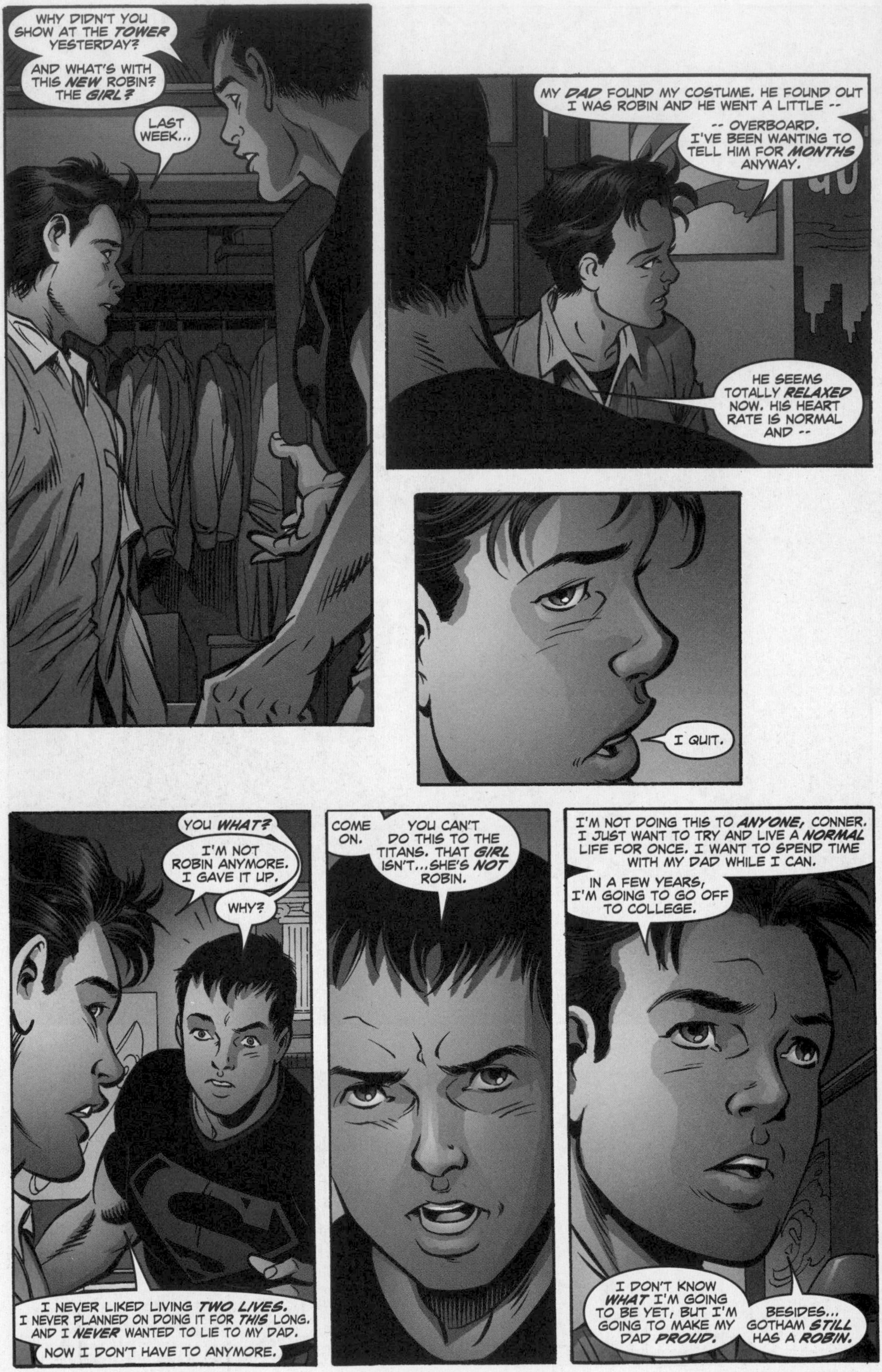
WHY DIDN'T YOU SHOW AT THE TOWER YESTERDAY?
AND WHAT'S WITH THIS NEW ROBIN? THE GIRL?
LAST WEEK...
MY DAD FOUND MY COSTUME. HE FOUND OUT I WAS ROBIN AND HE WENT A LITTLE --
-- OVERBOARD. I'VE BEEN WANTING TO TELL HIM FOR MONTHS ANYWAY.
HE SEEMS TOTALLY RELAXED NOW. HIS HEART RATE IS NORMAL AND --
I QUIT.
YOU WHAT?
I'M NOT ROBIN ANYMORE. I GAVE IT UP.
WHY?
I NEVER LIKED LIVING TWO LIVES. I NEVER PLANNED ON DOING IT FOR THIS LONG. AND I NEVER WANTED TO LIE TO MY DAD.
NOW I DON'T HAVE TO ANYMORE.
COME ON.
YOU CAN'T DO THIS TO THE TITANS. THAT GIRL ISN'T...SHE'S NOT ROBIN.
I'M NOT DOING THIS TO ANYONE, CONNER. I JUST WANT TO TRY AND LIVE A NORMAL LIFE FOR ONCE. I WANT TO SPEND TIME WITH MY DAD WHILE I CAN.
IN A FEW YEARS, I'M GOING TO GO OFF TO COLLEGE.
I DON'T KNOW WHAT I'M GOING TO BE YET, BUT I'M GOING TO MAKE MY DAD PROUD.
BESIDES... GOTHAM STILL HAS A ROBIN.

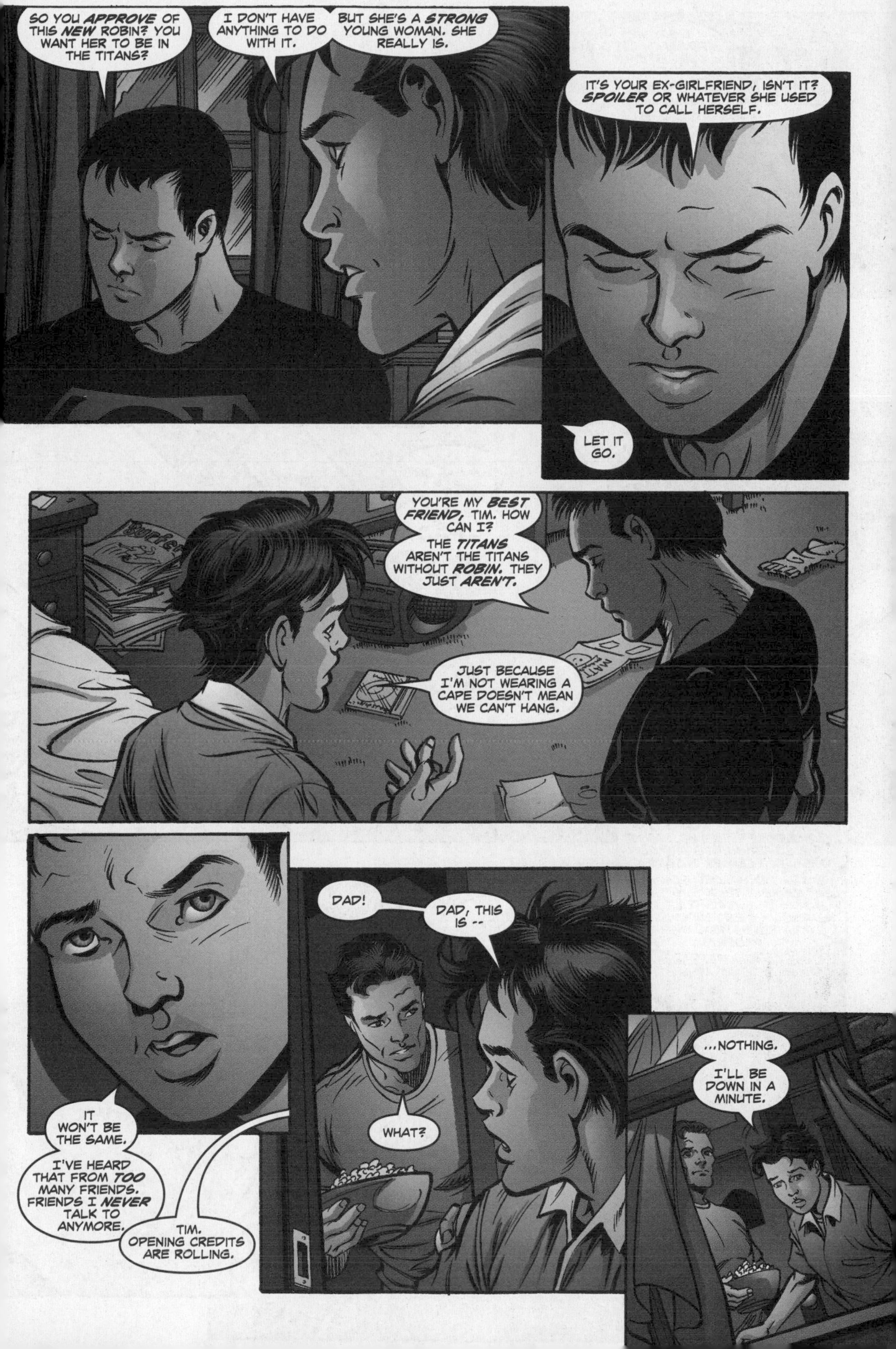

SO YOU APPROVE OF THIS NEW ROBIN? YOU WANT HER TO BE IN THE TITANS?
I DON'T HAVE ANYTHING TO DO WITH IT.
BUT SHE'S A STRONG YOUNG WOMAN. SHE REALLY IS.
IT'S YOUR EX-GIRLFRIEND, ISN'T IT? SPOILER OR WHATEVER SHE USED TO CALL HERSELF.
LET IT GO.
YOU'RE MY BEST FRIEND, TIM. HOW CAN I?
THE TITANS AREN'T THE TITANS WITHOUT ROBIN. THEY JUST AREN'T.
JUST BECAUSE I'M NOT WEARING A CAPE DOESN'T MEAN WE CAN'T HANG.
IT WON'T BE THE SAME.
I'VE HEARD THAT FROM TOO MANY FRIENDS. FRIENDS I NEVER TALK TO ANYMORE.
TIM. OPENING CREDITS ARE ROLLING.
DAD!
DAD, THIS IS --
WHAT?
...NOTHING.
I'LL BE DOWN IN A MINUTE.

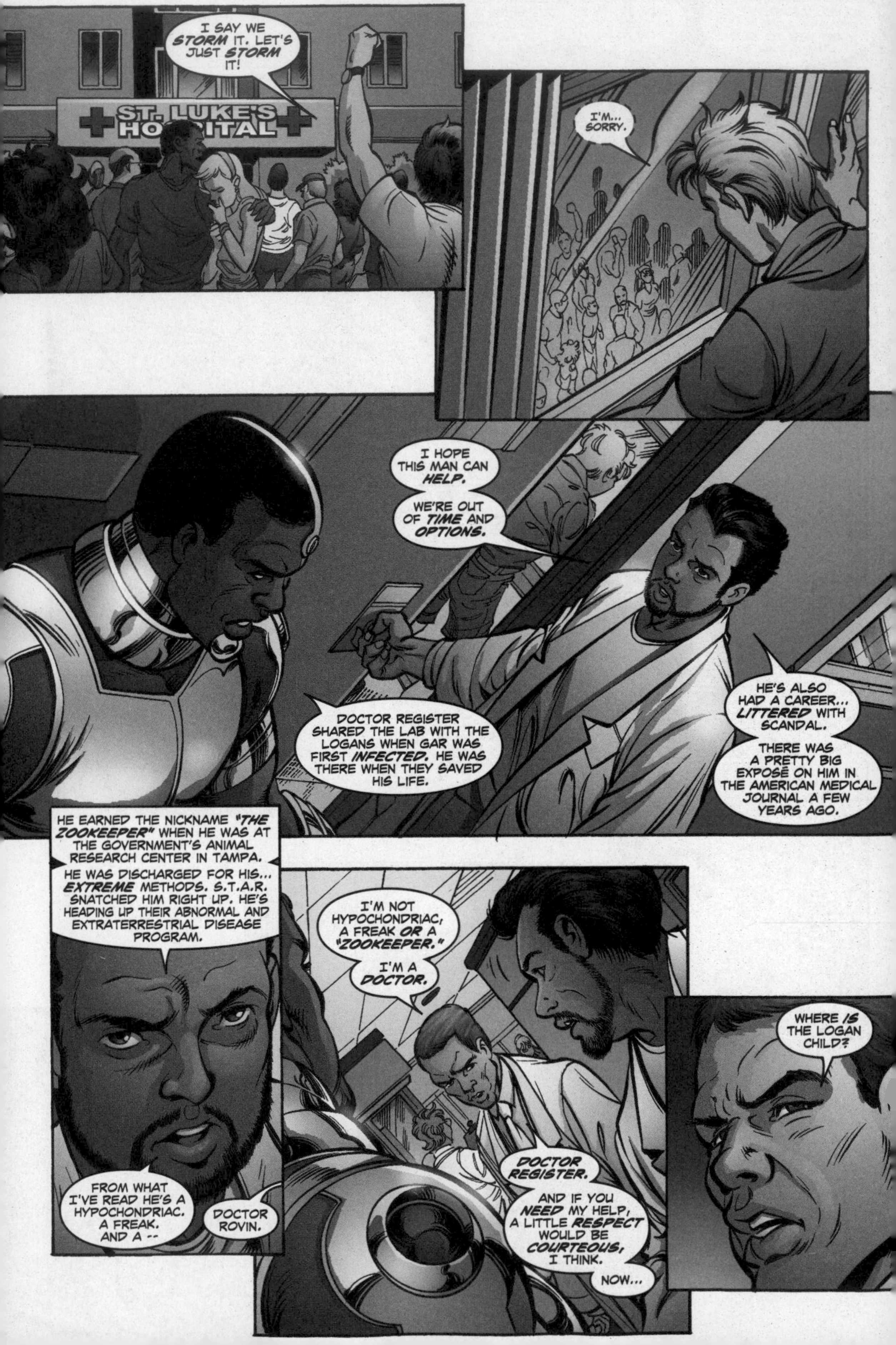

I SAY WE STORM IT. LET'S JUST STORM IT!
ST. LUKE'S HOSPITAL
I'M... SORRY.
I HOPE THIS MAN CAN HELP.
WE'RE OUT OF TIME AND OPTIONS.
DOCTOR REGISTER SHARED THE LAB WITH THE LOGANS WHEN GAR WAS FIRST INFECTED. HE WAS THERE WHEN THEY SAVED HIS LIFE.
HE'S ALSO HAD A CAREER... LITTERED WITH SCANDAL.
THERE WAS A PRETTY BIG EXPOSÉ ON HIM IN THE AMERICAN MEDICAL JOURNAL A FEW YEARS AGO.
HE EARNED THE NICKNAME "THE ZOOKEEPER" WHEN HE WAS AT THE GOVERNMENT'S ANIMAL RESEARCH CENTER IN TAMPA.
HE WAS DISCHARGED FOR HIS... EXTREME METHODS. S.T.A.R. SNATCHED HIM RIGHT UP. HE'S HEADING UP THEIR ABNORMAL AND EXTRATERRESTRIAL DISEASE PROGRAM.
FROM WHAT I'VE READ HE'S A HYPOCHONDRIAC. A FREAK. AND A --
DOCTOR ROVIN.
I'M NOT HYPOCHONDRIAC, A FREAK OR A "ZOOKEEPER."
I'M A DOCTOR.
DOCTOR REGISTER.
AND IF YOU NEED MY HELP, A LITTLE RESPECT WOULD BE COURTEOUS, I THINK.
NOW...
WHERE IS THE LOGAN CHILD?

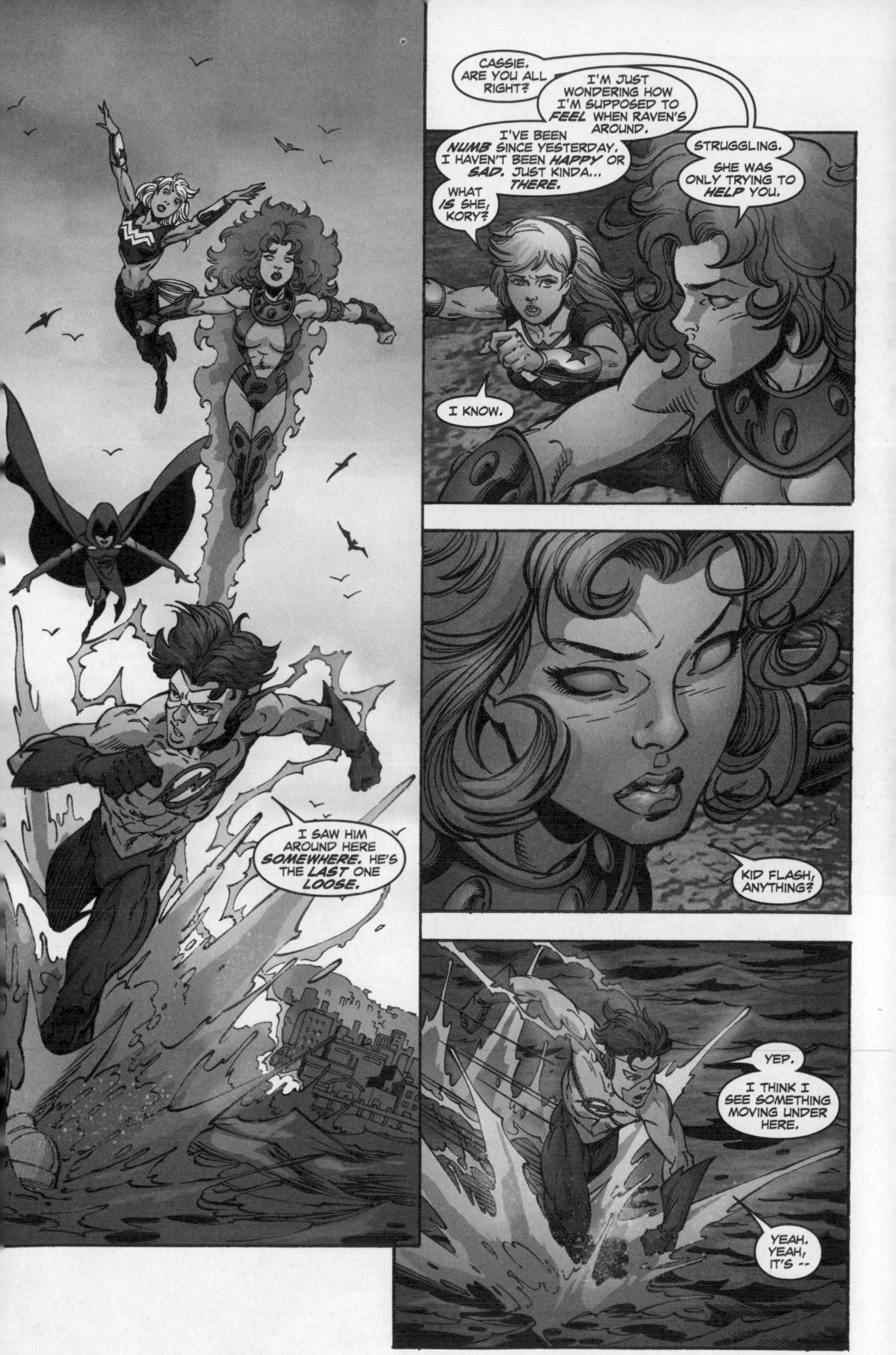

I SAW HIM AROUND HERE SOMEWHERE. HE'S THE LAST ONE LOOSE.
CASSIE. ARE YOU ALL RIGHT?
I'M JUST WONDERING HOW I'M SUPPOSED TO FEEL WHEN RAVEN'S AROUND.
I'VE BEEN NUMB SINCE YESTERDAY. I HAVEN'T BEEN HAPPY OR SAD. JUST KINDA... THERE.
WHAT IS SHE, KORY?
STRUGGLING.
SHE WAS ONLY TRYING TO HELP YOU.
I KNOW.
KID FLASH, ANYTHING?
YEP.
I THINK I SEE SOMETHING MOVING UNDER HERE.
YEAH. YEAH, IT'S --

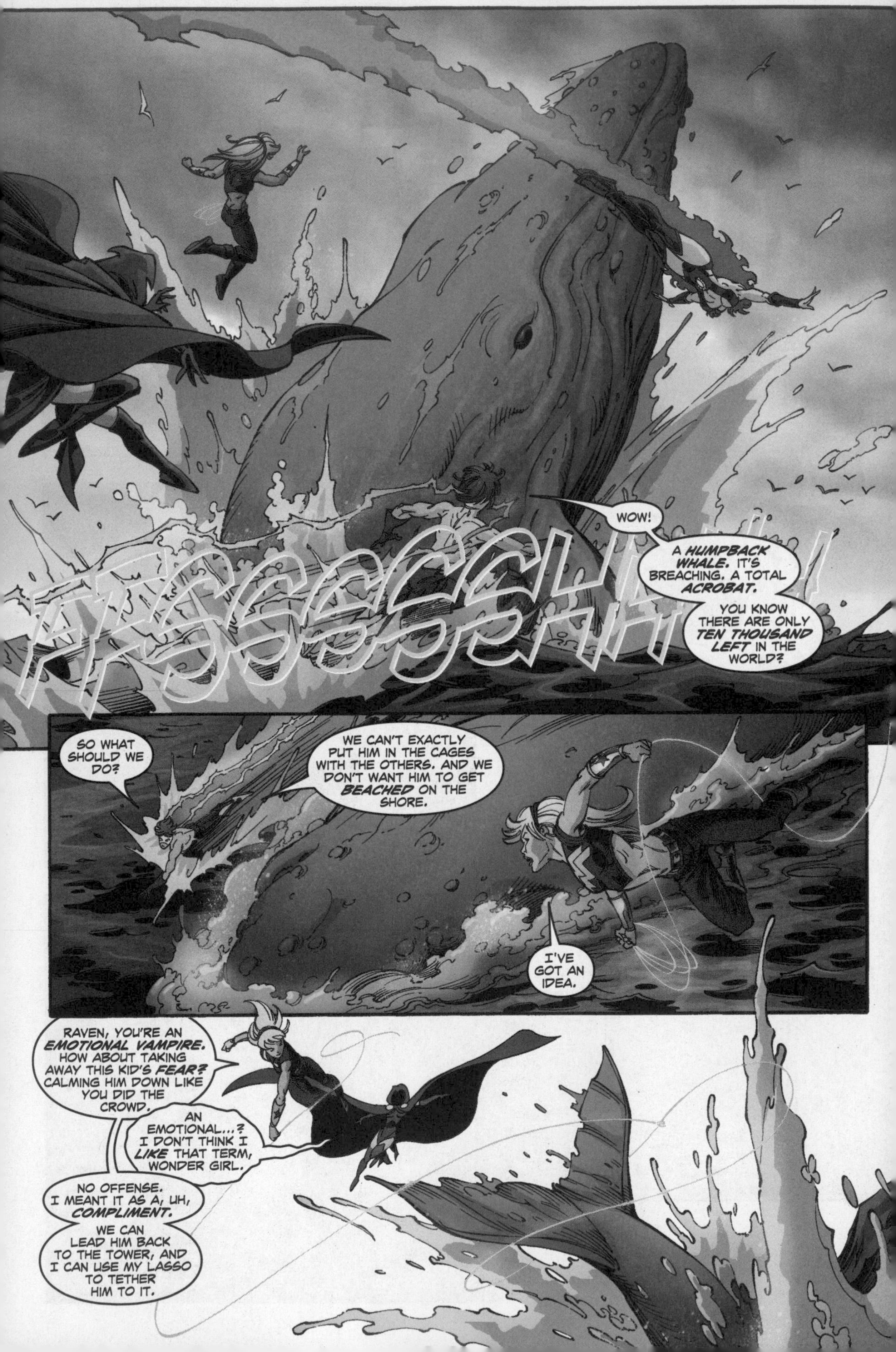
WOW!
A HUMPBACK WHALE. IT'S BREACHING. A TOTAL ACROBAT.
YOU KNOW THERE ARE ONLY TEN THOUSAND LEFT IN THE WORLD?
FSSSSSHHH
SO WHAT SHOULD WE DO?
WE CAN'T EXACTLY PUT HIM IN THE CAGES WITH THE OTHERS. AND WE DON'T WANT HIM TO GET BEACHED ON THE SHORE.
I'VE GOT AN IDEA.
RAVEN, YOU'RE AN EMOTIONAL VAMPIRE. HOW ABOUT TAKING AWAY THIS KID'S FEAR? CALMING HIM DOWN LIKE YOU DID THE CROWD.
AN EMOTIONAL...? I DON'T THINK I LIKE THAT TERM, WONDER GIRL.
NO OFFENSE. I MEANT IT AS A, UH, COMPLIMENT.
WE CAN LEAD HIM BACK TO THE TOWER, AND I CAN USE MY LASSO TO TETHER HIM TO IT.

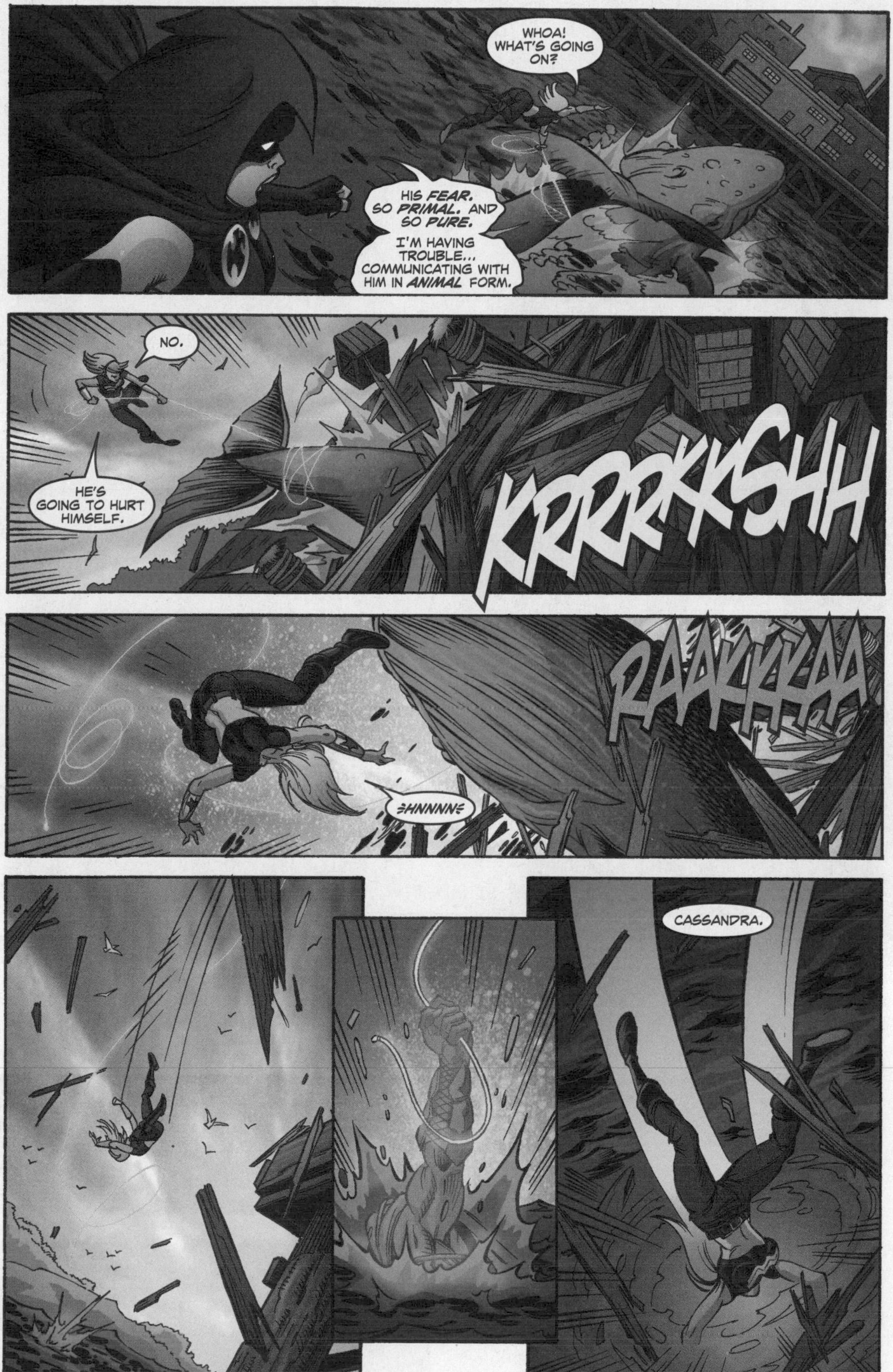
WHOA! WHAT'S GOING ON?
HIS FEAR. SO PRIMAL. AND SO PURE.
I'M HAVING TROUBLE... COMMUNICATING WITH HIM IN ANIMAL FORM.
NO.
HE'S GOING TO HURT HIMSELF.
KRRRKSHH
RAAKKKAA
HNNNN
CASSANDRA.

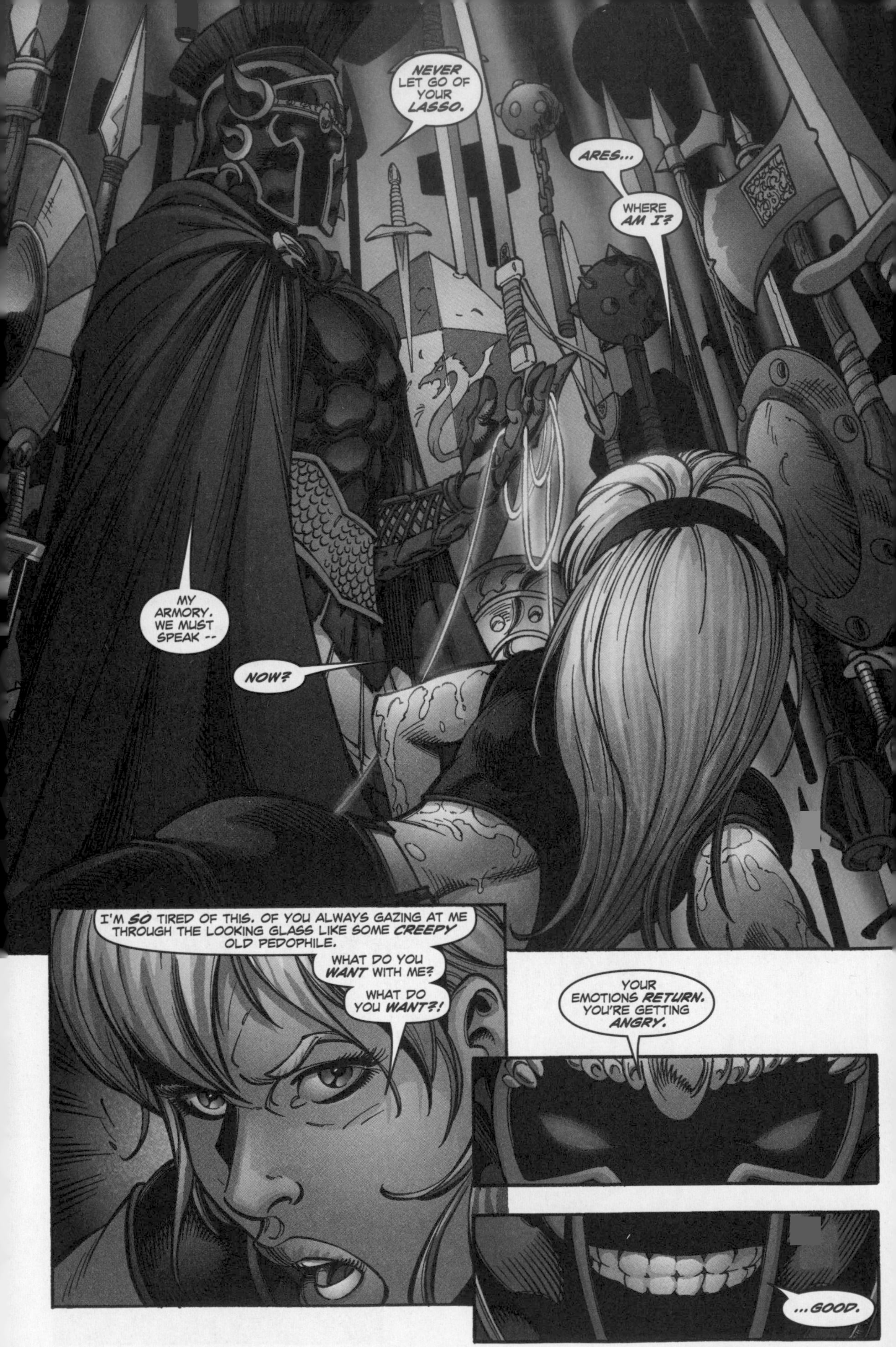
NEVER LET GO OF YOUR LASSO.
ARES...
WHERE AM I?
MY ARMORY. WE MUST SPEAK --
NOW?
I'M SO TIRED OF THIS. OF YOU ALWAYS GAZING AT ME THROUGH THE LOOKING GLASS LIKE SOME CREEPY OLD PEDOPHILE.
WHAT DO YOU WANT WITH ME?
WHAT DO YOU WANT?!
YOUR EMOTIONS RETURN. YOU'RE GETTING ANGRY.
...GOOD.

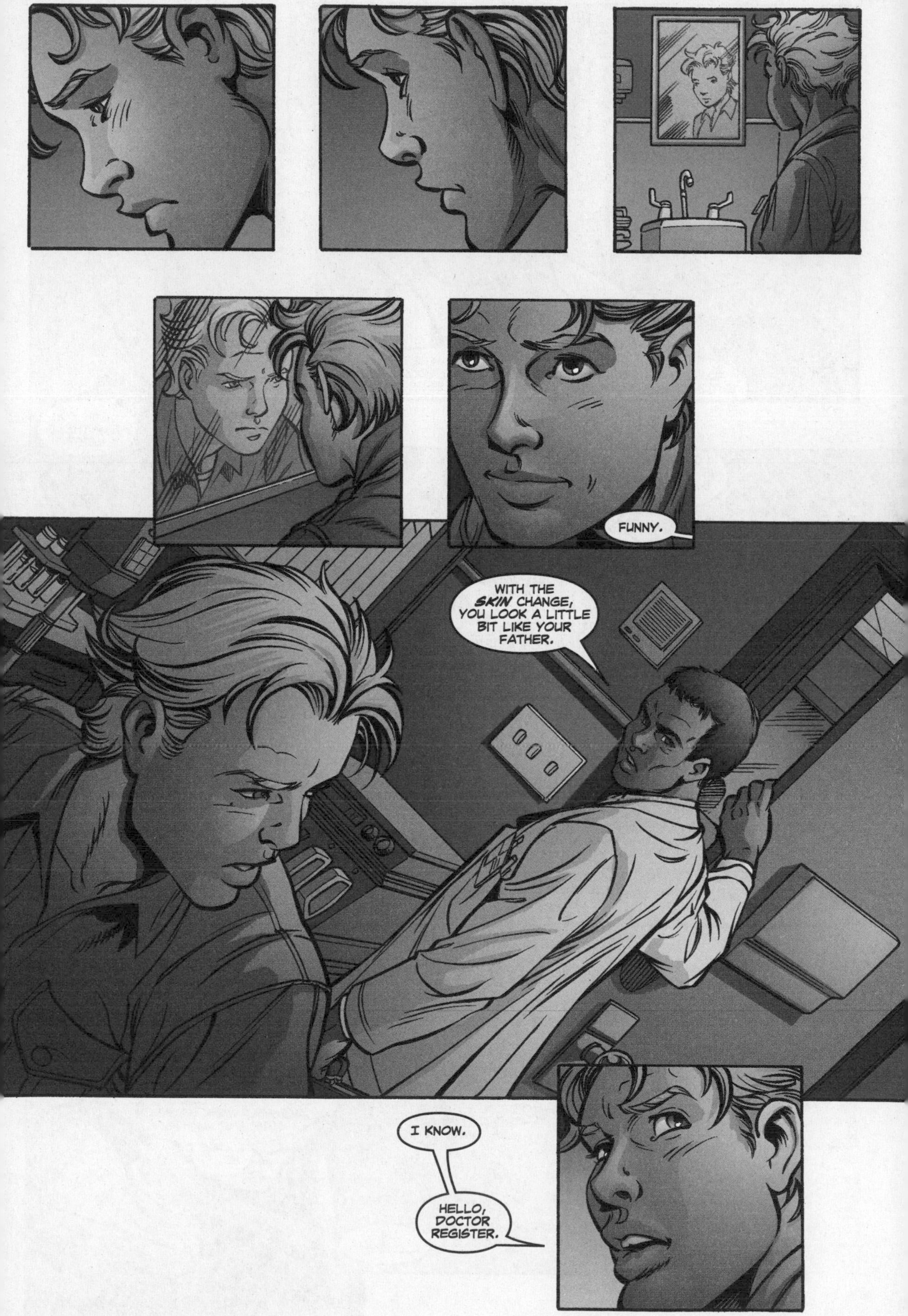
FUNNY.
WITH THE SKIN CHANGE, YOU LOOK A LITTLE BIT LIKE YOUR FATHER.
I KNOW.
HELLO, DOCTOR REGISTER.

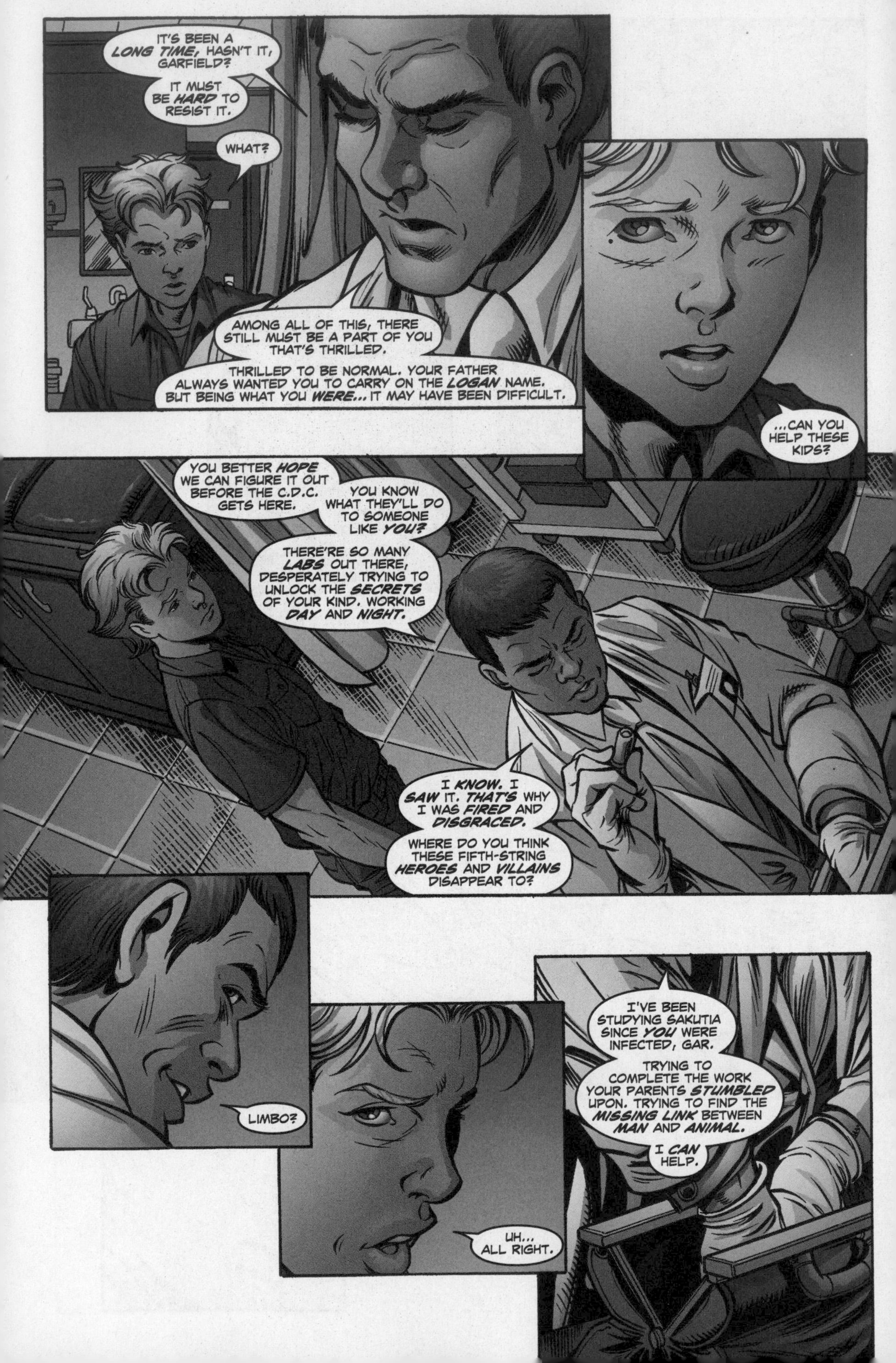
IT'S BEEN A LONG TIME, HASN'T IT, GARFIELD?
IT MUST BE HARD TO RESIST IT.
WHAT?
AMONG ALL OF THIS, THERE STILL MUST BE A PART OF YOU THAT'S THRILLED.
THRILLED TO BE NORMAL. YOUR FATHER ALWAYS WANTED YOU TO CARRY ON THE LOGAN NAME. BUT BEING WHAT YOU WERE... IT MAY HAVE BEEN DIFFICULT.
...CAN YOU HELP THESE KIDS?
YOU BETTER HOPE WE CAN FIGURE IT OUT BEFORE THE C.D.C. GETS HERE.
YOU KNOW WHAT THEY'LL DO TO SOMEONE LIKE YOU?
THERE'RE SO MANY LABS OUT THERE, DESPERATELY TRYING TO UNLOCK THE SECRETS OF YOUR KIND. WORKING DAY AND NIGHT.
I KNOW. I SAW IT. THAT'S WHY I WAS FIRED AND DISGRACED.
WHERE DO YOU THINK THESE FIFTH-STRING HEROES AND VILLAINS DISAPPEAR TO?
LIMBO?
UH... ALL RIGHT.
I'VE BEEN STUDYING SAKUTIA SINCE YOU WERE INFECTED, GAR.
TRYING TO COMPLETE THE WORK YOUR PARENTS STUMBLED UPON. TRYING TO FIND THE MISSING LINK BETWEEN MAN AND ANIMAL.
I CAN HELP.

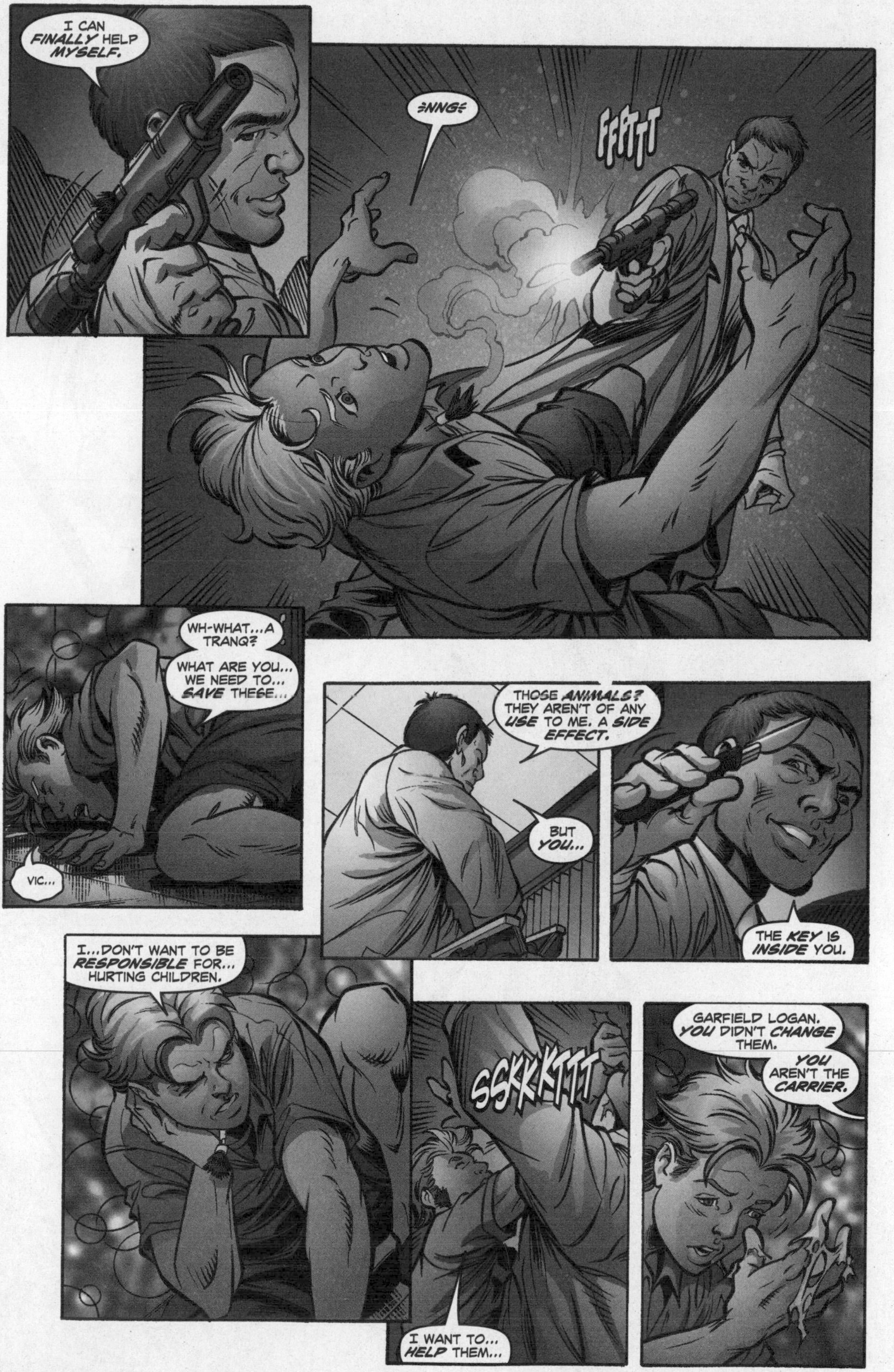
I CAN FINALLY HELP MYSELF.
NNG
FFFTTT
WH-WHAT...A TRANQ?
WHAT ARE YOU... WE NEED TO... SAVE THESE...
VIC...
THOSE ANIMALS? THEY AREN'T OF ANY USE TO ME. A SIDE EFFECT.
BUT YOU...
THE KEY IS INSIDE YOU.
I...DON'T WANT TO BE RESPONSIBLE FOR... HURTING CHILDREN.
SSKKKTTT
I WANT TO... HELP THEM...
GARFIELD LOGAN. YOU DIDN'T CHANGE THEM.
YOU AREN'T THE CARRIER.

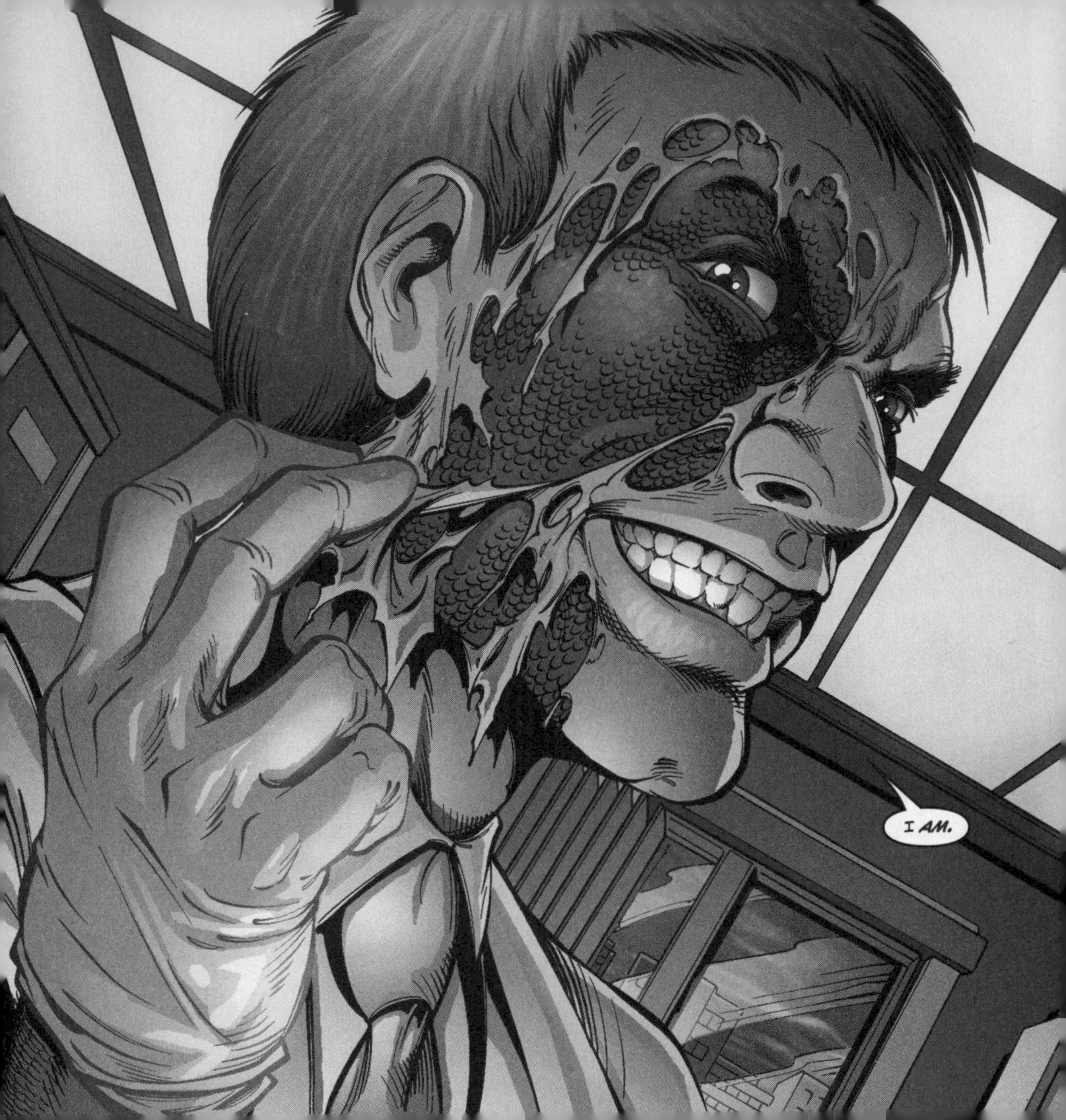
I AM.

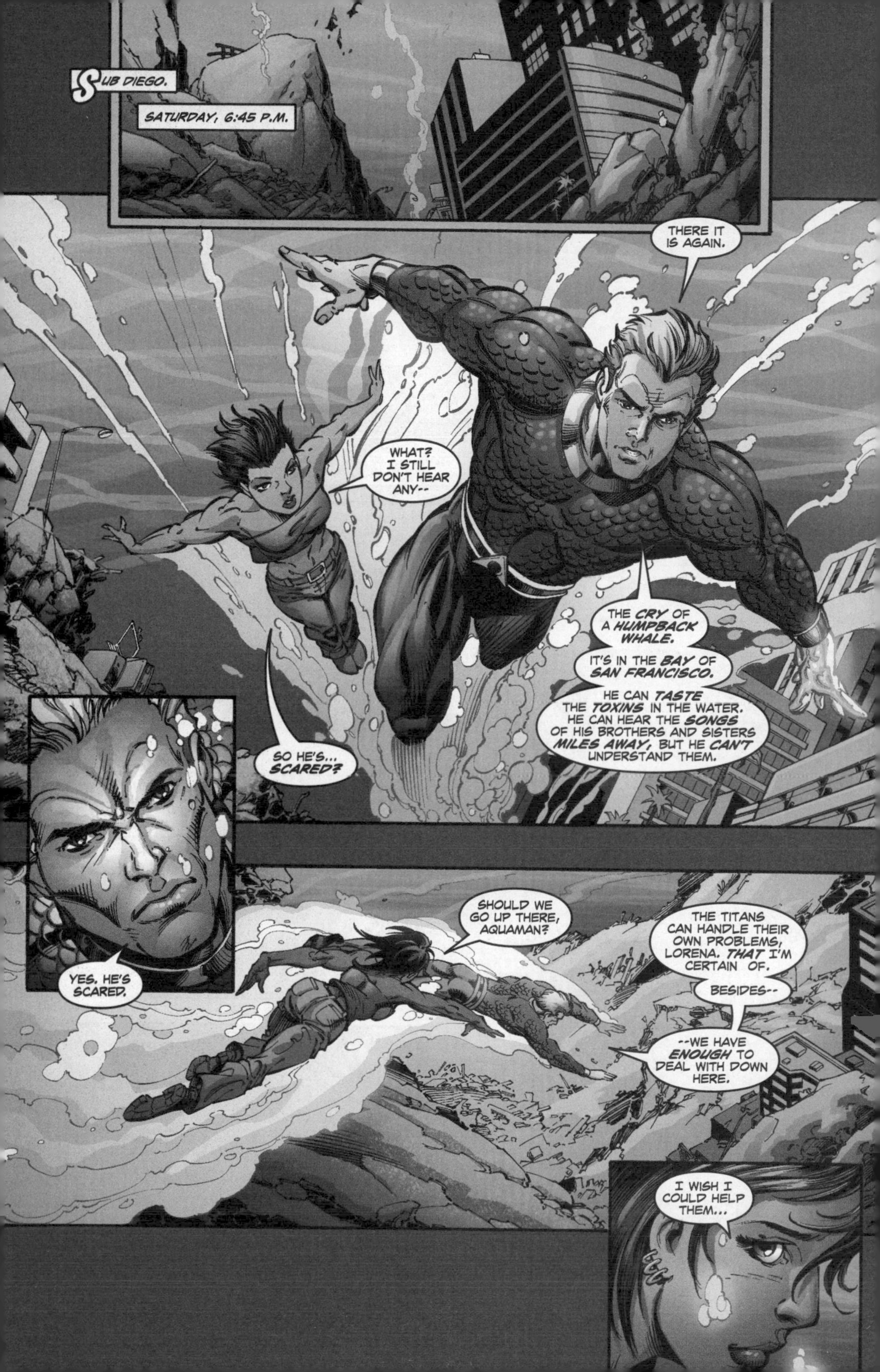
SUB DIEGO.
SATURDAY, 6:45 P.M.
THERE IT IS AGAIN.
WHAT? I STILL DON'T HEAR ANY--
THE CRY OF A HUMPBACK WHALE.
IT'S IN THE BAY OF SAN FRANCISCO.
HE CAN TASTE THE TOXINS IN THE WATER. HE CAN HEAR THE SONGS OF HIS BROTHERS AND SISTERS MILES AWAY, BUT HE CAN'T UNDERSTAND THEM.
SO HE'S... SCARED?
YES. HE'S SCARED.
SHOULD WE GO UP THERE, AQUAMAN?
THE TITANS CAN HANDLE THEIR OWN PROBLEMS, LORENA. THAT I'M CERTAIN OF.
BESIDES--
--WE HAVE ENOUGH TO DEAL WITH DOWN HERE.
I WISH I COULD HELP THEM...

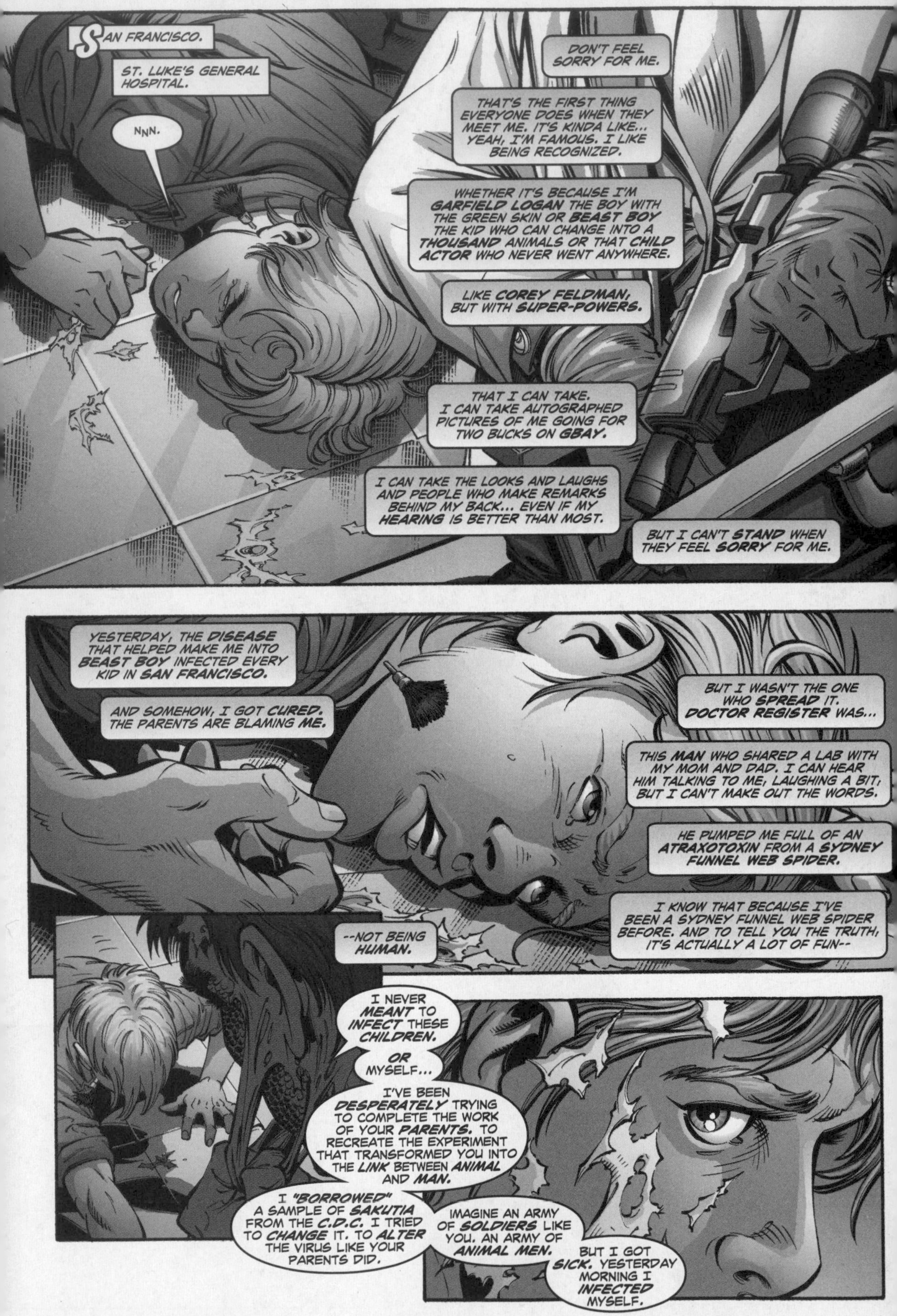
SAN FRANCISCO.
ST. LUKE'S GENERAL HOSPITAL.
NNN.
DON'T FEEL SORRY FOR ME.
THAT'S THE FIRST THING EVERYONE DOES WHEN THEY MEET ME. IT'S KINDA LIKE... YEAH, I'M FAMOUS. I LIKE BEING RECOGNIZED.
WHETHER IT'S BECAUSE I'M GARFIELD LOGAN THE BOY WITH THE GREEN SKIN OR BEAST BOY THE KID WHO CAN CHANGE INTO A THOUSAND ANIMALS OR THAT CHILD ACTOR WHO NEVER WENT ANYWHERE.
LIKE COREY FELDMAN, BUT WITH SUPER-POWERS.
THAT I CAN TAKE. I CAN TAKE AUTOGRAPHED PICTURES OF ME GOING FOR TWO BUCKS ON GBAY.
I CAN TAKE THE LOOKS AND LAUGHS AND PEOPLE WHO MAKE REMARKS BEHIND MY BACK... EVEN IF MY HEARING IS BETTER THAN MOST.
BUT I CAN'T STAND WHEN THEY FEEL SORRY FOR ME.
YESTERDAY, THE DISEASE THAT HELPED MAKE ME INTO BEAST BOY INFECTED EVERY KID IN SAN FRANCISCO.
AND SOMEHOW, I GOT CURED. THE PARENTS ARE BLAMING ME.
BUT I WASN'T THE ONE WHO SPREAD IT. DOCTOR REGISTER WAS...
THIS MAN WHO SHARED A LAB WITH MY MOM AND DAD. I CAN HEAR HIM TALKING TO ME, LAUGHING A BIT, BUT I CAN'T MAKE OUT THE WORDS.
HE PUMPED ME FULL OF AN ATRAXOTOXIN FROM A SYDNEY FUNNEL WEB SPIDER.
I KNOW THAT BECAUSE I'VE BEEN A SYDNEY FUNNEL WEB SPIDER BEFORE. AND TO TELL YOU THE TRUTH, IT'S ACTUALLY A LOT OF FUN--
--NOT BEING HUMAN.
I NEVER MEANT TO INFECT THESE CHILDREN.
OR MYSELF...
I'VE BEEN DESPERATELY TRYING TO COMPLETE THE WORK OF YOUR PARENTS. TO RECREATE THE EXPERIMENT THAT TRANSFORMED YOU INTO THE LINK BETWEEN ANIMAL AND MAN.
I "BORROWED" A SAMPLE OF SAKUTIA FROM THE C.D.C. I TRIED TO CHANGE IT. TO ALTER THE VIRUS LIKE YOUR PARENTS DID.
IMAGINE AN ARMY OF SOLDIERS LIKE YOU. AN ARMY OF ANIMAL MEN.
BUT I GOT SICK. YESTERDAY MORNING I INFECTED MYSELF.

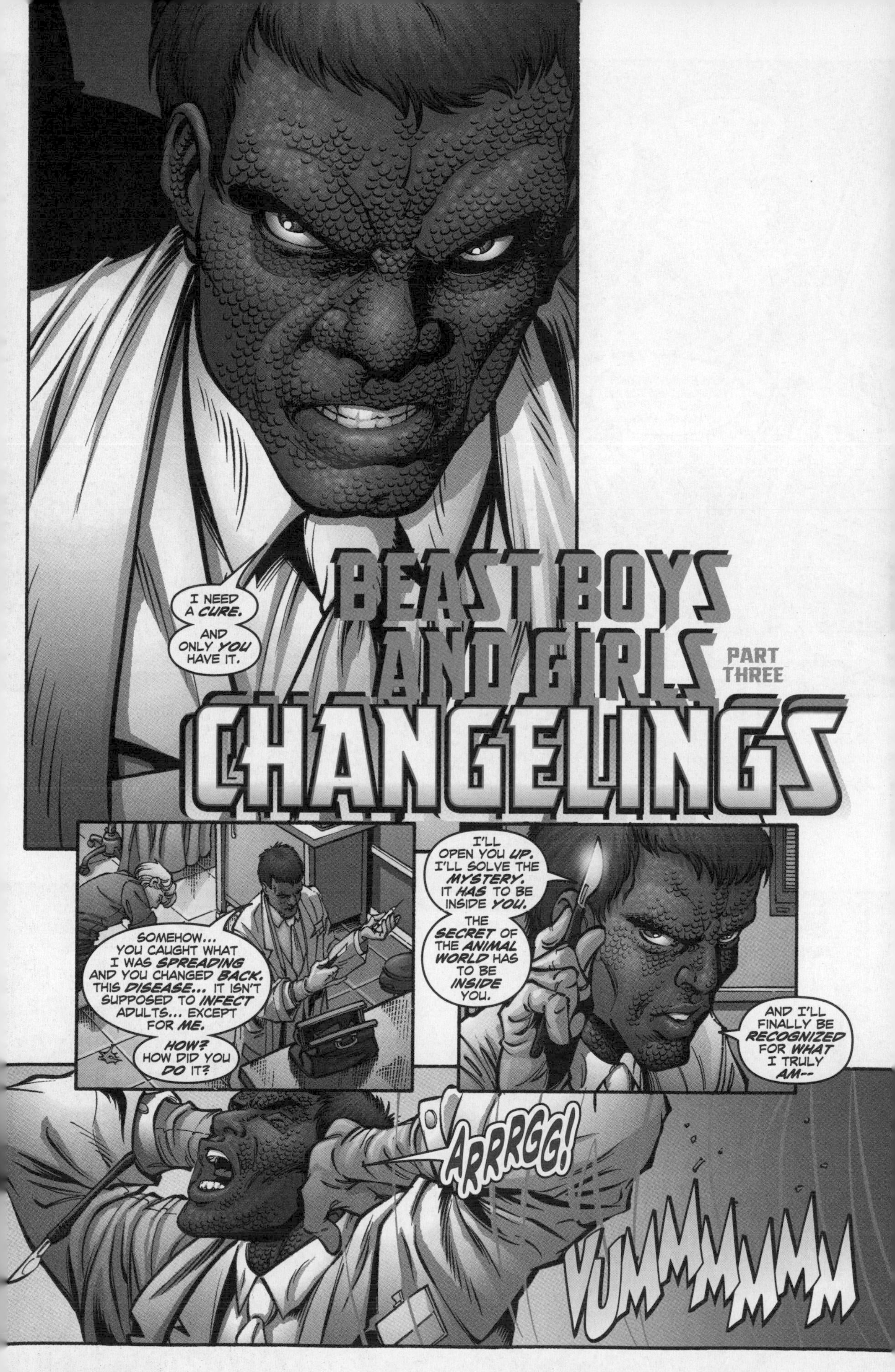
I NEED A CURE.
AND ONLY YOU HAVE IT.
BEAST BOYS AND GIRLS
PART THREE
CHANGELINGS
SOMEHOW... YOU CAUGHT WHAT I WAS SPREADING AND YOU CHANGED BACK. THIS DISEASE... IT ISN'T SUPPOSED TO INFECT ADULTS... EXCEPT FOR ME.
HOW? HOW DID YOU DO IT?
I'LL OPEN YOU UP. I'LL SOLVE THE MYSTERY. IT HAS TO BE INSIDE YOU.
THE SECRET OF THE ANIMAL WORLD HAS TO BE INSIDE YOU.
AND I'LL FINALLY BE RECOGNIZED FOR WHAT I TRULY AM--
ARRRGG!
VUMMMMMM

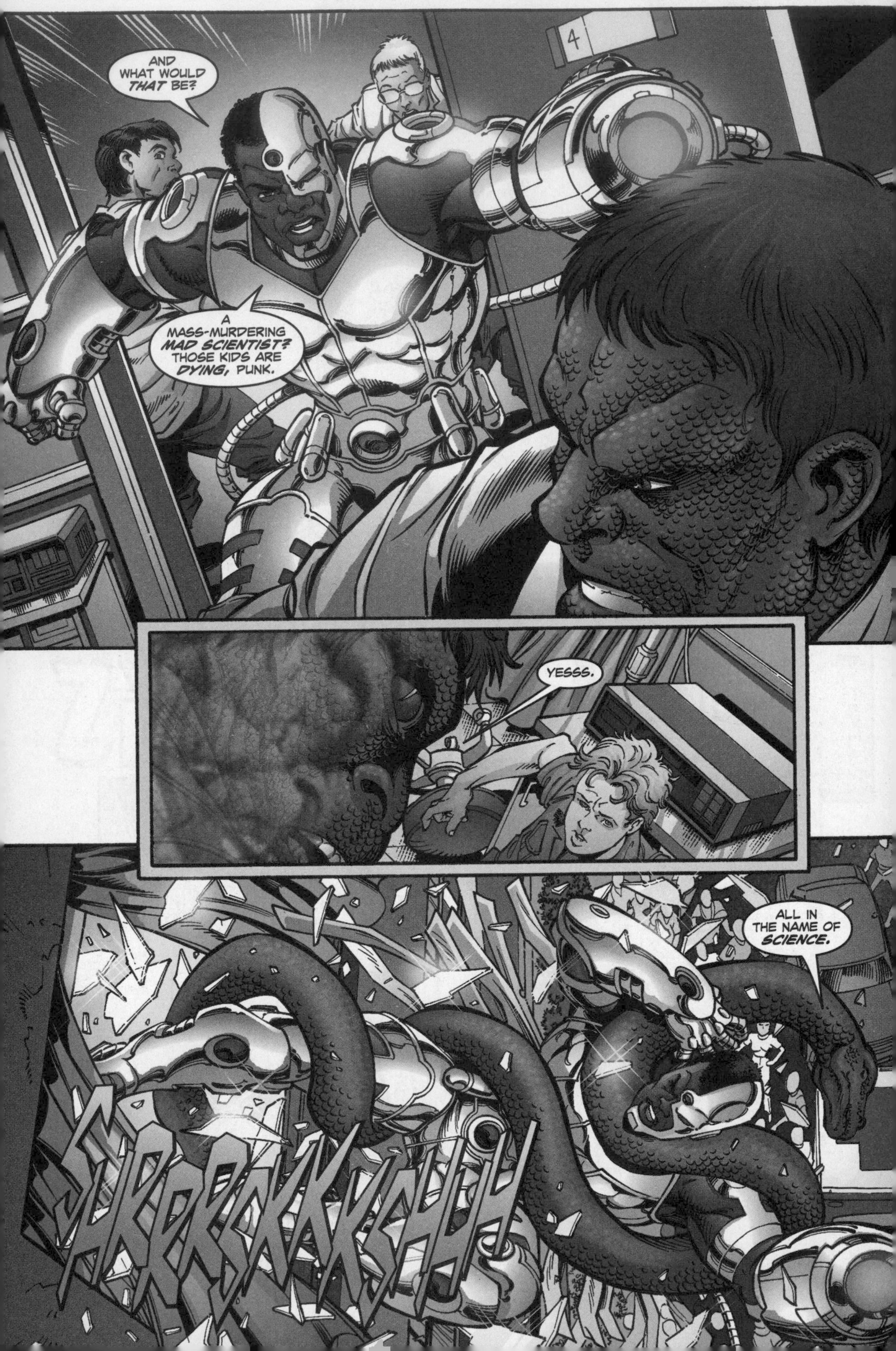
AND WHAT WOULD *THAT* BE?
A MASS-MURDERING *MAD SCIENTIST?* THOSE KIDS ARE *DYING*, PUNK.
YESSS.
ALL IN THE NAME OF *SCIENCE.*
SKRRRKKKSHH

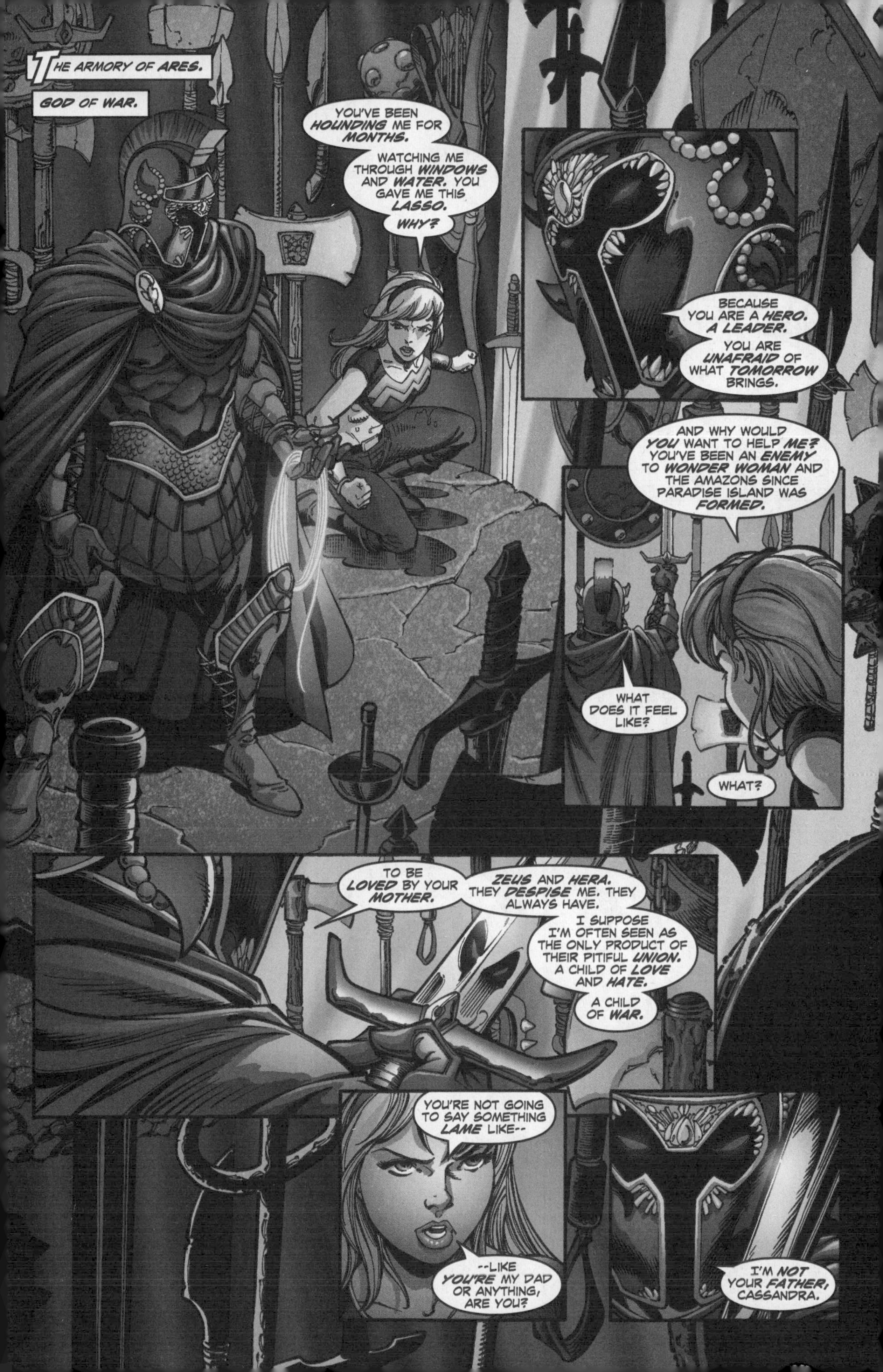
THE ARMORY OF ARES.
GOD OF WAR.
YOU'VE BEEN HOUNDING ME FOR MONTHS.
WATCHING ME THROUGH WINDOWS AND WATER. YOU GAVE ME THIS LASSO.
WHY?
BECAUSE YOU ARE A HERO. A LEADER.
YOU ARE UNAFRAID OF WHAT TOMORROW BRINGS.
AND WHY WOULD YOU WANT TO HELP ME? YOU'VE BEEN AN ENEMY TO WONDER WOMAN AND THE AMAZONS SINCE PARADISE ISLAND WAS FORMED.
WHAT DOES IT FEEL LIKE?
WHAT?
TO BE LOVED BY YOUR MOTHER.
ZEUS AND HERA. THEY DESPISE ME. THEY ALWAYS HAVE.
I SUPPOSE I'M OFTEN SEEN AS THE ONLY PRODUCT OF THEIR PITIFUL UNION. A CHILD OF LOVE AND HATE.
A CHILD OF WAR.
YOU'RE NOT GOING TO SAY SOMETHING LAME LIKE--
--LIKE YOU'RE MY DAD OR ANYTHING, ARE YOU?
I'M NOT YOUR FATHER, CASSANDRA.

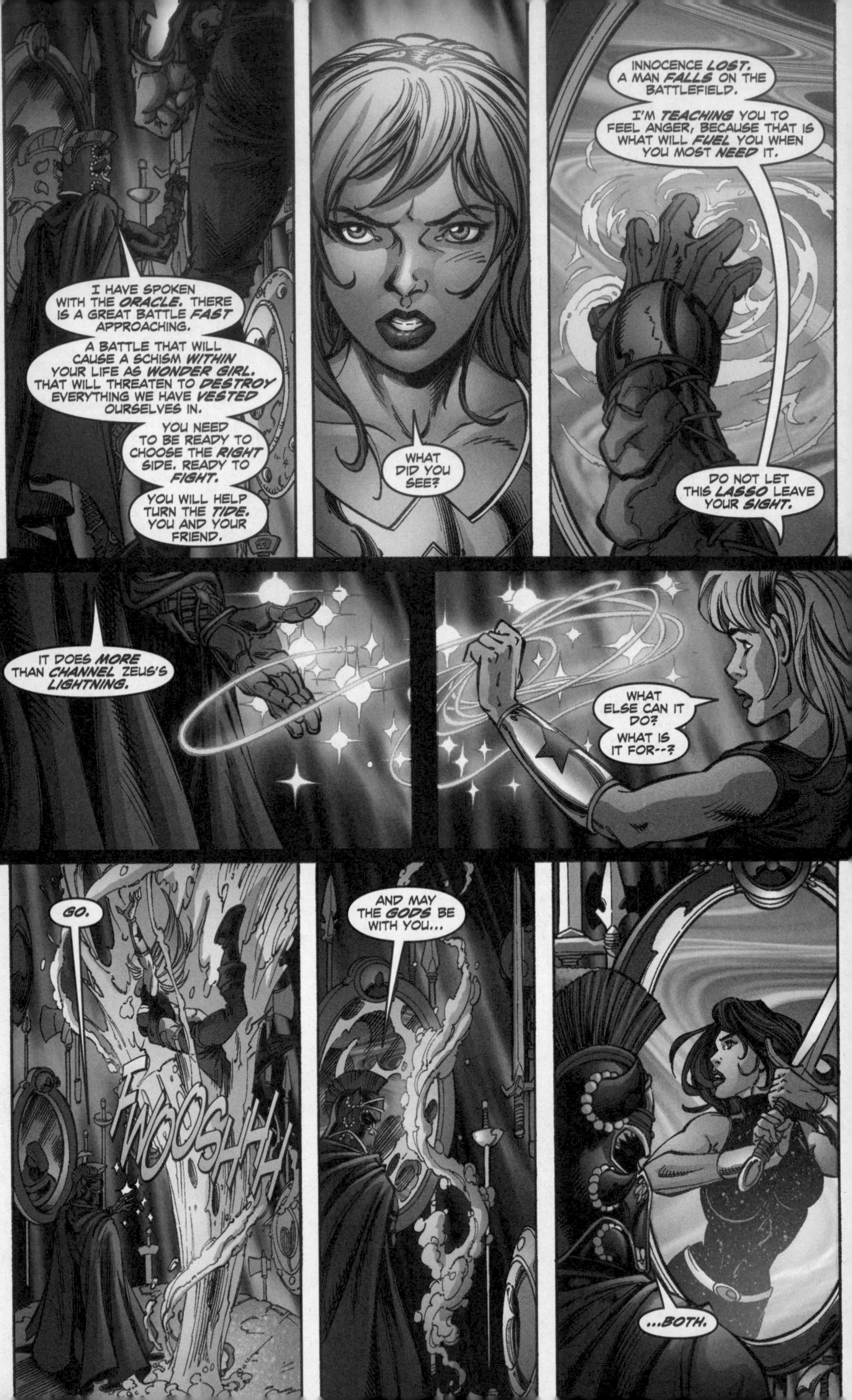
I HAVE SPOKEN WITH THE ORACLE. THERE IS A GREAT BATTLE FAST APPROACHING.
A BATTLE THAT WILL CAUSE A SCHISM WITHIN YOUR LIFE AS WONDER GIRL. THAT WILL THREATEN TO DESTROY EVERYTHING WE HAVE VESTED OURSELVES IN.
YOU NEED TO BE READY TO CHOOSE THE RIGHT SIDE. READY TO FIGHT.
YOU WILL HELP TURN THE TIDE. YOU AND YOUR FRIEND.
WHAT DID YOU SEE?
INNOCENCE LOST. A MAN FALLS ON THE BATTLEFIELD.
I'M TEACHING YOU TO FEEL ANGER, BECAUSE THAT IS WHAT WILL FUEL YOU WHEN YOU MOST NEED IT.
DO NOT LET THIS LASSO LEAVE YOUR SIGHT.
IT DOES MORE THAN CHANNEL ZEUS'S LIGHTNING.
WHAT ELSE CAN IT DO?
WHAT IS IT FOR--?
GO.
FWOOSHHH
AND MAY THE GODS BE WITH YOU...
...BOTH.

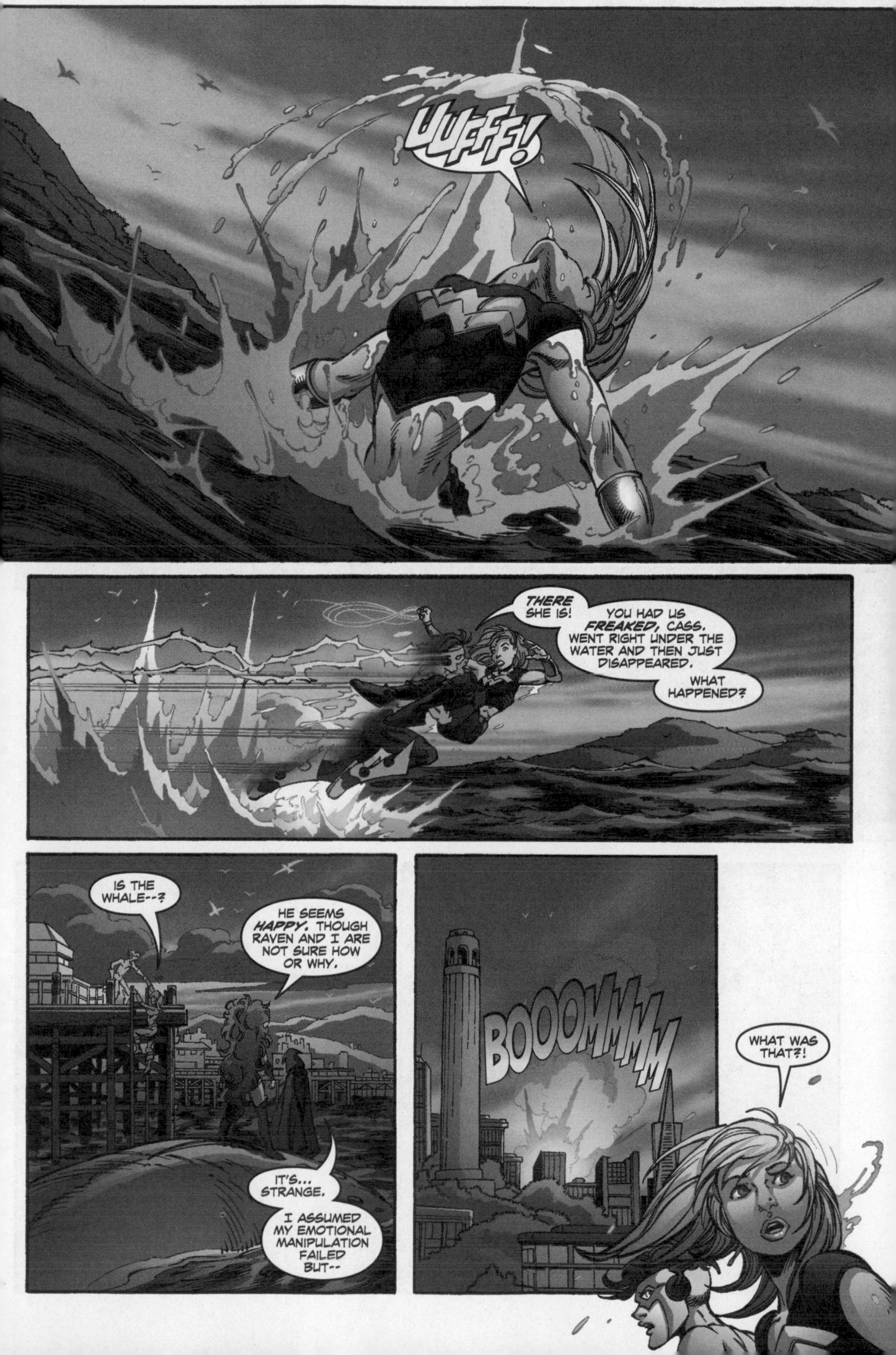
UUFFF!
THERE SHE IS!
YOU HAD US FREAKED, CASS. WENT RIGHT UNDER THE WATER AND THEN JUST DISAPPEARED.
WHAT HAPPENED?
IS THE WHALE--?
HE SEEMS HAPPY. THOUGH RAVEN AND I ARE NOT SURE HOW OR WHY.
IT'S... STRANGE.
I ASSUMED MY EMOTIONAL MANIPULATION FAILED BUT--
BOOOMMMM
WHAT WAS THAT?!

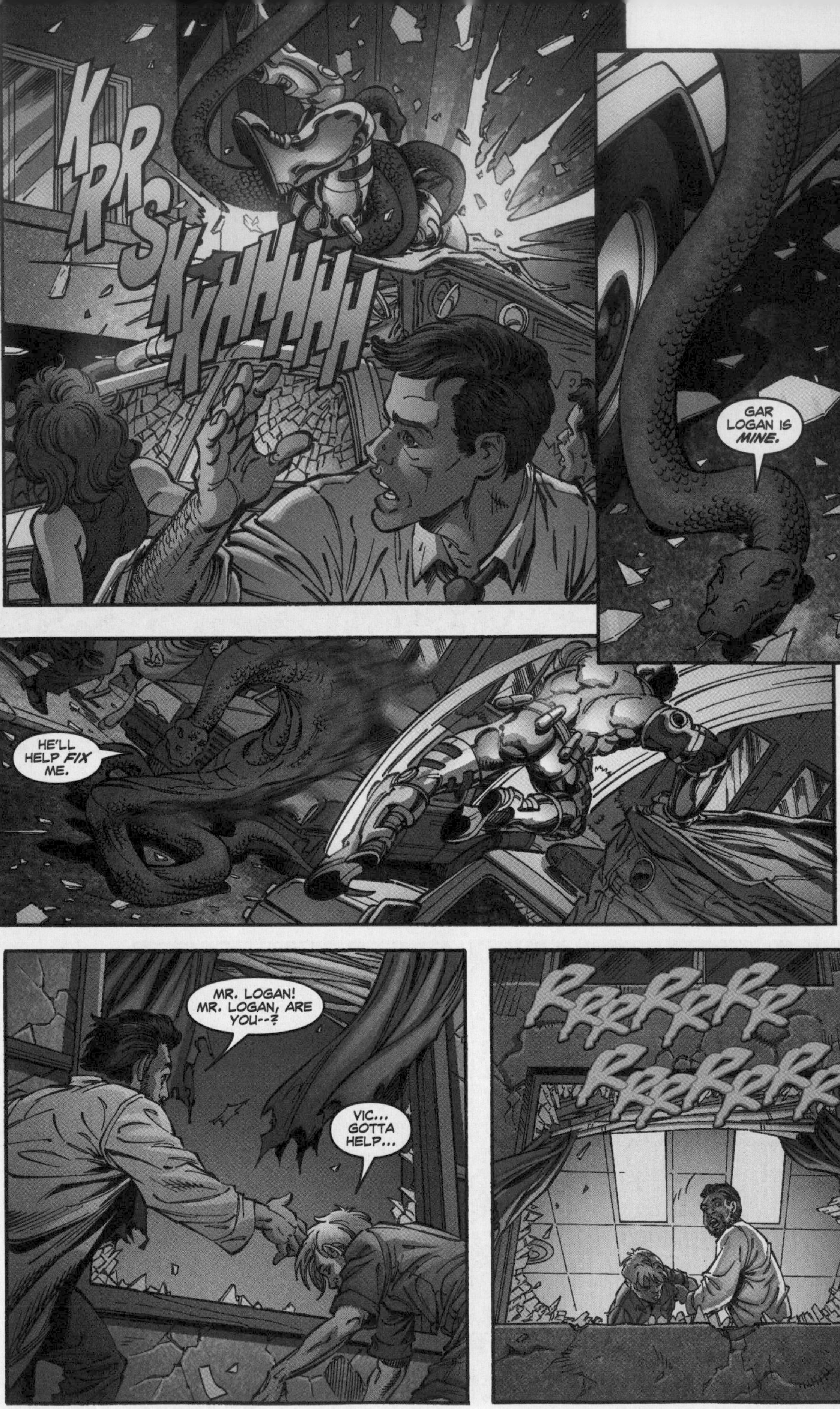
KRRSKKHHHHH
GAR LOGAN IS MINE.
HE'LL HELP FIX ME.
MR. LOGAN! MR. LOGAN, ARE YOU--?
VIC... GOTTA HELP...
RRRRRRR
RRRRRRR

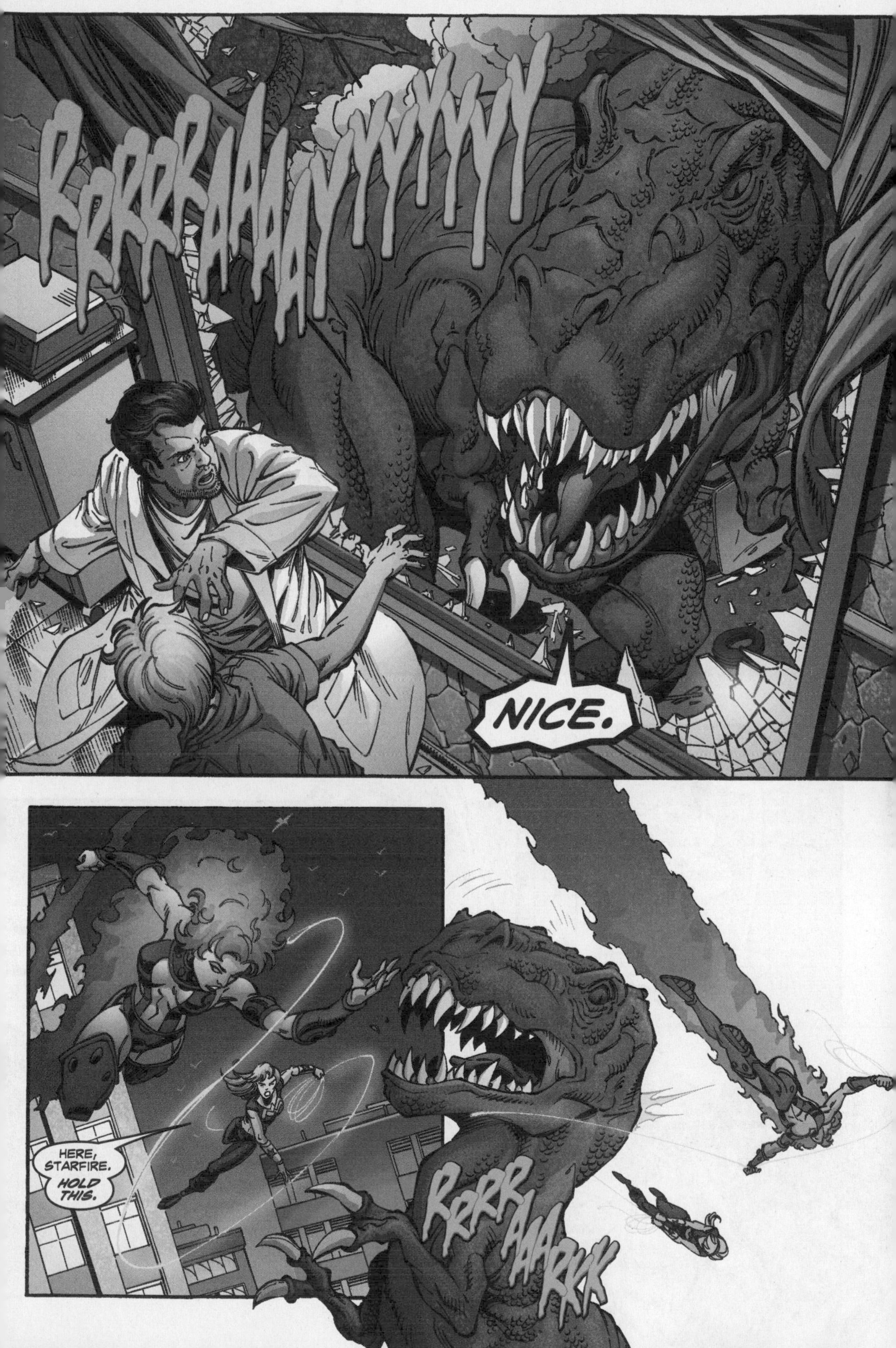
RRRRAAAAYYYYYYN
NICE.
HERE, STARFIRE. HOLD THIS.
RRRRAAARKK

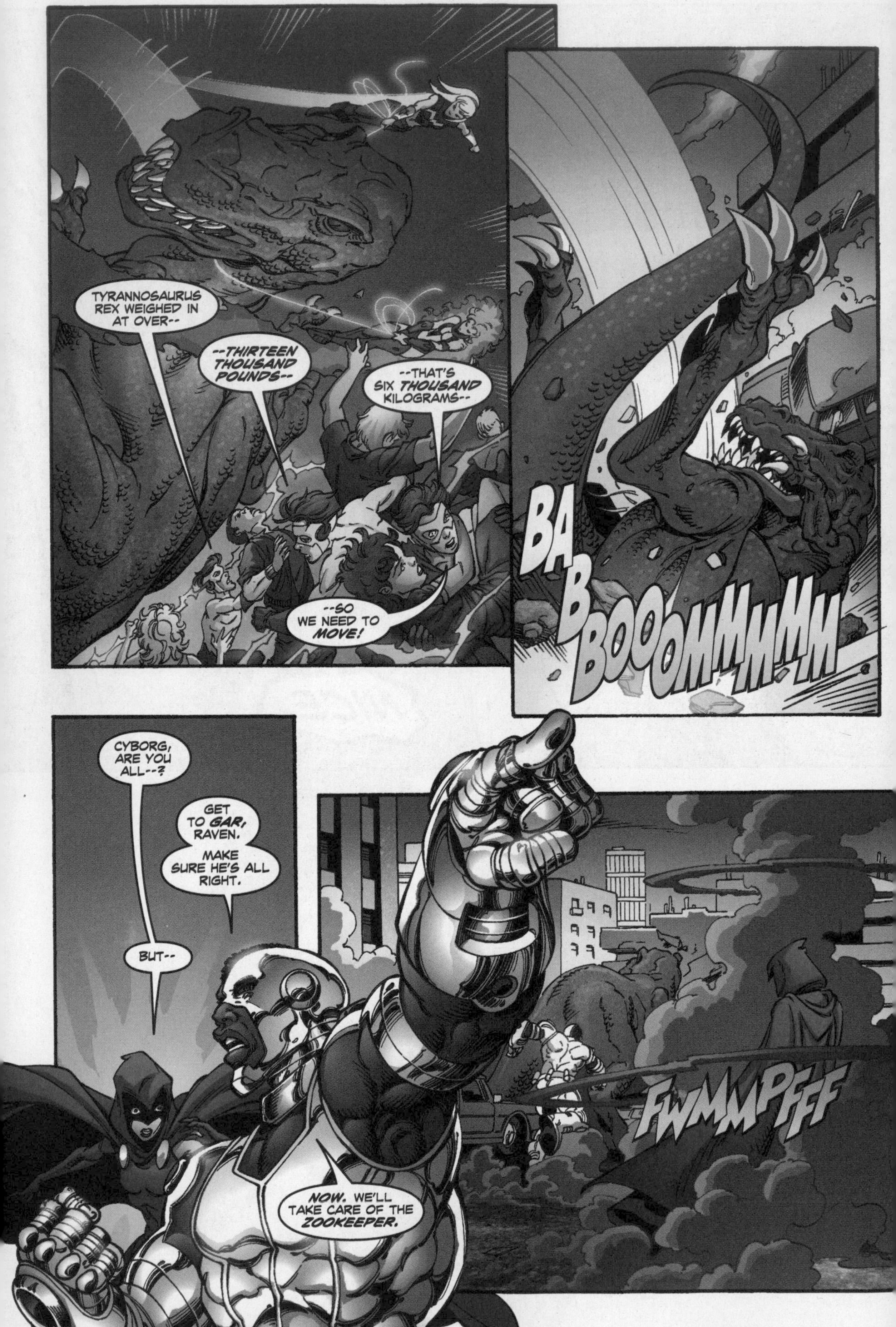
TYRANNOSAURUS REX WEIGHED IN AT OVER--
--THIRTEEN THOUSAND POUNDS--
--THAT'S SIX THOUSAND KILOGRAMS--
--SO WE NEED TO MOVE!
BA B BOOOMMMMM
CYBORG, ARE YOU ALL--?
GET TO GAR, RAVEN.
MAKE SURE HE'S ALL RIGHT.
BUT--
NOW. WE'LL TAKE CARE OF THE ZOOKEEPER.
FWMMPFFF

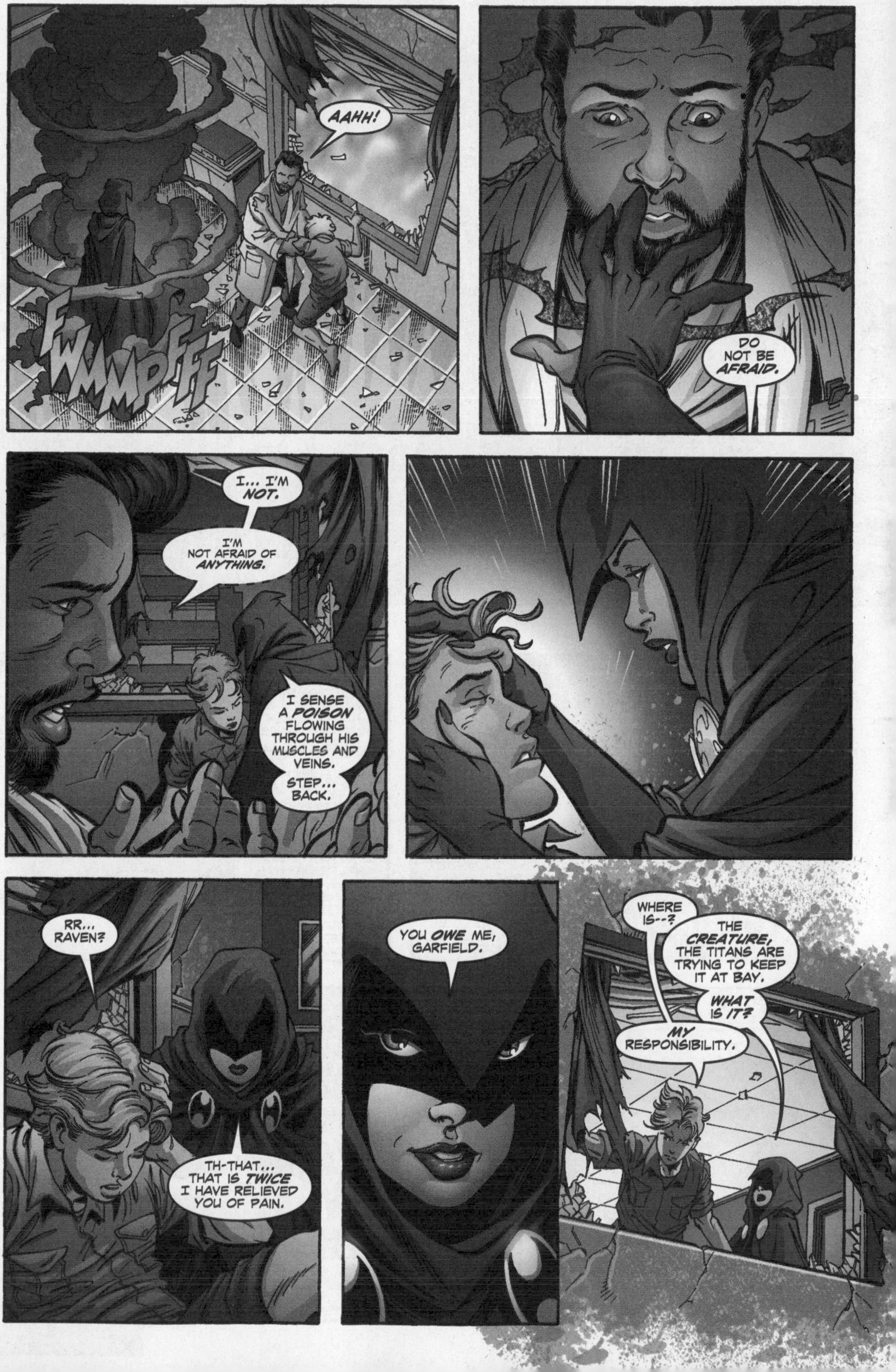
AAHH!
FWMMPFFF
DO NOT BE AFRAID.
I... I'M NOT.
I'M NOT AFRAID OF ANYTHING.
I SENSE A POISON FLOWING THROUGH HIS MUSCLES AND VEINS.
STEP... BACK.
RR... RAVEN?
TH-THAT... THAT IS TWICE I HAVE RELIEVED YOU OF PAIN.
YOU OWE ME, GARFIELD.
WHERE IS--?
THE CREATURE, THE TITANS ARE TRYING TO KEEP IT AT BAY.
WHAT IS IT?
MY RESPONSIBILITY.

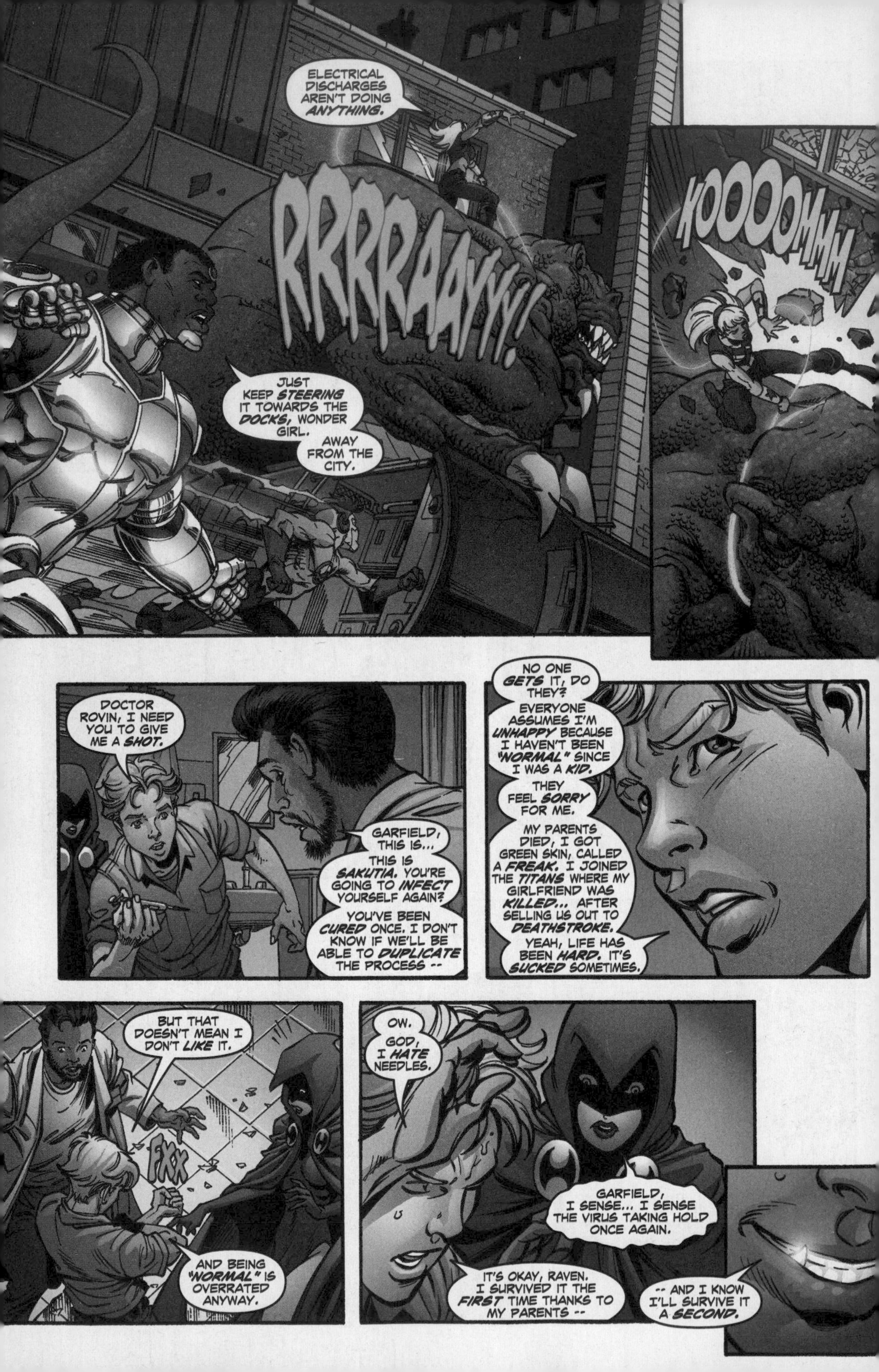
ELECTRICAL DISCHARGES AREN'T DOING ANYTHING.
RRRRAAYYY!
JUST KEEP STEERING IT TOWARDS THE DOCKS, WONDER GIRL.
AWAY FROM THE CITY.
KOOOOMMM
DOCTOR ROVIN, I NEED YOU TO GIVE ME A SHOT.
GARFIELD, THIS IS...
THIS IS SAKUTIA. YOU'RE GOING TO INFECT YOURSELF AGAIN?
YOU'VE BEEN CURED ONCE. I DON'T KNOW IF WE'LL BE ABLE TO DUPLICATE THE PROCESS --
NO ONE GETS IT, DO THEY?
EVERYONE ASSUMES I'M UNHAPPY BECAUSE I HAVEN'T BEEN "NORMAL" SINCE I WAS A KID.
THEY FEEL SORRY FOR ME.
MY PARENTS DIED, I GOT GREEN SKIN, CALLED A FREAK. I JOINED THE TITANS WHERE MY GIRLFRIEND WAS KILLED... AFTER SELLING US OUT TO DEATHSTROKE.
YEAH, LIFE HAS BEEN HARD. IT'S SUCKED SOMETIMES.
BUT THAT DOESN'T MEAN I DON'T LIKE IT.
FXX
AND BEING "NORMAL" IS OVERRATED ANYWAY.
OW.
GOD, I HATE NEEDLES.
GARFIELD, I SENSE... I SENSE THE VIRUS TAKING HOLD ONCE AGAIN.
IT'S OKAY, RAVEN. I SURVIVED IT THE FIRST TIME THANKS TO MY PARENTS --
-- AND I KNOW I'LL SURVIVE IT A SECOND.

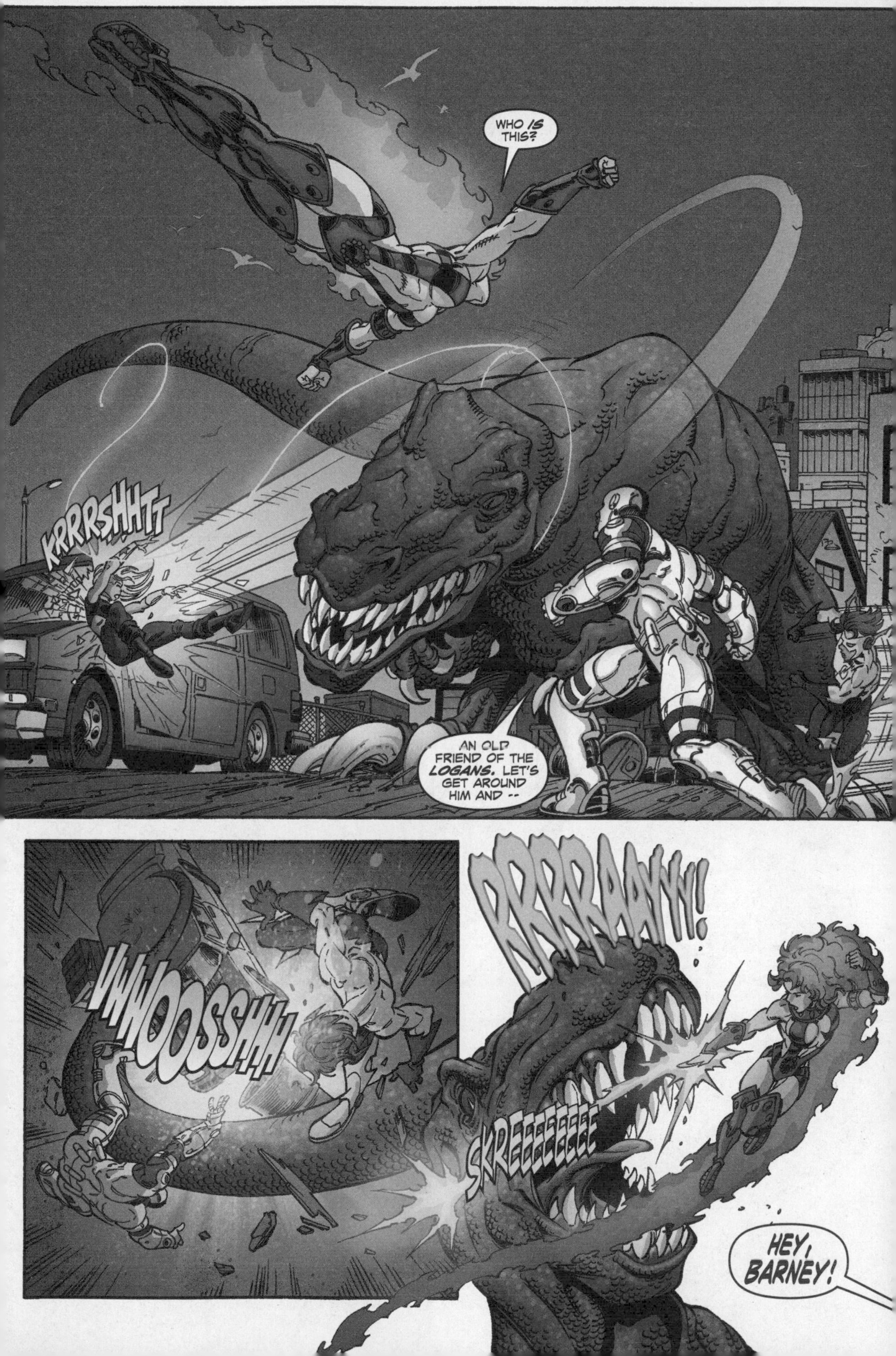

WHO *IS* THIS?
KRRRSHHTT
AN OLD FRIEND OF THE **LOGANS.** LET'S GET AROUND HIM AND --
RRRRAAYYY!
VWWOOSSHHH
SKREEEEEEEEE
HEY, BARNEY!

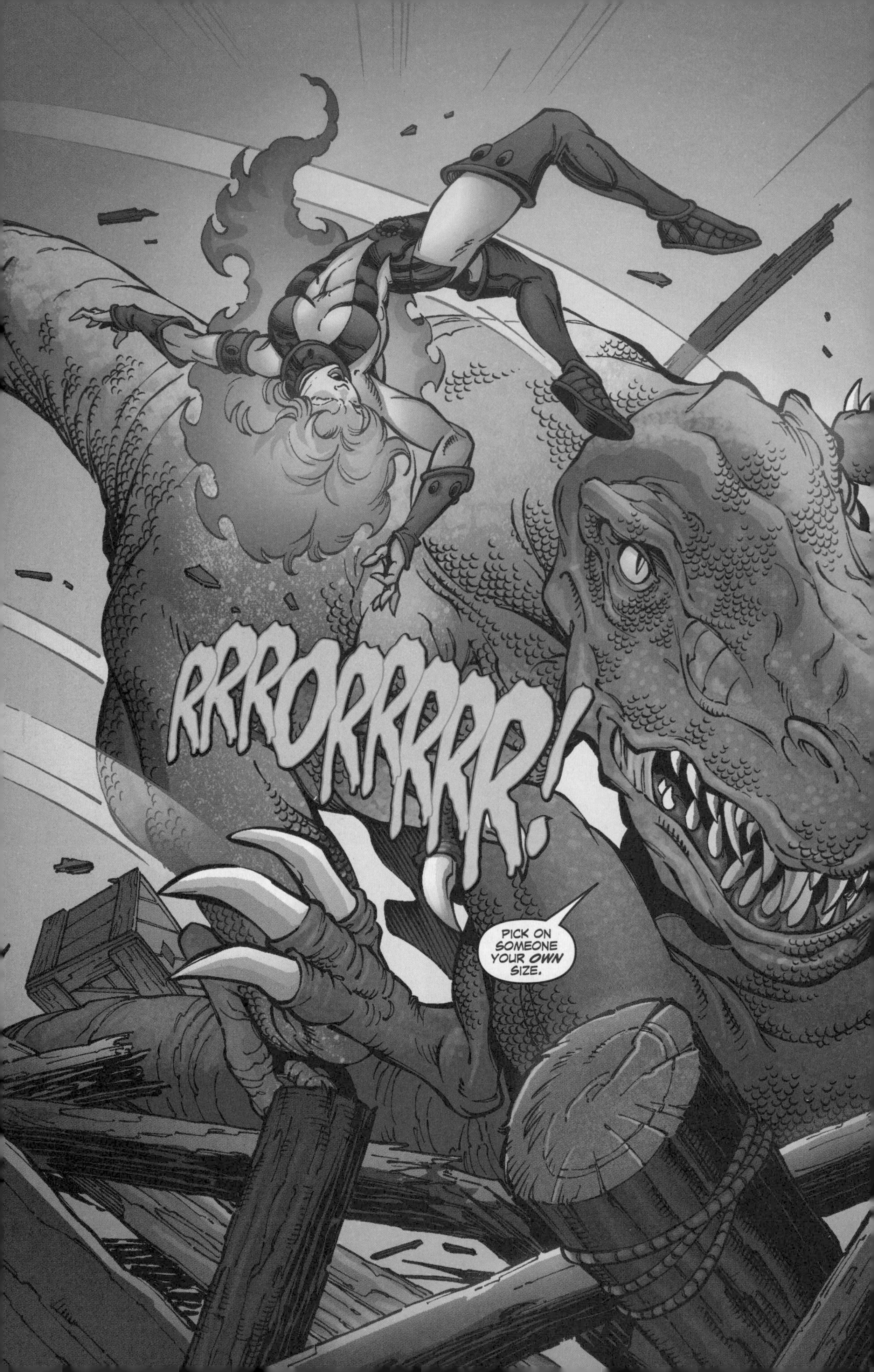
RRRORRRRRR!
PICK ON SOMEONE YOUR OWN SIZE.

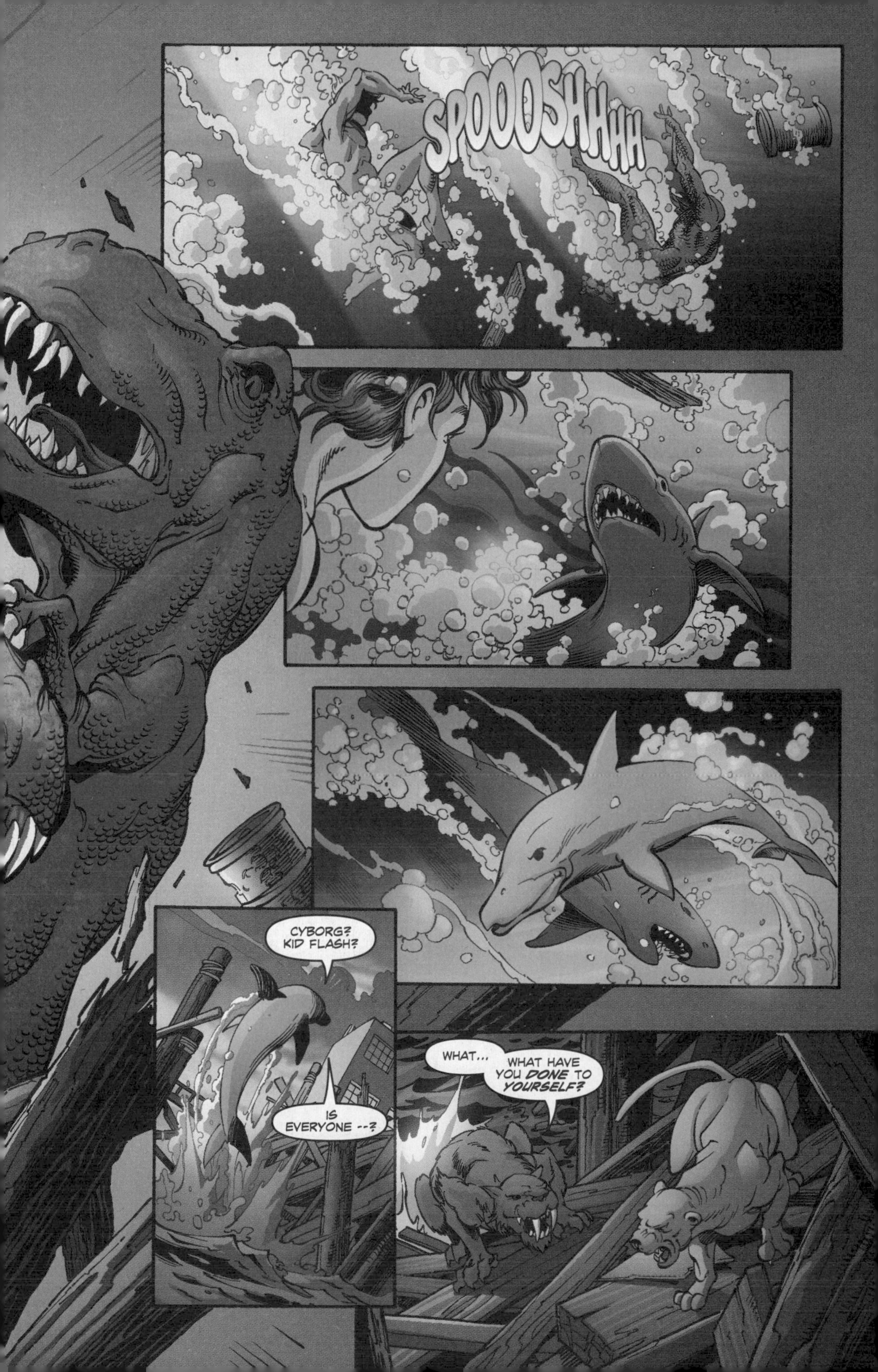
SPOOOSHHHH
CYBORG? KID FLASH?
IS EVERYONE --?
WHAT...
WHAT HAVE YOU *DONE* TO *YOURSELF?*

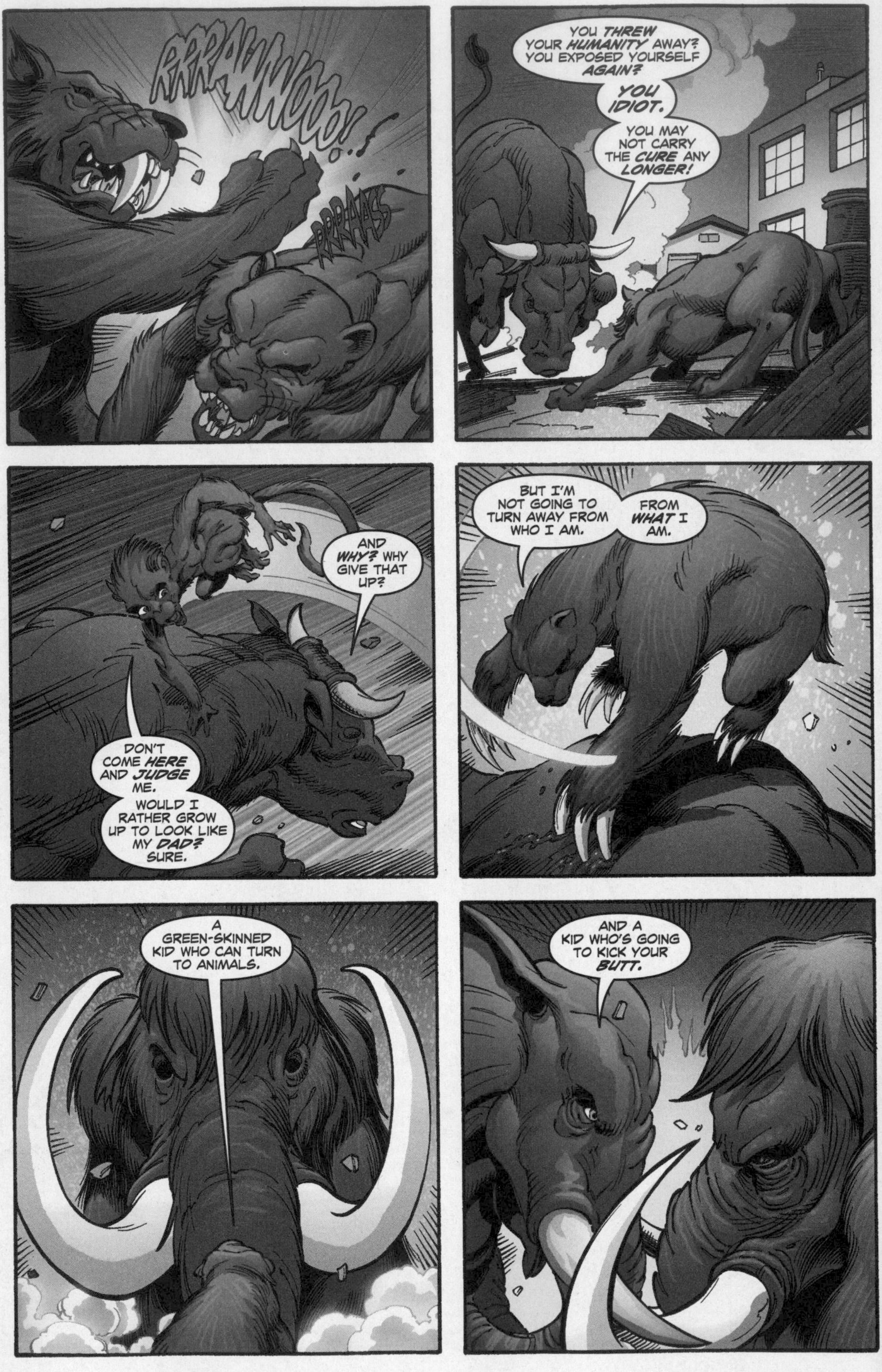
RRRAWWOOO!
PRRRAASS
YOU THREW YOUR HUMANITY AWAY? YOU EXPOSED YOURSELF AGAIN?
YOU IDIOT.
YOU MAY NOT CARRY THE CURE ANY LONGER!
AND WHY? WHY GIVE THAT UP?
DON'T COME HERE AND JUDGE ME.
WOULD I RATHER GROW UP TO LOOK LIKE MY DAD? SURE.
BUT I'M NOT GOING TO TURN AWAY FROM WHO I AM.
FROM WHAT I AM.
A GREEN-SKINNED KID WHO CAN TURN TO ANIMALS.
AND A KID WHO'S GOING TO KICK YOUR BUTT.

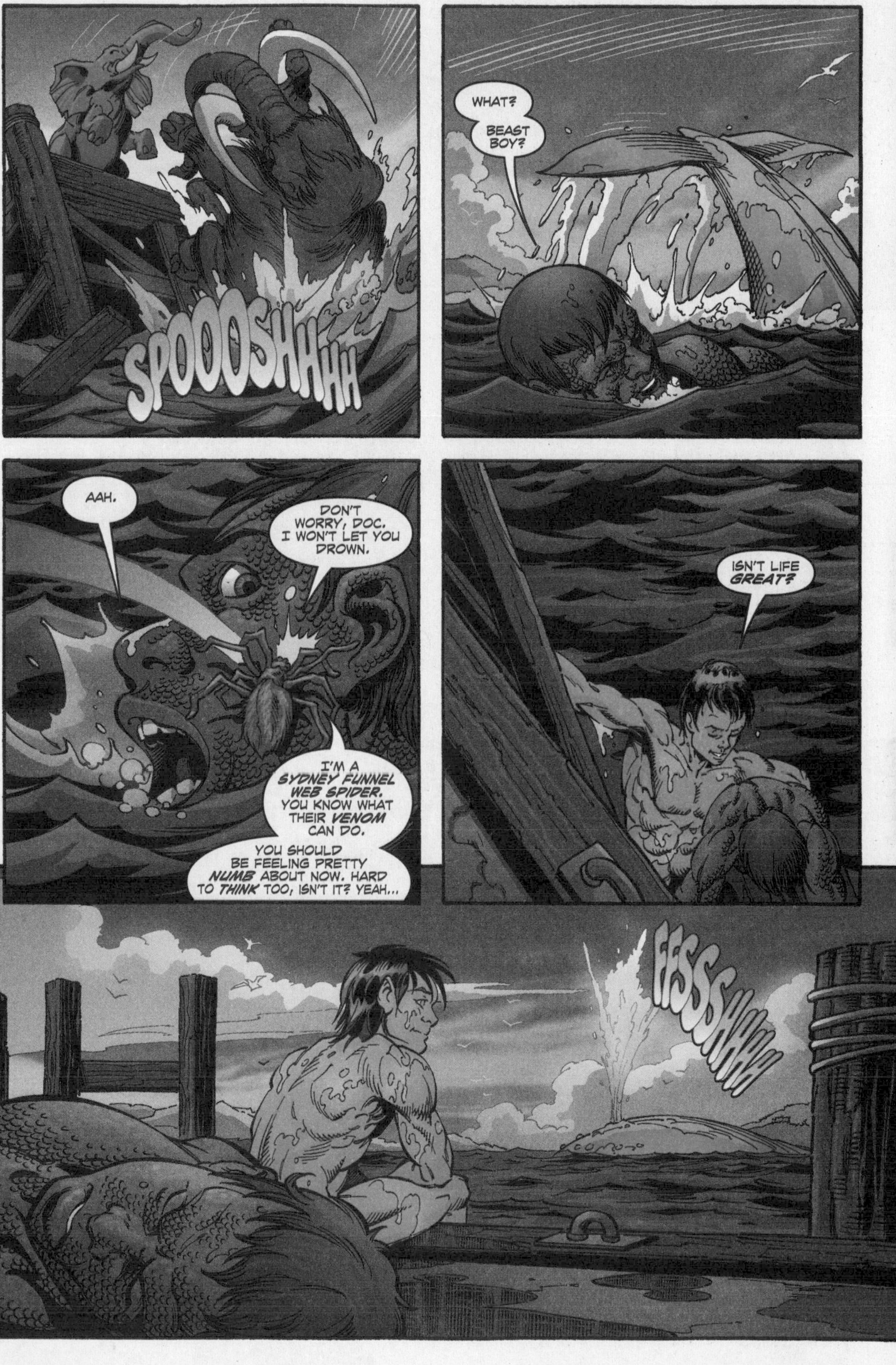
SPOOOSHHHH
WHAT?
BEAST BOY?
AAH.
DON'T WORRY, DOC. I WON'T LET YOU DROWN.
I'M A SYDNEY FUNNEL WEB SPIDER. YOU KNOW WHAT THEIR VENOM CAN DO.
YOU SHOULD BE FEELING PRETTY NUMB ABOUT NOW. HARD TO THINK TOO, ISN'T IT? YEAH...
ISN'T LIFE GREAT?
FFSSSHHHH

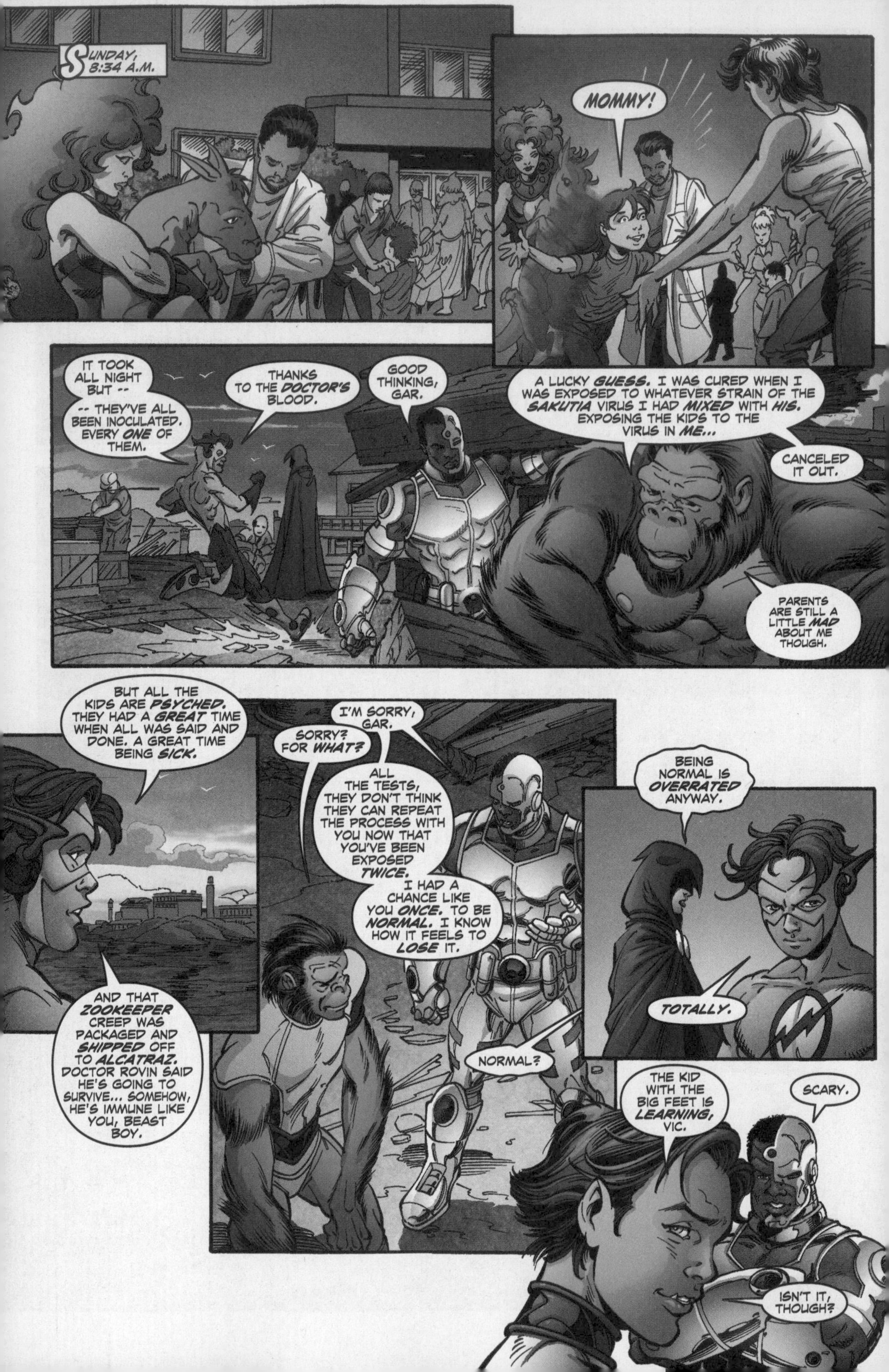
SUNDAY, 8:34 A.M.
MOMMY!
IT TOOK ALL NIGHT BUT --
-- THEY'VE ALL BEEN INOCULATED. EVERY ONE OF THEM.
THANKS TO THE DOCTOR'S BLOOD.
GOOD THINKING, GAR.
A LUCKY GUESS. I WAS CURED WHEN I WAS EXPOSED TO WHATEVER STRAIN OF THE SAKUTIA VIRUS I HAD MIXED WITH HIS. EXPOSING THE KIDS TO THE VIRUS IN ME...
CANCELED IT OUT.
PARENTS ARE STILL A LITTLE MAD ABOUT ME THOUGH.
BUT ALL THE KIDS ARE PSYCHED. THEY HAD A GREAT TIME WHEN ALL WAS SAID AND DONE. A GREAT TIME BEING SICK.
AND THAT ZOOKEEPER CREEP WAS PACKAGED AND SHIPPED OFF TO ALCATRAZ. DOCTOR ROVIN SAID HE'S GOING TO SURVIVE... SOMEHOW, HE'S IMMUNE LIKE YOU, BEAST BOY.
I'M SORRY, GAR.
SORRY? FOR WHAT?
ALL THE TESTS, THEY DON'T THINK THEY CAN REPEAT THE PROCESS WITH YOU NOW THAT YOU'VE BEEN EXPOSED TWICE.
I HAD A CHANCE LIKE YOU ONCE. TO BE NORMAL. I KNOW HOW IT FEELS TO LOSE IT.
NORMAL?
BEING NORMAL IS OVERRATED ANYWAY.
TOTALLY.
THE KID WITH THE BIG FEET IS LEARNING, VIC.
SCARY.
ISN'T IT, THOUGH?

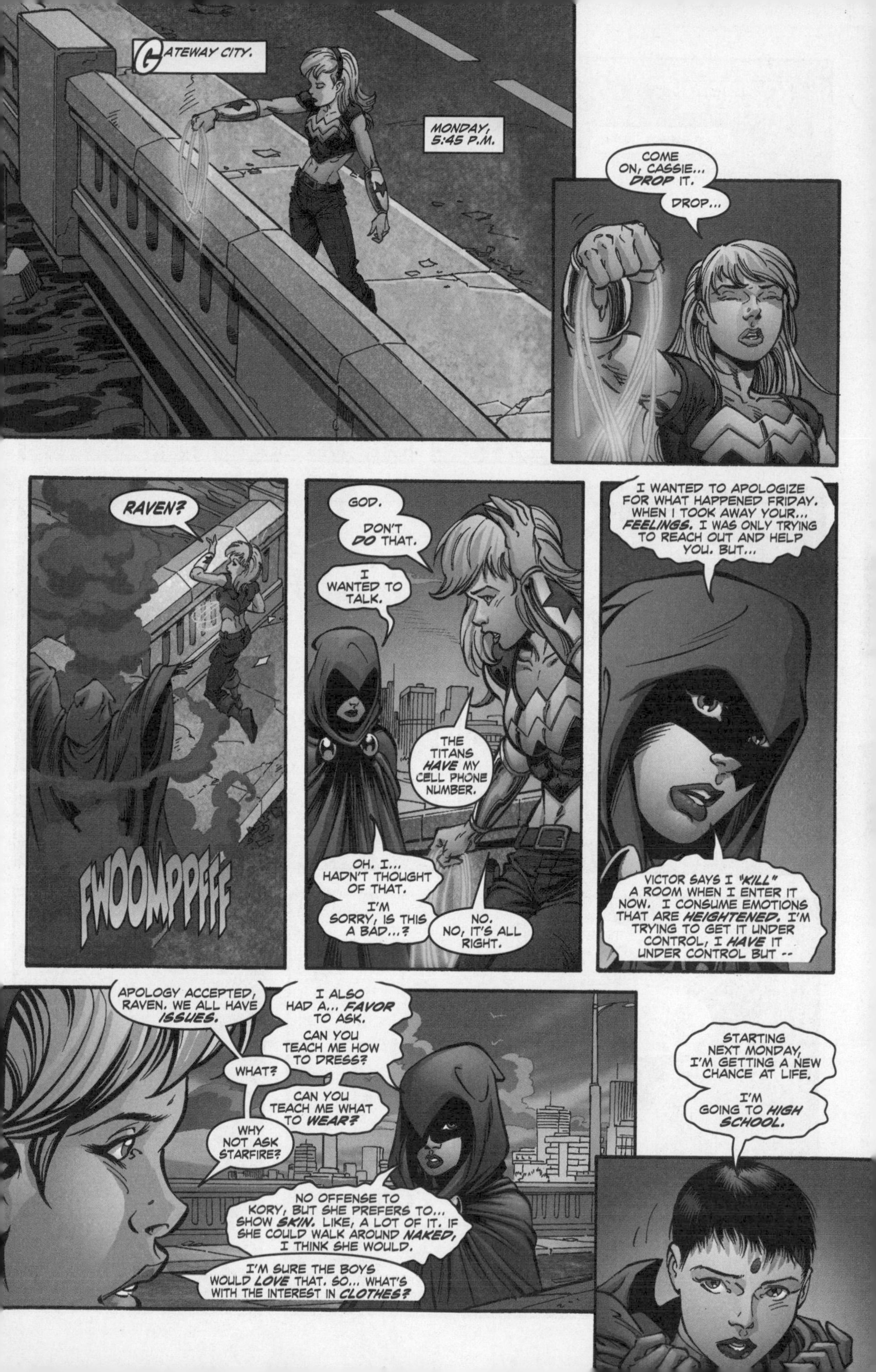
GATEWAY CITY.
MONDAY, 5:45 P.M.
COME ON, CASSIE... DROP IT.
DROP...
RAVEN?
FWOOMPFFF
GOD.
DON'T DO THAT.
I WANTED TO TALK.
THE TITANS HAVE MY CELL PHONE NUMBER.
OH. I... HADN'T THOUGHT OF THAT.
I'M SORRY, IS THIS A BAD...?
NO. NO, IT'S ALL RIGHT.
I WANTED TO APOLOGIZE FOR WHAT HAPPENED FRIDAY. WHEN I TOOK AWAY YOUR... FEELINGS. I WAS ONLY TRYING TO REACH OUT AND HELP YOU. BUT...
VICTOR SAYS I "KILL" A ROOM WHEN I ENTER IT NOW. I CONSUME EMOTIONS THAT ARE HEIGHTENED. I'M TRYING TO GET IT UNDER CONTROL, I HAVE IT UNDER CONTROL BUT --
APOLOGY ACCEPTED, RAVEN. WE ALL HAVE ISSUES.
I ALSO HAD A... FAVOR TO ASK.
CAN YOU TEACH ME HOW TO DRESS?
WHAT?
CAN YOU TEACH ME WHAT TO WEAR?
WHY NOT ASK STARFIRE?
NO OFFENSE TO KORY, BUT SHE PREFERS TO... SHOW SKIN. LIKE, A LOT OF IT. IF SHE COULD WALK AROUND NAKED, I THINK SHE WOULD.
I'M SURE THE BOYS WOULD LOVE THAT. SO... WHAT'S WITH THE INTEREST IN CLOTHES?
STARTING NEXT MONDAY, I'M GETTING A NEW CHANCE AT LIFE.
I'M GOING TO HIGH SCHOOL.

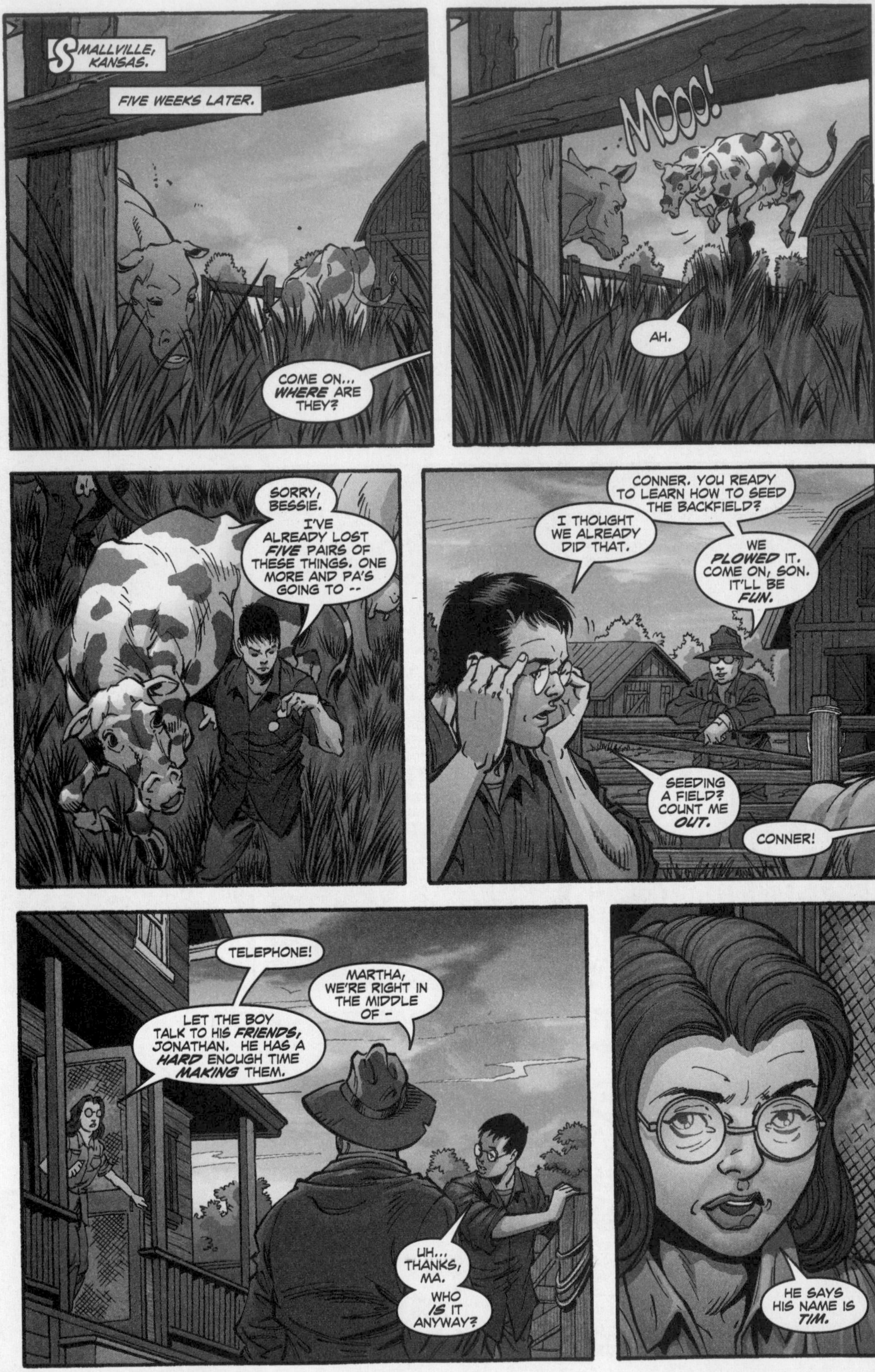
SMALLVILLE, KANSAS.
FIVE WEEKS LATER.
COME ON... WHERE ARE THEY?
MOOO!
AH.
SORRY, BESSIE.
I'VE ALREADY LOST FIVE PAIRS OF THESE THINGS. ONE MORE AND PA'S GOING TO --
CONNER. YOU READY TO LEARN HOW TO SEED THE BACKFIELD?
I THOUGHT WE ALREADY DID THAT.
WE PLOWED IT. COME ON, SON. IT'LL BE FUN.
SEEDING A FIELD? COUNT ME OUT.
CONNER!
TELEPHONE!
MARTHA, WE'RE RIGHT IN THE MIDDLE OF -
LET THE BOY TALK TO HIS FRIENDS, JONATHAN. HE HAS A HARD ENOUGH TIME MAKING THEM.
UH... THANKS, MA.
WHO IS IT ANYWAY?
HE SAYS HIS NAME IS TIM.

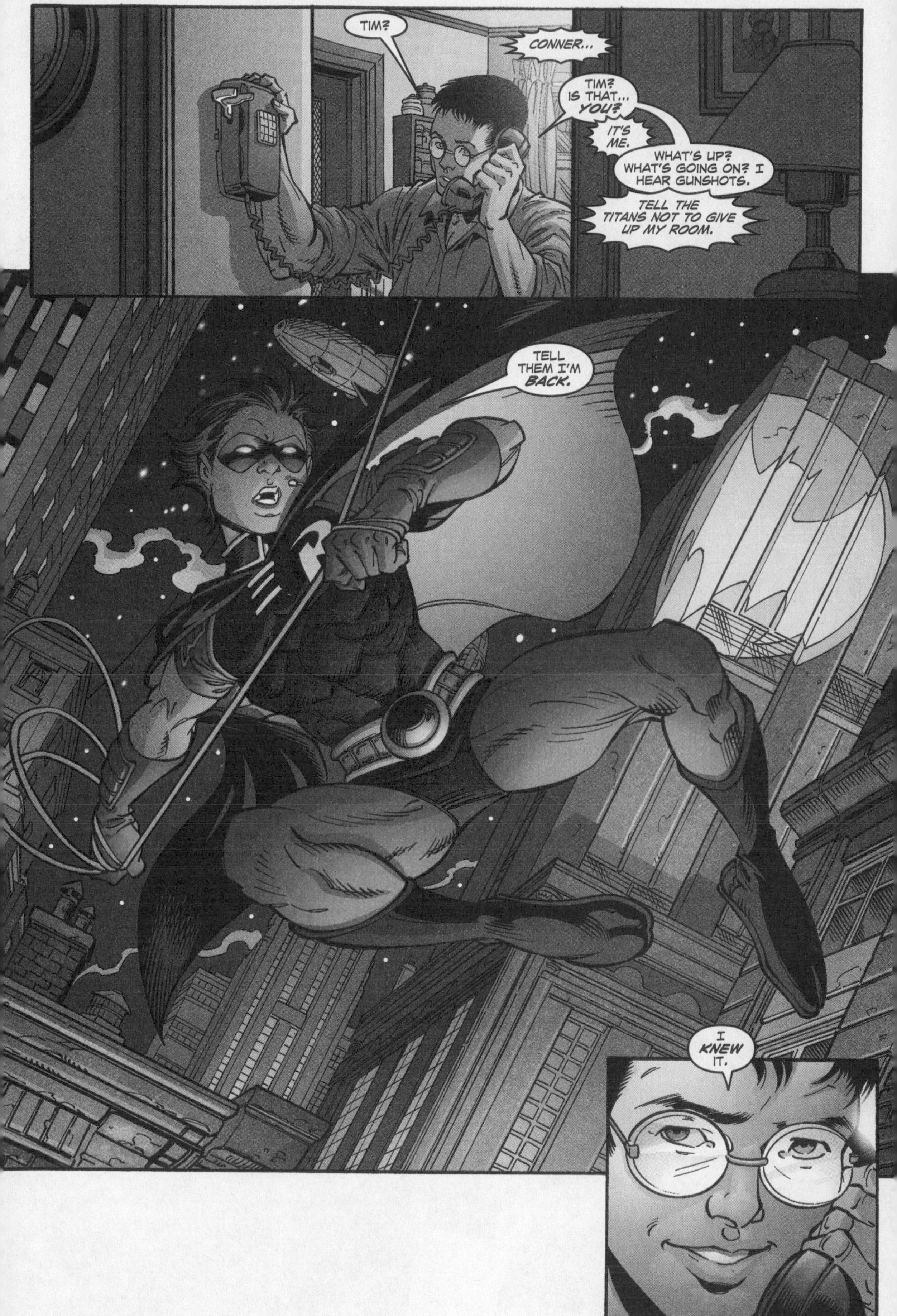

TIM?
CONNER...
TIM? IS THAT... YOU?
IT'S ME.
WHAT'S UP? WHAT'S GOING ON? I HEAR GUNSHOTS.
TELL THE TITANS NOT TO GIVE UP MY ROOM.
TELL THEM I'M BACK.
I KNEW IT.

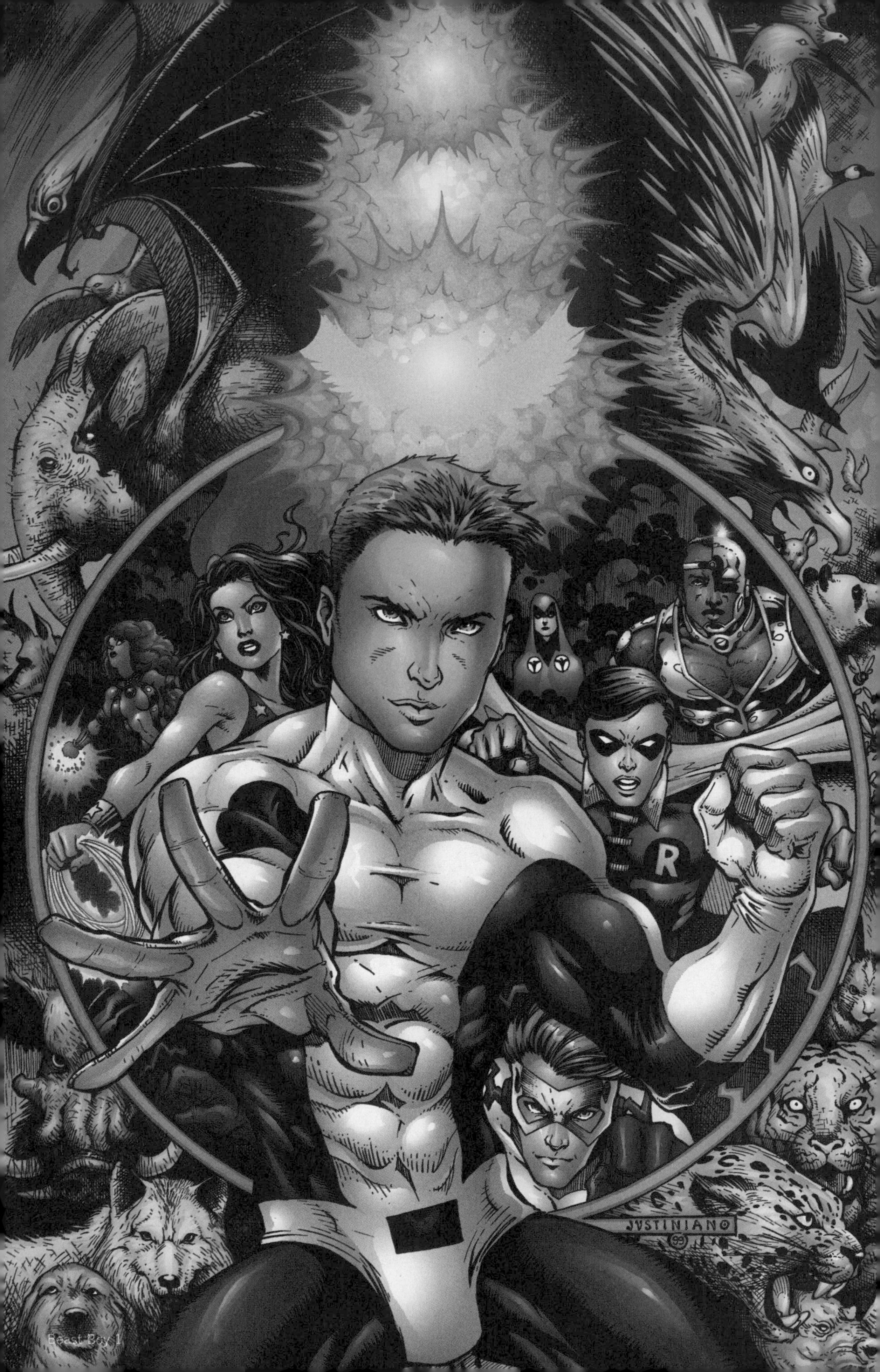
JUSTINIANO
99

Beast Boy 1

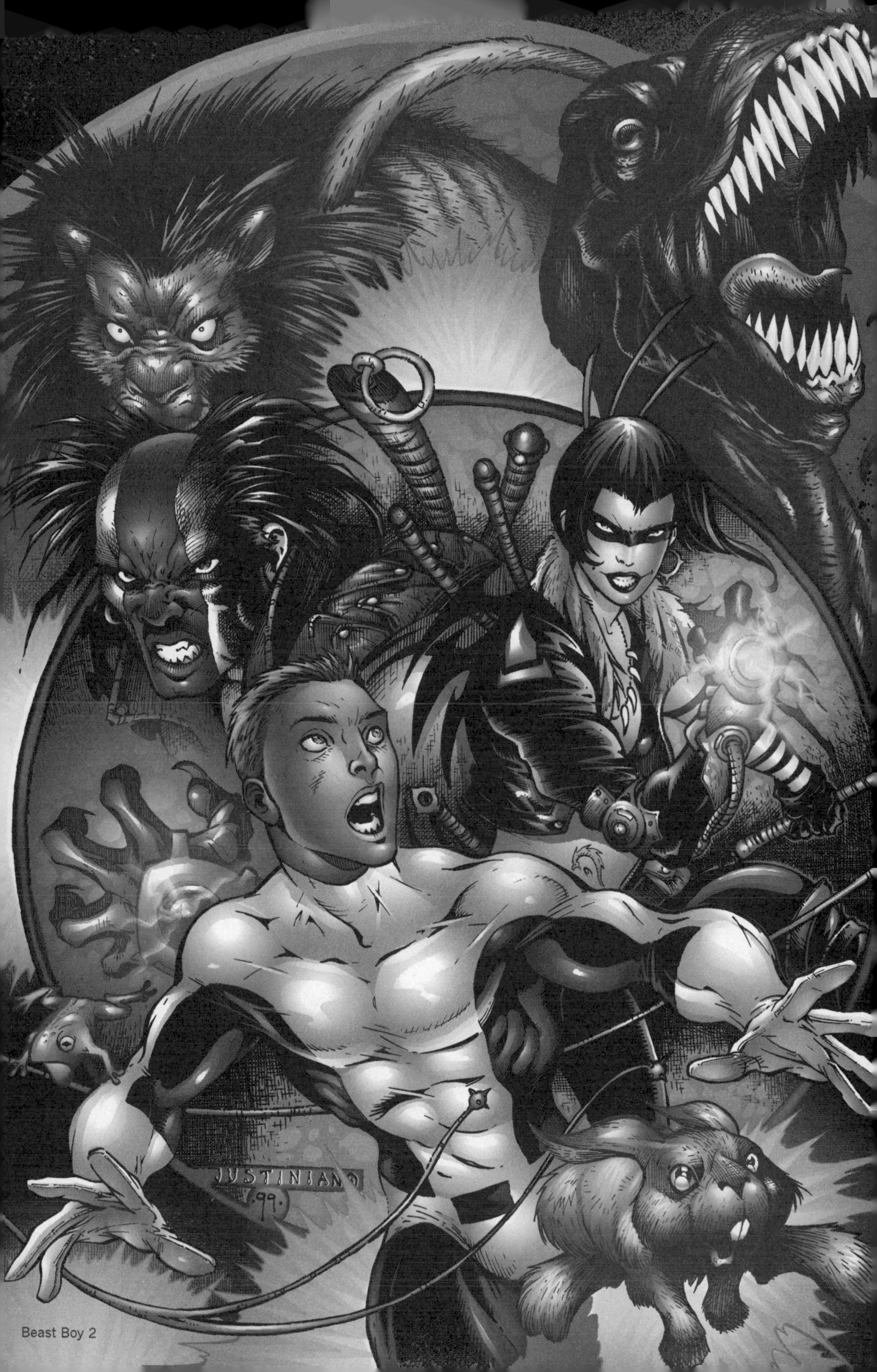
JUSTINIANO
'99
Beast Boy 2

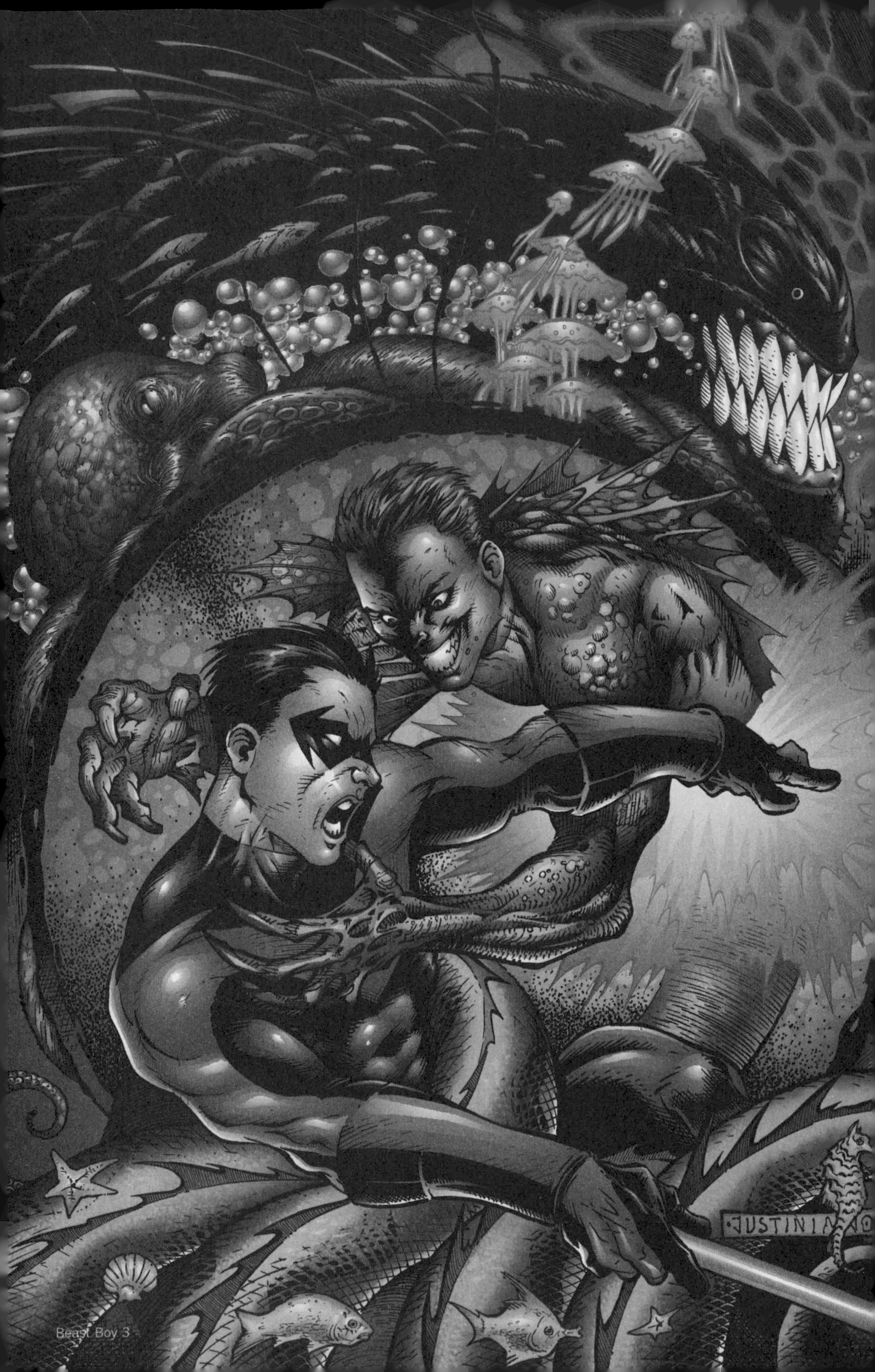
JUSTINIANO

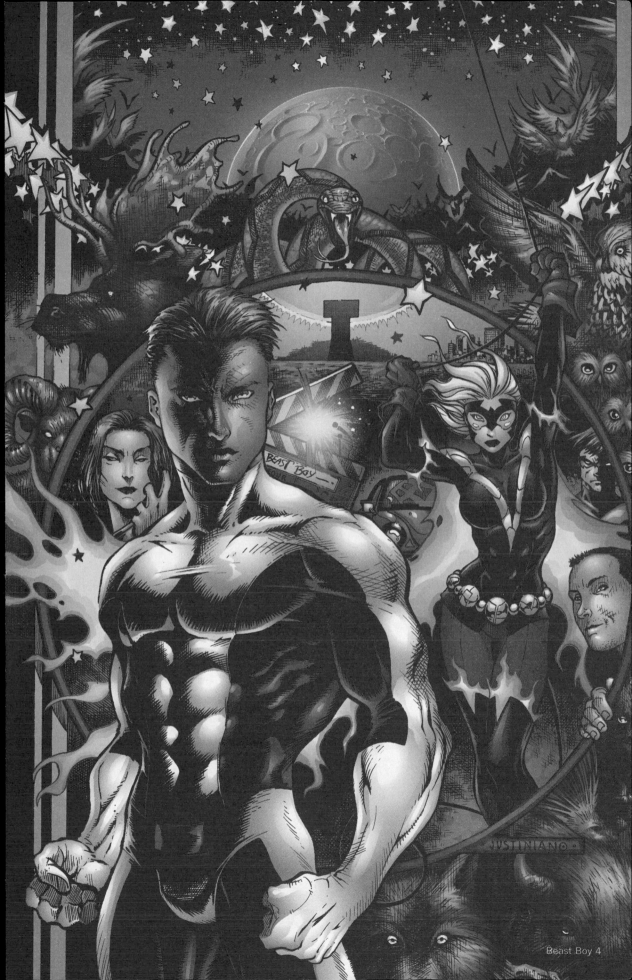

JUSTINIANO

Beast Boy 4

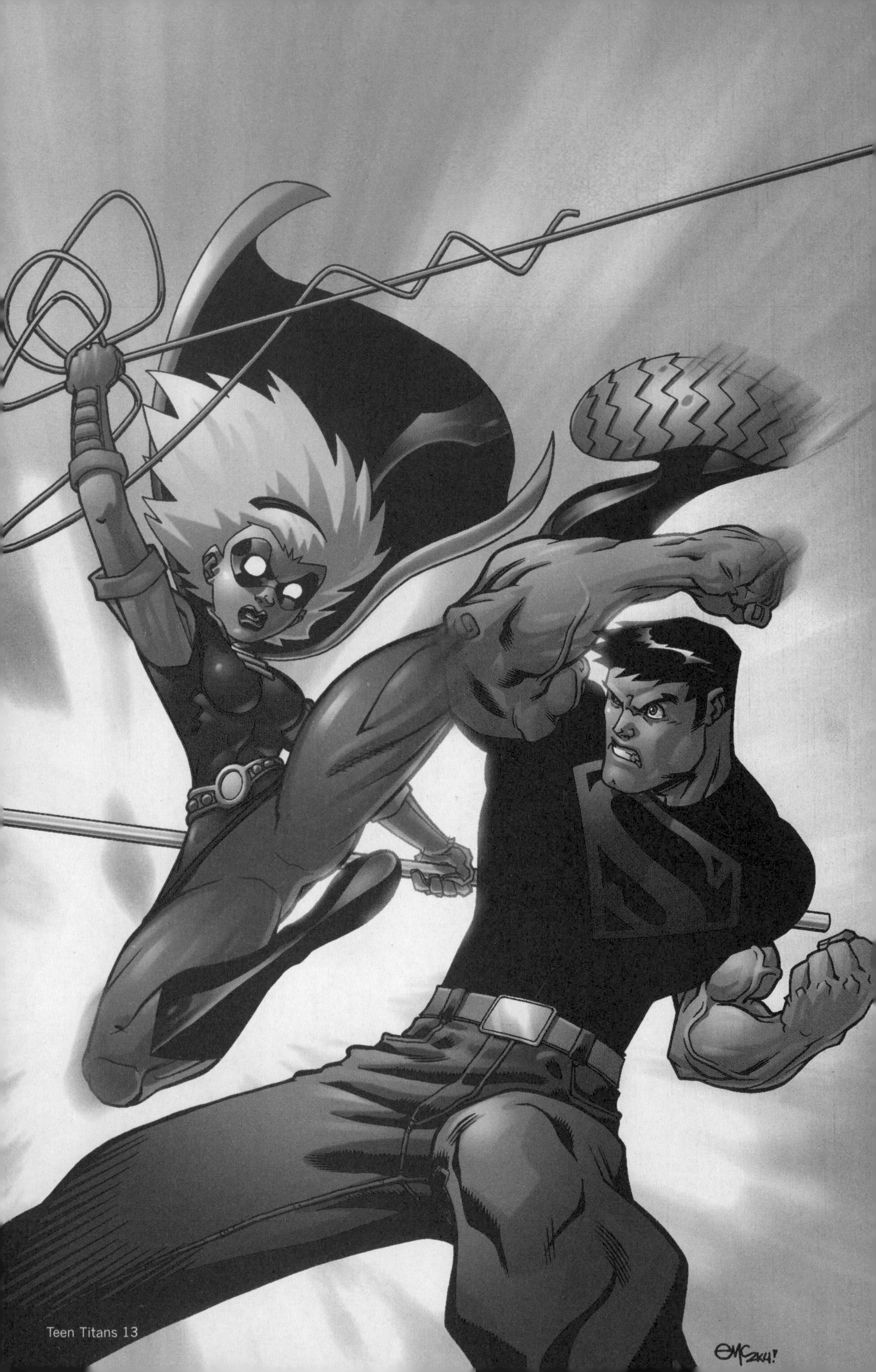
EMC 2K4!

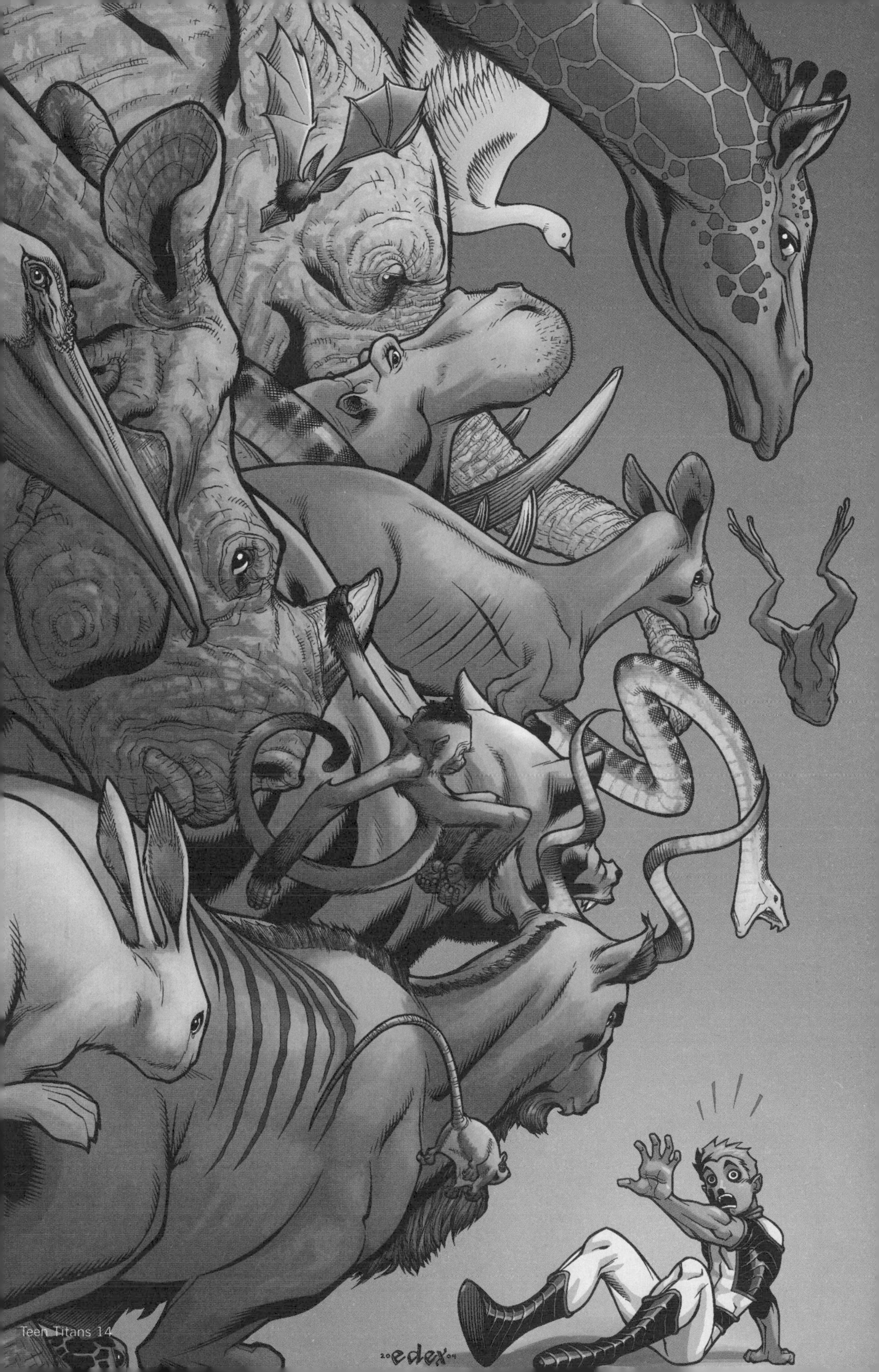

Teen Titans 14

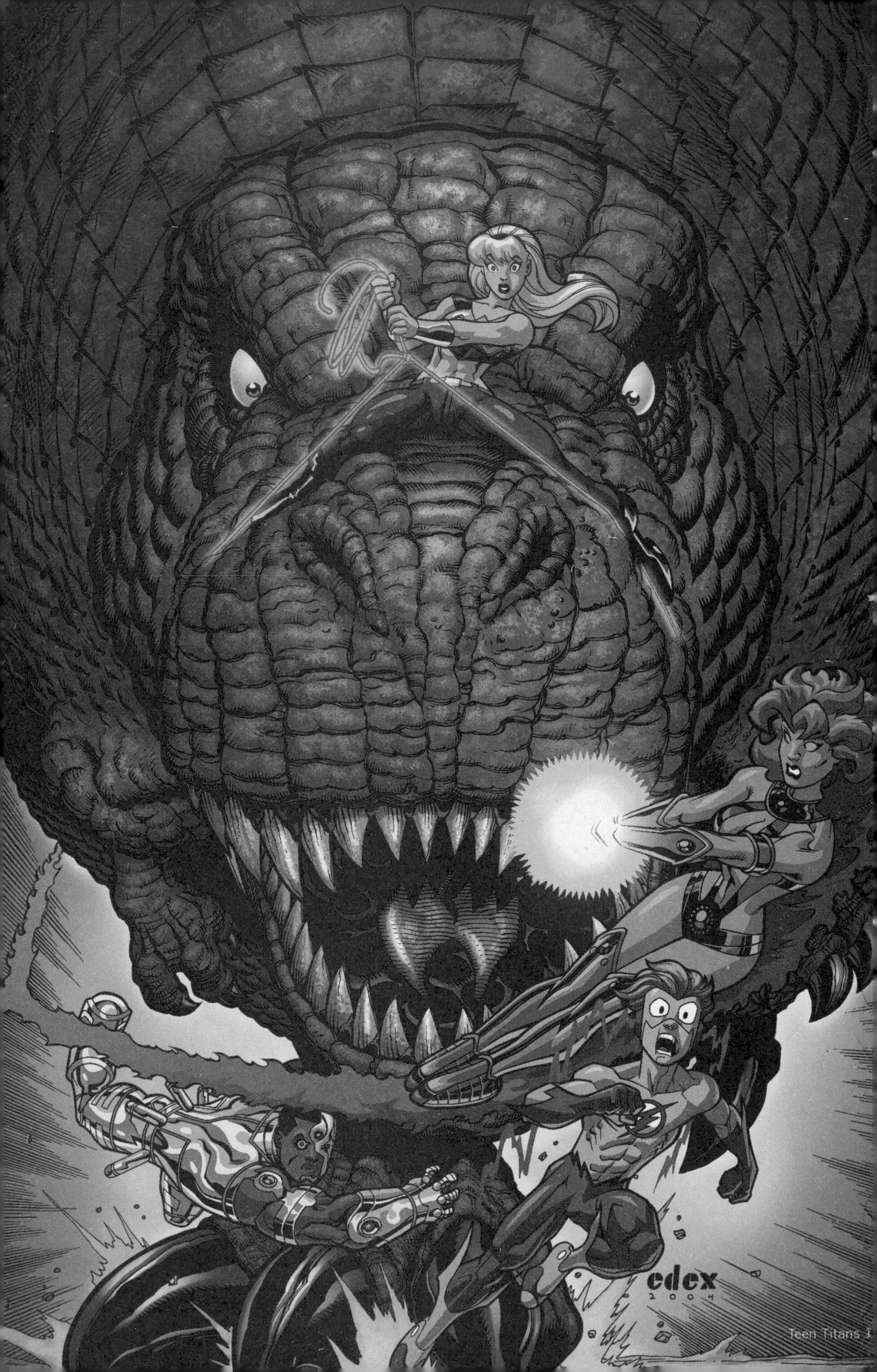
cdex
2004